12319

Contemporary Music Education

Third Edition

Third Edition

Contemporary Music Education

Michael L. Mark

Towson State University

Schirmer Books
An Imprint of Simon & Schuster Macmillan
NEW YORK
Prentice Hall International
LONDON MEXICO CITY NEW DELHI SINGAPORE SYDNEY TORONTO

Schirmer Books
An Imprint of Simon & Schuster Macmillan
1633 Broadway
New York, New York 10019

Library of Congress Catalog Card Number: 96-270

Printed in the United States of America

Printing number
‸ 4 5 6 7 8 9 10

Library of Congress Cataloging-in-Publication Data

Mark, Michael L.
    Contemporary music education / Michael L. Mark. — 3rd ed.
       p. cm.
    Includes bibliographical references and index.
    ISBN 0-02-871915-8 (alk. paper)
    I. School music—Instruction and study—United States.   I. Title.
MT3.U5M32   1996
780'.7'073—dc20   96-270
                                        CIP
                                       MN

Contents

List of Illustrations and Exhibits

Preface to the Third Edition

During the ten-year period between the second and third editions of this book, education reform has finally achieved enough substance to justify a measure of hope that all American schools will soon be able to offer a complete and excellent education to every child. As part of the ongoing educational reform movement, the music education profession has aspired to be included in schools as a true curricular subject. The Goals 2000 Act, passed by the United States Congress in 1994, was the realization of this goal; it specified the arts as one of the officially recognized core subject areas that should be part of the education of all children. Now that music education has finally achieved this elusive ambition, music educators begin a new phase in the history of their profession. They must demonstrate the unique value of their profession by ensuring that the national goals are reflected in the educational program of every American school. If this is done skillfully, and with insight, wisdom, and aesthetic sensitivity, it could mark the beginning of a new era for American music education.

The national education goals are only one example of how changes in American society have impacted on the profession of music education. To develop a broad and realistic view of the profession, music educators need to look beyond its boundaries to examine the social, economic, and political structure of the society that supports and nutures it. The third edition of this book focuses on many issues that come to the music education profession from the greater society, and to which the profession should, and must, respond. By learning about the social environment of their profession, music educators will better understand why things are as they are, and will be in a better position to make informed choices for the future.

My sincerest thanks to these colleagues for their generous assistance: Ann Blombach, Ohio State University; Leon Burton, University of Hawaii; Pamela Brasch, Suzuki Association of the Americas; Richard Carlin and Jonathan Wiener, Schirmer Books; Richard Colwell, New England Conservatory of Music; Roger Folstrom, The University of

Maryland College Park; J. Terry Gates, State University of New York at Buffalo; Richard Graham and Harriet Hair, University of Georgia; Olivia Gutoff, Maryland Music Educators Association; Sandor Havran, Educational Testing Service; Phyllis Hertz, Schulmerick Carillons; June Minckley, Florida State Department of Education; Allan Jones, Hartford, Connecticut, Public Schools; Gary S. Karpinski, University of Massachusetts at Amherst; Jeanne Ruviella and Eleanor Hofstetter, Towson State University; William Lee, International Association of Jazz Educators; Diana Mark, Esq; Richard Merrill and Alan Strong, Organization of American Kodály Educators; Ross Miller, Nazareth College of Rochester; Don Muro; Carol Myford, Educational Testing Service Center for Performance Assessment; Frank Phillips, Council of Chief State School Officers; Scott Shuler, Connecticut State Department of Education; Scott Stoner, ARTSEDGE, John F. Kennedy Center for the Performing Arts; Jack Taylor, Center for Music Research, Florida State University; James Undercofler, Minnesota Center for Arts Education; John Williams, former graduate student, Indiana University; Jean Wilmouth, Musik Innovations; Bruce Wilson, Special Collections in Music, The University of Maryland College Park; Cindi Wobig, American Orff Schulwerk Organization.

Preface to the First Edition

It is always important for educators to be aware of recent developments and trends in education. It is especially important at this particular time, when American education is in a state of intense, and in some cases overwhelming, change. Busy educators find it difficult to keep up with "what's new," and almost impossible to find the time to digest the origins, mechanics, and implications of trends. Every current trend does not affect every educator, but change in general does. Educators owe themselves, their students, and their profession a commitment to the present and the future. In order to fulfill that commitment it is imperative to understand what is happening now and to try and formulate implications for the future.

Music educators need to be aware of trends because the modes of response to society's educational needs change as society does. Because of the changing nature of music, music educators must be informed of how the profession remains contemporary and viable. In recent years changes in music education philosophy and methodology have brought happy results. Music educators who take the trouble to keep up with current trends and events do so with pride and hope for the future of the profession.

PART I

SOCIAL AND INTELLECTUAL
FOUNDATIONS OF
CONTEMPORARY MUSIC
EDUCATION

1

Historical Foundations of Music Education

Early American Music Education

Life was difficult for the first permanent English settlers in the New World. Having rebelled against political and church authority in England, the Pilgrims and Puritans had to find a new home where they could escape religious persecution and worship according to their beliefs. After the Pilgrims arrived in America in 1620, and the Puritans in 1630, they finally possessed the religious freedom they craved. They had brought with them their treasured musical traditions, especially the psalm singing that was central to their church service, but the challenges they had to overcome to create a new society in the wilderness prevented them from maintaining their musical skills. There was too much to do to create shelter and to feed and clothe themelves, and after the first generation, there were too few musically educated people. Succeeding generations may have had somewhat easier circumstances, but they, too, had to endure harsh realities. It was all but inevitable that musical standards declined in this atmosphere, and with lack of music instruction, each new generation was less musically skilled than the one before it.

Despite the harshness of the environment, the colonists recognized the importance of education to their future. The Massachusetts Bay Colony passed school laws early in its history. The first, the Massachusetts School Law of 1642, required town officials to compel parents to provide their children with an elementary education. The law did not establish schools; it merely set up minimum essentials of education and allowed each town to comply in the best way possible. The second law, the Massachusetts School Law of 1647, required that every township of at least fifty families appoint a teacher for the children, and that reading and writing be taught. Towns of 100 or more families were required to "set up a grammer schoole, the master thereof being able to instruct youth so farr as they may be fited for the university" [*sic*] (Harvard College was founded in 1636). Under this law, taxation for the purpose of paying a teacher was made legally permissible. The Massachusetts School Law of 1648 was more specific about what should be taught, and why:

> Forasmuch as the good education of children is of singular behoof and benefit to any Common-wealth; and whereas many parents and masters are too indulgent and negligent of their duty in that kinde. It is therefore ordered that the Select men of everie town, in the severall precincts and quarters where they dwell, shall have a vigilant eye over their brethren and neighbours to see, first that none of them shall suffer so much barbarism in any of their families as not to indeavor to teach by themselves or others their children and apprentices so much learning as may inable them perfectly to read the english tongue, and knowledge of the Capital lawes; upon penaltie of twentie shillings for each neglect therein. Also that all masters of families doe once a week (at the least) catechize their children and servants in the grounds and principles of Religion. . . . and further that all parents and masters do breed and bring up their children and apprentices in some honest lawfull calling, labour or imployment, either in husbandry, or some other trade profitable for themselves, and the Common-wealth, if they will not or can not train them up in learning to fit them for higher imployments.[1]

The legislatures of Connecticut, Plymouth, and New Hampshire enacted similar legislation within a few decades. Music was not considered a proper subject for study in the tax-supported schools at that time. That would not happen until the first half of the nineteenth century.

Musical traditions were transmitted orally in the New England colonies because most people were unable to read music. Having no music education system, succeeding generations could neither read notation nor sing with good tone quality, diction, and musicality. By the turn of the eighteenth century, many people, especially ministers, had expressed concern and alarm for the quality of congregational singing. Alice Morse Earle wrote: "Of all the dismal accompaniments of public worship in the early days of New England the music was the most hopelessly forlorn—not only from the confused versifications of the Psalms which were used, but from the mournful monotony of the few known tunes and the horrible manner in which these tunes were sung."[2] In 1721, Reverend Thomas Walter complained:

> The tunes are now miserably tortured and twisted and quavered in our churches, into a horrid medly of confused and disorderly voices. Our tunes are left to the mercy of every unskilled throat to chop

and alter, to twist and change, according to their infinitely diverse and no less odd humours and fancies. I have myself paused twice in one note to take a breath. No two men in the congregation quaver alike or together. It sounds in the ears of a good judge like five hundred tunes roared out at the same time, with perpetual interfearings with each other.[3]

THE DEVELOPMENT OF SINGING SCHOOLS

The response to the agitation caused by the critics of musical quality was seminal to the introduction of public music education. It was in the form of the "singing school," a movement in which itinerant singing masters provided their services to cities, towns, and villages for a fee. Classes were held for both children and adults in schools, churches, taverns, homes, or any other place where space was available. The singing masters taught the rudiments of music, and their pupils learned to read music from notation. Singing schools lasted from a couple of weeks to several months, after which the singing master traveled to the location of his next singing school. Entire families sometimes attended every time a singing school was held in their community. The singing master charged a fee for each student and earned additional income by selling tunebooks, most of which were compiled by himself or other singing masters.

Singing schools were highly regarded because they satisfied both musical and social purposes. People enjoyed singing and appreciated the pleasant social atmosphere in which they learned music reading and sang together.[4] The singing schools and other kinds of "night schools," including those for language, navigation, surveying, sewing, and cooking, fulfilled the need for practical education not yet met by the public schools. They probably came closer to true accountability than any public-school system in the second half of the twentieth century. The eighteenth-century night schools existed because people needed them, and teachers were able to earn their livelihoods (at least in part) because their students considered them necessary and effective. If the need for a particular subject did not exist, or if a teacher had not been successful in the past, then economic support was not forthcoming. No tax money was spent for these schools.

Singing schools did indeed help to improve the quality of singing in the churches. The movement lasted from the 1720s to the second half of the nineteenth century, and some singing schools still existed in isolated rural areas well into the twentieth century. The singing-school movement serves as an important example for contemporary educators in that they served a practical purpose, and they existed to meet a popular demand. It was a self-perpetuating movement: as people found more enjoyment in music, the demand for singing schools increased.

There was no formal methodology of teaching, but apparently the singing masters found a balance between pedagogy and performance that satisfied the public. During that period, the composers were also the teachers, and the earliest American school of composers, the "Yankee tunesmiths" (William Billings, Daniel Read, Oliver Holden, among others), were singing masters as well. The composers and their music were close to the people and were appreciated by them. Later generations of Americans became very much separated from composers, who were often put on a pedestal, revered, and known only to the part of the public that attended concerts. The Contemporary Music Project (see chapter 2) of the 1960s provided a historic service by placing composers and performers in public schools to make contemporary music a part of children's lives.

MUSIC INSTRUCTION IN PUBLIC SCHOOLS

Music was taught in schools in various parts of the country starting at the beginning of the nineteenth century. It was taught for a pragmatic reason: it was something children would need for both church and recreation. In 1838 Lowell Mason persuaded the Boston School Committee (board of education) to include music in the curriculum of the public schools as a regular subject. It was a major step forward because, for the first time, music instruction was to be supported by public taxes. In this way, it would be categorized with other curricular subjects. The School Committee report that recommended the addition of music in the schools justified the action with three reasons: music, like other school subjects, had to meet the criteria of being intellectually, morally, and physically beneficial to children. The report explained at length how music was beneficial for children in each of the three realms.[5] It also offered improved recreation, worship, and discipline as reasons for including music in the curriculum. The conclusion describes the effects that the study of music was expected to produce:

> In the language of an illustrious writer of the seventeenth century, "Music is a thing that delighteth all ages and beseemeth all states, a thing as seasonable in grief as joy, as decent being added to actions of greatest solemnity, as being used when men sequester themselves from action." If such be the natural effects of Music, if it enliven prosperity or soothe sorrow, if it quicken the pulses of social happiness, if it can fill the vacancy of an hour that would otherwise be listlessly or unprofitably spent, if it gild with a mild light the chequered scenes of daily existence, why then limit its benign and blessed influence? Let it, with healing on its wings, enter through ten thousand avenues the paternal dwelling. Let it mingle with religion, with labor, with the homebred amusements and innocent enjoyments of life. Let it no longer be regarded merely as the ornament of life. Let it no longer be regarded merely as the ornament of the rich. Still let it continue to adorn the abodes of wealth, but let it also light up with gladness, the honest hearth of poverty. Once introduce music into the common schools and you

make it what it should be made, the property of the whole people. And so as time passes away, and one race succeeds to another, the true object of our system of Public Education may be realized, and we may, year after year, raise up good citizens to the Commonwealth, by sending forth from our schools, happy, useful, well instructed, contented members of society.[6]

Music education has developed, matured, and flourished since 1838. The performance program has produced excellent choruses, bands, orchestras, small ensembles, and soloists; many teachers have been very successful with general music classes. However, music education, as a formal discipline within the public education structure, has not produced an adult population that is musically literate, appreciative, and participatory. The principal reasons are the lack of a common goal among music educators, and restrictive conditions that often impose limits on music programs. Music teachers, like all other teachers, must conform to the rules, regulations, traditions, and practices of the school systems that employ them. There have been notable exceptions, of course, and the fact that some regions of the United States have strong musical cultures is due, to some extent, to excellent school music programs.

Around the end of the nineteenth century, a pedagogical battle took place between music teachers who believed that the teaching of music reading should be a rote process and those who advocated a pure reading approach. The battle was beneficial to the profession because it made teachers think about methodology. Before coming to grips with method, however, teachers had to reflect on the most basic consideration: Why should the subject be taught at all? When the smoke of battle cleared around the turn of the twentieth century, some music educators began to realize that the "why" had never received proper consideration before teaching methods were developed. They had assumed that teaching children to read music to enable them to sing the great choral literature (which was a major goal at that time) was sufficient justification for music in public education. At the beginning of the twentieth century, when the child-centered movement in American education was taking hold, music educators finally began to agree that music education could be justified only in terms of helping children to enjoy music so it could become an important part of their lives. Samuel Cole said at a 1903 meeting of the National Education Association:

> The real purpose of teaching music in the public schools is not to make expert sight singers nor individual soloists. I speak from experience. I have done all these things and I can do them again; but I have learned that, if they become an end and not a means they hinder rather than help, because they represent only the abilities of the few. A much nobler, grander, more inspiring privilege is yours and mine; to get the great mass to singing and to make them love it.[7]

The time was right because the new child-centered approach valued the arts in education. The work of Friedrich Froebel, John Dewey, and Maria Montessori affected education in ways favorable to music and the other arts. Music appreciation was introduced into the curriculum, as were music literature, history, and theory. Instrumental music assumed an increasingly important place in the schools.

Although the American public is quite musical, its taste is decidedly for popular music. Both popular music and art music are important components of our society, and both enrich us in many ways. Many musically educated people enjoy both, although most musically uneducated people do not enjoy art music. For this reason, most symphony orchestras, opera companies, and other producers of art music lack adequate financial support. This implies that not enough of the public values art music sufficiently to assure its well being. Why is this so when music education has been offered for so long and to so many people?

Historic Problems of American Music Education

METHODOLOGY

Methodology continued to be a problem even after the child-centered curriculum was implemented in the early part of this century. Music teachers had to conform to a broader school philosophy and curriculum. Silberman states:

> The normal school movement viewed teachers as technicians rather than as autonomous professionals, and trained them accordingly. This view was solidified in the first few decades of this century, when superintendents of schools were caught up in the national fervor for "Scientific Management." Slavishly imitating the way they (sometimes mistakenly) thought corporate executives operated, superintendents tried to control the most minute details of school operation . . . teachers were production line workers whose every move had to be controlled and checked.[8]

Teachers who had so little freedom to operate independently were often unable to implement a successful child-centered aesthetic approach to music education. Despite having to use materials that were not especially conducive to true musical learning, music educators did help many children develop a true love of music. Their elementary graded music series, music appreciation books, and instrumental method books stressed cognitive learning and psychomotor development. The music in them, however, was not usually of high quality. Much of it was what we refer to as "educational music," derived from European musical traditions and arranged in nonauthentic fashion at a level of difficulty suitable for children. It did not necessarily engage the students' interest. Throughout most of this century the authors of educational music materials have, for the most part, failed to take advantage of the extensive body of excellent music that represents the classical and folk traditions.

LACK OF APPRECIATION FOR DIVERSITY

The population of the United States is extremely diversified, comprising people from virtually every national and ethnic background. Most of the early immigrants came from Western Europe, and Africans were brought to America as slaves soon after Europeans started to arrive. Later, Asians, Eastern and Central Europeans, and Hispanics began to immigrate, and by the end of the nineteenth century huge waves of immigrants from all parts of the world had poured into the United States. Despite the heterogeneity of the population it served, music education of the nineteenth century, and even of much of the twentieth century, was based especially on Western art music. Until the 1960s, music teachers attempted to "teach up" to what was considered a "cultured" level, meaning the music of the upper economic class. Western classical music was viewed as the best music, and teachers thought it proper to encourage students to aspire to it.

Beginning around the turn of the century, music education became a tool of the "melting pot." The phrase "melting pot" is derived from the famous line in Israel Zangwill's 1908 play, *The Melting Pot*: "America is God's Crucible, the great Melting-Pot where all the races of Europe are melting and re-forming." The melting pot concept appealed both to Americans who had been here for a long time and to many new Americans who were eager to assimilate so they could share in the wealth of their new country. Well-meaning societal leaders attempted to realize their ideal through many of America's institutions, including the workplace, the military, the streets, the media, and especially the schools. Music education played an important role in trying to homogenize a highly diverse population, and first- and second-generation Americans accepted the belief that it could help to elevate their children socially. It is not surprising that the national and ethnic musics of the more recent immigrants were not the stuff of school music programs. Most music educators, and probably most Americans whose families had arrived from Europe generations earlier, did not respect the music of the newcomers. Perhaps they were not even aware of it.

At that time, the music education profession did not attempt to find a reasonable balance between what was most meaningful musically to students and the "cultured" music derived from the European classical music heritage. This unbalanced approach probably failed to interest many pupils in art music, which requires knowledge, experience, and sophistication for most people to appreciate. Music educators were not to blame, though. They were helping to implement a massive social movement to assimilate immigrants and their children.

It has only been since the 1960s that the American education establishment has come genuinely to respect the heritage of every student. Social movements, legislation, and court decisions have finally persuaded us of the value and significance of social, ethnic, and cultural diversity in American society. Since the 1960s, American schools have attempted to teach about diversity, and the curriculum now is structured to reflect various cultural values and traditions.

PASSIVE LISTENING

Much earlier than the melting pot phenomenon, many Americans had become interested in listening to art music. In fact, we began to become a nation of listeners long before school music programs were plentiful enough to influence great numbers of people. Earlier, when people wanted music, they had to make it themselves because there were few places where they could hear it. In the first half of the nineteenth century, however, European concert artists discovered America and American audiences. They came here and toured, and Americans loved them. European recitalists, opera companies, and orchestras introduced millions of Americans to the best European art music. Americans idolized performers like Jenny Lind and Ole Bull. Their examples inspired American professional musicians, and eventually audiences had the opportunity to be captivated and enthralled by many excellent American touring organizations like the Theodore Thomas Orchestra and the Patrick Gilmore and John Philip Sousa bands.

Not surprisingly, the richness of American concert life led to passive participation. Music became a connoisseur art heard in concert halls, rather than an integral part of everyday life in which great numbers of people participated. School bands, orchestras, and choruses changed this somewhat throughout the twentieth century. Even so, despite their wealth of performing experiences as students, most of the children who participated did not continue to do so after completing their schooling. Some joined community bands, choruses, and orchestras, and for a time (until the 1930s) it was common for industry to sponsor choruses, bands, and orchestras comprised of its own employees; some industrial music ensembles still exist, but not to the extent of earlier years. This was a generous and humanistic aspect of some American industrial corporations, but most of these organizations have been replaced by piped-in "canned" music, selected for its ability to create an environment conducive to greater productivity.[a] The loss of so many of these participative activities is a loss to American society.

Live public concerts have been an important part of American musical life from the colonial period to the present, and throughout

---

[a]There are still many industrially sponsored musical organizations in Europe and Asia.

most of the twentieth century, music has been increasingly more accessible to all Americans, even in the most remote areas, through radio, television, and recordings. What we have come to call the "popular culture" arose with the advent of broadcast media and recordings, and much of the music that Americans have listened to from the early part of the twentieth century has been popular music. Considering that Americans prefer, for the most part, the kinds of music that have not traditionally been emphasized in school music programs, music educators need to question seriously how much they have actually affected the adult musical life of the nation. School music has endeavored to align itself more closely with the various musical tastes of the public since the late 1960s. Perhaps this practice will allow it to have more influence on the musical life of the nation in the future.

EMPHASIS ON PERFORMANCE

There has been great emphasis on performance in school music throughout most of this century, and student performance is often considered the educational product. Despite the emphasis on performance to the present, however, most music students do not continue to perform after graduating from school, nor do they develop enthusiasm for classical music in adulthood.

The technical quality of student performance is excellent, and it has set an example for much of the rest of the world. Large-ensemble performance, however, is somewhat restrictive for individual members, who learn to play second violin parts, third clarinet parts, tuba parts, and so forth, to the best of their abilities. The participants in the Yale Seminar (see chapter 2) pointed out that this does not really constitute music learning. The student musician who learns to play one particular part to a symphony or a Sousa march does not necessarily know anything else about the music, and has probably not developed much musical independence by playing that part in the ensemble. In that regard, performance in a chamber ensemble is usually more beneficial to students as they develop musically. Large-ensemble participation, on the other hand, is extremely gratifying to students, especially when the group performs for an appreciative audience or receives a high festival rating. The individual students are happy, proud, and satisfied and have derived pleasure from the experience. Yet, they often do not learn much about music from it.

MUSIC EDUCATION AS ENTERTAINMENT

Entertainment has often dominated the educational aspect of school music programs. This practice has been fueled by choice of music, musical competitions so intense that they rival athletic contests, and the flash and glitter of bright uniforms, colorful costumes, clever choreography, instruments in a variety of colors, all in a milieu that proclaims to the community, "We're here to entertain you and to show how well we can imitate professional entertainers." This view of student performance is so ingrained in some communities that willingness to fund their music programs often depends on the quality of entertainment and success in competitions.

Entertainment and competition are satisfying, wholesome, and healthy outlets that most people enjoy, and they should be part of school music programs. If they are the fundamental rationale for school music performance, however, the purpose of music education is questionable. Even if funding is based on these aspects of performance, ultimately such programs are endangered because boards of education can easily justify eliminating them in order to better support the more educational subjects. The arts education professional associations issued a joint statement on the subject in 1986:

> While all art has elements of entertainment, all entertainment is not art. If we lose the concept of distinction between the two, we lose the basis for discrimination about the relative purposes and values of aesthetic materials. At its extreme, such a condition creates an impossible context for providing rationales in support of serious arts education programs at the K–12 level.[9]

Jerrold Ross, Director of the National Arts Education Research Center, discusses the problem in pragmatic terms:

> Music education, which has always been described as the "loud speaker" when it comes to improving school public relations, needs to grow beyond that characterization (which, by the way, has rarely saved music programs in the schools as the budget axe swings in times of trouble) to something more accepted and valued by communities as disparate as East Harlem and East Lansing. How to advocate music beyond its value as entertainment for the community and how to involve parents and significant adults in a constructive way that helps the school to promote human values are questions that require immediate and continuous attention. . . . What needs to be understood . . . is that music education does not deserve recognition unless it is a principal player in connecting the aesthetic to other forms of human experience.[10]

Despite these problems, American music education has helped many millions of American children to learn about, participate in, and enjoy music. There are many other people, however, whose lives have not been touched by music even though they received music instruction in school. It is still the goal of the American music education profession to educate all children in music, and to provide the widest possible variety of musical experiences. Many things rally against good education at this time—a weak economy, social problems, and so on—but the same has been true at other times as well. Now, as then, educators must find ways to continue providing the highest possible quality of education to their students.

Changing Attitudes Toward Education

The U.S. mass education system, designed in the early part of the century for a mass production economy, will not succeed unless it not only raises but redefines the essential standards of excellence and strives to make quality and equality of opportunity compatible with each other.[11]

Dwight W. Allen, 1992

THE 1950s

American education in the 1950s was characterized by turmoil. The United States assumed a new role as one of two global superpowers after World War II, and by the early 1950s it was again caught up in world events. The Cold War and the Korean conflict created not only tension in all aspects of American life, but also a divisiveness in American society that was reflected in the educational structure. We feel the results of that divisiveness even now.

Fluctuating world and national conditions were so precarious in the 1950s that it was not possible to define the kind of world for which our schools were educating students. Sand and Miller stated:

1. Contemporary society is changing so fundamentally and rapidly that we have difficulty fitting ourselves in to the present and projecting ourselves into the future.
2. The almost incredible explosion of knowledge threatens to overwhelm unless we can find, and quickly, some intelligent solutions to problems created by the new and growing wealth of information.
3. Significant discoveries are being made about people and learning—discoveries that emphasize the vast range of differences among and within individuals and point to the great variety of ways in which people can learn. At a time when there is so much to be learned, and so urgent a need to learn it, we must create new teaching methods and adapt old ones to accelerate and enrich the teaching-learning process.[12]

Throughout the 1950s the schools were attacked from both the right and the left, with each side charging the entire educational system with anti-intellectualism. As the decade progressed, industrial, military, and educational leaders became increasingly aware of the fact that educational change was necessary to meet societal demands. A climate of urgency developed and was greatly intensified when, in October 1957, the Soviet

Union launched the first space satellite, Sputnik I. This shocked the American people, who were abruptly awakened to the fact that the Soviet Union had taken the lead in space technology, and by doing so had gained a military advantage that terrified the rest of the world. Thus, educational reform was needed not only for improved living standards, but to assure that we could remain technologically capable of defending ourselves from military attack.

Starting in 1958, the process of change in American education accelerated dramatically.[13] An analysis of change in New York State public schools indicated that the rate of innovation more than doubled in the fifteen months following the launch of Sputnik I. Change was spurred by vocal and provocative education critics like Vice Admiral Hyman G. Rickover, who directed the development of the United States Navy atomic submarine program. His was a strong voice in compelling American education to prepare students for the needs of a technological society. He wrote:

> Russia has built an educational system in record time which produces exactly the sort of trained men and women her rulers need to achieve technical supremacy. . . . Russia has no substandard teachers . . . students are studious, polite, well-disciplined, and earnest. . . . [Students] have no competing attractions, no comfortable homes, no playrooms, no jukeboxes, no senior proms, no dating, hardly any radio or TV, and no hot rods.[14]

Soviet Union's triumph in space technology indicated weakness in our society. To correct that deficiency, it was necessary to accord the highest status in our society to scientists and engineers, and to reorganize American education to strengthen science education. Rickover compared American and European education and found the American system lacking. European education, as he perceived it, provided the essential intellectual, cultural, and physical requirements. Students who were unable to meet requirements were shifted to vocational training. To Rickover, the American system wasted precious resources by attempting to educate everyone equally, regardless of ability. Activities like field trips, assemblies, artistic endeavors, and extracurricular activities were further evidence of waste. He strongly recommended that more money be spent on education, that science and math offerings be strengthened, and that all frills be eliminated from the curriculum.

Dr. James Bryant Conant, former president of Harvard University, was another influential education critic. Conant stressed the need for stronger math and science programs, but unlike Rickover, he recommended that students include music and art in their high school elective programs.[15] Rickover, Conant, and other critics helped make Americans aware of the importance of what were considered to be the most basic subjects: reading, mathematics, science, and foreign languages.

A particularly misguided education objective that emerged in the 1950s, and which still exists, has colored every reform movement to the present. The basic skills—reading, writing, mathematics—were emphasized so heavily that they became the major focus of education policy development, assessment, and funding. Many leaders lost sight of the fact that these skills are simply tools that open the gate to education. They are not an education in themselves.

National attention to education was further magnified when the federal government became involved. In 1960 President Eisenhower appointed eleven distinguished Americans to the Commission on National Goals. Education was one of the areas addressed by the commission. The final report, "National Goals in Education," known as the Gardner Report (prepared by John W. Gardner, president of the Carnegie Corporation), was a strong statement of educational philosophy and goals that served as a basis for change in American education. In 1961 President Kennedy established the White House Panel on Educational Research and Development (an advisory board to the U.S. Office of Education, the National Science Foundation, and his own science adviser) to help improve American education. The panel adopted three goals. The immediate goal was to address the issue of urban education, which was failing miserably in preparing students for their future roles in American society. The second was to improve instruction through new and daring curricula, and was to be paralleled by more effective recruiting and training of teachers. The third goal was to solve the problems caused by lack of understanding of the nature of learning.[16]

An important event occurred in 1959, when the Woods Hole (Massachusetts) Conference took place. Its purpose was to identify the problems of science education and to recommend solutions. The conference was convened by the Education Committee of the National Academy of Sciences and was supported by the Academy, the U.S. Office of Education, the Air Force, and the Rand Corporation. Educators, historians, physicists, biologists, psychologists, and mathematicians attended the ten-day conference. This was the beginning of a new trend in educational planning: the unified efforts of distinguished people in varied fields addressing themselves to the general improvement of education.[17] The Woods Hole Conference generated many other curriculum studies in academic subjects; a 1962 review listed ten projects in science, eleven in mathematics, one in language arts, two in foreign languages, and four in social studies. In 1961 the National Education Association sponsored a large-scale "Project on Instruction," which involved scholars in all disciplines.[18]

The federal government strongly supported change in education. The Cooperative Research Branch of the Office of Education disbursed approximately $10 million a year from 1956 to 1961 for 407 research projects. The National Science Foundation granted $159 million in

1960, $34 million of which went to teacher improvement institutes that served 31,000 teachers. In 1961 more than half of all funds granted by large foundations were for educational enterprises.[19]

The vast resources that were poured into education in the late 1950s and early 1960s were mostly for the improvement of curricular areas directly related to the perceived needs of the postindustrial technological society. The arts were not excluded from the movement, but neither did they receive generous support from it. The nation had focused its attention on what were considered to be the basic subjects, and many people thought of the arts as an educational "frill" that contributed little to children's needs. Some school systems went to frivolous extremes to create a sharp dichotomy between "solid" and "extraneous" courses: "One school system labels as 'food for thought' content of mathematics, science, English, history, and foreign language courses. Electives are called desserts and are used mainly to tempt the appetites of students who are not college bound."[20]

The implications of an unbalanced curriculum were clear to many educators. In 1959, the American Association of School Administrators (AASA) expressed support for a more complete curriculum:

> We believe in a well balanced school curriculum in which music, drama, painting, poetry, sculpture, architecture, and the like are included side by side with other important subjects such as mathematics, history, and science. It is important that pupils, as a part of general education, learn to appreciate, to understand, to create, and to criticize with discrimination those products of the mind, the voice, the hand, and the body which give dignity to the person and exalt the spirit of man.[21]

The National Education Association's Project on Instruction supported arts education. Its report stated that school priorities included skills in reading, composition, listening, speaking (both English and foreign languages), creative and disciplined thinking, and "fundamental understanding of the humanities and the arts, the social sciences and the natural sciences, and in literature, music, and the visual arts."[22] Despite the support of NEA, the perception of music education as a nonacademic subject persisted. Music educators realized the importance of being included in education reform, and worked to change that perception. The theme of the 1962 Music Educators National Conference (MENC) biennial meeting was music as an academic subject; its title was "The Study of Music: An Academic Discipline."

Scientists, alarmed by the curricular imbalance, added their voices to the chorus of support for arts education. The White House Panel on Educational Research and Development stated:

> Certain members of the Panel were convinced that there was a degree of correlation between excellence in scientific achievement

and the breadth of an individual's human experience. The best scientists, it was thought, were not necessarily those who had devoted themselves singlemindedly to their own field; somehow, familiarity with the arts and humanities sharpened a good scientist's vision.[23]

THE 1960s

The 1960s were a time of economic strength for education because the "baby boom" that followed World War II generated high enrollments. The maturation of that generation, combined with the social reforms of the 1960s, changed the character of American education profoundly. The sudden growth of the school population created a shortage of qualified teachers, and teacher education standards were reduced to bring more people into the profession. Combined with traditionally low teacher salaries, this tended to discourage people of the highest ability from entering the teaching profession.[b]

By the end of the 1960s portents of future problems were appearing. Like the period immediately preceding the Great Depression of 1929, it was a time of plenty for education, but educational quality continued to deteriorate. The gradual and insidious decline was augured by the downward trend of SAT scores. By the end of the 1960s, however, standards had not yet sunk to the point where educators and the public were overly alarmed. That was to happen in the next decade.

THE 1970s

Education in the 1970s was characterized by decline. During the early part of the decade, greatly increased oil prices severely affected world economic conditions. The ensuing inflation seriously hampered the ability of local school districts to maintain adequate funding levels. The states had similar problems and were unable to compensate for the shortages faced by local school districts. The federal government, now faced with new crises in social policy, foreign affairs, and the economy, diverted its attention and support away from education. This shift effectively ended a period of educational research and development that had been sponsored by government grants.

The government did not abandon education completely. It maintained research activities, but with very few funded projects and development activities. It did this in 1972 by replacing the Bureau of Research of the U.S. Office of Education with the National Institute of Education (NIE), which assumed responsibility for federal educational

---

[b]There is an irony in the contrasting methods of industry and education in attracting more workers when the labor supply is short. Industry raises salaries to make its jobs more attractive to workers. School systems, on the other hand, have traditionally dealt with teacher shortages by reducing professional and educational requirements for new teachers.

research. The federal government maintained that it continued to lead in research efforts: "While the direction of the education system remains primarily the responsibility of State and local governments, the Federal Government has a clear responsibility to provide leadership in the conduct and support of scientific inquiry into the educational process." NIE was established to "advance the practice of education, as an art, science, and profession; strengthen the scientific and technological foundations of education; and build an effective educational research and development system." Probably the most important function of NIE was the dissemination of research findings through its Educational Resources Information Center (see chapter 4). As valuable as this role is, and despite the strong leadership statement (above) in the legislation that created NIE, it actually allowed the federal government to reduce its direct involvement in education.

School enrollments declined to earlier levels because the children of the baby boom generation had completed their schooling. Fewer teachers were needed, and the number of music teaching positions declined significantly, as did positions in art and other subjects. One of the ways in which boards of education cut costs was to reduce the number of periods in the school day, thus decreasing the availability of electives. This compounded the problem because fewer students could take music in school. In addition, the student bodies of under-enrolled schools were often consolidated, thus further reducing the need for music teaching positions.

During this period of enrollment decline, educational quality continued to decrease as well. By the end of the decade, it was at such a low level that the nation realized that it had to deal with the problem quickly and effectively. In 1980 the average math SAT score had plunged to an all-time low of 466. Juvenile crime, drugs, and other social problems had created even more problems for the schools. Conditions were worse than they had been a decade earlier, and they had been extremely serious at that time. Equally important, public confidence in the nation's schools had dropped precipitously.

Earlier in the 1970s, as public awareness of the situation was beginning to grow, an accountability movement developed. Various accountability devices were implemented in schools as a panacea for declining performance. Although it did not prove to be a cure, the accountability movement helped clarify educational goals and objectives. It also provided a means of measuring the educational progress of individuals and the effectiveness of the educational system. Later in the decade, as the public became increasingly aware of the continuing decline of its educational system, calls for reform began to be heard from educators and from business, industry, the military, and the general public. The desire for reform developed into a "back-to-basics" movement, which, like earlier efforts, turned out to be an attempt to identify basic subjects, emphasize them, eliminate frills, and produce reasonably high learning and teaching standards.

THE 1980s

In the early 1980s a series of studies and reports on the plight of American education echoed the public alarm that was raised after the launch of Sputnik in 1957. By 1980 everybody recognized that something had to be done to improve American education. Although it was a national issue, the federal government did not have authority over education. In addition, most educational funding comes from the states and localities. With approximately 16,000 school districts in the United States, it is virtually impossible to achieve uniformity of quality on a national scale. The federal government can only identify problems, recommend solutions, offer some (but never enough) funding, and encourage the states and localities to find the will and resources to effect reform. Later, the federal government would find a way to become more directly involved in reform (see chapter 4).

Other factors contributed to the problems in American schools as well. The fifty years leading to the 1980s saw a drop in the number of school districts from 130,000 to 16,000. The percentage of classroom teachers in the total school staff declined from 96 percent to 86 percent, and the amount of school support from local governments declined from 83 percent to 43 percent. During the same period, the population almost doubled, and the per-student cost increased almost 500 percent.[24]

National Reports on American Education

In 1983, following years of increasingly harsh rhetoric about poor educational quality, several national reports informed the public about various studies that had been completed and their recommendations for proposed solutions to the problems.

THE NATIONAL COMMISION ON EXCELLENCE IN EDUCATION

The National Commission on Excellence in Education, a presidential commission, released a report titled *A Nation at Risk: The Imperative for Educational Reform* in April 1983. It echoed the calls for reform heard in 1957:

> If an unfriendly foreign power had attempted to impose on America the mediocre educational performance that exists today, we might well have viewed it as an act of war. As it stands, we have allowed this to happen to ourselves. We have even squandered the gains in student achievement made in the wake of the Sputnik challenge.

The report listed numerous defects in the educational system, making the point that, by any of a number of measures, the quality of American education had declined significantly. The current level of mediocrity was unlikely to produce an educated adult population capable of living productive and satisfying lives in the increasingly technological world community. As other nations overtook us in educational matters, the United States could be expected to fall behind economically, and the result would be a lower quality of life. (The findings of several sociological and economic studies have indeed shown that the quality of life in several other nations has surpassed that of the United States.) It recommended that elementary and secondary school curricula should include subjects that "advance students' personal, educational, and occupational goals, such as the fine and performing arts and vocational education."

MAKING THE GRADE: THE 20TH CENTURY FUND TASK FORCE ON FEDERAL ELEMENTARY AND SECONDARY EDUCATION POLICY

The 20th Century Fund Task Force released its report in May 1983. The task force called on "the executive and legislative branches of the federal government to emphasize the need for better schools and a better education for all young Americans." It recommended that (1) a national master teacher program be established to recognize and reward excellent teachers; (2) "the federal government clearly state that the most important objective of elementary and secondary education in the United States is the development of literacy in the English language"; and (3) various actions be taken by the federal government to improve science, math, and foreign language education and special education programs; to fund education; and to utilize research to improve education. The report did not mention music education, although one could easily infer the need for it:

> As we see it, the public schools, which constitute the nation's most important institution for the shaping of future citizens, must go further. We think that they should insure the availability of large numbers of skilled and capable individuals without whom we cannot sustain a complex and competitive economy. They should foster understanding, discipline, and discernment, those qualities of mind and temperament that are the hallmarks of a civilized polity and that are essential for the maintenance of a domestic tranquility in a poly-ethnic constitutional democracy. And they should impart to present and future generations a desire to acquire knowledge, ranging from the principles of science to the accumulated wisdom and shared values that derive from the nation's rich and varied cultural heritage.

THE NATIONAL SCIENCE BOARD COMMISSION ON PRECOLLEGE EDUCATION IN MATHEMATICS, SCIENCE, AND TECHNOLOGY

The Commission, a panel of the National Science Foundation, published its report in September 1983. It was entitled "Educating Americans for the 21st Century: A plan of action for improving mathematics, science and technology education for all American elementary and secondary students so that their achievement is the best in the world by 1995." The report urged the federal government to take a leadership role in education, warning that the United States "must not become an industrial dinosaur," and stated: "The nation that led the world into the age of technology is failing to provide its own children with the intellectual tools needed for the 21st century." The report also recommended a longer school day, more required courses for high school graduation and admission to college, and higher teacher pay:

> The Commission recognizes . . . the interrelationships among all areas of learning, and that there are also glaring deficiencies in the teaching and learning of English and foreign languages, history, political science, the classics, art, music and other areas of study important for life in the 21st century. Plans and programs to meet these problems are vital. The commission hopes such plans and programs will be developed with the same time schedule in mind.

THE COLLEGE BOARD STUDY

The document that offered the most support for arts education, and the most pragmatic of all the reports, was *Academic Preparation for College: What Students Need to Know and Be Able to Do*, published in 1983 by the College Board. The College Board publishes tests and provides other educational services for students, schools, and colleges. It is highly influential in such areas as college admissions and high school curriculum. The report is a part of the College Board Educational Quality Project, a long-term effort to improve the academic quality of secondary education and to assure that all students have equal opportunities for postsecondary education.

It identified English, the arts, mathematics, science, social studies, and foreign languages as the basic subjects:

> WHY? The arts—visual arts, theater, music, and dance—challenge and extend human experience. They provide means of expression that go beyond ordinary speaking and writing. They can express intimate thoughts and feelings. They are a unique record of diverse cultures and how these cultures have developed over time. They provide distinctive ways of understanding human beings and nature. The arts are creative modes by which all people can enrich their lives both by self-expression and response to the expressions of others.
>
> Works of art often involve subtle meanings and complex systems of expression. Fully appreciating such works requires the careful reasoning and sustained study that lead to informed insight. Moreover, just as thorough understanding of science requires laboratory or field work, so fully understanding the arts involves firsthand work in them.
>
> Preparation in the arts will be valuable to college entrants whatever their intended field of study. The actual practice of the arts can engage the imagination, foster flexible ways of thinking,

develop disciplined effort, and build self-confidence. Appreciation of the arts is integral to the understanding of other cultures sought in the study of history, foreign language, and social sciences. Preparation in the arts will also enable college students to engage in and profit from advanced study, performance, and studio work in the arts. For some, such college-level work will lead to careers in the arts. For many others, it will permanently enhance the quality of their lives, whether they continue artistic activity as an avocation or appreciation of the arts as observers and members of audiences.

WHAT? If the preparation of college entrants is in music, they will need the following knowledge and skills.

- The ability to identify and describe—using the appropriate vocabulary—various musical forms from different historical periods.
- The ability to listen perceptively to music, distinguishing such elements as pitch, rhythm, timbre, and dynamics.
- The ability to read music.
- The ability to evaluate a musical work or performance.
- To know how to express themselves by playing an instrument, singing in a group or individually, or composing music.[25]

THE PAIDEIA PROPOSAL

The Paideia Proposal was written by Mortimer Adler, who proposed that there be no electives in the curriculum, and that all students take the same three-part course of study. The three parts do not correspond to specific separate courses. The proposal recommended that organized knowledge be acquired in three broad areas: language, literature, and the fine arts; mathematics and natural science; and history, geography, and other social studies. He also recommended Socratic questioning to enlarge understanding of ideas and values, as well as discussion of books and other works of art, and involvement in music, drama, and visual arts.[26]

THE CARNEGIE FOUNDATION FOR THE ADVANCEMENT OF TEACHING

The Foundation released its report, written by its president, former United States Commissioner of Education Ernest Boyer, in 1983. It was entitled *High School: A Report on Secondary Education in America.* Boyer recommended that the first two years of high school be dominated by a core curriculum of required courses, including the arts: "The arts are an essential part of the human experience. They are not a frill. We recommend that all students study the arts to discover how human beings use nonverbal symbols and communicate not only with words but through music, dance, and the visual arts."[27]

A PLACE CALLED SCHOOL

A Place Called School, by John Goodlad, strongly supported arts education. Goodlad proposed that from 10 to 15 percent of each student's program be in the arts. Another 10 to 20 percent should be reserved for the development of student interests and talents; much of this time would be used for arts activities. Goodlad refuted the argument that there is not enough time in the school day for all of the subjects that need to be offered in a curriculum of high quality. He pointed out ways in which a great deal of time was wasted because of current practices, and recommended how subjects might be scheduled more efficiently and effectively.[28]

Summary of National Reports

Although each report emphasized a particular point of view, there were areas of commonality among them. In general, they agreed that the goals of education needed to be clarified. Those commissions interested in particular disciplines, such as math and science, tended to recommend goals that supported science and technology. Commissions that perceived education primarily as preparation for work tended to downplay the importance of education for personal fulfillment. There was agreement "that schools must continue to develop academic competencies, foster vocational skills and awareness, contribute to personal fulfillment and cultivate civic responsibility." There was also general agreement that all students should be required to complete a core curriculum, but not on what should constitute the core.[29]

Arts educators were pleased to note that most of the reports that were based on research and informed reflection supported arts education. The greatest disappointment to arts educators was *A Nation at Risk*, in which the arts were minimally supported, being subordinated to what the National Commission on Excellence in Education identified as the basic subjects. Paul Lehman stated:

> I wish that the press coverage and the public discussion of this document had reflected the emphasis it places on the arts. At the same time, I am deeply disappointed that the Commission assigned the arts to a second tier of priorities, clearly subordinate to the highest ranked fields of study. In this respect, *A Nation at Risk* is sharply at odds with most other major reports, which have included the arts among the basics.[30]

Responses to National Reports and Critics

Responses to the flurry of reports on the state of American education and their recommendations were many and varied. Fred Hechinger wrote, "The mass of proposals amid contradictory remedies could well neutralize each other. A confused public may grow impatient with all the talk and counter-talk and tune out again. Then, nothing would happen beyond some minor cosmetic readjustments."[31] Diane Ravitch warned about the ineffectiveness and danger of panaceas meant to improve education. In her history of American education from 1945 to 1980, she described the equal opportunity movement as the main focus for reform at all levels of education:

> Probably no other idea has seemed more typically American than the belief that schooling could cure someone's ills. As a result, sometimes schools have been expected to take on responsibilities for which they were entirely unsuited. When they have failed, it was usually because their leaders and the public alike had forgotten their real limitations as well as their real strengths.[32]

Ravitch's warning is supported by many studies from the 1960s to the 1980s that indicate that there is little relationship between the amount of money spent for education and improvement in the quality of education.

John Mahlmann, Executive Director of the Music Educators National Conference, wrote:

> We cannot allow the deafening roar of the educational critics to drown out the sounds of music in the schools. The report, *A Nation at Risk*, provides a balanced picture. However, in our haste to take remedial action to combat the "rising tide of mediocrity," which, the report charges, is eroding the allocational foundations of our society, it is possible that our good intentions can cause some serious oversights. So while we are "at risk" we will further exacerbate the situation, increase the risk, and stunt the chances for success if we are guilty of answering the call unaware of its emphasis on the important role of the arts in the education process. The real "risk" is not of failure to meet the challenges but in the dangers of overzealously attacking the system's balance of skill, knowledge and appreciation in all areas of learning.[33]

THE 1990s

The educational crisis of the previous forty years has continued into the 1990s. Now, as in the 1950s, excellence is more the exception than the rule. The dropout rate for high school students is above 25 percent. SAT scores have risen only slightly. American students have lower achievement levels than their counterparts in most other developed countries, and many are functionally unprepared to maintain and help move forward a technological society. Unreformed education is even a more serious matter in the 1990s than it was in the 1950s because new generations of students have been certified by their schools as educated when they actually lack basic literacy and numeracy skills. They are less able to cope with life in an advanced society than were their 1950s counterparts because there are fewer jobs for poorly educated people. These problems persist despite the fact that in 1990 the nation spent $215.5 billion on education, more than twice the amount spent ten years earlier.[34]

Nevertheless, progress has been made in the 1990s. Despite the long-standing problems, there is finally hope that true reform will occur. Early in the 1990s, the federal government renewed its involvement in education reform, which led to the most significant development in education reform since the 1950s: the enactment of federal legislation to adopt national educational standards. The national standards are expected to resolve a difficult issue that has always prevented national education reforms from succeeding. Diane Ravitch points out that, before the establishment of the standards, there had never been significant agreement on what students should learn in the various subjects, and at different grade levels. Other industrialized countries have been able to depend on their educational systems to prepare students effectively for adulthood. They can do this, in part, because they have decided what all of their students need to learn. The new national standards give us a way to decide what knowledge students in all states should have. Without this agreement, it is hardly possible even to agree on what problems need to be addressed.[35] The national standards, and their implications for music education, are discussed in chapter 2.

Conclusion

Almost everything new that has happened in music education from the 1970s to the 1990s has been the result of social issues that originated outside of the music education profession. The issues include national standards and goals, professional certification of music educators, multiculturalism, children-at-risk, practical applicability of the subject in the real-life world of society, assessment, technology, and decentralization and privatization of schools. All of these subjects are discussed in other parts of this book. Each is important, and if approached properly, will allow music educators to serve a greater variety of students in the future. Given the ever-increasing pace of change in our society, however, and unpredictable political pressures, it is possible that many of the activities in which we invest our energies today will be set aside prematurely as new areas of concern emerge.

What can be done to strengthen music education in the context of troubled schools? Fortunately, much can be done. It is possible that music education can help rejuvenate American education through efforts like the adoption of national standards by states and local school districts. This story will be told in later chapters.

NOTES

1 Sol Cohen, ed. *Education in the United States: A Documentary History*, vol. 1 (New York: Random House, 1974), 394–95.

2 Alice Morse Earle, *The Sabbath in Puritan New England* (Scribner's, 1896), quoted in Edward Bailey Birge, *History of Public Shool Music in the United States*, 2d ed. (Washington, DC: Music Educators National Conference, 1966), 4.

3 William Arms Fisher, *Notes on Music in Old Boston* (Oliver Ditson, 1918), quoted in Birge, *History of Public School Music*, 5.

4 Alice Morse Earle, *The Sabbath in Puritan New England*, quoted in Birge, 4.

5 "School Committee's Report," *Boston Musical Gazette*, no. 16 (5 December 1838): 123.; also reported in Birge, *History of Public School Music*, 40–50.

6 "School Committee's Report," *Boston Musical Gazette* no. 18 (26 December 1838): 137.

7 Birge, *History of Public School Music*, 61–62.

8 Charles E. Silberman, *Crisis in the Classroom* (New York: Random House, 1970), 437, 438.

9 *K–12 Arts Education in the United States: Present Context, Future Needs*. A briefing paper for the arts education community (Reston, VA: Music Educators National Conference. National Art Education Association, National Dance Association, National Association of Schools of Music, National Association of Schools of Art and Design, National Association of Schools of Theater, National Association of Schools of Dance, 1986), 6.

10 Jerrold Ross, "Research in Music Education: From a National Perspective." *Bulletin* of the Council for Research in Music Education, no. 123 (Winter 1994/1995): 126.

11 Dwight Allen, *Schools for a New Century: A Conservative Approach to Radical School Reform* (New York: Praeger, 1992), 2.

12 Ole Sand and Richard E. Miller, *Schools for the Sixties*, Report of the Project on Instruction, National Education Association (New York: McGraw-Hill, 1963), vii–viii.

13 Matthew B. Miles, "Educational Innovation: The Nature of the Problem," in *Issues in Education*, ed. Matthew B. Miles (New York: Bureau of Publications, Columbia University Teachers College, 1964), 8.

14 "Rickover, in Book, Attacks Schools," *New York Times*, 30 January 1959, 10.

15 James B. Conant, *The American High School Today* (New York: McGraw-Hill, 1959), 48.

16 Jerome S. Bruner, ed. *Learning About Learning: A Conference Report* (Washington, DC: U. S. Department of Health, Education and Welfare, Office of Education, 1966), iii.

17 A. Theodore Tellstrom, *Music in American Education: Past and Present* (New York: Holt, Rinehart, 1971), 243.

18 Miles, *Innovations in Education*, 3.

19 Ibid., 3–4.

20 Gordon Gardner, Leonard Grindstaff, and Evelyn Wenzel, "Balance and the Selection of Content," in *Balance in the Curriculum* (Washington, DC: Association for Supervision and Curriculum Development, 1961), 95.

21 American Association for School Administrators, *Official Report for the Year*

1958; Including a Record of the Annual Meeting and Work Conference on "Education and the Creative Arts" (Washington, DC: American Association of School Administrators, 1959), 248–49.

22 Ole Sand, "Current Trends in Curriculum Planning," *Music Educators Journal* 50, no. 1 (September 1963): 101. Reprinted by permission of Music Educators National Conference.

23 Irving Lowens, "MUSIC: Juilliard Repertory Project and the Schools," *The Sunday Star* (Washington, DC, 30 May 1971), p. E4. This is a report of the Yale Seminar working group on "Repertory in Its Historical and Geographic Contexts."

24. Milton Friedman, "Busting the State Monopoly," *Newsweek* (5 December 1983): 96.

25 Reprinted with permission from *Academic Preparation for College.* Copyright 1983 by College Entrance Examination Board.

26 Education Commission of the States, *A Summary of Major Reports on Education* (Denver: Education Commission of the States, 1983), 22.

27 Ernest L. Boyer, *High School: A Report on Secondary Education in America* (New York: Harper & Row, 1983), 304.

28 John I. Goodlad, *A Place Called School: Prospects for the Future* (St. Louis: McGraw-Hill, 1983).

29 *A Summary of Major Reports on Education*, 3.

30 Paul L. Lehman, "The Great Debate on Excellence in Education: What About the Arts," Seventh Annual Loyola Symposium (Loyola University, New Orleans, 1974).

31 Fred M. Hechinger, "Caution: Avoid Confusion on School Reforms," *Bulletin*, American Association for Higher Education 36, no. 1 (September 1983): 10.

32 Diane Ravitch, *The Troubled Crusade: American Education, 1945–1980* (New York: Basic Books, 1983).

33 John J. Mahlmann, "Don't Let the Education Critics Drown Out Music," *School Board News* (21 September 1983): 2.

34 Chuck Freadhoff, "Do Schools Need More Money?" *Investor's Business Daily* (September 20, 1991).

35 Diane Ravitch, *National Standards in American Education: A Citizen's Guide* (Washington, DC: Brookings, 1995).

2

Pivotal Events of the Contemporary Era

The contemporary era of music education began in the 1950s, when the profession was caught up in the tidal wave of educational change that swept across the country. Most of the profession's development since then has been in response to pressures exerted from outside of itself. The fact that it is able to respond effectively to the needs of the society that sponsors it is a great strength, and a confirmation of its vitality. If music education could not do this, it would quickly become irrelevant, and would probably decline and fade away.

A number of pivotal events have influenced American music education in the contemporary era. Most have been planned, organized, and implemented by professional associations, especially the Music Educators National Conference. These milestone events were responses to the demands of education reform that have continued from the 1950s to the present. As important as the events were in themselves, their greatest practical value was the publications that followed each of them. It is actually the publications that have influenced the course of music education history. They are discussed throughout this book.

The Contemporary Music Project

In 1957 the Ford Foundation began to explore the relationship between the arts and American society.[a] This was the first instance of a philanthropic institution taking upon itself the goal of improving the careers of artists on a national scale. The initiative came only seven years after the Ford

---

[a]Private philanthropic foundations provided the necessary support for many projects, especially those not appropriate for government support.

28

Foundation trustees had approved a major social science program that included neither the humanities nor the arts.[1] The foundation solicited ideas from leaders in the arts, one of whom, composer Norman Dello Joio, suggested a union between composers and public school music programs:

> Having lived the precarious life of a composer of serious music, I proposed the idea of putting young men of proven talent to work, doing what they should be doing, which was to write music. Since there were school situations in the country that offered outlets, such as choruses, bands, orchestras, and related performing groups, it seemed logical that placing someone in this setting to serve their needs and writing for the particular and specific groups would serve to give young men an outlet, bring to the young students a needed exposure to music of our time, stimulate teachers to expand their interests in a fresher repertory, and make a general community aware of the fact that composers were living beings, functioning right in their midst.[2]

Dello Joio's suggestion resulted in a Ford Foundation grant to establish the Young Composers Project in 1959. The project placed young composers (not over 35 years of age) in public school systems as composers-in-residence. According to Dello Joio, the project was intended to benefit both composers and school music programs. The composers were paid $5,000 per year to write music for specific performing organizations at various levels of experience and proficiency, with the assurance that their music would be learned and performed. This kind of experience would, of course, provide a healthy impetus to a young composer's career. The school systems would benefit by having composers tailor their music to students, writing for specific occasions, and adding a large body of new music to the school repertoire. Students and teachers would know composers as real people functioning among them, not elevated on a pedestal or hidden away in an ivory tower. Dello Joio expected that the students for whom new music would be written would develop respect and appreciation for contemporary music, and in time, a high regard for music of the past as well. Then, young people might no longer be satisfied with the insipid, often shallow, music that had long been a staple of many school music programs. During the first year of the Young Composers Project, twelve composers were placed in school systems across the country. From 1959 to 1962 thirty-one composers participated. The composers discovered that many music educators were poorly prepared to deal with contemporary music, and their reluctance to become involved with it was reflected by their students. Yet, teachers and students who gained firsthand experience with contemporary music from their young composers-in-residence proved to be very receptive to new music. It became apparent to the composers that music educators not involved in the Young Composers Project would benefit from a training program that would enable them to use contemporary music effectively in their own programs.

The National Music Council had planned to administer the project, but found that it was not staffed adequately for this complex job. In fact, its only employee was a half-time Executive Secretary. The Ford Foundation then had to take over, and found itself performing specialized tasks with insufficient expertise: selecting composers, matching them with appropriate schools, and other responsibilities that required particular knowledge, experience, and skills. The Ford Foundation officer for the arts, Chester D'Arms, decided to find another organization to handle the project. The final choice was between the American Musicological Society and the Music Educators National Conference, which, according to Allen Britton, were "unlikely adversaries because one group hardly knew of the existence of the other. The MENC deservedly won out because the AMS leadership failed to evidence much interest in the fate of school music or American composers."[3]

The MENC proposal included expansion of the project to include seminars and workshops on contemporary music and pilot programs in public schools. The Ford Foundation accepted the proposal, and in 1963 awarded a grant of $1,380,000 to organize what was named the Contemporary Music Project for Creativity in Music Education (CMP).[4] The earlier Young Composers Project was continued under the title Composers in Public Schools (CPS). At that time, the Ford Foundation elevated CPS status from a pilot program to one of its ten major programs. By 1968, forty-six more composers had been matched with public school systems.

MENC stated five goals for the Contemporary Music Project in its proposal to the Ford Foundation:

1. To increase the emphasis on the creative aspect of music in the public schools
2. To create a solid foundation or environment in the music education profession for the acceptance, through understanding, of the contemporary music idiom
3. To reduce the compartmentalization that now exists between the profession of music composition and music education for the benefit of composers and music educators alike
4. To cultivate taste and discrimination on the part of music educators and students regarding the quality of contemporary music used in schools.
5. To discover, when possible, creative talent among students.[5]

Among the first activities of the Contemporary Music Project was the establishment of sixteen workshops and seminars at several colleges throughout the country, designed to help teachers better understand contemporary music through analysis, performance, and pedagogy. In addition, six pilot projects were established in elementary and secondary schools to provide authentic situations for teaching contemporary music. Three of the projects took place in the Baltimore, San Diego, and Farmingdale, New York, schools. The programs in Baltimore and San Diego were in-service seminars for teachers using pilot classes at selected grade levels in a variety of schools. The composers conducted the pilot classes as laboratories for experimentation with methods and materials. The objectives of the project were to determine effective means of using contemporary music at different grade levels, to experiment with creative experiences for children, to identify appropriate contemporary music for these experiences, and to serve as in-service education for teachers.

In the Baltimore project, weekly seminars were held for music teachers to improve their ability to use various aspects of contemporary music, and to identify a body of music literature that they could use with children. The pilot classes were held in several schools: one in a poor section of the inner city; another in an old section of the city with average incomes; a school in a wealthy residential area; and an affluent suburban area school. The children analyzed, improvised, and composed contemporary music, and when the classes concluded, teachers judged the children's musical growth and their attitudes toward contemporary music to be substantially positive. The majority of seminar participants were music teachers, but classroom teachers were responsible for most of the daily musical experiences of the children. The program was extended for one year to address their needs. Three seminars on creativity were held during the 1964–65 school year. The topics were "Sounds Around Us," "Creative Interpretation of Contemporary Music," and "Improvisation and Composition." The seminars showed teachers how to encourage and guide children to compose in a free style and rearrange a given element of music to compose a piece.

The San Diego project included a two-hour weekly seminar for teachers and three pilot classes to implement the work of the seminars. The pilot schools included an upper-lower-class elementary, an upper-middle-class elementary, and a lower-class junior high. The highest priority was given to developing creative approaches to presenting recorded contemporary music. The work of the seminars and pilot classes resulted in the following conclusions:

1. Music in the twentieth century idiom is appropriate for and interesting to children at any age level. The earlier it is presented, the more natural the enthusiasm is likely to be. Young children should be exposed to the sound of contemporary music before they are able to intellectualize about it.

2. Activities related to contemporary music, such as compositions for percussion instruments, synthetic scales, and new sound sources,

provide a unique medium for creativity. The student with little or no background in theory and harmony can "create" with enthusiasm and success and, thus, gain a first-hand contact with music that he might otherwise miss.

3. Active involvement with the elements or compositional techniques employed contributes to a more effective listening experience for students at all age levels.

4. Basic goals and teaching techniques for the use of contemporary music at these levels do not differ appreciably from those used for the successful presentation of any music. Thus, a skillful teacher of music who possesses or acquires some knowledge of contemporary music literature should be able to apply it in the classroom situation. Greater emphasis on twentieth century music at the level of teacher education would help teachers feel more secure in presenting this music to children.

5. A background in "traditional" music is not necessary as a prerequisite for listening to twentieth century music; however, approaches need to be adapted to the background of the group.

6. One of the major goals in presenting twentieth century music to children should be to help them grow in listening discrimination, in order that they will gradually be able to be selective in their choice of contemporary music.

7. Additional contemporary selections that are short in length and simple in structure need to be located or composed, in order that they might be incorporated into the larger program of music education.[6]

The Farmingdale, New York, approach involved thirty-one musically talented children from grades 6 through 8. This project, held in the summer of 1964, demonstrated experimental techniques in twentieth-century musical idioms and developed musical skills through rhythmics, singing, improvisation, and composition. The students were divided into two groups. One explored musical creativity using then current techniques. The other approached musicianship through rhythm studies and movement based on the techniques of Emile Jaques-Dalcroze (see chapter 5). The participants concluded that the best method would be a combination of the two.

The Seminar on Comprehensive Musicianship was held at Northwestern University in 1965 to develop means of improving the education of music teachers. The seminar provided the impetus for the development of comprehensive musicianship (see chapter 5), which was soon to become a dynamic catalyst for change in music education. William Thomson stated:

> [There is] a quiet but certain revolution that now is pledged to strip the accumulation of words and procedures in our music teaching down to the true essentials, matters that are as relevant to all music, and with that as a beginning, to build up a new body of information

and sets of techniques which may enable the novice musician to develop as an intelligent and concerned listener, producer, and teacher of music—music of the past, present, and future.[7]

The Northwestern University seminar established basic principles for comprehensive musicianship, and developed methods and materials that were tested at six regional Institutes for Music in Contemporary Education. These institutes conducted experimental programs in thirty-six educational institutions.

In 1967 a symposium was held at Arlie House, in Warrenton, Virginia, to discuss the evaluation of comprehensive musicianship. The resulting document, *Procedures for Evaluation of Music in Contemporary Education*, offers guidelines for the evaluation of techniques and attitudes acquired through comprehensive musicianship studies. Comprehensive musicianship is described in chapter 5.

In 1968 the Ford Foundation granted MENC $1,340,000 to extend the Contemporary Music Project for an additional five years. MENC contributed $50,000 per year of its own money as an indication of its commitment. From 1968 to 1973 the Contemporary Music Project consisted of three programs: Professionals-in-Residence to Communities; the Teaching of Comprehensive Musicianship; and Complementary Activities.

The Professionals-in-Residence to Communities program was similar to the Young Composers Project, except that composers were assigned to communities rather than to school systems. The Teaching of Comprehensive Musicianship program developed approaches for teachers of comprehensive musicianship. The Complementary Activities program implemented and publicized the work of the Contemporary Music Project through consultative services to educational institutions at conventions and conferences, and through publications. These activities introduced thousands of music teachers all over the country to Contemporary Music Project philosophy, materials, and methods. The second national conference of this program identified the needs of the profession and related them to the CMP. As a result, CMP established its Forums on Contemporary Musicianship program. A variety of local and national forums brought together representatives of all aspects of the music profession to make plans for influencing the future of music in the United States.

When the Contemporary Music Project ended in 1973, its purpose had been fulfilled: "to provide a synthesis, a focus, for disparate activities in music, in order to give them a cohesion and relevance in our society, to its cultural and educational institutions and organizations."[8] The Contemporary Music Project had given direction, provided challenges, developed methodology and materials, and made the music education profession more open-minded toward change and innovation.

Louis G. Wersen, President of MENC, summarized the four main issues that represented to him the essence of all CMP programs:

1. The role of the teacher transcends the mere technical training of his students, and encompasses the development of their inner musicality.

2. The student should be encouraged to assume responsibility for his own musical growth, and in some cases the best thing for the teacher to do is simply to avoid inhibiting that growth.

3. The development of the teacher's musicality must be accomplished in his own schooling, and must continue in his subsequent career as a teacher.

4. The bringing together of a variety of musical and educational points of view to formulate the CMP programs is an exemplary technique to be followed in future efforts to improve music education.[9]

The Yale Seminar on Music Education

The Yale Seminar on Music Education took place at Yale University June 17–28, 1963, to identify and examine the problems facing music education. The initial impetus of the seminar came from the National Science Foundation (NSF), which had sponsored science curriculum development in the late 1950s. The success of NSF in science education was one of the factors leading to President Kennedy's appointment of the Panel on Educational Research and Development. The panel members, approaching the problems of science education from a broad perspective, were concerned about a curriculum overloaded with science courses. They recognized that many successful scientists were also accomplished musicians, and they believed that students would be stronger in science if they were exposed to the view of human experience as seen through the arts. The panel also recognized that school music had not produced a musically literate public, and recommended that the K–12 curriculum of previous decades be examined to discover why this was so.

The panel's recommendations resulted in a grant awarded to Yale University by the U.S. Office of Education Cooperative Research Program for a seminar called *Music in Our Schools: A Search for Improvement* (known informally as the Yale Seminar). Claude V. Palisca, Professor of Music at Yale University, was the seminar director. The participants, thirty-one musicians, scholars, and teachers, identified music materials and musical performance as areas that required close examination. The following discussion is taken from the proceedings of the seminar.

MUSICAL MATERIALS

The changes that took place in American education from the late 1950s on had little effect on music education. Generally, the music education profession had granted only limited recognition to contemporary music in its various innovative forms. Because there was little communication between musicologists and music educators, early Western and non-Western musics were seldom included in music education programs. The specific criticisms of the materials in use were as follows:

1. It is of appalling quality, representing little of the heritage of significant music.
2. It is constricted in scope. Even the classics of Western music—such as the great works of Bach, Mozart, Beethoven—do not occupy the central place they should in singing, playing, and listening. Non-Western music, early Western music, and certain forms of jazz, popular, and folk music have been almost altogether neglected.
3. It stunts the growth of musical feeling because it is so often not sufficiently interesting to enchant or involve a child to whom it is presumed to be accessible. Children's potentials are constantly underestimated.
4. It is corrupted by arrangements, touched-up editions, erroneous transcriptions, and tasteless parodies to such an extent that authentic work is rare. A whole range of songbook arrangements, weak derivative semipopular children's pieces, and a variety of "educational" recordings containing music of similar value and type, are to be strongly condemned as "pseudo-music." To the extent artificial music is taught to children, to that extent are they invited to hate it. There is no reason or need to use artificial or pseudo-music in any of its forms.
5. Songs are chosen and graded more on the basis of the limited technical skills of classroom teachers than the needs of children or the ultimate goals of improved hearing and listening skills. This is one of the causes of the proliferation of feeble piano and autoharp accompaniments and of "singalong" recordings.
6. A major fault of the repertory of vocal music stems from the desire to appeal to the lowest common denominator and to offend the least possible number. More attention is often paid to the subject matter of the text, both in the choice and arrangement of material, than to the place of a song as music in the educational scheme. Texts are banal and lack regional inflection.[10]

Despite the availability of a wealth of excellent music, the youth of America still preferred to listen to current popular music that lacked the inherent musical content of art music. School music education had done little to improve the situation. The materials of music education were not appreciably different from what they had been thirty years before the Yale Seminar.

PERFORMANCE

Musical performance standards had risen dramatically in the decades before the Yale Seminar, and performance in American school music programs was generally excellent. There was a surplus, however, of competent adult musicians who could not be absorbed into the musical professions. The seminar participants considered it important to find a way to utilize these musicians in teaching, performance, or other related professions so they would not be forced into nonmusical occupations.

The instrumental music program in American education had been extremely successful and contributed much to the growth of music in American culture. The ability to develop musical skills in children had been demonstrated by teachers many times over. Increasing sales of student-model musical instruments indicated that parents and children valued musical participation. Although many instrumental music programs fostered artistic maturity in individual students and in ensembles, superficial showmanship and mass activity often dominated. This did little to increase the musicality and musical appreciation of individual musicians. The Yale Seminar, therefore, saw the need to stimulate individual musical initiative and independence, rather than teamwork and technique.

The Recommendations of the Yale Seminar

DEVELOPING MUSICALITY

The basic goal of the K–12 music curriculum should be musicality. Many changes need to be made to achieve this goal. For example, practices in teaching performance, movement, musical creativity, ear training, and listening should all be examined. Creativity, as a means of developing musicality, should emphasize the performance of original student compositions. The repertory should be broadened to include the best of Western and non-Western music of all periods, as well as jazz, folk, and contemporary music. Children's ability to perceive and appreciate a wide variety of authentic music should not be underestimated, and less emphasis should be placed on music that is artificial in concept. An enlarged repertory should be made available in useful formats, perhaps in kits or packages with manuals and audiovisual aids. Sequential listening experiences need to be developed for elementary and junior high school students, and high school students should take music literature courses that require intensive experiences with representative works. Performance activities should include ensembles for which an authentic and varied repertory has been developed. This includes symphony, string and chamber orchestras, concert bands, and various sizes of choruses. Marching and stage bands should also be offered, not as ends in themselves, but to encourage students to participate in other ensembles. Small ensembles are especially important because they require more intense participation and are relevant for future adult musical activity. Keyboard instruction should also be available free of charge, and should be accompanied by basic musicianship and theory courses. Advanced theory and literature courses should be available to students who can benefit from them. These courses should be exploratory and structured to allow learning by discovery.

Advanced literature courses should concentrate on the analysis of a selected body of literature. The increasing disparity between professional and school music should be reduced by bringing musicians, composers, and scholars into the schools. Students should be given insights into how professionals think and work, and professionals should be given opportunities to help develop musicality in young people. This kind of program would also provide a link between schools and contemporary developments in the world of music. School music programs should also take advantage of professional and highly competent amateur musicians who might serve in various capacities, and community-centered ensembles that can lend support and assistance to school programs. The opportunities for advanced music study that exist in metropolitan centers should be made available to all talented students throughout the country. To serve these students, there might be regional cadres of teachers, a chain of state or national academies of music, drama, and dance, urban high schools of performing arts, and educational activities in community arts centers.[11]

The Yale seminar, unfortunately, had a serious flaw: it had too little representation from MENC, which was the only vehicle by which broad and sweeping changes could realistically be attempted. In fact, most of the Yale participants were unfamiliar with the content and methods of music education. They represented an impressive array of school and university faculty and administrators, professional musicians, and composers, but few were directly involved in school music education. The Seminar lacked the means and the leadership to carry out its proposals. It received little publicity, and its recommendations reached relatively few people. It did, however, help music education leaders decide to hold their own symposium to examine basic issues from the viewpoint of music education professionals.

AFTER THE YALE SEMINAR

Conscientious music educators could not deny the problems identified by the seminar, nor could they deny the wisdom of many of the suggestions. The time was right for change. Having no control over the music education profession, however, the seminar was powerless to effect change. Its most valuable contribution was to help create a professional climate that was conducive to change, in which the music education profession could seriously consider new practices and materials.

The Juilliard Repertory Project

Shortly after the Yale Seminar, Dean Gideon Waldrop of the Juilliard School of Music, having considered the seminar's recommendations, submitted a grant application to the U.S. Office of Education to develop a large body of authentic and meaningful music materials. This music was intended to augment and enrich the repertory available to teachers of music in the early grades. The Juilliard Repertory Project was established in July 1964 with the composer Vittorio Giannini as project director. Music educators opposed the project at first, fearing that Juilliard was planning a curriculum to be promoted as the most effective means of teaching music. Giannini assured them, however, that the intention was only to develop a library of first-rate music that could be used by any teacher, regardless of the method by which it was presented.

The project collected music of the highest quality for teaching music from kindergarten through sixth grade. Sensitive to the Yale Seminar criticism of the poor quality of music literature used in schools, all music accepted for the Juilliard Repertory Project accepted only music that had been evaluated and approved by school music teachers. Three groups compiled the repertory: research consultants (musicologists and ethnomusicologists), educational consultants (music educators), and testing consultants (public school elementary music teachers). Giannini appointed a research consultant for each of seven broad categories of music to create the *Juilliard Repertory Library*: Gustave Reese (pre-Renaissance), Noah Greenberg (Renaissance), Claude Palisca (Baroque), Paul Henry Lang (classical), Alfred Wallenstein (romantic), Norman Dello Joio (contemporary), and Nicholas England (folk music). There was so little contemporary music that could be used by school children that composers were invited to write music specifically for use in schools.

The research consultants chose appropriate, authentic music, and sent it to a panel of distinguished music educators—Allen P. Britton, Sally Monsour, Mary Ruth McCulley, and Louis G. Wersen—to select the pieces to be tested in practical classroom situations. Field tests were conducted in four moderate size communities (Amarillo, Texas; Ann Arbor, Michigan; Boulder, Colorado; and Elkhart, Indiana), two large cities (New York and Philadelphia), and one small town (Winfield, Kansas). Of more than 400 compositions tested, 230 vocal and instrumental works were ultimately included in the *Juilliard Repertory Library*, which was published by the Canyon Press (Cincinnati, Ohio). The *Reference Library* was large (384 pages) and expensive, and so Canyon Press also published it in eight separate volumes of vocal music and four of instrumental music. There was no overlap of content in these smaller, more affordable volumes, and each contained a cross-section of the entire collection.

The Juilliard Repertory Library Project satisfied not only the Yale Seminar requirement for high-quality and authentic music for school music programs, but also the recommendation that scholars and teachers join together to upgrade music education.

The Tanglewood Symposium

Music education leaders were displeased with the Yale Seminar. They did, however, recognize the many new problems that the profession needed to address, and so they decided it was time for serious introspection and planning. The Tanglewood Symposium took place from July 23 to

August 2, 1967, in Tanglewood, Massachusetts, the summer home of the Boston Symphony Orchestra. MENC sponsored it in cooperation with the Berkshire Music Center, the Theodore Presser Foundation, and the School of Fine and Applied Arts of Boston University. The purpose of the symposium was to discuss and define the role of music education in contemporary American society at a time when it was faced with rapid social, economic, and cultural change.

The music education profession needed to redefine its place in American society. In preparation for the symposium, the *Music Educators Journal* published position papers in 1967. The papers were to serve as the basis for discussion at the 1967 MENC Divisional Conferences and for the Tanglewood Symposium itself. To ensure a holistic and pluralistic view, participants were selected to represent several facets of society: sociologists, scientists, labor leaders, educators, corporate executives, and musicians. Three broad questions were presented:

1. What are the characteristics and desirable ideologies for an emerging postindustrial society?
2. What are the values and unique functions of music and other arts for individuals and communities in such a society?
3. How may these potentials be attained?

The weeklong symposium was devoted to discussions of value systems as they relate to the role of the arts in society, characteristics of contemporary society, contemporary music, the role of behavioral science, creativity, and means of cooperation between music education and other segments of society. It was followed by a postsession, attended by music educators and consultants, who formulated implications of the symposium, identified critical issues, and recommended appropriate actions.

THE SYMPOSIUM
Each participant in the postsession met with a different committee to explore specific issues. The committee topics were "A Philosophy of the Arts for an Emerging Society," "Music of Our Time," "Impact and Potentials of Technology," "Economics and Community Support for the Arts," and "The Nature and Nurture of Creativity."[12]

The committee that was assigned the topic "A Philosophy of the Arts for an Emerging Society" examined societal values and the role of music in the emerging society. Its issues included social change, the need to strengthen human values in the midst of change, and the effective utilization of change to support constructive values. Other issues, directed more specifically to the relationship between music education and social change, concerned the arts as a means of transition to new values, the need for higher-quality music, education as preparation for leisure, and music experiences for people of all ages. Another body of issues included the consideration of a new aesthetic compatible with the music of a

EXAMPLE 2.1. The Tanglewood Symposium

First Week—Basic Issues
   The Role of the Arts in a Changing Community
   Potentials for the Arts in the Community
   Toward the Year 2000
   Prospects for the Future
   Perspectives on Music and the Individual
   Economics and Community Support: Perspectives
   Music of Our Time

Second Week—Postsession Topics
   I.   A Philosophy of the Arts for an Emerging Society
       A. Values: Music as Means and Ends
       B. Music in the Emerging Society
   II. Music of our Time
   III. Impacts and Potentials of Technology
   IV. Economics and Community Support for the Arts
   V.   The Nature and Nurture of Creativity
   VI. Problems and Responsibilities
       A. Critical Issues
          1. Music and the Inner City
          2. Music Study for All Students in the High School
          3. Music for Teenagers
       B. Implications for Music in Higher Education and the
          Community
          1. College Admission, Testing and the Musically Talented
          2. Relations with other Disciplines—Inter- and Intra-
             Musical
          3. Music in the General Education of the College Student
          4. Goals of Aesthetic Education
          5. Creative Teaching of Music
          6. The Need for Highly Trained Specialists on Music
          7. Music and Libraries
          8. Continuing Education in Music
       C. Implications in the Music Curriculum
          1. The Music Curriculum for Children
          2. The Music Curriculum for Adults
          3. The Other Musics—Their Selection and Use
       D. Implications for the Education Process and for Evaluation
          1. Identification and Preparation of the Professional Music
             Educator
          2. Effective Utilization of New Technologies and
             Approaches in the Education Process
          3. Improvement of the Teaching Process in Group
             Instruction
          4. Measurement of Musical Behavior
          5. Accommodating Individual Differences in Learning
          6. Curriculum must Assume a Place at the Center of Music
  VII. The Tanglewood Declaration
  VIII. General Recommendations

technological society, the need to keep traditions and history alive while serving an emerging society, and the need for MENC to reexamine its various functions.

The committee considered several aspects of change in American life. Rising incomes, shorter working hours, and greater longevity were allowing people more opportunity to participate in the arts. Clearly, music education could be a long-term activity in which school is only an early stage. Americans had become globally oriented, and they were receptive to music of other cultures. The new technology had also helped people accept innovative sounds and unfamiliar kinds of music.

Unfortunately, the increasing intrusion of technology into peoples' lives afforded them few opportunities for individual development. The arts promote individuality and basic human values. This too, must be a consideration in determining the relationship between music education and society. Human values—the realization of what is important to individuals in terms of happiness, satisfaction, and well-being in the context of society—are neither taught nor imposed on people. They develop as the individual relates new experiences and perceptions to old ones. Education should enable the individual to explore, identify, and develop new humanistic values throughout life.

The nature of contemporary society forces us to realize that music that is new (electronic) or new only to Western listeners (music of exotic cultures) is aesthetically valid for large segments of the population. An aesthetic theory for contemporary society must encompass both new and foreign musics, and must also be sufficiently precise to serve a society that depends on scientific principles and measurements.

The role of the music educator in helping students to know a musical work places the discipline among the academic subjects. Music must be part of formal education because it is part of our cultural and social heritage. It is related to human nature and is one of the great challenges to the human mind.

Music educators need to prepare for tomorrow by anticipating future conditions: a different value system, a freer state of the art of music, a different kind of teaching and performing technology, and a higher level of student sophistication. The needs of the emerging society require education to extend beyond the public school level. Increasing affluence will allow adults to study and participate in the arts, and music educators will also participate in adult education. Music can help adults establish their relationship to a changing world.

Music and music education must be viewed as they relate to each other and to society. Four roles can be defined in the process of music: creators, distributors, consumers, and educators. Each has to find its place in the social structure. The committee concluded its report with several recommendations:

1. There should be a mechanism that allows the profession of music education to establish ongoing communication with all other relevant disciplines and interests.

2. MENC should bring to music teacher training the results of research in philosophy and the social sciences.

3. The music education profession should direct itself to the subject of leisure.

4. MENC should adopt a set of official positions as a basis for communication, policymaking, and guidance.

5. MENC should establish informal relationships with the Adult Education Association of the United States of America in order to foster cooperative activity and understanding.

6. MENC should direct its attention to studies of audiences. These studies should extend to the relationship between school and community.

7. A national commission on music education should be established to confront the issues treated by the symposium.

The committee on "Music of Our Time" examined the relationship between pluralism and music in American life. The committee acknowledged that Americans have a diversity of musical tastes. Music has so many dimensions now that new value judgments are needed. Because new music proliferates so rapidly and tastes often change, however, there is a question as to whether a hierarchy can and should be assigned to various kinds of music.

The committee on "Impact and Potentials of Technology" considered the changes brought about by the information explosion. Expanded technology has offered much more to education than educators have been able to use. The speed of technological change outstrips our ability to update educational practices. The committee made the following recommendations:

1. MENC should establish a committee on Advanced Educational Technologies, whose duties would be to keep the membership informed of new developments as they apply to music education and to bring the needs of music educators to the attention of industry.

2. Selected people from MENC should learn about computer concepts to enable them to evaluate projects and provide leadership; a training program in computer technology should be made available to music educators.

3. MENC should be concerned with the preparation of new teaching and in-service experiences in educational technology for working teachers.

The committee on "The Nature and Nurture of Creativity" discussed the nature of creativity and its manifestations in individuals. The committee report stated that "living life to the fullest suggests providing an environment for acquiring the skills needed for creative living." Creativity is latent in the human at birth, and the child's environment can stimulate or suppress its development. The schools must establish an open environment that encourages creativity and provides outlets for it.

The second broad area of committee reports was "Problems and Responsibilities." The "Critical Issues" committee dealt with music in inner-city schools and in general education. It recommended that teacher education programs in music be modified or expanded to include the special skills and attitudes needed for teaching inner city children and that a new music teacher education curriculum be formulated to attract teachers to inner city schools. Urban teachers should be trained in actual community situations. The committee also recommended that a commission be established to develop content and instructional processes to establish equality between high school music education and other subject areas and to reform teacher education programs to prepare music educators to teach music as a part of general education.

The committee on "Implications for Music in Higher Education and the Community" recommended that the profession promote recognition of precollege music study by higher-education admission boards, and that college admission standards be more flexible to recognize and honor creative efforts. It also suggested that MENC establish liaison committees with composition, musicology, and performance disciplines to encourage the exchange of ideas. Composers, performers, and other musicians should participate in professional music education meetings.

The committee on "Implications for the Music Curriculum" recommended a new elementary-level music curriculum, one that would have four major divisions: (1) understanding many types of music through guided listening or performance; (2) studying music through singing, playing instruments, movement, and combinations of these; (3) arranging and composing; and (4) understanding and using music notation. The committee also recommended that all junior high school students be required to take a general music course and that all high school students, even those who participate in performing ensembles, take at least one arts course. Instruments other than the standard orchestral instruments, especially social instruments like the guitar, should be taught.

The committee on "Implications for the Educational Process and for Evaluation" recommended that music educators find a way to identify potential for teaching music in young people. MENC should develop materials to assist high school counselors to identify potential music educators, and to help the students understand the advantage of an early commitment.

THE TANGLEWOOD DECLARATION

The Tanglewood Symposium is summarized in "The Tanglewood Declaration." It is a pivotal document that guided critical future developments in music education, and is quoted here in its entirety:

> The intensive evaluation of the role of music in American society and education provided by the Tanglewood Symposium of philosophers, educators, scientists, labor leaders, philanthropists, social scientists, theologians, industrialists, representatives of government and foundations, music educators, and other musicians led to this declaration:
>
> We believe that education must have as major goals the art of living, the building of personal identity, and nurturing creativity. Since the study of music can contribute much to these ends, WE NOW CALL FOR MUSIC TO BE PLACED IN THE CORE OF THE SCHOOL CURRICULUM.
>
> The arts afford a continuity with the aesthetic tradition in man's history. Music and other fine arts, largely nonverbal in nature, reach close to the social, psychological, and physiological roots of man in his search for identity and self-realization.
>
> Educators must accept the responsibility for developing opportunities which meet man's individual needs and the needs of a society plagued by the consequences of changing values, alienation, hostility between generations, racial and international tensions, and the challenges of a new leisure.

Music educators at Tanglewood agreed that:

1. Music serves best when its integrity as an art is maintained.

2. Music of all periods, styles, forms, and cultures belongs in the curriculum. The musical repertory should be expanded to involve music of our time in its rich variety, including currently popular teen-age music and avante-garde music, American folk music, and the music of other cultures.

3. Schools and colleges should provide adequate time for music in programs ranging from preschool through adult or continuing education.

4. Instruction in the arts should be a general and important part of education in the senior high school.

5. Developments in educational technology, educational television, programmed instruction, and computer-assisted instruction should be applied to music study and research.

6. Greater emphasis should be placed on helping the individual stu-

dent to fulfill his needs, goals, and potentials.

7. The music education profession must contribute its skills, proficiencies, and insights toward assisting in the solution of urgent social problems as in the "inner city" or other areas with culturally deprived individuals.

8. Programs of teacher education must be expanded and improved to provide music teachers who are specially equipped to teach high school courses in the history and literature of music, courses in the humanities and related arts, and music teachers equipped to work with the very young, with adults, with the disadvantaged, and with the emotionally disturbed.[13]

The Goals and Objectives Project

The Goals and Objectives (GO) Project of MENC was the first step toward realizing the recommendations of the Tanglewood Symposium. The GO Project identified the responsibilities of MENC as they pertain to future professional needs. The project began in 1969. Eighteen subcommittees were appointed to investigate specific aspects of music education:

1. Preparation for Music Educators
2. Musical Behaviors: Identification and Evaluation
3. Comprehensive Musicianship: Music Study in the Senior High School
4. Music for All Youth
5. Music Education in the Inner City
6. Research in Music Education
7. Logistics of Music Education Fact Finding
8. Fact Finding
9. Aesthetic Education
10. Information Science
11. Music for Early Childhood
12. Impact of Technology
13. Music in Higher Education
14. Learning Processes
15. Musical Enrichment of National Life
16. MENC Professional Activities
17. Professional Organization Relationships
18. Music of Non-Western Cultures[14]

Paul Lehman, director of this phase of the project, issued a draft statement of goals and objectives based on the eighteen reports, and in October 1970 the MENC National Executive Board made final revisions and formally adopted the goals and objectives. The broad goal of MENC was to conduct programs and activities to build a vital musical culture and an enlightened musical public. The goals of the profession were to carry out comprehensive music programs in all schools, to involve persons of all ages in learning music, to support the quality preparation of teachers, and to use the most effective techniques and resources in music instruction.[15]

Of the thirty-five objectives listed below, the MENC National Executive Board identified eight priority objectives on which the organization would focus its efforts in the immediate future (they are marked with asterisks).

*1. Lead in efforts to develop programs of music instruction challenging to all students, whatever their sociocultural condition, and directed toward the needs of citizens in a pluralistic society

*2. Lead in the development of programs of study that correlate performing, creating, and listening to music and encompass a diversity of musical behaviors

*3. Assist teachers in the identification of musical behaviors relevant to the needs of their students

*4. Advance the teaching of music of all periods, styles, forms, and cultures

5. Promote the development of instructional programs in aesthetic education

6. Advocate the expansion of music education to include preschool children

7. Lead in efforts to ensure that every school system requires music from kindergarten through grade 6 and for a minimum of two years beyond that level

8. Lead in efforts to ensure that every secondary school offers an array of music courses to meet the needs of all youth

9. Promote challenging courses in music for the general college student

10. Advocate the expansion of music education for adults both in and out of school

*11. Develop standards to ensure that all music instruction is provided by teachers well prepared in music

12. Encourage the improvement and continual updating of preservice and in-service education programs for all persons who teach music

*13. Expand its programs to secure greater involvement and commitment of student members

14. Assist graduate schools in developing curricula especially designed for the preparation of teachers

15. Develop and recommend accreditation criteria for the use of recognized agencies in the approval of school and college music program and in the certification of music teachers

16. Support the expansion of teacher education programs to include specializations designed to meet current needs

*17. Assume leadership in the application of significant new developments in curriculum, teaching-learning patterns, evaluation, and related topics, to every area and level of music teaching

18. Assume leadership in the development of resources for music teaching and learning

19. Cooperate in the development of exemplary models of desirable programs and practices in the teaching of music

20. Encourage maximum use of community music resources to enhance educational programs

*21. Lead in efforts to ensure that every school system allocates sufficient staff, time, and funds to support a comprehensive and excellent music program

22. Provide advisory assistance where music programs are threatened by legislative, administrative, or other action

23. Conduct public relations programs to build community support for music education

24. Promote the conduct of research and research-related activities in music education

25. Disseminate news of research in order that research findings may be applied promptly and effectively

26. Determine the most urgent needs for information in music education

27. Gather and disseminate information about music and education

28. Encourage other organizations, agencies, and communications media to gather and disseminate information about music and education

29. Initiate efforts to establish information retrieval systems in music and education and to develop data bases for subsequent incorporation into such systems

30. Pursue effective working relationships with organizations and groups having mutual interests

31. Strengthen the relationships between the conference and its federated, associated, and auxiliary organizations

32. Establish procedures for its organizations' program planning and policy development

33. Seek to expand its membership to include all persons who, in any capacity, teach music

34. Periodically evaluate the effectiveness of its policies and programs

35. Ensure systematic interaction with its membership concerning the goals and objectives of the conference.[16]

As a result of the GO Project, MENC appointed two commissions to help implement the recommendations. The MENC National Commission on Organizational Development was established "to prepare recommendations of needed changes in the organization, structure, and function of the conference including all of its federated and affiliated units."[17] The MENC National Commission on Instruction was "to plan, manage, and coordinate a wide variety of activities, following the operational pattern that has proved highly successful for the Commission on Teacher Education."[18] Existing bodies, like the Music Education Research Council, the Publications Planning Committee, the public relations program, and the *Music Educators Journal*, managed the other objectives of the GO Project.[19] Entire issues of *MEJ* were devoted to single topics that had been treated as issues by the symposium. They included youth music, electronic music, music in urban education, and music in special education. Many sessions of national, regional, and state conferences brought to music educators ideas and methods for practical approaches to fulfillment of the Tanglewood recommendations as they applied to specific teaching situations.

During the 1970s the majority of members of the MENC National Executive Board stated that they were influenced in varying degrees in their decision making by the GO Project. According to one board member, the GO Project provided a forum for "brainstorming" in consideration of the needs of American society and of young people.[20]

The Development of Professional Standards

THE SCHOOL MUSIC PROGRAM: DESCRIPTION AND STANDARDS

In 1974, the National Commission on Instruction published a booklet entitled *The School Music Program: Description and Standards*. It was a response to the suggestion of the Tanglewood Symposium that MENC provide leadership in developing high-quality music programs in all schools. It describes the ideal school music program as a benchmark against which lay people and professionals can compare the programs in their own schools, and presents standards for curriculum, staffing, facilities, and equipment, and levels of support.[21] Paul Lehman wrote:

> *The School Music Program: Description and Standards* . . . has been used extensively by superintendents and principals, state departments of education and state supervisors of music, music educators, and laymen. It has been referred to and quoted by various groups concerned with accreditation or certification, and it has been cited in innumerable curriculum guides. It has been the most popular publication in the history of MENC.[22]

The second edition (1986) presented MENC goals for 1990:

1. By 1990, every student, K–12, shall have access to music

instruction in school. The curriculum of every elementary and secondary school, public or private, shall include a balanced, comprehensive, and sequential program of music instruction taught by qualified teachers. At the secondary level, every student shall have an opportunity to elect a course in music each year without prerequisites and without conflicts with required courses.

2. By 1990, every high school shall require at least one unit of credit in music, visual arts, theater, or dance for graduation.

3. By 1990, every college and university shall require at least one unit of credit in music, visual arts, theater, or dance for admission.[23]

MENC reported its progress toward these goals in its 1988 publication, *Arts in Schools: State by State*.[24]

The two editions of *The School Music Program* represent the response of the music education profession to the national movement for increased quality in education. By identifying standards and achievement levels, MENC demonstrated to the public that the music education profession considered its work to be consequential and that it was resolved to improve itself.

National Standards for Arts Education

The standards published in the two editions of *The School Music Program* were valuable to the profession, but they were really a prelude to an even greater achievement: *The Goals 2000: Educate America Act* (see chapter 4). For the first time, standards were written for arts education as a statutory core curricular subject. Regardless of how effective previous standards had been, they had been written for a profession that was still trying very hard to convince the American people that music should be a curricular subject. The Goals 2000 Congressional mandate made writing the *National Standards for Arts Education* a much different kind of job than developing the earlier standards.

National Standards for Arts Education contains content standards for dance, music, theater, and visual arts. Every content standard is followed by several achievement standards describing how students are to demonstrate mastery of the content standards. The goals are not intended to be a curriculum. Instead, curriculum is to be developed locally on the basis of the goals. The standards are grouped into grade levels: K–4, 5–8, and 9–12. Within each grade level section, they are grouped in four divisions—creation and performance; cultural and historical context; perception and analysis; and the nature and value of the arts. The authors state: "They ask that students should know and be able to do the following by the time they have completed secondary school:

- *They should be able to communicate at a basic level in the four arts disciplines*—dance, music, theatre, and the visual arts. This includes knowledge and skills in the use of the basic vocabularies, materials, tools, techniques, and intellectual method of each arts discipline.

- *They should be able to communicate proficiently in at least one art form*, including the ability to define and solve artistic problems with insight, reason, and technical proficiency.

- *They should be able to develop and present basic analyses of works of art* from structural, historical, and cultural perspectives, and from combinations of those perspectives. This includes the ability to understand and evaluate work in the various arts disciplines.

- *They should have an informed acquaintance with exemplary works of art from a variety of cultures and historical periods*, and a basic understanding of historical development in the arts disciplines, across the arts as a whole, and within cultures.

- *They should be able to relate various types of arts knowledge and skills within and across the arts disciplines*. This includes mixing and matching competencies and understandings in art-making, history and culture, and analysis in any arts-related project.

As a result of developing these capabilities, students can arrive at their own knowledge, beliefs, and values for making personal and artistic decisions. In other terms, they can arrive at a broad-based, self-grounded understanding of the nature, value, and meaning of the arts as a part of their own humanity.[25]

The music content standards are as follows:

GRADES K–4

1. Singing, alone and with others, a varied repertoire of music
2. Performing on instruments, alone and with others, a varied repertoire of music
3. Improvising melodies, variations, and accompaniments
4. Composing and arranging music within specified guidelines
5. Reading and notating music
6. Listening to, analyzing, and describing music
7. Evaluating music and music performances
8. Understanding relationships between music, the other arts, and disciplines outside the arts
9. Understanding music in relation to history and culture

GRADES 5–8

1. Singing, alone and with others, a varied repertoire of music
2. Performing on instruments, alone and with others, a varied repertoire of music

3. Improvising melodies, variations, and accompaniments

4. Composing and arranging music within specified guidelines

5. Reading and notating music

6. Listening to, analyzing, and describing music

7. Evaluating music and music performances

8. Understanding relationships between music, the other arts, and disciplines outside the arts

9. Understanding music in relation to history and culture

GRADES 9–12 (each standard specifies two achievement levels—proficient and advanced)

1. Singing, alone and with others, a varied repertoire of music

2. Performing on instruments, alone and with others, a varied repertoire of music

3. Improvising melodies, variations, and accompaniments

4. Composing and arranging music within specified guidelines

5. Reading and notating music

6. Listening to, analyzing, and describing music

7. Evaluating music and music performances

8. Understanding relationships between music, the other arts, and disciplines outside the arts

9. Understanding music in relation to history and culture[26]

Music educators, especially those who teach at the elementary level, have an additional opportunity to help their students meet the national standards. Because there are few dance and theater teachers in elementary schools, music teachers will probably play a major role in achieving the goals in those areas. Music educators should review the dance and theater goals to determine which of them are already incorporated in their own curricula. Many, especially those who use movement and dramatic activities, will find that they are already meeting several dance and theater goals.

Summary

The pivotal events that have occurred from the 1950s to the 1990s indicate that the music education profession has gone through a period of self-definition. The Tanglewood Symposium was probably the most critical event because it made the profession take stock of itself, examine its relationship to the greater society, and begin to plan its future in a more organized fashion than in the past. The goals that the profession set for itself were worthy, but societal changes, economics, technology, and many other factors have changed some of them, made others obsolete, and led to the creation of new ones.

Probably the most important goal was the official acceptance of music as a curricular subject. Now that the goal has been achieved, music educators must continue defining their profession in terms of the national goals. Their curricula and teaching practices must demonstrate to skeptical state and local educational policymakers that music is indeed a basic educational subject. Despite the vastly improved environment for arts education, the profession must deal with the fact that there is no Congressional mandate for school systems to adopt the standards. Only if states and local school districts implement them voluntarily, or adopt their own versions of them, can they make a difference. It is clear that the profession must continue to work toward inclusion in the curriculum at the state and local levels. This is discussed further in chapter 4.

NOTES

1 W. Neil Lowry, Introduction, in *The Arts and Public Policy in the United States* (Englewood Cliffs, NJ: Prentice-Hall, 1983), 11.

2 Norman Dello Joio, letter to author, 6 February 1977.

3 Allen P. Britton, "MENC: Remembrances and Perspectives," *The Quarterly Journal of Music Teaching and Learning* V, no. 2 (Summer 1994): 7.

4 Ibid.

5 "CMP in Perspective," *Music Educators Journal* 59, no. 9 (May 1973): 34.

6 *Experiments in Musical Creativity: CMP 3* (Washington, DC: Music Educators National Conference, 1966), 60–61. Reprinted by permission of the Music Educators National Conference.

7 William Thomson, "New Math, New Science, New Music," *Music Educators Journal* 53 (March 1967): 30. Reprinted by permission of the Music Educators National Conference.

8 "Contemporary Nusic Project: Comprehensive Musicianship," *Music Educators Journal* 59, no. 9 (May 1973): 47.

9 Louis G. Wersen, "New Directions for Music Education," *Music Educators Journal* 54, no. 7 (March 1968): 66–67. Reprinted by permission of the Music Educators National Conference.

10 Irving Lowens, "Music: Julliard Repertory Project and the Schools," *The Sunday Star* (Washington, DC, 30 May 1971), p. E4. This is a report of the Yale Seminar working group on "Repertory in Its Historical and Geographical Contexts."

11 Claude V. Palisca, *Music in Our Schools: A Search for Improvement* (Washington, DC: U.S. Department of Health, Education and Welfare, Office of Education, 1964).

12 From *Documentary Report of the Tanglewood Symposium*. Copyright 1968 by Music Educators National Conference. Used with permission.

13 From Robert A. Choate, ed., *Documentary Report of the Taglewood Symposium*. Copyright 1968 by Music Educators National Conference. Used with permission.

14 From "The GO Project: Where Is It Heading?" *Music Educators Journal* 40, no. 6 (February 1970): 44–45. Copyright 1970 by Music Educators National Conference. Used with permission.

15 Ibid.

16 From "Goals and Objectives for Musical Education," *Music Educators Journal* 57, no. 4 (December 1970): 24–25. Copyright 1970 by Music Educators National Conference. Used with permission.

17 "MENC Forms Two Commissions," *Music Educators Journal* 57, no. 8 (April 1971): 47–48. Reprinted by permission of the Music Educators National Conference.

18 Ibid., 47.

19 "MENC Forms Two Commissions," 47.

20 James A. Middleton, letter to author, July 1979. Quoted in "The GO Project: Retrospective of a Decade," *Music Educators Journal* 67, no. 4 (December 1980): 42–47.

21 National Commission on Instruction, *The School Music Program: Description and Standards* (Vienna, VA: Music Educators National Conference, 1974), ix.

22 Paul R. Lehman, *The School Music Program: Description and Standards*, 2d ed. (Reston, VA: Music Educators National Conference, 1986), 7.

23 Ibid.

24 Daniel V. Steinel, comp. and ed., *Arts in Schools: State by State*, 2d ed. (Reston, VA: Music Educators National Conference, 1988).

25 From *National Standards for Arts Education*, 18–19. Copyright 1994 by Music Educators National Conference. Used with permission.

26 From *National Standards for Arts Education*. Copyright 1994 by Music Educators National Conference. Used by permission. The complete National Arts Standards and additional materials relating to the Standards are available from Music Educators National Conference, 1806 Fulton Drive, Reston, VA 22091.

3

Intellectual Currents in the Contemporary Era

The sine qua non *of education is not keeping kids off the streets or teaching them how to march in line, both of which are nice things to be able to do, but actually, to learn and to understand. The purpose of education should be to enhance understanding—understanding of the world, and understanding of yourself and your own experiences.*

Howard Gardner, 1994[1]

Philosophy and Psychology

The contemporary era of music education has seen major advances into new philosophical and psychological territory. These movements have been complementary to each other and fortuitous for music education. The simultaneous support of music education from the perspective of two separate disciplines was not entirely accidental. Aesthetic education, based on aesthetics, a branch of philosophy, and cognitive psychology both developed around the beginning of the contemporary era. The work of several distinguished philosophers and psychologists has tended to validate arts education as a basic subject in schools. A 1964 statement by the American Society for Aesthetics relates philosophy and psychology: "The term 'aesthetics' is understood to include all studies of the arts and related types of experience from a philosophic, scientific, or other theoretical standpoint, including those of psychology, sociology, anthropology, cultural history, art criticism, and education."[2]

Philosophy of Music Education

There was no coherent philosophy early in the contemporary era of music education. Progressive education had declined shortly before, and by the early 1950s its philosophical basis was no longer relevant. Without a common curricular underpinning, music, like other disciplines, began to operate in an isolated manner, rather than as an integral part of a coherent curriculum. This complicated the process of developing a new foundational belief because an educational philosophy should integrate the diverse segments of the school curriculum. Gradually, however, the profession has generally accepted a philosophy upon which to base practices. Bennett Reimer wrote:

> The profession as a whole needs a formulation which can serve to guide the efforts of the group. The impact the profession can make on society depends in large degree on the quality of the profession's understanding of what it has to offer which might be of value to society. There is an almost desperate need for a better understanding of the value of music and of the teaching and learning of music. An uncomfortable amount of defensiveness, of self-doubt, of grasping at straws which seem to offer bits and pieces of self-justification, exists now in music education and has always seemed to exist. It would be difficult to find a field so active, so apparently healthy, so venerable in age and widespread in practice, which is at the same time so worried about its inherent value. . . . The tremendous expenditure of concern about how to justify itself—both to itself and to others—which has been traditional in this field, reflects a lack of philosophical "inner peace." . . .[3]

Reimer's statement echoes, to a disquieting degree, a similar statement made eighty-five years earlier, at a time when music education was undergoing a similar metamorphosis. The lack of inner peace is not new to American music education. Daniel Hagar wrote:

> The importance of music as a branch of school education is, in this country, poorly appreciated, even in communities that recognize it as one of their school studies. Under the most favorable auspices music is too generally regarded as inferior in value to the more common branches; as designed to afford recreation rather than mental culture. Hence it too often enters the school-room with words of apology, doubtful of its right to enter, and humbly grateful for the modicum of time and attention there grudgingly conceded to its claims.[4]

The Historical Basis of Music Education Philosophy

Music education has been discussed throughout Western intellectual history not only by those who taught music, but, more important, by intellectual, religious, political, and educational leaders. From the time of ancient Greece until the nineteenth century, the great majority of writings about the philosophy of music education is by societal and intellectual leaders. Plato's ideal society deeply valued music education for its ability to maintain and continue what he felt were critical cultural values and traditions. He wrote in *Protagoras*:

> The music masters by analogous methods instill self-control and deter the young from evil-doing. And when they have learned to play the lyre, they teach them the works of good poets of another sort, namely the lyrical which they accompany on the lyre, familiarizing the minds of the children with the rhythms and melodies. By this means they become more civilized, more balanced, and better adjusted in themselves and so more capable in whatever they say or do, for rhythm and harmonious adjustment are essential to the whole of human life. . . .[5]

Aristotle also concluded that education in music served the citizen well:

> It is evident, then, that there is a sort of education in which parents should train their sons, not as being useful or necessary, but because it is liberal or noble. . . [the ancients'] opinion may be gathered from the fact that music is one of the received and traditional branches of education. . . .[6]

Two millenia later, early American music education was based on a utilitarian rationale. The teaching of music could not have existed in the early days of this country for the sole purpose of aesthetic development. Spanish and French conquerors, in what are now the southwestern and north central United States, brought teachers from their own countries to indoctrinate the natives in European practices and values. This was accomplished, in great part, through music education. Early in the eighteenth century, musicians established the singing school movement along the eastern seaboard to improve music in worship, thereby enhancing the quality of church services. Lowell Mason, arguing that music met the same moral, physical, and intellectual requirements as other school subjects, persuaded the Boston School Committee to adopt music as a curricular subject in 1838. The report of a subcommittee of the Boston School Committee described the extramusical basis for acceptance of music as a curricular subject:

> Judged then by this triple standard, intellectually, morally, and physically, vocal Music seems to have a natural place in every system of

instruction which aspires, as should every system, to develope [sic] man's whole nature. . . . Now the defect of our present system, admirable as that system is, is this, that it aims to develope the intellectual part of man's nature solely, when for all the true purposes of life, it is of more importance, a hundredfold, to feel rightly, than to think profoundly."[7]

The fact that music was measured by the same moral, physical, and intellectual standards as other subjects and was judged to be capable of making a unique contribution to each is significant. The aesthetic impact of music was believed to be of utilitarian value in the education of the citizen. Throughout the nineteenth century and into the twentieth, music was introduced into public school systems across the country, justified on essentially the same rationale that was used in Boston in 1838.

When progressivism provided the philosophical basis for American schooling throughout much of the first half of the twentieth century, music assumed an even stronger position in public schools. Progressive education changed music instruction radically and gave it a secure place in the curriculum, in part because of its effectiveness in the development of socialization skills in children. This, too, is a utilitarian justification.

The Development of an Aesthetic Basis for Music Education Philosophy

By the middle of the twentieth century, music educators had assumed the role of spokespersons for their own profession. Since that time, there has been a more or less steady withdrawal from a utilitarian philosophy of music education. It has been superseded by a philosophy based on the aesthetic component of music. Allen Britton, of the University of Michigan, and Charles Leonhard, of the University of Illinois, were the foremost early leaders of the movement away from the utilitarian philosophy. In the 1950s nationwide concern for the quality of education threatened to redirect educational resources from music to other subjects. Both Britton and Leonhard sought to develop a more principled rationale, one based on the inherent nature of music, to replace the old utilitarian justifications.

Leonhard wrote:

When we speak of a philosophy of music education, we refer to a system of basic beliefs which underlies and provides a basis for the operation of the musical enterprise in an educational setting. . . . The business of the school is to help young people undergo meaningful experience and arrive at a system of values that will be beneficial to society. . . . While reliance on statements of the instrumental value of music may well have convinced some reluctant administrator more fully to support the music program, those values cannot stand close scrutiny, because they are not unique to music. In fact, many other areas of the curriculum are in a position to make a more powerful contribution to these values than is music.[8]

A few years later Bennett Reimer commented: "If music education in the present era could be characterized by a single, overriding purpose, one would have to say this field is trying to become 'aesthetic education.' What is needed in order to fulfill this purpose is a philosophy which shows how and why music education is aesthetic in its nature and its value."[9]

Basic Concepts in Music Education

A significant development occurred in 1954, when MENC organized the Commission on Basic Concepts. The Commission was created in recognition of the need for a solid philosophical foundation for music education. In addition to music educators, the members represented the disciplines of philosophy, psychology, and sociology because MENC recognized that the Commission had to reflect a diversity of viewpoints. The National Society for the Study of Education (NSSE) published the commission's work as its fifty-seventh yearbook.[a] It came out in 1958 under the title *Basic Concepts in Music Education*.[10] In *Basic Concepts*, music educators, psychologists, philosophers, and sociologists presented a variety of positions relative to their disciplines; they were needed by a profession seeking a new intellectual basis. Allen Britton cited historical justification for music education, but criticized the practice of referring to ancillary values of music instruction as a basis for contemporary justification:

> Music, as one of the seven liberal arts, has formed an integral part of the educational systems of Western civilization from Hellenic times to the present. Thus, the position of music in education historically speaking, is one of great strength. Unfortunately, this fact seems to be one of which most educators, including music educators, remain unaware. As a result, the defense of music in the curriculum is often approached as if something new were being dealt with. Lacking the assurance which a knowledge of history could provide, many who seek to justify the present place of music in American schools tend to place too heavy a reliance upon ancillary values which music may certainly serve but which cannot, in the end, constitute its justification. Plato, of course, is the original offender in this regard, his general view that the essential value of music lies in its social usefulness seems to be as alive today as ever.[11]

---

[a]The National Society for the Study of Education publishes a two-volume yearbook, each volume on a different topic. The 35th yearbook, *Music Education* (1936), was the first to be dedicated to music.

The impact of *Basic Concepts in Music Education* on the profession was so great that it set the agenda for future intellectual developments in music education. Music education professors incorporated it into their course syllabi, and philosophers and psychologists referred to it as they developed the intellectual support system for music education in the contemporary era.

A Utilitarian Position

The problems created by the substandard national economic conditions of the 1970s stimulated renewed philosophic introspection. Controversy over utilitarian-versus-aesthetic philosophical positions reemerged with occasional articles reflecting the need to maintain some utilitarian beliefs in the ancillary values of music education. The philosophical statement of the Bergenfield, New Jersey, music education program is an example of a utilitarian approach:

> The PHILOSOPHICAL PURPOSE of the music department is to dedicate itself, first foremost, to the support furtherance of the GENERAL PHILOSOPHY of the Bergenfield Board of Education and the individual schools particularly in the phases of character education and the development of better citizenship, preparing young people for life in a free, democratic society in which they will have the opportunity the responsibility to make choices.[12]

The Bergenfield music educators carried forth the justification that supported music during the years of progressive education, when music education was highly valued as a component of the curriculum—a view stated much earlier by several respected music educators:

> The general aim of education is to train the child to become a capable, useful, contented member of society. The development of a fine character and of the desire to be of service to humanity are results that lie uppermost in the minds of the leaders of educational thought. Every school subject is valued in proportion to its contribution to these desirable ends. Music, because of its powerful influence upon the very innermost recesses of our subjective life, because of its wonderfully stimulating effect upon our physical, mental, spiritual natures, because of its well-nigh universality of appeal, contributes directly to both of these fundamental purposes of education. By many of the advanced educators of the present day, therefore, music, next to the "three R's" is considered the most important subject in the public school curriculum.[13]

Despite the age of this statement, it reflects one of the core issues of music education in the 1990s—why society needs music education. Schwadron wrote:

The *real* problems in contemporary music education which are daily concerns are to a considerable extent value-centered. We are coming to realize that a new or alternate approach is needed for the construction of value-oriented curricular designs. The context of this emerging curriculum will focus on issues relevant to the nature of music and to the lives of the students. It will lead students to ask fundamental questions, to engage in intriguing musical activities, to seek answers based on personal reflection, inquiry, discovery, and research; it will help them formulate their values of music on both logical and introspective levels. Does it not follow that educators should themselves be encouraged to explore these matters for both general or practical classroom purposes and the self-examination of personal value systems, prejudices, tolerances, etc.? . . . It seems very odd that the why of music has been investigated by those like Dewey, Mursell, Langer, and Meyer and yet categorically avoided by those directly responsible for daily musical instruction. . . .[14]

Renewed Interest in Aesthetic Education

Except for *Basic Concepts*, the writings of Bennett Reimer and Abraham Schwadron, and other occasional articles and reports, relatively little was published on the subject of music education philosophy from the 1950s until the 1990s. Early in the 1990s, however, there was a resurgence of interest in the subject. In 1990 Estelle Jorgensen chaired The Philosopher\Teacher in Music Symposium at Indiana University. This event brought together music educators and philosophers to present their views on a number of philosophical issues. It led to the founding of the Music Education Philosophy Special Research Interest Group (SRIG), one of eleven SRIGS (see chapter 8) approved by the Music Education Research Council (MERC) of MENC. MERC approval not only constitutes official recognition for philosophical research, but it also provides the opportunity to sponsor sessions on music education philosophy at MENC in-service conferences. A second outcome of the symposium was the founding of the *Philosophy of Music Education Review*, a semiannual periodical. This journal was needed because there were too few research outlets for the amount of intellectual foment taking place in the 1980s. A second symposium on music education philosophy, chaired by David Elliott, was held at the University of Toronto in 1994.

Renewed interest in music education philosophy inspired many music educators to study the branch of philosophy known as aesthetics. Often, they went to the sources of Reimer's work: John Dewey, Susanne Langer, and Leonard Meyer. Reimer wrote: "The ability to enjoy music aesthetically—that is, for its intrinsic power to cause feelingful responses—is ubiquitous. Human capacities for aesthetic experience in general and musical experience in particular are conceived as robust, natural, primal to the human condition, and not limited to 'art and music of the elite.'"[15]

The direction taken by music education philosophers in the 1990s is, in large part, the study of aesthetics and its applications to music education. New positions, however, have also been formulated. For example, David Elliott, in *Music Matters: A New Philosophy of Music Education*,[16] challenges the aesthetic basis of music education philosophy. Elliott argues that musical compositions are not aesthetic objects, but that music should be viewed as a four-dimensioned human activity. He states: "Music is a tetrad of complementary dimensions involving (1) a does, (2) some kind of doing, (3) something done, and (4) the complete context in which doers do what they do." He calls music a "diverse human practice," and describes how music education should be structured on this understanding.

The revitalized interest in music education philosophy has also generated several other books on the subject. The second edition of Bennett Reimer's landmark work, *A Philosophy of Music Education*, was published in 1989. Richard Colwell edited *Basic Concepts in Music Education II* (1991).[17] Bennett Reimer and Jeffrey Wright published *On the Nature of the Musical Experience* in 1992.[18] This book presents many viewpoints on the musical experience and includes a section on implications for future research in music education philosophy. Also in 1992, the National Society for the Study of Education published its ninety-first yearbook—*The Arts, Education, and Aesthetic Knowing*,[19] edited by Bennett Reimer and Ralph Smith. One of the most important contributions of this book is its illumination of the relationship between aesthetic learning and cognitive psychology.

Can Philosophy Be Put into Practice?

Because of the lack of central authority over education in the United States, it is doubtful that there will ever be an absolute reconciliation of philosophic positions. One position might gain ground, but by the time it actually begins to influence classroom practicies, a new belief begins to overtake it. Continuing discussions and disagreements, often resulting in appropriate compromise, might well be the healthiest and most productive paradigm for the music education profession. As is true of any discipline, it is in the best interest of the music education profession for philosophers to debate long-held beliefs and to propose new doctrines.

Cognitive Psychology

The contemporary era of music education corresponds with a new era in the psychology of human development. Ulrich Neisser defined cognitive psychology as "the study of human cognition as it occurs in natural purposeful activity within the ordinary environment."[20] Until the 1950s, psychologists based their work on such learning theories as Gestalt and associationist theory. The rise of cognitive psychology in the 1960s supplanted learning theories for most psychologists and educators, and the term "psychological theory" has replaced "learning theory." George Mandler wrote: "The various tensions and inadequacies of the first half of the twentieth century cooperated to produce a new movement in psychology that first adopted the label of information processing and after became known as modern cognitive psychology. And it all happened in the five year period between 1955 and 1960."[21]

Representatives of several disciplines participated in the development of cognitive psychology. Neuroscientists, anthropologists, early scholars in artificial intelligence, and philosophers all contributed to the new view of human development. Psychology and linguistics were the disciplines most central to what was called the "cognitive revolution." One of the early beliefs of cognitive psychology was that there is a strong analogy between human and computer behavior, and artificial intelligence was a central issue. Philosopher Hilary Putnam explained that a problem could be solved by a variety of computer programs operating on different machines, and so the software, or thinking process, can be viewed separately from its hardware environment. Analogously, all humans share the same anatomy and physiology, but not all humans exhibit the same patterns of thinking or of problem solving. Human bodies are similar, but the thought processes of each individual are not.

Cognitive Psychology and Arts Education

PROJECT ZERO

The work of philosopher Nelson Goodman was highly influential in applying cognitive development to arts education. His book *Languages of Art*, published in 1968, discussed the symbolic nature of the arts and how they are perceived. Goodman's interest in aesthetics carried over into arts education. In 1967 he founded Project Zero[b] at Harvard University and became its codirector. Since that time, Project researchers have investigated such areas as "the artistic and aesthetic development of children, aesthetic perception of works of art, problem solving and creation in the arts, and practical problems of curriculum construction and evaluation."[22]

Since the 1970s, both psychologists and music education researchers have focused their efforts on musical cognition, and several

---

[b]According to Howard Gardner, Goodman, with his wry sense of humor, said, "Well, nobody knows anything about this, so I'm going to call our group Project Zero." From a speech to Young Audiences, Indianapolis, IN, March 1994.

specialized interest areas have emerged. They enhance our understanding of how people perceive, create, and perform music. Some of the important books on cognitive psychology in music are *The Psychology of Music* (Diana Deutch, ed.), *Music Cognition* (W. Jay Dowling), *The Development of Thought in Sound* (Mary Louise Serafine), *The Musical Mind: The Cognitive Psychology of Music* (John Sloboda), and *Developmental Psychology* (Hargreaves).

The Theory of Multiple Intelligences

Howard Gardner, codirector of Project Zero, developed the theory of multiple intelligences, which has strongly supported the concept of the arts as basic education. He explained "intelligence" as follows:

> When we define intelligence, we talk about solving a problem, which is part of everybody's definition. We also talk about making something. If you're intelligent, you can make things. You can make works of art, you can create scientific theories. You can teach a good class, organize a meeting, run a business. Those are all signs of intelligence, but they are a hundred percent absent on any IQ test. And, we also talk in our definition about intelligence as being something that's valued in a community. Nothing is intelligent or non-intelligent by itself, it's intelligent if it leads to some kind of a problem solving or product making activity that's valued.[23]

In *Frames of Mind: The Theory of Multiple Intelligences* he wrote:

> There is persuasive evidence for the existence of several *relatively autonomous* human intellectual competences, abbreviated hereafter as "human intelligences." These are the "frames of mind" of my title. The exact nature and breadth of each intellectual "frame" has not so far been satisfactorily established, nor has the precise number of intelligences been fixed. But the conviction that there exist at least some intelligences, that these are relatively independent of one another, and that they can be fashioned and combined in a multiplicity of adaptive ways by individuals and cultures, seems to me to be increasingly difficult to deny.[24]

Gardner identifies the seven primary intelligences as linguistic, musical, logical-mathematical, spatial, bodily kinesthetic, interpersonal, and intrapersonal. He wrote, "Of all the gifts with which individuals may be endowed, none emerges earlier than musical talent."[25] Other psychologists have also identified several autonomous intelligences that include the musical, or artistic.

Philip Phenix asserts that the arts are one of six independent "realms of meaning," all of which must be acquired by each individual in order to function well in society. His realms of knowledge include Symbolics (ordinary language, mathematics, nondiscursive symbolic form), Empirics (physical science, biology, psychology, social science), Esthetics (music, visual arts, arts of movement, literature), Synnoetics (personal Knowledge), Ethics (moral knowledge), and Synoptics (history, religion, philosophy):[26]

> The six realms may be regarded as comprising the basic competences that general education should develop in every person. A complete person should be skilled in the use of speech, symbol, and gesture, factually well informed, capable of creating and appreciating objects of esthetic significance, endowed with a rich and disciplined life in relation to self and others, able to make wise decisions and to judge between right and wrong, and possessed of an integral outlook. These are the aims of general education for the development of whole persons.[27]

Elliot Eisner, in *Learning and Teaching: Ways of Knowing*, identifies the aesthetic, scientific, interpersonal, intuitive, narrative and paradigmatic, formal, and spiritual as the seven modes of thinking.[28]

In *Knowledge and the Curriculum* Paul Hirst lists mathematics, physical sciences, human sciences, history, religion, literature and the fine arts, and philosophy as the seven forms of knowledge needed by students to have a liberal education.[29] Harry Broudy, with B. Othanel Smith and Joe R. Burnett, classified the arts as one of six "categories of instruction" for students to develop the "cognitive and evaluative maps" needed to function in a modern mass society.

All of these psychologists agree that the aesthetic is a specific and separate area of knowledge. Progressive education treated the arts as tools for learning other subjects. Conversely, cognitive psyhchology values the arts for their unique contributions to human learning and life.[30]

Franz Roehmann warns that Gardner's theory of multiple intelligences (and by implication, those of other psychologists) is unproven. He writes: "It is, in fact an idea that has (again) regained the right to be discussed seriously. . . . Those who interpret Gardner's work might consider the mind more in terms of multiple potentials and less in terms of multiple intelligences. . . . We are a long way from understanding what human intelligence is and how it functions."[31]

Arts Propel

Gardner directed a major project called Arts Propel. PROPEL is a not-quite-exact acronym for Production (making music by singing, playing an instrument, or composing), Perception (listening to music), and Reflection (thinking about what one does, both in words and in the appropriate symbol system). Its genesis was a project in visual art education sponsored by the Getty Center for Education in the Arts that began in 1982 to promote visual art as an integral part of basic education. In 1985 the Center published *Beyond Creating: The Place for Art in America's Schools*.[32] This influential book recommended a new mode of instruction called Discipline-based Art Education (DBAE). DBAE consists of knowing how (art production), knowing about (art history and culture), knowing why (art criticism), and knowing of and within (aesthetics). DBAE was intended to expand the traditional emphasis in assessment on skill development.[33] Mittler and Stinespring describe a practical DBAE situation:

> A visitor walking into an art classroom today might find students working with a variety of media and techniques in their efforts to solve a studio problem based on implementing certain elements and principles of design or reflecting concepts employed by Picasso's cubism. But that visitor could just as easily stroll into the same classroom to discover students critiquing a painting by Paul Gauguin, or discussing the influence of Japanese printmakers on the French impressionists, or reporting on the impact of Henry Moore's work on the sculptors who followed.[34]

DBAE has generated a great deal of controversy because art educators do not agree on whether skill or content should be the basis of their subject. The music education concept closest to DBAE is comprehensive musicianship (see chapter 5), and a similar controversy exists in music education.

The skill-content debate has never been settled, and perhaps never will, but it reflects concern on the part of arts educators for one of the most basic aspects of their discipline. The same concern was reflected in music in the form of Arts Propel, which began in 1985 as a joint project between Project Zero, the Pittsburgh (Pennsylvania) Public Schools, and the Educational Testing Service. The Rockefeller Foundation provided funding. Initially, the project was intended to formulate a means of assessing artistic learning in middle and high schools, but it later expanded to include curriculum modules. Arts Propel emphasized process, "primarily process as production which necessarily involves the cognitive components of perception and reflection."[35]

In Arts Propel, process incorporates assessment. "Domain projects," similar to curricular units, are organized on central ideas in the arts, such as how to learn from a musical performance. Domain projects were designed to integrate production, perception, and reflection. Process folios are an integral component. A process folio, similar to a composer's notebook, is a collection of the student's work that leads up to the finished product. Folios might include notes on how the student thought of the project, early drafts, and critiques of the work in progress. Assessment is an important aspect of the process folio. This process is similar to that used by professional musicians and artists. Rather than treating music as an abstract subject, the student experiences it in a real life manner. It is an authentic approach that involves students in several areas of music learning. It also reflects the tenets of cognitive psychology.

How Does Cognitive Psychology Support Music Education?

For decades, MENC and other organizations have promoted music as a basic subject, but its successes have been due more to effective advocacy than to an objective factual base that is well-grounded in research. Music educators know inherently that music is basic, and that education can be complete only if it includes the study of music. It is very difficult, however, to translate their conviction into a persuasive argument. Now studies in cognitive psychology affirm that musical intelligence affords a view of the world and a way of knowing that are not experienced through other subjects. With the advent of cognitive psychology, psychologists and music education scholars are compiling a body of scientific literature that supports the claim.

More and more, cognitive psychology is helping educators align educational practices with scientifically derived knowledge about learning and teaching. The subject became a matter of public interest with the 1994 publication of a controversial book about intelligence testing: Herrnstein and Murray's *The Bell Curve*.[36] *The Bell Curve* was provocative because it suggested racial differences in terms of intelligence. It did, however, raise the consciousness of the public about the issue of intelligence testing. Two highly debated questions resurfaced with the publication of this book: What is intelligence, and what do IQ tests actually measure? Many educational decisions are still based on IQ scores, but cognitive psychology informs us that IQ tests only measure some intelligences, basically those that rely on verbal and quantitative abilities, and neglect others. Standardized IQ tests are controversial for many reasons, but the major problem they pose for music education is that they ignore musical intelligence. Robert Deluty writes:

> Perhaps an unintended consequence of the controversy swirling around *The Bell Curve* will be to draw attention to some truly important issues in the study of intelligence, including: Why are only some intelligences valued in our society? What are the costs and benefits of such differential valuation? And, most important, how can the multiple intelligences be fostered so that individuals and societies achieve a greater array of goals and fulfill a wider range of potentialities?[37]

One manifestation of cognitive psychology is the teaching of various subjects as they relate to authentic real-life experiences, rather than as abstract subjects. English, math, science, and other subjects are all taught in this manner. The fact that similar systems are used with other school subjects validates its use for music instruction.

The Synergy of Philosophy and Psychology

It is always difficult in a time of change to arrive at sufficient agreement to be able to base classroom practices and materials on a new school of thought. Diane Ravitch writes: "Pedagogical practice follows educational philosophy, and it is obvious that we do not yet have a philosophical commitment to education that is sound enough and strong enough to withstand the erratic dictates of fashion."[38] This statement was true for music education, as it was for other disciplines. Yet, following the philosophical work of Britton, Leonhard, Schwadron, and especially Reimer, and the contributions of many cognitive psychologists, classroom practices have changed. Many of the materials and practices of contemporary music education reflect belief in aesthetic education and the principles of cognitive psychology.

Jerome Bruner and the Development of Conceptual Learning

The educational practices that developed early in the history of cognitive psychology were called "conceptual learning." Prior to the 1960s, the process of education utilized various approaches to rote learning. Children were expected to memorize specific information conveyed by teachers and books. They were assumed to have comprehended a subject after having learned the appropriate facts about it. This assumption was challenged after a significant early event in the history of conceptual education: the Woods Hole Conference (see chapter 2). It was this science education conference that inspired Jerome Bruner's *The Process of Education*. Only ninety-seven pages in length, this book was the impetus for curriculum development in all subject areas and helped to change the nature of instruction in American schools. *The Process of Education* discusses four important themes related to teaching and learning.

The first theme is the role of structure in learning and how it can be made central in teaching. Bruner asks, "What are the implications of emphasizing the structure of a subject, be it mathematics or history—emphasizing it in a way that seeks to give a student as quickly as possible a sense of the fundamental ideas of a discipline?"[39] Bruner states that to make exposure to a subject genuinely meaningful, students must develop true understanding of the subject:

The teaching and learning of structure, rather than simply the mastery of facts and techniques, is at the center of the classic problem of transfer. . . . If earlier learning is to render later learning easier, it must do so by providing a general picture in terms of which the relations between things encountered earlier and later are made as clear as possible.[40]

The second theme concerns readiness for learning. Psychologists and educators suspected that children could begin to study difficult subjects at a younger age than had been realized. The discussion is introduced by the now-famous proposition, "The foundations of any subject may be taught to anybody at any age in some form." The acceptance of the proposition signified recognition that the schools wasted "precious years by postponing the teaching of many important subjects on the ground that they are too difficult." Bruner explains:

It is only when . . . basic ideas are put in formalized terms as equations or elaborated verbal concepts that they are out of reach of the young child, if he has not first understood them intuitively and had a chance to try them out on his own. The early teaching of science, mathematics social studies and literature should be designed to teach those subjects with scrupulous intellectual honesty, but with an emphasis upon the intuitive grasp of ideas and upon the use of these basic ideas. A curriculum as it develops should revisit these basic ideas repeatedly, building upon them until the student has grasped the full formal apparatus that goes with them.[41]

The third theme is intuition:

The intellectual technique of arriving at plausible but tentative formulations without going through the analytic steps by which such formulations would be found valid or invalid conclusions. . . . The shrewd guess, the fertile hypothesis, the courageous leap to a tentative conclusion—these are the most valuable coin of the thinker at work, whatever his line of work.[42]

The fourth theme is the desire to learn, and how such desire may be stimulated:

Ideally, interest in the material to be learned is the best stimulus to learning rather than such external goals as grades or later competitive advantage. While it is surely unrealistic to assume that the pressures of competition can be effectively eliminated or that it is wise to seek their elimination, it is nonetheless worth considering how interest in learning per se can be stimulated.[43]

Bruner's work, as well as that of many others who found new meanings in his ideas, had profound impact on curriculum development in the 1960s. In fact, it began a new movement, which was called "conceptual learning" at that time. Music educators studied the implications of conceptual learning, developed new ideas about teaching and learning music, and gradually created new practices and curricular materials. Russell Getz, president of MENC, stated:

> One of the greatest changes for better music teaching was the gradual acceptance by general music teachers of the concept approach, as compared to previous efforts, which were often more concerned with associative properties of music. Instead of emphasizing story-telling through program music and correlating music with geography, social studies, mathematics, and science, the heart of music education has become the study of music itself, the components of pitch, duration, dynamics, and timbre, and the resultant concomitants such as melody, harmony, rhythm, instrumentation, style, and form.[44]

Another important book that described a conceptual approach to music education was published in 1967. *The Study of Music in the Elementary School—A Conceptual Approach*, edited by Charles Gary,[45] provides a definition of "concept" on which the rest of the book is predicated:

> A concept is a relatively complete and meaningful idea in the mind of a person. It is an understanding of something. It is his own subjective product of his way of making meaning of things he has seen or otherwise perceived in his experiences. At its most abstract and complex level it is a synthesis of a number of conclusions he has drawn about his experience with particular things. A conceptual statement is a description of the properties of a process, structure, or quality, stated in a form which indicates what has to be demonstrated or portrayed so a learner can perceive the process, structure or quality for himself.[46]

The book also discusses the development of musical concepts:

> [It] requires that children think musically. Since each child develops his own concepts individually, it is necessary for him to discover for himself what is in the music. If the teacher presents the child with a body of predetermined facts, there can be a gap between the lesson that is taught and the lesson that is learned. But when the child is making his own investigation of the music and when the processes of his investigation are consistent with the essential nature of the music, there will be no such gap. Too often information is simply poured

into the minds of children, thereby depriving them of the exciting experience of discovering it for themselves.[47]

One of the major contributions of *The Study of Music* is its discussion of concepts about rhythm, melody, harmony, form in music, forms of music, tempo, dynamics, and tone color. It also relates the conceptual learning of music to the general music and instrumental music programs.

Summary

The combination of aesthetic education and cognitive psychology holds promise for a solid foundation for music education if educational policy makers are aware of how they validate music as a basic subject. The advocacy efforts of the professional arts education organizations already reflect this information. Ideally, this knowledge will become so ingrained in the American psyche that, eventually, advocacy will no longer be necessary.

NOTES

1 Howard Gardner, "The ARTS PROPEL Approach to Education in the Arts," *Kodály Envoy* 22, no. 2 (Winter 1994): 4.

2 "The Revival of Aesthetics," *Report of the Commission on The Humanities* (New York: The American Council of Learned Societies, 1964), 53. The *Report* was sponsored jointly by the American Council of Learned Societies, the Council of Graduate Schools in the United States, and the United Chapters of Phi Beta Kappa.

3 Bennett Reimer, *A Philosophy of Music Education* (Englewood Cliffs, NJ: Prentice-Hall, 1970), 3.

4 Daniel B. Hagar, "President Hagar's Address." *NEA Proceedings* 24 (1885): 369.

5 Plato, *Protagoras*, from *The Collected Dialogues of Plato*, ed. Edith Hamilton and Huntington Cairns (Princeton: Princeton University Press, Bollingen Foundation, distributed by Pantheon Books, 1961), 322.

6 Aristotle, *Politica*. *The Works of Aristotle*, vol. 10 (London: Oxford University Press, 1921), 1338: 10–35.

7 Report of the select committee of the Boston School Committee, 24 August 1837.

8 Charles Leonhard, "The Philosophy of Music Education—Present and Future," in *Comprehensive Musicianship: The Foundation for College Education in Music* (Washington, DC: Music Educators National Conference, 1965), 42, 43, 45.

9 Bennett Reimer, *A Philosophy of Music Education* (Englewood Cliffs, NJ: Prentice-Hall, 1970), 2.

10 Nelson B. Henry, ed., *Basic Concepts in Music Education*, Fifty-seventh Yearbook of the National Society for the Study of Education, part 1 (Chicago: University of Chicago Press, 1958).

11 Allen Britton, "Music in Early American Public Education: A Historical

Critique," in *Basic Concepts in Music Education*, ed. Nelson Henry (Chicago: National Society for the Study of Education, 1958), 195.

12 "Music Thrives in Bergenfield, N.J.," program of presentation at the Music Educators National Conference In-service Conference, Kiamesha Lake, New York, 31 March 1981.

13 Horatio Parker, Osbourne McConathy, Edward Bailey Birge, and W. Otto Miessner, *The Progressive Music Series*, Teacher's Manual, 2 (Boston: Silver, Burdett, 1916), 9.

14 Abraham A. Schwadron, "Philosophy in Music Education: Pure or Applied Research?" *Bulletin* of the Council for Research in Music Education, no. 19 (Winter 1970): 26.

15 Bennett Reimer, *A Philosophy of Music Education*, 2d ed. (Englewood Cliffs, NJ: Prentice-Hall, 1989), 144–46.

16 David Elliott, *Music Matters: A New Philosophy of Music Education* (New York: Oxford University Press, 1994).

17 Richard J. Colwell, ed. *Basic Concepts in Music Education II* (Niwot: University Press of Colorado, 1991).

18 Bennett Reimer and Jeffrey E. Wright, eds. *On the Nature of Musical Experience* (Evanston, IL: Center for the Study of Education and the Musical Experience, Northwestern University, 1992).

19 Bennett Reimer and Ralph A. Smith, eds. *The Arts, Education, and Aesthetic Knowing* (Chicago: National Society for the Study of Education, 91st Yearbook, part 2, 1992).

20 Ulrich Neisser, *Cognitive Psychology* (New York: Appleton Century-Crofts, 1967), quoted in Marilyn P. Zimmerman, "Psychological Theory and Music Learning," *Basic Concepts in Music Education II*, 163.

21 George Mandler, "What is Cognitive Psychology? What Isn't?" Address to the American Psychological Association Division of Philosophical Psychology, Los Angeles, 1981.

22 George Geahigan, "The Arts in Education: A Historical Perspective," in *The Arts, Education, and Aesthetic Knowing* (Chicago: National Society for the Study of Education, 1992), 15.

23 Speech to Young Audiences, Inc., Indianapolis, IN, March 1994.

24 Howard Gardner, *Frames of Mind: The Theory of Multiple Intelligences* (New York: Basic Books, 1983).

25 Ibid., 99.

26 Philip H. Phenix, *Realms of Meaning: A Philosophy of the Curriculum for General Education* (New York: McGraw-Hill, 1964).

27 Ibid., 8.

28 Elliot Eisner, ed. *Learning and Teaching: The Ways of Knowing*, 84th Yearbook of the National Society for the Study of Education, part 2 (Chicago: National Society for the Study of Education, 1985).

29 Paul Hirst, *Knowledge and the Curriculum* (London: Routledge & Kegan Paul, 1974), 64.

30 George Geahigan, "The Arts in Education: A Historical Perspective," in *The Arts, Education, and Aesthetic Knowing*, ed. Bennett Reimer and Ralph A. Smith (Chicago: National Society for the Study of Education, 1992), 11.

31 Franz L. Roehmann, "On Philosophies of Music Education: Selected Issues

Revisited," *The Quarterly Journal of Music Teaching and Learning* 2, no. 3 (Fall 1991): 41.

32 *Beyond Creating: The Place for Art in American Schools* (Los Angeles: Getty Center for Education in the Arts, 1985).

33 Jessica Davis and Howard Gardner, "The Cognitive Revolution: Consequences for the Understanding and Education of the Child as Artist," in *The Arts, Education, and Aesthetic Knowing*, ed. Bennett Reimer and Ralph A. Smith (Chicago: National Society for the Study of Education, 1992), 114.

34 Gene A. Mittler and John A. Stinespring, "Intellect, Emotion, and Art Education Advocacy," *Design for Arts in Education* 92, no. 6 (July/August 1991): 16.

35 Ibid., 115.

36 Richard Herrnstein and Charles Murray, *The Bell Curve: Intelligence and Class Structure in American Life* (New York: Free Press, 1964).

37 Robert H. Deluty, "The Klutzy Professor: Is He Smart or Stupid?" *The Sun* (Baltimore), 4 November 1994, p. 27A.

38 Diane Ravitch, "Why Educators Resist a Basic Required Curriculum," in *The Great School Debate*, ed. Beatrice Gross and Ronald Gross (New York: Simon & Schuster, 1985), 203.

39 Jerome S. Bruner, *The Process of Education* (Cambridge, MA: Harvard University Press, 1960), 3.

40 Ibid., 12.

41 Ibid., 12.

42 Ibid., 13, 14.

43 Ibid., 14, 15.

44 Russell P. Getz, "Music Education in Tomorrow's Schools: A Practical Approach," in *The Future of Musical Education in America* (Rochester, NY: Eastman School of Music Press, 1984), 24, 25.

45 Charles L. Gary, ed., *The Study of Music in the Elementary School—A Conceptual Approach* (Washington, DC: Music Educators National Conference, 1967).

46 Asahel D. Woodruff, unpublished paper; quoted in Gary, *The Study of Music in the Elementary School*, 2.

47 Ibid., 3.

4

Advocacy: Connecting Public Policy and Arts Education

Until very recently, public policy and arts education[a] were seldom if ever mentioned in the same sentence—if, indeed, they were even linked in the same discussion.

Harold M. Williams, 1993
President and Chief Executive Officer
The J. Paul Getty Trust

Public Policy

Most of the important developments of the last decade have resulted from the responses of the arts education profession to public policy issues. Arts educators who wish to truly understand why their profession has developed as it has must be knowledgeable of the public policy arena because so many of the decisions that affect their professional lives are made there.

There are forces in our environment that we might wish were not there, but which demand a response. Public policy is the predominant environmental force for public education, as it is for all public endeavors. For as long as music and art have been curricular subjects in the United States, their direction and focus have been subject to the controls imposed by public policy. For many years, those controls were benign-

---

[a]The term "arts education" is used instead of "music education" throughout this chapter because most public policy matters that affect music education actually address all of the arts disciplines in the curriculum. In this context, arts education means music, visual art, dance, and theater.

73

fully neglectful. Although policy guided arts education, it was not overly intrusive, and arts educators were more or less in charge of their own professional destiny. This empowered the profession to develop on its own terms, and to flourish and prosper.

Public policy itself is also subject to environmental forces to which federal, state, and local policymakers must respond. Some of the forces that directly affect educational policy are economic conditions, quality of life, and court decisions that determine how schools deal with equity issues of minorities, gender, underprivileged and disabled students, and children at risk. A plethora of social and economic issues has forced policymakers to ration their limited resources severely since the 1970s, and public policy has not been favorable toward arts education since then. The high cost of arts instruction has proved too much to bear in some school systems, especially those where the rationale for arts education was not convincing to policymakers. The convergence of environmental forces has compelled many school districts to reduce or eliminate their arts programs. At the same time, the inclusion of the arts in the national goals for education, a public policy established by Congress in 1994, affords reason to hope for better times ahead. Whether change occurs for the better depends on the environmental forces that face arts education in the future, and how the profession responds to them.

Arts educators need to understand the relationship between their profession and the numerous and complex facets of government. The Constitution grants certain powers to the federal government and Congress creates laws to exercise those powers. Because the United States Constitution does not mention education, it is not a federal responsibility. Instead, education is left to the states. The states are not required to offer public education, but there is universal agreement that education is one of the most important functions of state government, and every state mandates it. By law, educational opportunity must be offered equally to all students within each state. If a state mandates music and art in the curriculum, it must be offered to every student in every school district. If the state does not require it but an individual school system does, then it must be offered to every student in that school system.

State laws guide the establishment of local school authority and specify its responsibilities. For example, a local board of education has the authority to appoint a superintendent to be the chief administrator of the school system. On the recommendation of the superintendent, the board appoints teachers and administrators and approves the budget, capital projects, and policies by which the school system operates.

Federal laws are administered by federal agencies that operate within the executive branch of the government. The administration of most federal education matters is the responsibility of the United States Department of Education (DOE), which establishes policies and regulations to support congressional legislation. DOE distributes federal money to states for support of such programs as school lunches, affirmative action, and education for the handicapped, but it is state education law, created by the state legislature, that determines how the money is to be distributed and utilized within the state (in keeping with federal guidelines and policies).

Education law varies from state to state, and so arts education is mandated in some states and left to local authorities in others. Depending on the policy of the local board, arts education can include music, visual art, drama, and dance, or it may be any one subject or a combination of subjects. Local policy also dictates whether arts instruction is provided by arts education specialists or by general classroom teachers. Ideally, arts education specialists should be responsible for the various arts disciplines. That is one of the goals of arts advocacy.

Most arts educators, by nature of their interests, education, and training, are relatively unfamiliar with public policy as it affects their professional lives. Being complex, undergoing frequent change, and often appearing to defy logic, it is a difficult field to know. Yet, because of its impact on their livelihood, and because it is possible to influence public policy, arts educators can benefit greatly by understanding the democratic process as it applies to education. Writing about the importance of policy to arts education, Lawrence Castiglione commented:

> If those in the fields of the arts and arts education do not want to be regarded merely as cultural ornaments and would rather be serious players in the high-stakes game of government and corporate funding, they should begin to develop and study policy that affects them. So long as the arts and arts education compete for public funds or supplicate private granting agencies, policy studies will be demanded by those who grip the purse strings.[1]

Advocacy for Arts Education

W. McNeil Lowry discussed the difference between "policy" and "advocacy":

> Public policy in the arts is the sum of private and governmental interests (of which individual patrons, foundations, corporations, and national and local arts councils are examples) with particular or general values in mind. Advocacy is any argument, action, publication, or coalition promoting increased contributed income for the arts.[2]

Advocacy is similar to lobbying, but there is a fundamental difference. Lobbying is a legally defined activity practiced by licensed professionals who are paid to influence legislators for specific causes. Advocacy is done by nonprofit organizations[b] whose tax status prohibits them from some activities that professional lobbyists engage in. Advocacy is the means by which the needs of a specific cause are made known to legislators, government administrators who make policies to implement laws, public boards that control public education, school administrators, and the electorate, which has ultimate control over public policy by means of the voting process. The purpose of arts education advocacy is to inform decision makers of the importance of arts education, the effects of legislation and public policy on it, and what kinds of legislation and policy are needed to improve or correct a particular situation.

Traditionally, the arts education associations have interfaced with the government on behalf of individual arts educators by means of advocacy. A 1986 briefing paper to the arts education community stated: "Clearly, the advocacy movement is on the cultural formation scene in force. The arts education community must relate to the advocacy movement as positively as possible without giving up the intellectual ground on which the whole notion of serious education in the arts disciplines is based."[3]

Formal advocacy in music education began when MENC appointed Joan Gaines as director of its new public relations program in 1966. Gaines said that music educators need to advance their subject by interpreting music education as ideas, processes, and relationships. She traveled extensively to spread the message of music education to the public, and coached music educators in making their own public relations efforts more effective. Her print advertisements and radio and television announcements blanketed the country. She was also an advisor to every MENC project for several years. Gaines authored *Approaches to Public Relations for the Music Educator* in 1968, and was the guiding force behind the January 1972 issue of *Music Educators Journal*, which focused on public relations.

When the national economy declined in the early 1970s, MENC recognized a greater need to promote music education to policy makers rather than to the general public. It refocused its efforts from public relations to government relations, although it has continuously maintained a strong public relations program as well. MENC began its government relations efforts by working with legislators and their staffs and

---

[b]Nonprofit organizations are those approved by the Internal Revenue Service (IRS) for special tax status because they provide an important public service that the government itself does not, or cannot offer. Nonprofit status allows the organization relief from tax liability because its income is not distributed as profit to shareholders, but instead is put back into the organization's operations. The Music Educators National Conference (MENC), like most nonprofit associations, is a 501(c)3 organization. The designation refers to section 501(c)3 of the United States Tax Code.

presenting government relations workshops for state and divisional MENC units. Charles Moody, an MENC staff member in the 1970s, was active in training many MENC members in government relations. These workshops have been a routine part of national, regional, and state music education conferences ever since. The word "advocacy" gradually replaced "government relations" because it describes MENC activities more accurately.

MENC participated actively in legislative agendas and took formal positions in a number of diverse federal issues.[c] Several MENC Presidents have served the organization well with their testimony on Capitol Hill.

By the 1980s MENC had acquired considerable expertise in advocacy. Advocacy for arts education at the federal and state levels is normally undertaken by coalitions representing the various arts disciplines because public policy usually affects them all collectively.[d] Coalitions also have the advantage of greater political clout because they represent more constituents than a single discipline. Samuel Hope points out: "Unity has been the rallying cry of the American arts advocacy movement for nearly thirty years. A fundamental principle of arts advocacy remains that unity is essential for effectiveness."[4]

MENC and the American Council for the Arts (ACA) called together thirty-one leaders of arts and arts education organizations for a meeting in 1986 at the Pew Memorial Trust in Philadelphia. The Ad Hoc National Arts Education Working Group was formed at this meeting. A product of the meeting was "The Philadelphia Resolution," which stated the basic principles agreed upon by all of the organizations:

---

[c]For example: the reauthorization of the Elementary and Secondary Arts Education Program; the establishment of the Cabinet level Department of Education; the 1979 White House Conference on the Arts; the Career Education Act of 1978; legislated authority to conduct a baseline survey of the status of arts education in the schools, which resulted in *Toward Civilization*; and the need for a White House Conference on Education in 1980. MENC also provided expert witnesses to testify at several Congressional hearings. One, *The Arts Are Fundamental to Learning* (1977), was a joint hearing before the Subcommittee on Select Education of the Committee on Education and Labor, House of Representatives, and the Special Subcommittee On Education, Arts and Humanities of the Committee on Human Resources of the U. S. Senate. Another was entitled *To Permit the Use of Title IV-B ESEA Funds for the Purchase of Band Instruments*. Following this hearing, Congress agreed to permit the purchase of band instruments with Title I funds.

[d]The earliest arts education coalition, formed in the early 1970s, included the professional organizations for dance, art, music, and theater, and was known as DAMT. A more contemporary coalition is described by John Mahlmann in "Maximizing the Power of Coalitions," *Association Management* 47, no. 9 (September 1995): 32–39.

> WHEREAS, American Society is deeply concerned with the condition of elementary and secondary education; and
> WHEREAS, the arts are basic to education and have great value in and of themselves and for the knowledge, skills and values they impart; and
> WHEREAS, the arts are a widely neglected curriculum and educational resource in American schools; and
> WHEREAS, numerous national reports have cited the arts as one of the most basic disciplines of the curriculum; and
> WHEREAS, every American child should have equal educational opportunity to study the arts as representations of the highest intellectual achievements of humankind; and
> WHEREAS, the undersigned individuals, representing a broad cross-section of national arts organizations, agree:
> THAT EVERY elementary and secondary school should offer a balanced, sequential, and high quality program of instruction in arts disciplines taught by qualified teachers and strengthened by artists and arts organizations as an essential component of the curriculum;
> THAT WE PROMOTE public understanding of the connections between
> the study of the arts disciplines, the creation of art, and the development of a vibrant, productive American civilization;
> THAT WE URGE inclusion of support for rigorous, comprehensive arts education in the arts development efforts of each community;
> THAT WE PURSUE development of local, state and national policies that result in more effective support for arts education and the professional teachers and artists who provide it.[5]

The ad hoc coalition continued to meet after the Philadelphia event and eventually produced another document, "Concepts for Strengthening Arts Education in Schools," to present to their individual boards. In 1988 the group became the National Coalition for Education in the Arts (NCEA). Its mission was "to develop and monitor policy affecting education in the arts." The coalition existed for three years, during which time it participated in a symposium known as "Toward a New Era in Arts Education." This event was also convened by MENC and the ACA.[e] "Toward a New Era" was held in November 1987 at the Interlochen Arts Center in Michigan.[6] The proceedings of the symposium, including "The Interlochen Proposal," are published in *Toward a New Era in Arts Education*.[7] The Proposal states:

> WHEREAS education must focus on the child, how the child learns and interacts in the school environment, and

---

[e]Costs were underwritten by the Interlochen Arts Center, the National Endowment for the Arts, and the Sears Roebuck Foundation.

WHEREAS each child deserves the opportunity to develop all dimensions of his or her being; and

WHEREAS each child should have the opportunity to explore a diversity of subjects and fields:

THEREFORE, to achieve these goals, arts educators must collaborate with a broad range of colleagues in the arts, humanities, and sciences to develop a school agenda that improves the total life of the school and allows each child to reach his or her full potential. We must participate in an overall effort to improve education in the schools.

WHEREAS all members of society should be knowledgeable and interactive in all art forms; and

WHEREAS a variety of levels of involvement and achievement in the arts are appropriate:

THEREFORE, American schools, K–12, should provide arts education for all students every day. Instruction in the arts should encompass visual arts, music, dance, theater, and creative writing. It should be accorded resources of time, money, and personnel equivalent to other basic subject areas, and the same level of expertise. Every school should have an in-school sequential arts program that serves all the children.[8]

It was the National Coalition for Education in the Arts that successfully advocated inclusion of arts education in the Goals 2000 Act.

There were other sources of moral support for arts education as well. In 1984 the American Assembly convened a meeting of representatives of government, business, universities, foundations, associations, the arts (graphic, plastic, and literary), artistic direction and administration, and patrons and critics of the arts. One of the recommendations of this broadly representative group was for the support of arts education:

Appreciation of the arts is by and large developed through the educational system. The beginnings of attitudes and opinions about the importance of the arts have the same locus. We cannot hope to establish the centrality of the arts to this society or their value to the individual without a clear recognition of this fact. More support for the arts in education is needed, especially at the local level.[9]

Music Education Coalitions

Following the triumphant conclusion of the advocacy effort that produced the national arts education standards, a Music Education Summit was held in Washington, DC, in 1994. The participants discussed how their organizations could cooperate in a wide range of music education issues. The summit was sponsored by the National Coalition for Music Education. The participants are listed here to illustrate the remarkable breadth of interests represented in the music education profession:[10]

American Bandmasters Association

American Choral Directors Association

American Federation of Musicians

American Guild of Handbell Ringers, Inc.

American Guild of Organists

American Music Conference

American Orff-Schulwerk Association

American School Band Directors Association

American Society of Composers, Authors and Publishers

American String Teachers Association

American Symphony Orchestra League

Association of Concert Bands of America, Inc.

Bands of America, Inc.

Broadcast Music, Inc.

Chamber Music America

College Music Society

Foundation for Music Based Learning

Gordon Institute for Music Learning

Guitar and Accessories Music Marketing Association

International Association of Electronic Keyboard Manufacturers

International Association of Jazz Educators

Music Educators National Conference

Music Industry Conference

Music Teachers National Association

National Academy of Recording Arts & Sciences, Inc.

National Association for Music Therapy, Inc.

National Associations of Band Instrument Manufacturers

National Association of Music Merchants

National Association of School Music Dealers

National Association of Schools of Music

National Association of Teachers of Singing

National Band Association

National Black Music Caucus

National Federation of Music Clubs

The National Flute Association

National Music Council

National Piano Foundation

National School Orchestra Association

Organization of American Kodály Educators

Percussive Arts Society

Phi Mu Alpha Sinfonia Fraternity

Piano Manufacturers Association International

Sigma Alpha Iota

SPEBSQSA, Inc.

Suzuki Association of the Americas

Sweet Adelines International

The VoiceCare Network

Women Band Directors National Association

The state music education associations have also been involved in advocacy for many years. Many have formed statewide coalitions since the national coalitions were created. These organizations endeavor to educate policy and decision makers such as state legislators, school boards, and principals about music education. The state coalitions also undertake specific issues that affect music education within a particular state.

Other Advocacy Efforts

Professional arts education organizations are not the only advocates for arts education. In 1979 the prestigious Arts Education and Americans Panel, chaired by David Rockefeller, Jr., published *Coming to Our Senses*, with no author indicated. *Coming to Our Senses* described the status of arts education in the nation at that time, and offered a dire warning for the future of American culture if the arts were not taken more seriously in education. Rockefeller wrote: "If we want our world to be still, gray and silent, then we should take the arts out of school, shut down the neighborhood theatre, and barricade the museum doors. When we let the arts into the arena of learning, we run the risk that color and motion and music will enter our lives."[11] The analysis of the problems of the arts and arts education in contemporary American society was followed by specific recommendations based on three principles:

1. The fundamental goals of American education can be realized only when the arts become central to the individual's learning experience, in or out of school and at every stage of life.

2. Educators at all levels must adopt the arts as a basic component of the curriculum deserving parity with all other elements.

> 3. School programs in the arts should draw heavily upon all available resources in the community: the artists, the materials, the media, and the total environment.[12]

As in the early 1960s, when scientists spoke for a balanced curriculum that included the arts, scientists again came to the aid of arts education. The following is the testimony of Glen Seaborg, Professor of Chemistry at the University of California at Berkeley, and former Chairman of the U.S. Atomic Energy Commission, in a 1977 hearing before the Subcommittee on Select Education of the Committee on Education and Labor (House of Representatives) and the Special Subcomittee on Education, Arts and Humanities of the Committee on Human Resources of the United States Senate. Seaborg was a member of the Panel that oversaw the creation of *Coming to Our Senses*:

> As one of two scientists on the 25 member Panel on the Arts, Education and Americans, I have gained a special insight into an important facet of American education. The meetings, the briefings, the demonstrations, the conversations with my fellow Panelists have put into perspective the place that the arts hold today in our educational system at all levels. It is clear that the quality and quantity of arts education is not commensurate with its importance, not equal to the potential of a field that can give insight to all other areas of learning. An increased emphasis in our educational system on all the art subjects is needed as we begin our country's Third Century.
>
> Art is all encompassing. And in the late Twentieth Century all subjects are interrelated. I can see especially clearly the relationship between science and the arts. The symmetries of natural science, the synthesis of new theories from added information, the design of experiments, all have their counterparts in art forms. The arts have their laboratories in the form of museums, art galleries, etc. Radio, television, video tape, renovation and preservation of classic paintings, lasers in art, holography, high fidelity recording, electronics in music are but a few of the ways in which science and the arts can enhance each other.
>
> It is to be hoped that the publication of *Coming to Our Senses* will not only point out the significance of the arts in American education, but that as a consequence all art forms will receive appropriate attention, recognition and implementation in our educational system.

In 1988 Charles Fowler's book *Can We Rescue the Arts for America's Children? Coming to Our Senses—10 Years Later*[13] was published. Fowler provides an in-depth analysis of the status of arts education in the decade following the publication of *Coming to Our Senses*. His conclusion is dispiriting:

What has happened since this milestone [the publication of *Coming to our Senses*]?

Are the arts any more significant in education today than they were 10 years ago? Apparently, the arts have not gained much new status in American schooling. The brutal fact is that American education has not yet come to its senses in those intervening years, not nearly. In truth, I believe we are farther away from that august agenda today than we were in 1977 when the panel report was published.[14]

Both books were commercial publications that reached wide audiences throughout the country.

In 1990 MENC, the National Association of Music Merchants, and the National Academy of Recording Arts & Sciences, Inc. created the National Commission on Music Education. The Commission heard testimony in public forums in Los Angeles, Chicago, and Nashville in 1990, and at a national symposium in Washington in 1991. In that year, MENC published the Commission's report, *Growing Up Complete: The Imperative for Music Education*.[15] *Growing Up Complete* was a key element in the effort to have the arts included in the *Goals 2000* legislation, and was distributed to Congress, the White House, parent groups, arts and education organizations, major corporations, advocacy groups, and individuals concerned about the role of the arts in education. The commission members included, among others, Steve Allen, Leonard Bernstein, Ernest L. Boyer, Dave Brubeck, Rep. Thomas J. Downey, Morton Gould, Karl Haas, Whitney Houston, Senator James M. Jeffords, Shari Lewis, Henry Mancini, Barbara Mandrell, Marilyn McCoo, Rep. Raymond McGrath, Robert Merrill, Dudley Moore, Luciano Pavarotti, Itzhak Perlman, and André Previn.

The Federal Government and Arts Education: A Brief Review

The federal government was marginally involved in education until the 1950s, and then only in regard to issues that transcended the states. For example, before mid-century, the government provided limited federal aid for vocational and agricultural education programs and facilities, rehabilitation and training of war veterans, school lunch programs,[f] and health service education.

The states have traditionally viewed federal involvement in education with suspicion and considered it intrusive. Attitudes began to change, however, when the growing discontent with public education in the late 1950s was heightened by the flight of Sputnik in 1957 (chapter

---

[f]School lunch programs was a federal issue because in the late 1940s, the military had to reject many recruits who were malnourished.

1). Even before Sputnik, however, the federal government had begun to perceive the need for it to be involved in education, had created programs to support educational improvement.

The United States Department of Education

The administration of federally funded programs is a massive undertaking. The agency responsible for most federal education programs is the Department of Education, but for those parts of the discussion concerning the events of the 1950s and 1960s, the previous designation of DOE, the U.S. Office of Education, is used here. USOE was comprised of several bureaus, including the Bureau of Elementary and Secondary Education; the Bureau of Adult, Vocational, and Library Programs; the Bureau of Education for the Handicapped; and the Bureau of Research.[g]

USOE created the Educational Resources Information Center (ERIC) to disseminate research results. ERIC provides policy, coordination, training, funds, and general services to clearinghouses at universities and other institutions throughout the country, each of which is responsible for a specific area of education. Music topics are assigned to the social studies area. Each clearinghouse acquires, abstracts, indexes, and analyzes educational information appropriate to its area and reports materials to ERIC for publication and dissemination. Materials are announced in two monthly publications—*Research in Education* (*RIE*), a journal of abstracts, and *Current Index to Journals in Education* (*CIJE*), an index to more than 600 education journals. The clearinghouses also prepare bibliographies and interpretative summaries of reviews of new and important documents in education.

Legislation That Supports Arts Education

THE NATIONAL ADVISORY COMMITTEE ON EDUCATION ACT OF 1954

This Act established a committee to recommend areas of national concern that might be addressed by the U.S. Office of Education, which was then a branch of the Department of Health, Education, and Welfare. Music, having been identified as a "critical subject" of national concern, was eligible to receive support from the National Defense Education Act (NDEA) of 1958 (Fig. 4.1).

---

[g]The Bureau of Research is a good example of the complexity of the federal government and its changing bureaucratic organizational structure. In 1970 the Bureau of Research was replaced by the National Center for Education Research and Development (NCERD). In 1972 NCERD was succeeded by the National Insistute of Education (NIE), which assumed responsibility for federal educational research and development projects. NIE was later replaced by the current structure, which includes the Office of Research, the National Center for Education Statistics, Programs for Improvement of Practice, and the Office of Information Services. These offices were allocated $63.6 million in 1987, but the arts received none of that amount.

EXAMPLE 4.1. National Defense Education Act of 1958

OUTLINE OF PERTINENT TITLES

Title II

Authorized loans to college students with the provision that up to 50% of the amount would be forgiven at the rate of 10% a year for each year that the student taught in the public schools.

Title III

Authorized matching grants for public schools and loans to private schools for the purchase of equipment used in teaching science, mathematics, and foreign languages.

Title IV

Authorized 5,500 three-year graduate fellowships for students enrolled in new or expanded programs.

Title V

Provided state education agencies with funds for guidance, counseling, and testing and for guidance and counseling training.

Title VI

Authorized a program for the development of educational utilization of television and related communications media.

Title VII

Expanded vocational education by providing funds to the states for training skilled technicians in science-related occupations.

THE NATIONAL DEFENSE ACT OF 1958

The NDEA sponsored, among other things, experimentation and dissemination of information on the effective utilization of media for educational purposes. Public Law 87–474[h] established grants for the construction of educational television broadcasting facilities (Fig. 4.1).

THE HIGHER EDUCATION FACILITIES ACT OF 1963

This act provided grants and loans for new educational facilities, including electronic music studios. The use of television in education held so much promise that in the late 1950s and early 1960s the Ford Foundation Fund for the Advancement of Education also provided generous financial support for educational television. The foundation financed a variety of experiments to develop television as a functional educational tool that could reach more students with fewer teachers. This was expected to help alleviate the critical shortage of qualified teachers.

---

[h]The numbering system of public laws signifies which Congress passed the legislation and the number of the specific bill. Thus, P. L. 87–474 was the 474th bill to be passed into law by the 87th Congress.

THE ELEMENTARY AND SECONDARY EDUCATION ACT OF 1965 (P.L. 89-10)

The Elementary and Secondary Education Act (ESEA) was highly significant for American education in general, but it also provided support for specific music education projects. The law authorized more than $1.3 billion to be channeled into classrooms to strengthen elementary and secondary school programs for educationally deprived children in low-income areas, provide additional school library resources, textbooks, and other instructional materials, finance supplementary educational centers and services, broaden areas of cooperative research, and strengthen state departments of education. The most significant section of ESEA to music education was Title I, which was prefaced as follows: "An ACT to strengthen and improve educational quality and educational opportunities in the Nation's elementary and secondary schools."[16] Until 1973, under the terms of Title I, school districts all over the country received funds (matching funds, in most cases) with which to establish programs to equalize educational opportunities for children of low-income families. Many school districts were able to hire music teachers and purchase instruments and equipment for schools in low-income areas, which were identified by means of well-defined guidelines. Funds were allocated only to those particular schools, and the educational experiences they made possible were supplementary to the services already provided by the individual school districts. Title I enabled great numbers of children to participate in music and the other arts. During fiscal year 1966, approximately one-third of the 8.3 million children participating in the program were involved in music or art (Fig. 4.2).[17]

In 1973 USOE revised the terms of Title I to provide greater support for the development of basic skills, especially in reading and mathematics. Most state education departments interpreted this to mean remedial aid in those areas. Under this interpretation, music and art could be approved for Title I funding only if they related in some way to the development of reading, writing, or mathematics skills. This effectively reduced the involvement of arts education in Title I programs.

ESEA Title III authorized funds for supplementary educational centers and services. Its three basic functions were to improve education by enabling communities to provide services not then available to children, to raise the quality of educational services already offered, and to stimulate and assist in the development and establishment of high quality elementary and secondary school educational programs that could serve as models for regular school programs.[18] An example of an ESEA Title III program is the Interrelated Arts Program (IAP), formerly an ESEA Title III Elementary Arts Teacher Training Project, which was established in the Montgomery County, Maryland, public schools. The goals for the original project were:

> To train classroom teachers in the arts and to provide in-class support which will enable them to more fully meet their responsibilities for the education of their students.

FIGURE 4.2 Elementary and Secondary Education Act of 1965

TITLE I
  Established a three year program of grants to local education agencies for the education of disadvantaged children. The distribution formula allocated 50% of each state's average expenditure per school age child (5-17) to school districts in which at least 3% of the enrollment, or 100 children, came from families with an annual income less than $2,000.

TITLE II
  Authorized a five-year program to purchase library resources, texts, and other instructional materials for the use of children and teachers in public and private schools.

Title III and Title IV
  Authorized grants directly to local and regional organizations for the establishment of supplementary educational centers and regional laboratories. Title IV also provided for university related research and development centers.

Title V
  Established grants to strengthen state departments of education.

The training of classroom teachers is designed to:
1. Build the teachers' confidence in the arts, increase their aesthetic awareness, and develop their understanding of arts processes, concepts, and skills through active involvement in the arts;
2. Develop the teachers' understanding of how the arts contribute to the child's emotional, intellectual, and physical development and how the arts relate to each other and to other subject areas;
3. Develop the teachers' skills in designing and providing classroom activities which incorporate the arts.[19]

Funding for the project was renewed for a second period after the initial period expired. Upon the second expiration, the Board of Education, recognizing the value of the program, voted to continue it with local funding (Fig. 4.3).

ESEA Title IV authorized $100 million over a five-year period for national and regional research facilities, expansion of existing research and development programs, and a training program for educational researchers. Title IV benefited music education researchers by supporting the Special Training Project in Research in Music Education in 1968. This project was awarded to the Music Education Research Council (MERC) of MENC. Title IV also created regional laboratories to develop and implement research data. Two of the laboratories, the Central

FIGURE 4.3. ESEA Title III Elementary Arts Teacher Training Project Montgomery County (Maryland) Public Schools

OUTLINE OF ACTIVITIES
PHASE I

Fall/Spring 1974–75

Two Arts Teams

Support 12 Pilot Schools (110 K–3 teachers)
(each team supports 6 schools from 3 administrative areas)

- conduct monthly arts workshops for the principals, K–3 teachers, and arts specialists from 12 pilot schools, and for participants from the 1973 Street 70 Creativity Workshop
- Individual team members visit participating K–3 teachers in their classrooms an average of 2 half-days per month
- conduct workshops at PTA meetings in pilot schools

Each pilot school receives Title III funds for one eight-hour teacher assistant.

Conduct In-Service Training for Arts Specialists
- conduct 3 countrywide workshops—1 each for art, music, and physical education specialists
- consult with specialists in pilot schools when possible

Support Private School Programs (7 K–3 Teachers)
- teachers from St. John the Evangelist attend monthly workshops and are visited regularly by arts team

Collect Arts Activities for Bank
- publish a newsletter
- design framework for arts activities

Design a Staff Development Program
· define instructional goals for participating teachers

Phase I Outcomes:
13 Schools' K–3 staff received training
2 Arts teams trained
Arts activities collected; preliminary framework designed for activities bank.

OUTLINE OF ACTIVITIES
PHASE II

Summer, 1975

4-Week Workshop, Interrelated Arts in the Classroom
Conducted by 2 arts teams
Participants:
· at least 2 K–3 teachers from each of the 12 new pilot schools
· interested K–3 teachers from original pilot schools
· interested arts specialists from pilot schools
· other MCPS K–3 teachers and arts specialists (total 31 participants)
· 40 K–3 children
Principals of pilot schools will attend 1 week of workshop

Fall/Spring, 1975–76

Three Arts Teams

Support 18 Pilot Schools (est. 127 K–3 Teachers)
· Conduct fall in-service interrelated arts course for K–3 teachers and arts specialists from pilot schools.
· Conduct 1½-hour arts workshops monthly in each pilot school.

(*cont.*)

FIGURE 4.3. (*continued*)

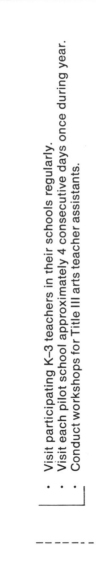

- Visit participating K–3 teachers in their schools regularly.
- Visit each pilot school approximately 4 consecutive days once during year.
- Conduct workshops for Title III arts teacher assistants.

Each of 6 new pilot schools receives Title III funds for one three-hour teacher assistant.
Each of 12 original pilot schools receives MCPS funds for one three-hour teacher assistant.

Conduct arts workshops for interested non-pilot schools

Conduct in-service training for arts specialists
- conduct workshops
- consult regularly with specialists in pilot schools

Support Private School Programs
(2 schools, 14 K–3 teachers)
- fall in-service course conducted by teams include K–3 teachers from private schools
- consult with school staffs to design follow-up training

Develop Arts Activities Bank
- continue publishing newsletter
- define learner objectives for K–3 integrated arts program
- develop bank of 50 sample arts activities

Design a Staff Development Program
• 3 programs designed, based upon instructional goals previously defined

Phase II Outcomes:
24 Schools' K–3 staff have received training
3 Arts teams trained
18 Teacher assistants trained
Preliminary arts activities bank developed
Preliminary staff development program designed

OLTLINE OF ACTIVITIES
PHASE III

Summer, 1976

4-Week Institute, Interrelated Arts in the Classroom
Conducted by 6 arts team members and consultants
Participants
  • Interested K–6 teachers from 18 pilot schools
  • Interested specialists from pilot schools
  • Other MCPS K–6 teachers and specialists
  (total 40 participants)
  • 60 K–6 children
Elementary principals invited to sessions

4-week Curriculum Development Workshop
Curriculum writer/evaluator and 4 arts team members
Refine staff development objectives and assessments
Develop model for arts package development

(cont.)

FIGURE 4.3. (continued)

Fall/Spring 1976-77

Three Arts Teams

Support 18 Pilot Schools (est. 150 K–6 teachers)
- Conduct fall in-service interrelated arts course
- With each participating school staff, develop project goals for year.
- With each participating teacher, co-design, and deliver services.
- Conduct monthly, centralized workshops for 2nd and 3rd year teachers.
- Identify school staff members to assist in training teachers.
- Consult regularly with arts specialists.

Each pilot school receives MCPS funds for one three-hour teacher assistant (pending budget approval of County Council).

Conduct arts workshops for teacher assistants in pilot schools.

Conduct orientation sessions for MCPS staff, community groups (est. 30 sessions).

Conduct arts workshops for interested non-pilot schools related to school staff goals (est. 30 schools).

Conduct workshops for arts specialists.

Conduct workshops for MCPS Administrators (est. 115 administrators).

Support Private School Programs (est. 2 schools, 20 K–6 teachers)
- Conduct fall in-service interrelated arts course
- Consult with school staff to design additional services

Refine and Pilot Arts Activities Bank

Develop Arts Support Materials for at least 2 existing MCPS curriculum guides.

Disseminate Information on Project

. design and distribute brochure

. conduct out of county workshops

. design and develop training video-tapes, slide packages, and film.

Establish Contacts with Community Arts Resources

. Assess local needs and resources

. Assist schools in working with local artists and art groups

Refine Staff Development Program

. Define objectives and assessments for classroom teacher training in arts.

. Describe procedures and necessary supports for implementation

. Evaluate effectiveness of program

. Write final report and suggest method for expanding program to secondary level

Phase III Outcomes

Over 50 schools K–6 staff have received training

115 MCPS administrators participated in workshops

18 teacher assistants trained

3 arts teams trained

Arts activities bank published and piloted

Arts supported materials developed

Introductory brochure distributed

Training materials developed

Staff development program defined, evaluated

Final report written and published

Source: Montgomery County Public Schools, Rockville, Maryland, under ESAE, Title III

Atlantic Regional Educational Laboratory (CAREL) in Washington, DC, and the Central Midwestern Regional Educational Laboratory (CEM-REL) in St. Louis, Missouri, were especially concerned with aesthetic education. Their goals and operations were somewhat similar to those of IMPACT (Interdisciplinary Model Programs for Children and Teachers), which is discussed later in this chapter.

ESEA supported many other arts projects in addition to those discussed above. In 1966 alone, the Arts and Humanities Program sponsored forty-eight research projects in music, forty-six in art, eighteen in theatre and dance, four in the arts in general, and eleven in the humanities.[20] Some of the music projects were the Yale Seminar, the Juilliard Repertory Project, some programs of the Contemporary Music Project, and the Manhattanville Music Curriculum Program (see chapter 5).

The 1978 ESEA reauthorization bill stipulated that "the arts should be an essential and vital component for every student's education." This was the first federal legislation to offer direct support for arts education. The bill created a grants program to "encourage and assist state and local educational agencies and other public and private agencies, organizations, and institutions to establish and conduct programs in which the arts are an integral part of elementary and secondary school curricula." The elation of the arts education community was short-lived, however, as the Education Consolidation Act of 1981 merged all categories and programs. Twenty percent of the monies for the twenty-nine categorical aid programs, including the arts, was absorbed into block grants for states and 80 percent for local school districts. This reflected the priorities of President Reagan, who transferred as much federal authority as possible to the state and local levels. The states and localities had complete discretion in reallocating the money. The original twenty-nine programs fell by the wayside because the states and local districts had different priorities from those of the Department of Education. The block grant program signaled a serious decline in the federal government's involvement in education. Its interest was not renewed until the publication of *A Nation at Risk* in 1983.

THE INTERNATIONAL EDUCATION ACT OF 1966
The International Education Act of 1966 (P.L. 89-698) provided grants to institutions of higher education to establish and operate centers for research and training in international studies. Shortly thereafter, several colleges and universities founded institutes for comparative music education. Comparative music education is still a topic of great interest to many music educators, and is a major focus of the International Society for Music Education (ISME).

THE EDUCATION PROFESSIONS DEVELOPMENT ACT OF 1967
The Education Professions Development Act (EPDA) of 1967 (P.L. 90-35) was intended to improve the quality of teaching and to help overcome

the shortage of trained teachers by implementing training and retraining programs. Interdisciplinary Model Programs in the Arts for Children and Teachers (IMPACT) was established in 1970 under EPDA. Its purposes were to demonstrate that school activities in the arts can transform the traditional curriculum into one that emphasizes the integration of the arts into the mainstream of human experience; aid students in becoming sensitive to qualitative experiences as sources for artistic ideas; explore the similarities and differences in the ways that professionals in the arts develop their ideas; and challenge students to make effective use of their creative resources.[21]

The DAMT group—MENC, the National Art Education Association, the American Theater Association, and the Dance Division of the American Association for Health, Physical Education, and Recreation—established a plan of operation for IMPACT. Other organizations joined later. The USOE Arts and Humanities Program committed part of its Artists-in-Schools Program to the five sites in which IMPACT operated. The John D. Rockefeller III (JDR 3) Fund Arts Education program supported a program for IMPACT personnel during its first year, provided coordination services, and sponsored a tour of the IMPACT schools for the executive secretaries and presidents of the four arts education associations.

The program's specific objectives were:

1. To reconstruct the educational program and administrative climate of the school in an effort to achieve parity between the arts and other instructional areas and between the affective and cognitive learnings provided in the total school program

2. To develop educational programs of high artistic quality in each art area, that is, the visual arts, music, dance, and drama, in each of the participating schools

3. To conduct in-service programs, including summer institutes, workshops, demonstrations, and other similar activities, for teachers, administrators, and other school personnel so they can implement programs exemplifying high aesthetic and artistic quality in their own schools

4. To develop ways of integrating the arts into all aspects of the school curriculum as a means of enhancing and improving the quality and quantity of aesthetic education offered in the school, and as a principal means for expanding the base for affective learning experiences in the total school program

5. To invite a number of outstanding artists, performers, and educators into the school system to enhance the quality of the arts experiences of children.[22]

IMPACT was implemented in five locations ranging from single schools to a consortium of three school districts. When it ended in 1972, evaluators found that teachers who were not arts specialists had become more confident of their abilities to use the arts in teaching, and children had the opportunity to learn in an aesthetic environment. Test results indicate that students who participated in IMPACT programs were significantly above grade level in reading and other skills several years after their arts experiences. They also showed that students developed self-esteem through their arts experiences and that their attitudes toward school improved.

THE PUBLIC BROADCASTING ACT OF 1967

The Public Broadcasting Act of 1967 (P.L.90-129) created a corporation for public broadcasting responsible for funding noncommercial radio and television stations, program production groups, educational television networks, and construction of educational radio and television facilities. This act did not immediately affect music education, but public broadcasting has been a strong influence in developing childrens' musical tastes, and has therefore indirectly influenced music education practices and materials.

The National Foundation on the Arts and the Humanities

The enactment of P.L. 89-209 in 1965 created the National Foundation on the Arts and the Humanities as an independent federal agency in the executive branch of the government. Congress declared:

> The practice of art and the study of the humanities requires constant dedication and devotion and . . . while no government can call a great artist or scholar into existence, it is necessary and appropriate for the Federal Government to help create and sustain not only a climate encouraging freedom of thought, imagination, and inquiry, but also the material conditions facilitating the release of this creative talent.[23]

The National Endowment for the Arts (NEA) and the National Endowment for the Humanities (NEH) are components of the National Foundation on the Arts and the Humanities.[24]

THE NATIONAL ENDOWMENT FOR THE HUMANITIES

The National Endowment for the Humanities sponsors some projects that involve the arts:

> According to the Act which established the Endowment, the humanities include, but are not limited to, the following fields: history, philosophy, languages, linguistics, literature, archeology, jurisprudence, history and criticism of the arts, ethics, comparative religion, and those aspects of the social sciences employing historical or philosophical approaches. . . . Because man's experience has been princi-

pally preserved through books, art works, and other cultural objects, the humanities are often defined in terms of specific academic disciplines. However, the concerns of the humanities extend, through the classroom, the library, and the media, to encompass a host of social, ethical, and cultural questions which all human beings confront throughout the course of their lives.[25]

THE NATIONAL ENDOWMENT FOR THE ARTS

NEA awards grants for the creation of new art works and for production and performance of new or established works. Its grants support eight categories of arts—theater, visual arts, literature, dance, music, general arts, architecture and design, and education and public media. Until recently, NEA has been only minimally involved in arts education. The Artists-in-Schools program, its major link with arts education, had granted funds to artists to work in schools, and over a million students in thousands of schools participated in the arts with professionals through this program. Artists-in-Schools never persuaded arts educators, however, that NEA was seriously involved in arts education because of the difference between educational activities in which children create art and those that they observe as audience members. Many educators considered it to be more of an employment program for professional artists than an educational program for students.

The National Alliance for Arts Education

The National Alliance for Arts Education (AAE) was established in 1973 by the John F. Kennedy Center for the Performing Arts and the USOE, in cooperation with MENC, the National Art Education Association, the American Theater Association, and the National Dance Association. The Alliance for Arts Education was created in response to the Congressional mandate that the Kennedy Center, as a national symbol of excellence in the arts, become a vehicle and focal point for strengthening the arts in education at all levels (Fig. 4.4).

The Alliance for Arts Education gives young people access to the Kennedy Center as performers and as audience members, makes the Center's performances and services available to people all over the country, helps the Center become a vehicle for strengthening the arts in education at the national, state, and local levels. AAE sponsors many activities that focus attention on music education and provide opportunities for young people to perform, including showcase series to present the best student work in music, drama, and other arts at the Kennedy Center.

Another way in which the Alliance carries out its Congressional mandate is by encouraging leaders in the arts in each state to establish individual state Alliance for Arts Education Committees to promote arts education as an integral part of public elementary and secondary edu-

FIGURE 4.4. AAE Organizational Chart

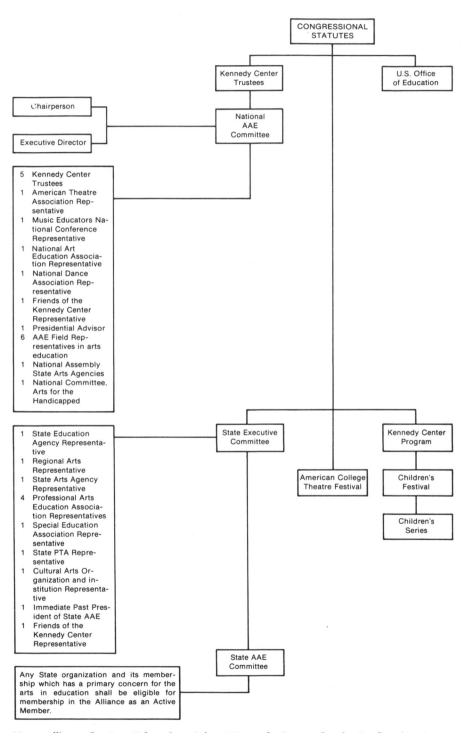

Note: Alliance for Arts Education, John F. Jennedy Center for the Performing Arts

cation. Virtually all of the states have Alliance for Arts Education chapters, but the specific goals vary among them. For example, the Constitution of the Maryland Alliance for Arts Education states:

> The basic purpose of the Maryland Alliance for Arts Education . . .
> shall be to encourage and strengthen the arts in all educational
> processes in the state. This shall be done by: (1) organizing, unifying
> and promulgating an alliance of organizations supportive of the arts
> in the State of Maryland; (2) facilitating coordination and coopera-
> tion among appropriate state groups and agencies; (3) cooperating
> with appropriate agencies of the Federal Government, particularly
> the John F. Kennedy Center for the Performing Arts and the United
> States Department of Education in order to encourage their nation-
> al aims and purposes and promote the cause of arts education
> throughout the United States.[26]

Some positive indications for future support of arts education at the federal level emerged in the early 1980s. The Congressional Arts Caucus was established to offer symbolic and legislative recognition of the arts. In 1983 the leaders of the Caucus, Representative Thomas Downey (NY) and Representative James Jeffords (VT), introduced a resolution urging "all citizens to support efforts which strengthen artistic training and appreciation within our Nation's schools." Senator Edward Kennedy (MA) introduced a companion resolution in the Senate. Passage of the resolutions raised hopes that they would "stimulate a nationwide effort to promote and enhance the status of arts in education."[27] Unfortunately, that was not to be, at least not yet.

New Federal Initiatives for Arts Education

Until recently, there was no federal policy on arts education. The arts are the responsibility of the National Endowment for the Arts, which for many years was interested only in the presentation of the arts, and education was the responsibility of United States Department of Education. Neither supported arts education. James Backas described the situation in 1981:

> Because of the budgeting and funding structure of the federal gov-
> ernment, responsibility for an area of national activity is assigned to
> a specific agency. If the national activity does not fall conveniently
> within the purview of a single agency, it is assigned to several, each
> with a piece of the responsibility. "The arts," for example, are
> assigned to the National Endowment for the Arts, and "arts educa-
> tion" is assigned to the Department of Education. . . . Although arts
> education belongs to both the world of the arts and the world of edu-
> cation . . . it does not receive assistance from several federal agencies;

in fact, it receives meaningful assistance from none. The major reason for this is that the nation's schools and colleges have traditionally been considered the responsibility of state and local governments, and the federal agency to which education has been assigned, the Department of Education, offers only supplementary assistance to state and local education authorities.[28]

In 1983 Frank Hodsell, Chairman of the National Endowment for the Arts, announced in a speech to arts education leaders that he planned to explore the feasibility of creating a stronger link between NEA and arts education. The next year, in cooperation with the National Assembly of State Arts Agencies, NEA held a series of five regional meetings "to help identify and disseminate techniques, strategies and resources for promoting arts education from kindergarten through 12th grade." The goal was to identify exemplary programs that could be described in a practical guide for others who wanted to develop similar programs.[29] Within a decade this modest beginning would lead to much deeper involvement by the National Endowment for the Arts.

In 1986 the National Council on the Arts recommended to Hodsell that NEA adopt new guidelines for increasing the agency's involvement in arts education. The recommendation came at an opportune time, when the interest of the public in education reform had been fueled by the negative, critical national reports on education. The NEA Arts-in-Education program emerged shortly after that. It evolved from the 1969 Artists-in-Schools Program, which in 1980 became the Artists-in-Education Program. Arts-in-Education was more than a cosmetic change of name: it was a radical realignment of NEA interests and goals. The first paragraph of its guidelines stated:

> The study of the arts is basic to nurturing perceptive and committed audiences and artists of the future and assists in developing intellectual skills and understanding of civilization. The study of the arts should include substantive components, such as the development of artistic skills and knowledge, art history, criticism, aesthetics, and analysis as well as experiential and appreciation components.

The Arts-in-Education Program works with the states through two funding categories: State Arts in Education Grants and Arts in Schools Basic Education Grants. A third category, Special Projects, makes awards to a variety of organizations, including education agencies, school districts, institutions, and organizations. The program:

1. aims at concentrating public attention on the need for sequential, curriculum-based instruction in the arts for all elementary and secondary school students.

2. encourages the arts agency system to promote improved arts education among state and local education agencies.

3. encourages cooperation by using all the arts resources of each state.

4. relies on consultation with K–12 arts education specialists and higher education arts faculties.[30]

Despite the involvement of NEA in arts education, Congress did not officially recognize the new liaison betwen government and education. The Arts and Humanities Act of 1980, which reauthorized the original legislation for five years (until 1985), contained no reference to education. The national reports on education of the early 1980, however, stirred the interest of Congress in education, and when Congress considered the NEA reauthorization bill in 1985, it requested that NEA complete a study of the state of arts education. The Endowment produced a thorough and excellent study entitled *Toward Civilization: A Report on Arts Education*. This 1988 report to Congress and the public made painfully clear that the arts were not considered serious academic subjects, that knowledge and skills in the arts were not seen as educational objectives, and that those responsible for deciding what is taught had never clarified to the public what constitutes arts education because they themselves had never agreed. *Toward Civilization* recommended:

- A comprehensive definition of arts education—one that would value both knowledge and skills in the arts;

- Efforts to make the arts a part of basic education, meaning that arts instruction would have adequate time, personnel, and other resources; would be taught sequentially; and would be viewed as serious learning with academic standards and the means of appropriately assessing student achievement; and

- Partnerships, like that between the NEA and the U.S. Department of Education [below], would help advocate for increased arts education and provide the comprehensive type of arts education called for in the report.[31]

After the publication of *Toward Civilization*, NEA sponsored partnerships and collaborative efforts at the state level to address the problem. The activities involved state arts agencies, departments of education, and other state-level agencies and organizations. These projects were supported by the NEA Arts-in-Schools Basic Education Grants program. The agency also supported efforts to increase interaction between arts organizations and arts education. To promote cooperation between the arts education disciplines, in 1989 the NEA Arts in Education Program began to underwrite some costs of the National Coalition for Education in the Arts (NCEA). More than twenty-five organizations now belong to NCEA, which began in 1986 when the American Council for the Arts and the Music Educators National Conference brought together the leaders of national organizations for discussions. NCEA publications such as *Arts and School Reform* and *Advocacy Through Partnership: Advancing the Case for Arts Education* have been influential in gaining support for arts during a time of radical school reform.[32]

Together, NEA and the Department of Education developed policies and programs to establish a role for the federal government in supporting arts education. This particular collaboration has had excellent results, including the creation of the National Arts Education Research Center in 1979, with divisions at New York University and The University of Illinois (until 1990). The purpose of the Center is to study and assess arts education. Ultimately, this information is expected to help make sequential arts education available to all students. The Illinois center was funded for three years, and it completed nine projects in several areas of arts education. Among them are important surveys of the status of arts education in American schools.

The combined efforts of DOE and NEA have also produced a national arts education research agenda, described in their joint publication, *Arts Education Research Agenda for the Future*. The monograph emerged from a national arts education conference that concluded with the drafting of several research questions about curriculum, instruction, assessment, evaluation, teacher education, media and technology, policy, funding, and collaboration.[33] It was the second monograph on arts education research published by the federal government. The first, *Research in Arts Education: A Federal Chapter* (1976), reviewed studies supported by federal monies in the 1960s and early 1970s. *Arts Education Research Agenda for the Future* could well be the basis for future influential research studies. One would hope that at least some of these studies will be supported with federal funds.

ARTSEDGE

The John F. Kennedy Center for the Performing Arts entered into a cooperative agreement with the National Endowment for the Arts, with additional funding provided by the U.S. Department of Education, to develop a national arts and education information network. This technology-based initiative is focused on the development of an online community of professionals and advocates for the arts in education, as well as a new knowledge base of information and resources that will ensure a prominent place for the arts in education reform. The ARTSEDGE Information Gallery is accessible to the public through the Internet (Fig. 4.5).[34]

FIGURE 4.5. ARTSEDGE—Prototype Phase Design

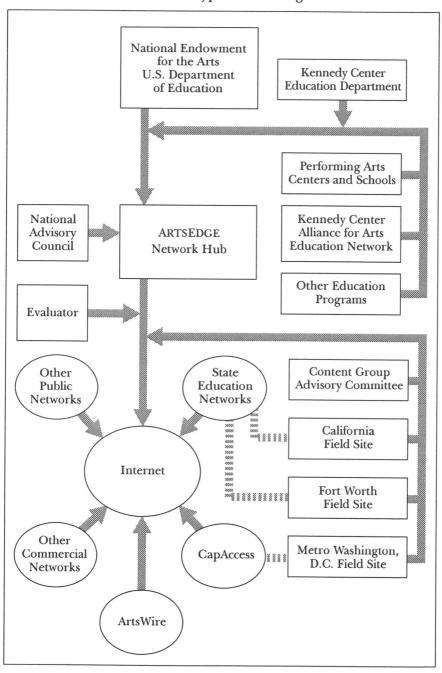

Courtesy of the Education Division, John F. Kennedy Center for the
Performing Arts

Goals 2000: Educate America Act

This is a remarkable departure. Today we can say, America is serious about education; America cares about the future of every child; and America will lead the world in the 21st century. . . .

President Clinton, March 31, 1994, to the children of the
Zamorano Fine Arts Academy Elementary School, San Diego,
at the Goals 2000: Educate America Act signing ceremony

Of all the education projects the federal government has initiated or participated in, the most significant for arts education is the establishment of national standards for arts education. The federal government appears to have committed itself to the improvement of arts education, but like every project resulting from legislation, it remains to be seen whether serious support for the improvement of education will continue on a long-term basis. The national standards and assessment are products of a Congressional act entitled *Goals 2000: Educate America Act* (PL 103-227), which originated in the six National Education Goals established by President Bush and the state governors in 1990. Congress passed the *Goals 2000 Act* during the administration of President Clinton. Section 2 (Purpose) states:

The purpose of this Act is to provide a framework for meeting the National Education Goals established by title I of this act by—

(1) promoting coherent, nationwide, systemic education reform;

(2) improving the quality of learning and teaching in the classroom and in the workplace;

(3) defining appropriate and coherent Federal, State, and local roles and responsibilities for education reform and lifelong learning;

(4) establishing valid and reliable mechanisms for—

(A) building a broad national consensus on American education reform;

(B) assisting in the development and certification of high-quality, internationally competitive content and student performance standards;

(C) assisting in the development and certification of opportunity-to-learn standards; and

(D) assisting in the development and certification of high-quality assessment measures that reflect the internationally competitive content and student performance standards;

(5) supporting new initiatives at the Federal, State, local, and school levels to provide equal educational opportunity for all students to meet high academic and occupational skill standards and to succeed in the world of employment and civic participation;

(6) providing a framework for the reauthorization of all Federal education programs by—

(A) creating a vision of excellence and equity that will guide all Federal education and related programs;

(B) providing for the establishment of high-quality, internationally competitive content and student performance standards and strategies that all students will be expected to achieve;

(C) providing for the establishment of high-quality, internationally competitive opportunity-to-learn standards that all States, local education agencies, and schools should achieve;

(D) encouraging and enabling all State educational agencies and local educational agencies to develop comprehensive improvement plans that will provide a coherent framework for the implementation of reauthorized Federal education and related programs in an integrated fashion that effectively educates all children to prepare them to participate fully as workers, parents, and citizens;

(E) providing resources to help individual schools, including those serving students with high needs, develop and implement comprehensive improvement plans; and

(F) promoting the use of technology to enable all students to achieve the National Education Goals;

(7) stimulating the development and adoption of a voluntary national system of skill standards and certification to serve as a cornerstone of the national strategy to enhance workforce skills; and

(8) assisting every elementary and secondary school that receives funds under this Act to actively involve parents and families in supporting the academic work of their children at home and in providing parents with skills to advocate for their children at school.

The states and localities have an important role in implementing the standards. The states are expected to appoint state panels that include the governor and the chief state school officer, the chairperson of the state board of education, chairpersons of appropriate authorizing committees of the state legislature, teachers, principals, administrators, college deans, representatives of teachers' organizations, parents, business and labor leaders, community-based organizations, local boards of education, and state and local officials.[35] The panel is to conduct statewide hearings and develop a state reform plan, which must be approved by the U.S. Department of Education. The state departments of education are then eligible to apply for planning grants to implement the goals. There must also be local reform plans to fulfill the state plans.

The part of the Act of most immediate interest and importance to the arts education community is Title I—National Education Goals, entitled "Student Achievement and Citizenship." The third of eight goals under this title states:

By the year 2000, all students will leave grades 4, 8, and 12 having demonstrated competency over challenging subject matter including English, mathematics, science, foreign languages, civics and government, economics, *arts* [author's italics], history, and geography, and every school in America will ensure that all students learn to use their minds well, so they may be prepared for responsible citizenship, further learning, and productive employment in our Nation's modern economy.[Fig. 4.6]

The arts had not been included among the core subjects in the original bill, and it was only after extensive advocacy efforts that Secretary of Education Richard Riley agreed to include them. This was the most con-

Figure 4.6 Goals 2000: Educate America Act

OUTLINE OF TITLES

Title I
Establishes National Education Goals
Title II
Establishes a mechanism for building national consensus for education improvement, reporting on progress toward achieving the National Education Goals, and reviewing the voluntary national content standards, voluntary national student performance standards, and voluntary national opportunity-to-learn standards certified by the National Education Standards and Improvement Council.
Title III
Improve the quality of education by improving student learning through a long-term broad-based effort to promote coherent and coordinated improvements in the system of education through the Nation and at the State and local levels.
Title IV
Parental assistance
Title V
National Skill Standards Board
Title VI
International Education Program
Title VII
Safe Schools
Title VIII
Minority -Focused Civics Education
Title IX
Educational Research and Improvement, called the "Educational Research, Development, Dissemination, and Improvement Act of 1994."

sequential, far-reaching achievement for the MENC advocacy program to date. The inclusion of world-class standards in the legislation demonstrates the high level of sophistication of the MENC advocacy program. The Implementation Task Force for the National Standards for Arts Education is a further example of maturity in advocacy. The task force released seven different versions of its "Education, Standards, and the Arts" brochures in the fall of 1994, each directed toward a specific constituency: business people, state legislators, artists, school administrators, state education officials, school board members, and parents. The brochures provide specific information on how each group can help implement the National Standards for Arts Education. Paul Lehman clarified the importance of advocacy by arts education organizations:

> The standards project has given arts educators control of the agenda in the debate over arts education. It has enabled arts educators to lead the discussion. This was not the case previously. In past years, for example, initiatives in arts education were routinely taken by advocacy groups or other organizations with no competence or experience in arts education, and not surprisingly, nothing worthwhile or permanent happened. But now MENC has seized the initiative and has proven that it's a major force on the Washington scene. Don't underestimate the significance of that achievement.[36]

Passage of the *Goals 2000* legislation on March 31, 1994, by the 103rd Congress was only part of the process. The world-class arts education standards then had to be written. This massive undertaking was the responsibility of the Consortium of National Arts Education Associations, which consisted of the Music Educators National Conference, the American Alliance for Theater and Education, the National Art Education Association, and the National Dance Association. A. Graham Down, of the Council for Basic Education, chaired the group. The National Endowment for the Arts, the National Endowment for the Humanities, and the Department of Education provided $1,000,000 for the arts group to develop standards for curriculum content and for student achievement.

Each organization appointed a team to write standards for its own discipline. The members of the Music Task Force were Paul Lehman (chair), June Hinckley, Charles Hoffer, Carolynn Lindeman, Bennett Reimer, and Scott Shuler. The Task Force presented a working draft to the MENC membership in the September 1993 issue of the *Music Educators Journal* with an invitation for comments. The final standards draft was brought to the National Committee on Standards in the Arts, which approved the music standards in early 1994. Finally, Secretary Riley accepted the complete set of arts education standards at a press conference on March 11, 1994. The *Goals 2000* legislation also created the National Education Standards and Improvement Council (NESIC) to certify the voluntary standards. It is responsible for approving all of the national education standards as well as the standards of those states that wish NESIC certification.

The arts standards were the first to be developed and accepted among all of the disciplines. The standards, and their proposed assessment, are discussed in chapter 9. With their completion, those states that wish to develop their own content standards (as they are referred to in the original legislation) can begin doing so. State standards can be based on the national standards, but do not have to be. Like the national standards, they too will be approved by NESIC. States are not mandated to adopt the standards, and may choose not to do so. Those that do not, however, may be ineligible for some government education funding programs in the future (Fig. 4.7).

FIGURE 4.7. The Key Components of Goals 2000

FEDERAL LEVEL

U.S. Department of Education
Provides funding, technical
assistance, research, and
dissemination

Goals Panel and NESIC
Provide voluntary model
standards and assessments, and
certification of states on request.

State Level
Broad-based State Planning Panel
Appointed by Governor and Chief State School Officer
Funds and Assists Local Planning Panels

Local Level
Broad-based, appointed by Local Education Agency
Develops local improvement plans for approval by State Panel
Submits plan to State Education Agency for funding approval

Schools
Receive pass-through funding to implement local plans

The Secretary's Fund for Innovation in Education (DOE) awards competitive grants as an incentive to state departments of education to create frameworks for implementing the standards and to develop state content standards. The brief history of this fund is encouraging to arts educators because the Curriculum Framework in Science and Mathematics and its standards (generated by the 1991 competition) are now used in math and science textbooks, and it is possible that arts education will be treated in a similar manner. The summary statement in the request for proposals indicates the new commitment of the federal government to education reform:

The Secretary announces absolute priorities for Fiscal Years 1994 and 1995 for the Fund for Innovation in Education: Innovation in Education Program. The Secretary takes this action to focus Federal financial assistance on State content standards as the starting point for systemic school improvement. The priorities will assist projects to develop and implement State content standards, kindergarten through grade 12 (K–12), in English, history, geography, civics, foreign languages, and the arts, together with new approaches to teacher education and certification appropriate to the content standards.[37]

The 1994 competition resulted in over $5,000,000 being awarded for seventeen projects to develop state content standards. Five of the projects were for multidisciplinary approaches that included the arts.

The adoption of the arts standards received a great deal of favorable publicity in the media. It was jarring, then, when Albert Shanker, President of the American Federation of Teachers (AFT), published a disapproving, condescending opinion about the arts standards. His statement was especially surprising because the AFT had officially supported the creation of world-class standards, and many of its members are arts education specialists. Ironically, Shanker himself was a member of the National Commission for Standards in the Arts. He appears to have missed both the point and the spirit of educational reform, at least where the arts are concerned:

Some groups will propose standards that are unrealistic—like the arts-education standards that recently appeared. It's true that the arts are sadly neglected in most schools these days, but it's ridiculous to create standards that call for youngsters graduating from high school to "compose music in several distinct styles" and "choreograph a duet demonstrating an understanding of choreographic principles, processes, and structures." Most youngsters don't have that kind of talent—or interest. A wish list is not a set of standards.[38][i]

Despite Shanker's curious assertion, congressional enactment of world-class standards is a highly significant achievement of the music education profession in the area of public policy, and one that will allow the profession to contribute to school reform efforts. It will probably serve as a platform for future advocacy efforts, which are likely to be directed at state and local standards adoptions. In the summer and fall of 1994, shortly after the

---

[i] The statement is Shanker's personal opinion and does not represent the official AFT position. This was clarified in a telephone call to the Public Information Office of the American Federation of Teachers on August 22, 1994. When the President of a national organization writes for a national magazine without disclaimer, the general public would normally take the statement to be official policy of the organization.

legislation was enacted, the National Endowment for the Arts and the United States Department of Education convened meetings for representatives of "over 100 national arts, arts education, museum education, higher education, parent organizations, businesses, foundations and government agencies." The meetings were to develop a plan to support the arts as it gains recognition as a member of the core curriculum, and to help schools and students in achieving the national goals.[39]

Assessment of the Standards

The arts education standards are not only the first to be approved, but they are also the first to be selected for national assessment. The assessment, originally planned for 1996, was postponed until 1997. The confluence of standards and assessment gives arts educators a vehicle "to thoughtfully question . . . assumptions about learning in the arts, identify appropriate adjustments to meet the needs of a changing world, and provide a means for measuring the effectiveness of the process."[40] NAEP and the 1997 assessment are discussed in Chapter 9.

State Issues

By the middle of the 1970s the economy had declined so severely that it generated "taxpayer revolts" in several states. The impact on education was harsh. The most visible of these events is the 1978 passage of Proposition 13 in California. Proposition 13 tied state government spending to economic growth. High tax rates had imposed such a heavy burden on California residents that they welcomed the opportunity, in the form of Proposition 13, to vote for an initiative that promised economic relief. Proposition 13 reduced property taxes, but it also drastically reduced the financial resources available to the state, county, and local governments. As a result of Proposition 13, it became impossible to maintain previous levels of such government services as police and fire protection, street and highway maintenance, parks and recreation, libraries, and education. Public education in California had not been funded generously prior to 1978, and support for arts education had declined steadily for several years. Proposition 13 aggravated the already serious situation in school districts throughout the state. Arts education suffered, as did other curricular areas; teaching positions were eliminated, equipment could not be maintained or replaced as needed, and educators' morale plummeted.[41][j]

---

[j]A new issue, Proposition 187 (1994), denies many public services, including free public education, to illegal immigrants in California. As of this writing, the legality of the proposition is under court challenge.

Proposition 13 was followed by similar initiatives in twenty-five other states. The most severe for education was Proposition 2-1/2 in Massachusetts (1980). In 1979 the Massachusetts property tax was nearly twice the national average. Proposition 2-1/2 mandated that property taxes be limited to 2.5 percent of the assessed valuation of communities, and that increases be limited to 2.5 percent annually thereafter. Communities were unable to provide public services at previous levels, and public works suffered. In the first year, 17,263 municipal employees were laid off across the state. Education suffered even more than other public agencies because local school boards lost fiscal autonomy. Previously, they had been able to make their own budgets and set the necessary tax rates, but Proposition 2-1/2 shifted school budgets to municipal governments. Many school employees were laid off throughout the state, and at least 700 music teaching positions were eliminated. In some communities entire school music programs were lost. By the 1981–82 school year more than one out of five music teaching positions had disappeared.[42] In the second year of Proposition 2-1/2, more than 90 percent of the schools responding to a survey indicated that they had made cuts in their music programs, and 70 percent of the departments had been forced to reduce or eliminate some programs in the music curriculum. In addition, the director of music position was eliminated in almost 20 percent of the school systems, and some music programs were put under the authority of supervisors of other subjects.[43] By the third year of Proposition 2-1/2 (1983–84), the situation showed signs of stabilizing and, in some cases, even improving. Although cuts in music programs continued, a number of school systems either reinstated previously eliminated areas of the music curriculum or expanded the program with new courses. These actions, however, did not counterbalance the hundreds of positions that were eliminated in 1981.[44]

Other Policy Issues

Time and Learning

In 1991 Congress enacted the Education Council Act (P.L. 102-62), which established the National Education Commission on Time and Learning to examine how American schools use time, and to compare results with the use of time in other countries, especially Japan and Germany. This issue is critical because the adoption of national standards by school systems will require significantly more instruction time. The Commission published its report, *Prisoners of Time*, in 1994. The report states: "The degree to which today's American school is controlled by the dynamics of clock and calendar is surprising, even to people who understand school operations." It points out that almost all schools begin and end at fixed times of the day, operate within a nine-month school year, structure daily studies in six periods (about 5.6 hours), and goes on to say:

> Despite the obsession with time, little attention is paid to how it is used: in 42 states examined by the Commission, only 41 percent of secondary school time must be spent on core academic subjects. The results are predictable. The school clock governs how families organize their lives, how administrators oversee their schools, and how teachers work their way through the curriculum. Above all, it governs how material is presented to students and the the opportunity they have to comprehend and master it.[45]

Prisoners of Time describes how the traditional school day, originally intended for academic subjects, must now be divided to embrace "a whole set of requirements for what has been called 'the new work of the schools'—education about personal safety, consumer affairs, AIDS, conservation and energy, family life, driver's training—as well as traditional nonacademic activities." The Commission recognized that the new national standards would need much more time in school than is now available for them, and recommends that sufficient time be made available for the core subjects.[46] Paul Lehman, representing the Consortium of National Arts Education Associations at a Commission hearing, asserted that 15 percent of school time should be devoted to arts instruction.[47] Now that the arts have been officially recognized as core curricular subjects by the United States Department of Education, it is likely that they will benefit from the recommendations, but only after school time is restructured to provide the kind of schedule necessary to to teach core subjects effectively.

Decentralization of School Governance

School boards have debated governance issues for years, and some have made radical changes that have had major impact on arts education. A case in point is decentralization, or the transfer of policy-making authority from a central office to local communities within a school system. The policy areas are usually personnel, curriculum, and budget. Many boards of education are elected bodies, and directly reflect the educational wishes of communities. This is done in large school systems to allow more people to participate in the direct governance of their schools. It also reduces the amount of red tape that citizens need to negotiate when they want to contact school board members. The federal government encouraged and promoted local participation in policy-making by funding such programs as the Model Cities Program and Title III of the Elementary and Secondary Education Act of 1965. There are two general types of decentralization: community control and site based management.

COMMUNITY CONTROL

Community control places policy and personnel decisions in the hands of community boards or neighborhood associations. Some large cities have many boards of education that legislate and govern the administration of the schools in particular sections of cities. In 1969 New York City apportioned its school system into thirty-two school districts and a single high school division. Other cities, such as Washington, DC, and Chicago, retain a strong central bureaucracy that delegates authority to local administrative offices. At the time of this writing, there is a debate about further decentralizing the New York City schools. Current Mayor Rudolph W. Giuliani plans to "strip the board of education's central headquarters of most of its responsibilities, redistributing functions to local school boards, borough offices, or other city and private agencies."[48]

SITE-BASED MANAGEMENT

Site-based management transfers authority that was previously held by central administrators to principals. The central office retains authority to appoint principals and maintains control over some policy areas. The effects of both community control and site-based management have been somewhat negative for music programs. Those school systems that had strong music programs before decentralization usually had a music supervisory staff to coordinate the music programs in all of the schools. In those school systems that retained a central bureaucracy after decentralization, supervisory personnel were usually reclassified as consultants, with no actual authority. Building principals hold authority, and they may or may not be supportive of music education. In many cases, principals are subjected to strong pressure to improve student literacy and numeracy performance, and they tend to use their resources for those areas. They often decide either to reduce instructional time by arts specialists, or to have no arts specialists on their staffs.

School authority is delegated in other ways as well. For example, task forces are sometimes appointed to provide policy-making guidance for local boards of education, or neighborhood councils are organized to provide local input. Thus, policymakers act on the counsel of laypeople who do not have the appropriate experience to evaluate the total educational program.

The transfer of authority to lower administrative levels brings to light the kind of irony that often occurs in policy-saturated areas. When an enterprise is governed by so many layers of policy, from federal to individual schools, contradictory policies are likely to occur. In this case, we see federal policy fostering new national standards that can guide curriculum development, as opposed to local-level decision-making about curriculum. The conflict between national standardization and the authority of each building principal to decide which subjects to include in the curriculum is likely to create tense scenarios in the future, as supporters of arts education deal with principals whose primary interest is raising reading and mathematics performance levels.

Alternative Schools

Many policymakers have concluded that the decline in public school academic performance cannot be reversed because the myriad social and economic problems facing American society prevent any kind of significant, large-scale improvement. Claudia Wallis writes: "Fundamental change is needed in American education and to make it, schools must break free of stultifying regulation and bureaucracy. Fifty years of top-down reform have not done the trick."[49] Creative alternatives to the traditional public school paradigm have been implemented with varying degrees of success. These approaches to the problems of American education are significant to arts educators because for the most part, they focus on basic skills—reading and mathematics—rather than on broader educational goals. They either neglect the arts or assign them a marginal role in the curriculum.

SCHOOL PRIVATIZATION

Privatization is the extension of school decentralization to the extreme. Its two predominant forms, contract schools and charter schools, are radical departures from the traditional model of school governance. Privatization means that the government turns over control of schools to a private company or a special-interest group. Both contract and charter schools receive the same amount of per-pupil funding as do the public schools with which they compete.

CONTRACT SCHOOLS

School systems occasionally contract with private education delivery companies to take over public schools and improve their performance. This had been done on a small scale in several cities before 1993, when the Board of Education of Baltimore, Maryland, contracted with Education Alternatives, Inc. (EAI), a for-profit company, to operate eight elementary schools, one middle school, and one high school. EAI also contracted to operate one school in Miami, Florida, in 1993. In 1994 the company signed a contract to operate the entire Hartford, Connecticut, school system of thirty-two schools with 26,000 students. This is the first instance of a city contracting with a private firm to operate all of its schools.

　　EAI contracts specify the levels of improvement to be achieved in reading and mathematics scores, and the assessment techniques used to measure student achievement. They also target attendance, attitude, and school appearance. Despite the controversial nature of for-profit contract schools, Walter Amprey, Baltimore City superintendent of schools, articulated high expectations for the private-public partnership: "The genie is out of the bottle. This is proliferating nationwide."[50k]

Some EAI schools have teams of arts consultants who spend a week at each school before going on to the next one. In Hartford, however, the board of education had reduced its arts programs before it contracted with EAI, in violation of the state curriculum mandate. When EAI assumed control of the schools, no provision was made for arts education. At the time of this writing, parents of the Hartford EAI students have brought the issue to court.

Another for-profit company, the Edison Project, operates three schools in Massachusetts. The founding president of the Edison Project is Benno Schmidt, former president of Yale University.

It is too early to evaluate the success of arts education in contract schools, but it does not seem likely that for-profit companies will be willing to cut into their profits by supporting expensive curricular areas that are not required.

CHARTER SCHOOLS

Special education interests underlie the chartering of special schools by groups of teachers, parents, business groups, universities, or museums. These schools are created by the sponsoring parties and approved by the state department of education. Charter schools operate autonomously, rather than under the policies and regulations of local school districts, and they are funded by the state. Since Minnesota passed the first charter school law in 1991, at least ten other states have followed suit. It is likely that many more charter schools would open if state laws permitted, but most states are unable, or unwilling, to assume the cost of educating students who would otherwise be funded by local school districts. If charter schools prove to be successful, however, it is likely that more states will enact laws permitting their creation.

As of 1994 Massachusetts has approved fifteen public charter schools. The Benjamin Franklin Classical Charter School emphasizes academics, and the Boston University Charter School serves homeless youths and wards of the state. The Fenway II Charter School was established by teachers. It is a member of the Coalition for Essential Schools of Brown University, and serves children who have not succeeded in traditional schools. In 1995 California had at least sixty charter schools, and Colorado twelve. Kansas and Arizona recently became charter school states through their state legislative processes. Charter schools have stimulated public school systems to seek new ways to operate that will satisfy

---

[k]The Baltimore City Board of Education terminated its contract with EAI in December, 1994, because of financial exigency.

community members who might otherwise consider seeking charters. Some school districts that are in direct competition with charter schools have already opened alternative schools.

Like other forms of decentralization, privatized schools can either hold great promise for arts education or be detrimental. It remains to be seen whether the arts will find places in these schools, but since the schools are usually established to correct deficiencies or improve performance in particular areas of the public school curriculum, arts education might not be of great concern to school administrators. On the other hand, being model schools, they could welcome the educational benefits of arts education. Given the recent arts education advocacy successes, these schools might well be future targets for advocacy.

MAGNET SCHOOLS

Magnet schools have existed for decades, but their numbers have increased as pressure mounts for higher-quality education, and as competition from private alternative schools becomes more intense. Magnet schools offer specialized programs for students with similar interests and abilities. They provide a range of high-level programs, from the arts to technology. Many magnet schools have multiple focuses, such as music (or performing arts), foreign languages, and computer science. Other specialties, such as applied engineering, mass communication, environmental science, and mathematics are offered at different magnet schools. Most magnet schools are high schools, but many are middle and elementary schools.

The obvious advantage of magnet schools is that they provide the higher level, more intense, education needed by students with special interests and abilities. Magnet schools have proved their ability to do this and have satisfied many parents who might otherwise have sought other kinds of alternative schools. The disadvantage is that the highly talented students are often drawn away from comprehensive schools. When the most advanced performers choose to attend magnet schools, they leave behind bands, orchestras, and choruses that cannot perform at the same high level as before. Students who remain in those schools no longer have their peer role models for excellence, and this tends to reduce educational quality. Unfortunately, the migration to magnet schools by talented musicians can be a death knell for music programs in comprehensive schools. As their quality declines they become susceptible to criticism and reduction in resources. Boards of education that are criticized for lack of arts education opportunities can point to magnet schools with pride, although students in comprehensive schools might be denied quality music programs.

HOME SCHOOLING

Still another alternative to traditional schooling is home schooling, which is legal in every state. As many as a half million children are educated at home by parents or other family members who must meet basic educational goals and use a curriculum with written materials.[51] The socialization aspect of public schools is missing in the home schooling environment, but parents find ways to make up for it through after-school clubs and athletic activities. Arts education in home schooling is as diverse as the many homes in which it takes place. There does not appear, however, to be a role for professional arts educators.

Crisis Intervention

Crisis intervention was an early advocacy activity that is not used much any more because it became apparent, over the years, that by the time a crisis had developed it was usually too late to do anything about it. Now arts education associations are adept at policy analysis, and they try to stay far enough ahead of events to avoid crises. Some examples of crisis intervention are presented here for their historical interest, and to demonstrate how communities and organizations have pulled together the necessary resources to protect and preserve music programs.

It has not always been this way, though. In 1972 the Chicago superintendent of schools proposed a 1973–1974 budget that was $98.5 million less than that of the current year. The reduced budget would have eliminated the music, art, and physical education programs in the Chicago schools. When the media and the public learned of the proposed action, they began a strong advocacy campaign. The Chicago Musicians Union, the area music dealers, the National Association of Music Merchants, the American Music Conference, the Chicago Orchestra Association, and *Down Beat* magazine organized to fight the cuts. Members of the music industry and music teachers provided a budget of $24,000 (although only $11,000 was actually collected). A campaign called Save Our Music Education Citizens' Committee (SOME) was formed to carry out three objectives: (1) to restore music to the school budget at the level of January 1, 1972; (2) to persuade the Board that music was a necessary course of instruction for all public school students; and (3) to prepare a foundation for the improvement of the quality of music instruction in the Chicago schools. There was a strong media campaign to support the endangered programs, and a number of public figures advocated the maintenance of the programs. The House of Representatives of the State of Illinois adopted House Resolution No. 609, which stated:

> This House was shocked to hear that the Chicago Board of Education has seen fit to do away with the Music, Art and Physical Education classes for elementary and secondary Chicago schools. . . . Be it resolved . . . that we do recommend that the Chicago Board of Education . . . do see fit to return to their budget the $3.7 million allocated for these very important educational classes. . . .

At the two-day public hearing held by the Board of Education, 300 persons testified. Of these, 198 spoke specifically for music education. Benny Goodman provided testimony at the invitation of SOME, as did Charles Gary, Executive Secretary of MENC. A few days later, to dramatize the impact of the loss of the music program, more than 5,000 music students participated in a Parade of Silence, marching to the sound of muffled drums, carrying their instruments in cases, and wearing black armbands. The result of the well-planned and effective community effort was the restoration of the music program to the Chicago public schools. Although not every community action has been successful, the Chicago experience provides evidence that the public wants music in the schools, and that advocacy can be successful.[52]

Following the passage of Proposition 13, music education administrators in several parts of California joined together to strengthen the position of arts education in the state. They succeeded in having a fine arts requirement added to the secondary curriculum in many school districts and in persuading the University of California to recognize high school arts credits for admission. The music education administrators developed a five-year legislative plan to address the needs of music and arts education in their state:

> Goal I: California Music Educators Association (CMEA) shall establish as a high priority the expansion of legislative action.
> - Objective 1: Identify and develop strong community liaison relationships to support CMEA legislative action goals and objectives.
> - Objective 2: Involve the total CMEA membership in expanded legislature action.
> - Objective 3: Continue annual legislative conference.
> - Objective 4: Develop funding for legislative action, at the level of $5,000 annually.
>
> Goal II: CMEA shall develop a unified voice for the arts at the state level.
> - Objective 1: Identify and establish a working coalition with arts advocacy groups.
>
> Goal III: CMEA legislative action and advocacy efforts shall be focused on: (1) improvement of general funding for schools; (2) teacher preparation; (3) continuance of the state-funded Exemplary Arts Program; and, (4) mandates for the arts as an element of basic education.
> - Objective 1: Secure passage of legislation that will improve the general funding level for schools.
> - Objective 2: Prior to certification, all multiple-subject K–8 classroom teachers shall demonstrate proficiency in teaching of the visual and performing arts.

• Objective 3: Continue the SB1735 (Senate Bill) Exemplary Arts Program

• Objective 4: Achieve, through legislation, mandated programs in the visual and performing arts as elements of basic education.

• Objective 5: Achieve, through resolution of the State Board of Education, the requirement for one year of instruction in visual and performing arts for high school graduation.

Another example of crisis intervention was provided by music educators in Memphis, Tennessee. In 1981 the city school system faced a $30 million deficit, and the entire elementary general music and orchestra programs (elementary through high school) were threatened with elimination. The music education program was well known to the public and respected by it because of years of effective public relations. When the threat to the music program became known, numerous letters and telephone calls flooded the school board. The local media also supported the music program. The result was that 60 percent of the elementary music program was retained, as was all of the orchestra program. According to music consultant Tommie Pardue:

> We have relied too long on the sounds of our students' music to carry our message. Take every opportunity to define the values of your program to parents, community, and administrators. Learn to speak in language that they understand. Give your public the tools to become strong music supporters. . . . The happy ending [is]. . . . during the fall of 1982 Memphis citizens voted to increase our local sales tax by three-fourths of a cent, providing $13 million for our school budget. For this school year sixteen elementary positions have been added to the system's music staff.[53]

NOTES

1 Lawrence V. Castiglione, "Evaluating Policy Analyses in Arts Education and Art," *Design for Arts in Education* v. 92, no. 6 (July/August 1991): 2.

2 W. McNeil Lowry, Introduction to *The Arts and Public Policy in the United States* (Englewood Cliffs, NJ: Prentice-Hall, 1984), 20–21.

3 *K–12 Arts Education in the United States: Present Context, Future Needs: A Briefing Paper for the Arts Education Community*. Presented for discussion and comment by Music Educators National Conference, National Art Education Association, National Dance Association, National Association of Schools of Music, National Association of Schools of Art and Design, National Association of Schools of Theatre, National Association of Schools of Dance (January 1986, reprinted 1989).

4 Samuel Hope, "The Need for Policy Studies in Arts Education," in David Pankartz and Kevin Mulcahy, *The Challenge to Reform Arts Education: What*

Role Can Research Play? (New York: American Council for the Arts, 1989), 74.

5 John T. McLaughlin, ed., *Toward a New Era in Arts Education* (New York: American Council for the Arts, 1988), 7.

6 David B. Pankratz and Kevin V. Mulcahy, *The Challenge to Reform Arts Education: What Role Can Research Play?* (New York: ACA Books, 1989), xi–xiii.

7 *Toward a New Era in Arts Education* (New York: American Council for the Arts, 1988).

8 McLaughlin, 119

9 Final Report of the Sixty-Seventh Asmerican Assembly, in *The Arts and Public Policy in the United States.*

10 "National Music Education Summit Participating Organizations," *Teaching Music* 2, no. 3 (December 1994): 48.

11 David Rockefeller, Jr., *Coming to our Senses: The Significance of Arts for American Education.* The Arts, Education and Americans Panel (New York: McGraw-Hill, 1979), back cover.

12 *Coming to our Senses: The Significance of the Arts for American Education* (New York: McGraw-Hill, 1977), 248.

13 Charles Fowler, *Can We Rescue the Arts for America's Children? Coming to our Senses—10 Years Later* (New York: American Council for the Arts, 1988).

14 Fowler, xiv.

15 The National Commission on Music Education. *Growing Up Complete: The Imperative for Music Education* (Reston, VA: Music Educators National Conference, 1991).

16 The United States Office of Education, *The Elementary and Secondary Act of 1965: An Analysis* (Washington, DC: United States Office of Education, April 1965), quoted in William P. Lineberry, ed., *New Trends in Schools* (New York: Wilson, 1967), 88–89.

17 Paul R. Lehman, "Federal Programs in Support of Music," *Music Educators Journal* 55, no. 1 (September 1968): 53.

18 Lineberry, 93–94.

19 ESEA Title III Elementary Arts Teacher Training Project Statement of Goals, Montgomery County Public Schools (Rockville, Maryland, mimeographed).

20 John I. Goodlad, et al., *The Changing School Curriculum* (New York: The Fund for the Advancement of Education, 1966), 84.

21 David Boyle, ed., *Arts IMPACT: Curriculum for Change* (University Park, PA: Pennsylvania State University Press, 1973), 11.

22 Ibid., 3.

23 National Endowment for the Arts, *Guide to Programs* (Washington, DC: National Endowment for the Arts, 1975), 3.

24 Ibid.

25 National Endowment for the Humanities, *Program Announcements* (Washington, DC: National Endowment for the Humanities, 1976), 1–2.

26 Constitution and Bylaws of the Maryland Alliance for Arts Education, mimeographed.

27 "Congressional Call for Arts in the Schools," *Music Educators Journal* 70, no. 8 (April 1984): 11.

28 James Backas, "The Environment for Policy Development in Arts Education," *Proceedings of the 56th Annual Meeting* (Reston, VA: National Association of Schools of Music, 1981), 5.

29 Joe N. Prince (Artists in Education Program, NEA) and Geoffrey Platt, Jr. (National Assembly of State Arts Agencies), memorandum to members of Alliance for Arts Education, 18 April 1984.

30 "The New National Endowment for the Arts-in-Education Program: A Briefing Paper for the Arts Education Community." Reston, VA: Music Educators National Conference, National Art Education Association, National Dance Association, National Association of Schools of Music, National Association of Schools of Art and Design, National Association of Schools of Theatre, National Association of Schools of Dance (November 1986).

31 Nancy Langan, "Arts in Education: From National Polict to Local Community Action." National Assembly of Local Arts Agencies *Monographs* 3, no. 3 (Washington, DC: National Assembly of Local Arts Agencies, April 1994), v.

32 Ibid.

33 *Arts Education Research Agenda for the Future* (Washington, DC: National Endowment for the Arts and U. S. Department of Education, 1994), v.

34 Scott Stoner, Director, ARTSEDGE, memorandum to author, October 31, 1994.

35 National Endowment for the Arts, *Goals 2000: Opportunities for the Arts* (May 1994), 7, 8.

36 Paul Lehman, "The National Standards: From Vision to Reality." *Music Educators Journal* 58, no. 2 (September 1994), special insert.

37 Fund for Innovation in Education: Innovation in Education Program—State Content Standards for English, History, Geography, Civics, Foreign Languages, and the Arts. *Federal Register* 59, no. 69 (April 11, 1994), Notices.

38 Albert Shanker, "Where We Stand" (advertisement). *New Republic* (May 16, 1994).

39 National Endowment for the Arts, United States Department of Education, *The Arts and Education. Partners in Achieving Our National Education Goals*, 1995.

40 Frank Philip, "Council of Chief State School Officers begins National Assessment of Education Progress Project on Arts Education Assessment." *Special Research Interest Group in Measurement and Evaluation* (Boston University [Winter, 1993]), 3.

41 Rosemarie Cook, Music Consultant, Los Angeles County Public Schools, interview with author, Downey, California, 11 January 1984.

42 Michael A. Hiltzik, "Proposition 13 Fever Became National Epidemic," *Los Angeles Times*, 6 June 1983, 3, 14.

43 John J. Warrener, "The Effects of Proposition 2-1/2 on the Position of Music Supervisor in Massachusetts," *Massachusetts Musical Educator* 31, no. 4 (Summer 1983): 29.

44 John J. Warrener, letter to author, May 1, 1984.

45 National Education Commission on Time and Learning, *Prisoners of Time* (Washington, DC: U. S. Government Printing Office, 1994), 7, 8.

46 Ibid.

47 Ibid., 21.

48 Diane Williams Hayes, "NYC School Reform Plan Being Hotly Debated," *Black Issues in Higher Education* 11, no. 11 (August 11, 1994): 21.

49 Claudia Wallis, "A Class of Their Own," *Time* 144, no. 18 (October 31, 1994): 55.

50 Gary Gately and Michael Dresser, "EAI Omits Poor Scores as Invalid." *Baltimore Sun*, 18 November 1994, p. 18A.

51 Nancy Gibbs, "Home Sweet School," *Time* 144, no. 18 (October 31, 1994): 62–63.

52 Charles Suber and Better J. Stearns, "Music Alert: the Chicago Story" (Washington, DC: Music Educators National Conference, 1972).

53 Tommie Pardue, "Stay Public," *Music Educators Journal* 70, no. 5 (January 1984): 27–28.

Part II

THE MUSIC CURRICULUM

5

Music Education Methods

Performance in the General Music Class

Conceptual education (see chapter 3) stimulated a new emphasis on performance activities in general music classes in the early 1960s. Since then, instrumental study has been integrated into general music because it is an excellent vehicle for conceptual learning. The electronic revolution was one of the stimuli to classroom instrument performance activities. Electronic keyboards made it possible for groups of students to learn to play the piano together because the keyboards cost less than pianos, were smaller, and lent themselves to class instruction in ways that were not possible with acoustic pianos. They are used in music classes not only to develop keyboard skills, but to teach theory and harmony, and for ensemble experiences. The electronic keyboard makes it possible for teachers to assist individuals within a large group of students in a single period of time. The same is true of class guitar instruction. Although acoustic guitars are used in some school music programs, most teachers favor electronic guitar laboratories. The handbell choir has also gained considerable popularity since the 1970s. Students develop musical concepts through handbell playing, and gain performing experience with them. They often participate in school handbell choirs whose curricular status is similar to that of other musical ensembles.[1]

Arts in Education

Another development of the 1970s was the trend known as arts in education, in which the arts are incorporated into the educational program of the school. Arts in education included the visual arts, music, dance and movement, theater, folk art, creative writing, architecture, costume and fashion design, crafts, poetry, film, television and radio, and photography."[2] Ideally, the Arts in Education program is an essential part of the

125

curriculum in which the arts are integrated into the instruction received by every child. According to Lee, "In such a curriculum the arts are taught on the same level as and experienced together with disciplines such as English, mathematics, and foreign languages. They are not embellishments to the curriculum, nor are they isolated from the basic subject areas; they are part of the core of the educational program."[3] The Pittsburgh, Pennsylvania, public schools provide an example.

> [The Pittsburgh Comprehensive Arts Program] is primarily concerned with the development of each child's capacity and ability to perceive and respond to the expressive qualities of art. . . . Springing from the educational theories of Pestalozzi, Montessori, Dewey, Piaget, Bruner, and others, the Comprehensive Arts curriculum embraces the eclectic theory of intellectual development, suggesting that the learning process, when truly effective, involves the totality of the learner's personality. With the developing of aesthetic sensitivity as the goal, growth in the affective domain—the area of subjective attitudes such as feeling, taste, and valuing—is the primary concern.

Although the term "Arts in Education" is no longer current, the practice was, and perhaps still is, the ideal. The economic exigencies of the past several decades, however, have not spared the arts, and it is unfortunate that the educational agenda is often more responsive to budget limitations than to educational needs of children. The curricular approaches that follow, nevertheless, exemplify many of the principles of Arts in Education.

Music in Open Education

Perhaps more than any other approach to arts education, open education embodied the spirit of arts in education. Charles Silberman wrote:

> The arts play a radically different role in the open classroom than the traditional school. Painting, sculpture, music dance, crafts—these are not frills to be indulged in if time is left over from the real business of education; they are the real business of education as much as reading, writing, math, or science. For the arts are the language of a whole range of human experience; to neglect them is to neglect ourselves and to deny children the full development that education should provide.[4]

AN ABANDONED EDUCATIONAL MOVEMENT
Open education was a major movement in American education that began to fade in the 1970s and disappeared in the 1980s, despite its long and distinguished history. It declined because it was intended to educate

the children of an earlier time, rather than those of a technologically advanced society beset with myriad social problems. Open education put children's individual interests first, allowing them actively to learn in ways that were natural to them. It was never meant for children who acquire much of their information and knowledge passively from the media. The arts played a central role in open education, and its demise was a loss for arts education. The child's interest was the basis of learning; music, painting, sculpture, drama, and movement were used to a greater extent in open classrooms than in traditional classrooms. Children developed language skills and cognitive knowledge through the arts. The immediate objective of art in the open classroom was for children to use their natural art abilities to express and communicate experience.

Many open education ideas and techniques have survived in more contemporary forms. Music educators who wish to know about the long and distinguished history of the movement, and its philosophy and techniques, should consult the 1975 MENC publication, *Individualized Instruction in Music*,[5] a compilation of writings on music in open education.

Approaches to the Music Curriculum

Most of the approaches described in this chapter incorporate conceptual learning materials, techniques, and practices. Until the 1960s basal music series did not contain sequential music reading programs; they were actually little more than song books. At a time when educators and psychologists recognized that subjects must be learned through their unique structures, music educators needed innovative ways to approach music teaching and learning conceptually. William C. Hartshorn's speech, delivered at the 1962 MENC biennial meeting, urged music educators to view their subject as an academic discipline. The conference was entitled "The Study of Music: An Academic Discipline." Hartshorn said, "What does it mean to study music as an academic discipline? It means that music will be studied as a process of inquiry into its nature, meaning, and structure, rather than as the accumulation of predetermined facts about it."[6] In 1965 MENC published *Music in General Education*,[7] which describes general music as a means of conceptual learning.

Visionary music educators began to investigate how music education could be transformed into a discipline based on knowledge of child development and other psychological principles. Some developed American approaches. Others recognized possibilities in foreign curricula; they traveled overseas, studied methods that appeared to be relevant for American needs, and some of them dedicated their professional lives to helping American music educators adopt the new methods.

The Dalcroze Method

Emile Jaques-Dalcroze (1865–1950) studied at the Conservatoire of Music in Geneva, in Paris under Lo Delibes, and in Vienna under Anton Bruckner and Robert Fuchs. In 1892 he was appointed Professor of Harmony at the Geneva Conservatoire. Dalcroze realized early in his teaching career that the preparation of musicians emphasized the training of individual faculties to develop excellence in technique, but with little regard for musical expression. The education of musicians almost entirely neglected the basic ability to express oneself musically:

> The students were taught to play instruments, to sing songs, but without any thought of such work becoming a means of self-expression, and so it was found that pupils, technically far advanced, after many years of study were unable to deal with the simplest problems in rhythm and that their sense for pitch, relative or absolute, was most defective; that, while able to read accurately or to play pieces memorized, they had not the slightest power of giving musical expression to their simplest thoughts or feelings, in fact were like people who possess the vocabulary of a language and are able to read what others have written, yet are unable to put their own simple thoughts and impressions into words.[8]

Dalcroze regarded technique only as a means to produce art. The goal of music education should not be to train performers technically, but to develop their musical faculties. The musicality of the individual should be the primary consideration in specialized musical study.

Dalcroze believed that it was necessary to make students aware of musicality through tone and rhythm. Because tonal sense could only be developed through the ear, he emphasized vocal exercises and singing. He found that students sang more musically when they beat time themselves, and so he wrote "gesture songs," which combined music with movement. Contrary to the common practice of the time, Dalcroze utilized movement education, and made the coordination of movement and music the basis of his method. At first he only employed the arm movements used by conductors. The next step was to develop a series of arm movements to express various meters from 2 to 12 beats per bar. He devised body and leg movements that corresponded with various note values from whole notes to 12 beats.

The conservatory took a dim view of his innovative teaching, although his supporters appreciated it, and he had to form a voluntary experimental class that met after hours, away from the conservatory. In 1905 he demonstrated his method at the Solothurn Music Festival, where it was received warmly. Until then the method was intended for the early education of musicians. When he studied psychology, with the help of his friend, psychologist Claparede, however, he recognized that the method held great potential for teaching children. Dalcroze wrote:

> It is true that I first devised my method as a musician for musicians. But the further I carried my experiments, the more I noticed that, while a method intended to develop the sense for rhythm, and indeed based on such development, is of great importance in the education of a musician, its chief value lies in the fact that it trains the powers of apperception and of expression in the individual and renders easier the externalization of natural emotions. Experience teaches me that a man is not ready for the specialized study of an art until his character is formed, and his powers of expression developed.[9]

Dalcroze presented his first training course for teachers in 1906, and awarded the first diploma in 1909. He granted diplomas to his students to distinguish them from other teachers who used his method, but whom he himself did not train. People in many countries imitated the method, but they were unlikely to meet Dalcroze's standards. Spector writes:

> [Dalcroze deserves] credit not for his selection of talented students, but for his ability to create, to form, that talent. It was not just a question of talent itself; Dalcroze found the way to bring out the best qualities in each student to the highest degree. Often it resulted in what appeared to be the emergence of a great (or a hidden) talent or capability.[10]

Placido de Montoliu brought the Dalcroze method to the United States in 1913, after he completed his studies with Dalcroze. He taught in Bryn Mawr and Ardmore, Pennsylvania, Baltimore, Maryland, and Greenwich, Connecticut. Within a few years, Marguerite Heaton and Suzanne Ferriére started teaching the Dalcroze method in New York. In 1926 Paul Boepple and several other instructors, all of whom held Dalcroze diplomas, arrived at the New York school. When Boepple became director in 1928, it was renamed the American Institute of Dalcroze Eurythmics. As the method gained popularity, several nearby schools took advantage of the opportunity to have their students study Dalcroze. They included the Damrosch Institute of Musical Art (which later became the Juilliard School of Music), Hunter College, New York University School of Musical Education, Teachers College of Columbia University, and the New York Institute for Education of the Blind.[11]

The method also spread to other cities across the country, although not in its authentic form. Many teachers who tried to adhere to the authentic form found that it was not appropriate for their students. Karl Gehrkens wrote:

> As a system of rhythmic training, the greatest obstacle to the success
> of the method has been the attitude of some of the Dalcroze teach-
> ers themselves. They have often insisted that the system must be
> taught in its entirety to be effective and that if it cannot be worked
> completely and exactly in accordance with its inventor it must not be
> adopted at all.[12]

The techniques were adapted for American circumstances, and many
teachers have since been influenced by derivations of it. Charles Hoffer
wrote:

> The use of "walking" and "running" as designations for quarter and
> eighth notes is one common example in the elementary schools. By
> the 1930s a number of college music schools or physical education
> departments were requiring courses in eurhythmics, the term often
> used for Dalcroze-like instruction. The interest in it seemed to level
> off at that point and then decline. A modest renewal of interest in it
> has taken place since 1970. About twenty colleges offer some instruc-
> tion in the approach, with five of them giving a Dalcroze certificate.[13]

The Method

EURHYTHMICS

The term "eurhythmics" was coined by John Harvey of the University of
Birmingham (England). It is a loose translation of the French word
"rythmique," which has no English cognate. "Eurhythmics"[14] is commonly thought to be the Dalcroze method, but it is only one of its three
components. The other parts are ear training (solfege) and improvisation. Eurhythmics consists of exercises for the physical response to
music. Students become sensitive to rhythm by responding with their
entire bodies. They internalize musical concepts through rhythmic
movement. According to Dalcroze:

> It is my object, after endeavoring to train the pupil's ear, to awaken
> in him by means of special gymnastics, the sense of his personal
> body-rhythm, and to induce him to give metrical order to the spon-
> taneous manifestations of his physical nature. Sound rhythms had to
> be stepped, or obtained by gestures; it was also necessary to find a
> system of notation capable of measuring the slightest nuances of
> duration, so as to respond to both the demands of the music and to
> the bodily needs of the individual.[15]

Students move freely to music in eurhythmics classes. The teacher,
and sometimes students, improvises at the piano. The students walk,
run, and skip, creating individual movements expressive of the music
they hear. Every person interprets differently what he or she hears, and

so the movements of each student are individualistic. Students develop movements that range from simple physical responses to complex combinations in which the arms conduct the meter, while the feet move in syncopated patterns and the head nods on certain beats. The following exercises were adapted by Jo Pennington in the book *The Importance of Being Rhythmic: A Study of the Principles of Dalcroze Eurhythmics Applied to General Education and to the Arts of Music, Dancing, and Acting*, which is based on Dalcroze's book *Rhythm, Music and Education*.

EXERCISE 1. FOLLOWING THE MUSIC, EXPRESSING TEMPO AND TONE QUALITY

The teacher at the piano improvises music to which the pupils march (usually in a circle) beating the time with their arms (3/4, 5/8,12/8, etc.) as an orchestra leader conducts, and stepping with their feet the note values (that is, quarter notes are indicated by normal steps, eighth notes by running steps, half notes by a step and a bend of the leg, a dotted eighth and a sixteenth by a skip, etc.).

The teacher varies the expression of the playing, now increasing or decreasing the intensity of tone, now playing more slowly or more quickly; and the pupils "follow the music" literally, reproducing in their movements the exact pattern and structure of her improvisation.

EXERCISE 4. NOTE VALUES, SYNCOPATION

In the exercise to demonstrate note values, the pupils march one step for each beat while the teacher plays quarter notes; two for each beat in eighth notes; three for triplets, and so on. The values of whole and half notes are also represented, the half note by a step and a bend, and the whole note by a step followed by three or more movements of the leg without stepping. Exercises in syncopation require more training. The teacher plays an even tempo—say quarter notes in four-four time. The pupils at a command walk in syncopation for one measure or more—stepping either just before or just after the beat . . . anticipating the beat or retarding it. As their *feet* take steps just *off the beat*, their *arms* must continue to beat the time regularly, each movement being made *on the beat*. This exercise then is one in concentration, mental and physical control (coordination) and in the understanding of the musical principles of polyrhythm and syncopation.

EXERCISE 7. "REALIZATION" OF RHYTHMS

As explained in the program, to "realize" in the Dalcroze sense means to express in bodily movements all the elements of the music save sound. In this exercise the teacher plays a series of measures and the pupils, after listening to them, realize in their movements the rhythm which they have heard—expressing the note values, the meter, the shading, the quickness or slowness—they reproduce the rhythm in movement as definitely as though it were written in ordinary musical notation. In fact that is usually the next step in the exercise. This exercise combines several important elements of Dalcroze eurhythmics: ear training; the musical analysis of rhythm; memory and concentration; and the physical response necessary to the execution of the rhythm in movement.

EXERCISE 9. INDEPENENCE OF CONTROL

This exercise is one in polyrhythm, the pupil expressing several rhythms at the same time. He may perhaps beat three-four time with the left arm and four-four with the right at the same time walking twelve-eight with the feet. There are many variations of this though in the beginning pupils find it sufficiently difficult to beat two with one arm and three with the other, especially since each arm must "remember," so to speak, the accent that falls on the first beat of its own measure. Another form of this exercise is to have the pupils march one measure while beating time for another; as three with the arms and four with the feet. These are worked out mathematically at first but soon the pupils learn to keep in their muscular and mental consciousness the pulse of the two rhythms simultaneously.

EXERCISE 10. RHYTHMIC COUNTERPOINT

Rhythmic counterpoint is an exercise in the appreciation of unplayed beats. The teacher improvises a short theme, let us say simply two half notes and a quarter in five-four time. The pupil, instead of stepping on the first, third and fifth beats of the measure, will do the counterpoint by stepping on the *second* and *fourth*. Or, if told to do the counterpoint in eighth notes, he will fill in every unplayed eighth note beat. This is an exercise in inhibition and in the accurate analysis of time values. A more complicated form of exercise is the realization of theme and counterpoint simultaneously. For example, the pupils may learn a simple melody for a theme and then proceed to sing this melody while executing a rhythmic counterpoint, as a sort of accompaniment, with steps, or with gestures. This is a very interesting exercise to watch, as first one hears the note played by the teacher and following it the steps taken by the pupils to fill in the measure, the whole making a sound pattern as well as a rhythmic pattern.[16]

Ear Training, or Solfège

Dalcroze believed that the study of solfège helped students develop their abilities to listen, hear, and remember. The first exercises are in the key of C; they help the student develop a tonal memory for C. Various hearing and singing exercises are mastered, after which the student goes on to other keys. The purpose of ear training is to develop what Dalcroze called "inner hearing":

> Solfège sessions are a part of each Dalcroze class. Students sing intervals and songs with syllables, and improvise vocally. In learning pitch

relationships, students may sing one or more measures aloud, then one or more measures silently. Or, when ending one song and beginning another, students may sing the final pitch of the first song, then the beginning pitch of the second, naming the interval between them. The piano is used to test accuracy of the interval. Many times during a solfège session, students are asked to sing the syllable *do*, which in the European fixed-do system is always C. Students are expected to work toward acquisition of absolute pitch.[17]

Improvisation

Improvisation is usually done at the piano. This helps students develop the same freedom at the piano that they have in their bodily responses to music. They are assigned extemporaneous playing exercises in given tempi:

> For example, as children are moving freely to music improvised by the teacher, one child may be asked to move toward the piano, improvise a "flute part" in the high register or a "drum part" in the lower as the teacher continues his playing in the middle register, all without interruption of the pulse or the movement activity of the rest of the class.[18]

Dalcroze used improvisation liberally in his theoretical harmony classes. He would have students improvise melodies or melodic fragments as part of their development of comprehension of intervals. Improvisation also helped them become familiar with harmony.

The Use of Eurhythmics in Special Education

Dalcroze recognized the value of his method to students who had special needs. He himself taught students with exceptional ability and those with physical handicaps, especially the blind. He taught blind students in Barcelona, using special exercises to develop consciousness of space of objects that could not be seen. Dalcroze included several exercises for blind students in his book *Eurhythmics, Art and Education*, some of which follow:

> *Exercises for Developing the Sense of Space and the Muscular Sense.* Two rows of pupils facing each other. Each pupil in the first row, with outstretched arms, touches the palm of the hand of a pupil in row 2. One step backwards, then again one step forward, clapping the hand that has been released. . . . Then two steps, three steps, eight steps, twelve steps. . . .
>
> *Exercises for Developing Tactile Sensibility and Muscular Consciousness.* Realize on the arms of a sighted pupil the *crescendos* and (decrescen-

dos) of muscular innervation, in their relation to fullness of gesture—then execute these dynamic nuances oneself. Control is easy to establish if, in moving his arms, the pupil can place the end of his finger on different steps of a ladder or on pegs planted in the wall and serving as guide-marks.

Exercises for Developing the Auditory Faculties in their Relation to Space and the Muscular Sense. The pupils, standing anywhere in the room, guide themselves by the voice of the master. He moves about, uttering a sound or beating a drum from time to time; they walk in the direction of the sound. . . . The master plays the piano, the pupils, attracted by the sound, make their way towards the piano, to right or left, pass round it, retreat from it during the decrescendo, etc.[19]

The Orff Approach

Carl Orff's (1885–1982) approach to music education for children developed from his own radical musical-theatrical style of composition. His eclectic interest in folk song, nineteenth-century popular song, dance and theater music, and music of the medieval, Baroque, and Renaissance periods led to his comprehensive theory of music pedagogy. The approach is an experiential method based on rhythm and improvisation. It builds on the rhythms of strolling, skipping, running, swaying, and stomping, and the universal children's chant on the minor third.

During his early years of his career in Munich, Dalcroze's dance-movement (eurhythmics) theories influenced him. In 1924 Orff, with the dancer Dorothea Gunther, founded the Gunther Schule, an innovative ensemble of dancers and musicians that developed and trained teachers in new forms of movement and rhythm. Many of their students were preparing to be physical education teachers. Orff encouraged creativity by means of Dalcroze's principles, and improvisation was a major part of the Gunther Schule program.

With the help of Curt Sachs and Karl Maendler, Orff developed an instrumental ensemble at the Gunther Schule, which he described as follows:

In due course the Gunther school boasted an ensemble of dancers with an orchestra of their own. Music and choreography were supervised by Gunild Keetman and Maja Lex, respectively. Dancers and players were interchangeable. Suitable instruments (flutes, cymbals, drums, etc.) were integrated into the dance itself. The diverse and varied instruments employed included recorders, xylophones, and metallophones of all ranges, glockenspiels, kettledrums, small drums, tomtoms, gongs, various kinds of cymbals, triangles, tune bells; and sometimes also fiddles, gambas, spinettinos, and porta-tives.[20]

The ensemble traveled throughout Germany, playing for educational conferences and teachers' meetings, and generating interest in the work of the Gunther Schule. Orff planned to test the approach on a large scale in German schools, but World War II prevented him from doing so.

The Gunther Schule was completely destroyed during the war, but later, a Bavarian radio official discovered an out-of-print recording from the school. His interest in the record led to the gradual rekindling of national interest in Orff's work. When Orff reflected on the method he had developed a few years earlier, he realized that rhythm education might be more effective if begun in early childhood rather than in the adult years. He explored this new idea and concluded that elemental music, that is, primeval or basic music evolving from speech, movement, and dance, should be the basis of early childhood music education. Orff, with his lifelong associate Gunild Keetman, began to test his ideas in nursery schools and kindergartens.

A radio broadcast series in 1948, in which children performed elemental music on a small complex of Orff instruments, engendered widespread interest in music that had universal appeal to children. In 1949 Klauss Becker opened Studio 49, a workshop in which he improved the design of the instruments, and built new ones.

Between 1950 and 1954 Orff published his five-volume *Music for Children*. The approach, called *Schulwerk*, was a compilation and complete revision of his prewar work. It attracted international interest. *Music for Children* was translated into eighteen languages, and the exercises were adapted to the indigenous rhythms and music of the many countries that imported his techniques. Since 1961, the Orff Institute of the Hochschule "Mozarteum" in Salzburg, Austria, has had students from forty-eight countries.[21]

The Orff approach is not a method. Brigitte Warner explains:

> Orff and Keetman never intended to write a textbook with detailed lesson plans. Such an approach would negate the Orff-Schulwerk philosophy, which, after all, is based on the inherent creativity not only of the child but of the teacher as well. Instead, they provided us with exercises in speech, rhythm, melody, and harmony, all of which serve as guidelines to a sequential development of the musical concepts. These exercises are meant to be points of departure and motivation for improvisation.[22]

She reminds teachers that the curriculum is the sequence of musical activities that they select.

The American (actually Canadian) adaptation of *Music for Children*, by Doreen Hall and Arnold Walter, consists of five volumes and a teacher's edition. It corresponds to the original *Schulwerk* in progression of subject matter, but the material itself has been selected or written especially for English-speaking children.

Orff believed that rhythm should evolve from dance movement, melody from speech rhythms, and sonority from layers of rhythms. His work as a composer was greatly influenced by his teaching. He regarded rhythm to be the fundamental musical element and the basis of melody, contrary to the then-current concept of melody as the basis of rhythm. Orff's music is straightforward and insistent. Harmony is subordinate to the interaction of melody, rhythm, and sonority, as in folk songs. His infusion of musical theater with musical and visual forms led him to create *Carmina Burana* (1936), a scenic/oratorio named after the thirteenth-century manuscript collection of Latin folk poems at Benediktbevern in southwest Germany. It is his most successful composition and is performed frequently.

THE APPROACH

Orff held that music education should be patterned on the evolutionary stages of humankind. Children develop musicality by reliving the historical development of music. He used the word "elemental" to refer both to the music of early humans and to the music of young children. It is neither sophisticated nor refined music, but natural and capable of development. Improvisation, an important part of elemental music, must be introduced at the child's level before it can be developed into a mature form. To Orff this meant beginning with rhythm and allowing other musical elements to grow out of it. He devised simple rhythms and chants to serve as the basis for sequential developmental activities. Speech patterns familiar to children are their first musical materials. The patterns come from chants, games, and the vocal sounds that are already part of the child's vocabulary. Pupils chant, clap, dance, and sing the patterns. Bergethon and Boardman wrote:

> The essence of Orff's instructional plan is to help children built a vocabulary of rhythmic, melodic, and harmonic patterns that they can use in creating their own music. This they acquire through a progressive sequence of performance activities: speaking, moving, singing, and playing.[23]

Orff's emphasis on rhythm suggested to him the need for percussion instruments in music education. Working with instrument makers, he developed an ensemble of percussion and stringed instruments that included xylophones (soprano, alto, and bass), glockenspiels (soprano and alto), metallophones (soprano, alto, and bass), drums, cymbals, woodblocks, rattles, viola da gambas, and lutes. The instruments are designed to create the proper instrumental timbre for the music contained in the *Schulwerk*. Although the instruments can be played with no training, children develop sufficient technique to play them correctly so they can be used expressively. The *Schulwerk* includes many exercises and ensemble arrangements for such usage.

Children are encouraged to imitate and improvise both vocally and instrumentally. They create their own music both from inner feelings and in imitation of the sounds of their environment. They learn to become sensitive to sounds and to use them as sources for the development of other sounds. Rhythm serves as sources for imitation, answers to contrasting rhythms, and melodic invention:

> Rhythm patterns, melodies, and ostinato figures are tried out and played on the instruments played earlier. These instruments are anything but toys. They are carefully selected and contrasted, they are in fact replicas of medieval ensembles, as meaningful to children now as they were to grownup people in those days. They are difficult enough to be a challenge to a child yet simple enough to make improvisation possible. . . . and that is what Orff wants more than anything else—*to enable* children to improvise, to invent their own rhythms, melodies, and accompanying figures.[24]

Ostinati are important because children are secure in repetitive patterns. This is why Orff's accompaniments feature ostinati so preeminently.

Early experiences are informal and often are based on children's games. Children enjoy them as they build a solid musical foundation by evaluating music and improving its sequence, structure, and other properties. The first melody encountered by children in the Orff approach is the falling minor third (also true of the Kodály concept). Children chant names of classmates and familiar words to develop feeling for tempo, direction, meter, and dynamics in relation to melody. They notate their music, inventing their own systems under the guidance of the teacher.

New intervals and rhythmic patterns are added gradually. Once students learn the pentatonic scale, a repertory of pentatonic tunes follows. Orff thought it important to limit children to the pentatonic scale in the early stages of instruction because it is easier for them to be creative in this mode. If a seven-note scale were used, the children might imitate music they already know, rather than creating their own.[25]

The first harmony lessons use drones of open fifths, which Orff called "Borduns." Borduns are effective when played against pentatonic melodies and are conducive to improvisation. They also lend themselves to ostinati. More sophisticated harmony evolves from the melodic movement of Borduns. When rhythm and melody have become part of the children's vocabulary, studies in form and improvisation are introduced. Alternations between chorus and soloist provide the contrast that delineates form. Canons are also used abundantly.

The *Schulwerk* is organized as follows:

Volume I.   Pentatonic Nursery Rhymes and Songs

Volume ll.   Major: Bordun (the fourth and seventh scale degrees are introduced)

Volume lll.   Major: Triads (tonic and supertonic, tonic and submediant)

Volume IV.   Minor: Bordun (Aeolian, Dorian, and Phrygian modes)

Volume V.   Minor: Triads (first and seventh triads, first and third triads, and other degrees)

The First International Symposium on Orff-Schulwerk was held in May 1967 in Bellflower, California. Funded as a federal project under Title III, it was a one-week demonstration involving six California school districts. The California Orff-Schulwerk Institute was one result of the Bellflower symposium.

Orff Education Now

Orff-Schulwerk has expanded in recent years to include music therapy. Many members of the American Orff-Schulwerk Association (AOSA) are music therapists who find practical applications of Orff-Schulwerk techniques in their own work. The Summer 1994 issue of *The Orff Echo* is dedicated to music therapy. Orff himself wrote "The Schulwerk and Music Therapy" for the *Echo* in 1964.[26]

The American Orff-Schulwerk Association, the professional organization for Orff educators, is an auxiliary member of MENC. Its address is P.O. Box 391089, Cleveland, OH 44139–8089. AOSA publishes *The Orff Echo* four times each year, as well as guidelines for Orff-Schulwerk. It approves Orff teacher training courses, and listed fifty-three colleges, universities, and conservatories offering approved courses in 1994. Approval is based on number of contact hours, content of course, and qualifications and number of instructors. Courses are designed according to the official standards described in *Guidelines for Orff-Schulwerk Training Courses: Levels II, III*.

The Kodály Concept

Kodály believed that Hungarian music education should be designed to teach the spirit of singing to everyone, to educate all to be musically literate, to bring music into every day for use in homes and in leisure activities, and to educate concert audiences. He was concerned with the creative, humanizing enrichment of life through music and regarded the goal of music literacy for everyone as the first step toward his ideal.[27]

Loraine Edwards

Zoltán Kodály was a dedicated musician and a fervent nationalist who aspired to reestablish the national music culture of his beloved Hungary. He sought to awaken his countrymen to their rich cultural heritage by giving them the means to know, enjoy, and take pride in indigenous Hungarian, or Magyar, music. He wanted twentieth-century Hungary to be as musical as it had been a century earlier, when music was a normal part of everyday life activity. Kodály recognized that this could be accomplished only if the schools accepted the responsibility of making musical literacy the national standard. He created his pedagogical system to help the schools reawaken the musicality of the Hungarian people. Kodály said: "It is much more important who is the music teacher in Kisvárda than who is the director of the opera house in Budapest . . . for a poor director fails once, but a poor teacher keeps on failing for thirty years, killing the love of music in thirty batches of children."[28]

Kodály was born on December 15, 1882, in Kecskemet, Hungary, to parents who were amateur musicians. As a child, he learned the piano and violin, sang in a cathedral choir, and often visited the cathedral music library to study its scores. He attended the Budapest Academy of Music and became a composer. Kodály was aware that his countrymen knew little about their indigenous music and what made it distinctly and uniquely Hungarian. He saw that published versions of Hungarian folk music were poorly edited and arranged, and were not authentic, and so from 1906 to 1908 Kodály, with his lifelong friend Béla Bartók, wandered the country collecting native folk songs. They assembled a body of authentic literature to help reestablish Hungarian nationalistic pride. Under Kodály's guidance, this literature became part of a pedagogical system that was developed to help the schools reawaken the musicality of the Hungarian people.

THE CONCEPT

The Kodály concept is a developmental curriculum built on singing, reading and writing music, ear training, improvisation, and listening. Movement and rhythm games help children recognize and feel the basic beat and rhythm patterns aurally and visually. This leads students to notate simple rhythms using stem notation. The names "ta" and "ti" are assigned to quarter and eighth notes so they can be sung in rhythmical-ly. Emil Chevé had devised the rhythm syllables in nineteenth-century France, and Kodály adapted the system for his own use.

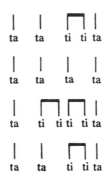

Children sing the rhythms, clap them, and move to them. Rhythms are derived from children's song literature and speech patterns, and children respond to rhythm phrases with their own improvised phrases. This develops feeling for meter, pulse, accent, and balance. As rhythm experiences become more complex, students develop both increasingly acute sensitivity to rhythm and beat and skill in rhythm reading.

Rhythm and melody are taught together with a structured sequence of rhythm and melodic experiences. Kodály believed that if children did not develop good intonation habits and skills at a young age, they would not be able to improve them later. He recognized that children typically do not sing half steps in tune. Rather than encourage faulty intonation, the musical literature of his approach consists of pen-tatonic songs and exercises, which do not contain half steps. Kodály found that children are musically and intellectually capable of mastering a body of music literature built on that scale.

American children do not usually sing pentatonic Hungarian songs, and this caused a problem in adapting the system for American usage. When American music educators addressed themselves to the Kodály method, however, they found ample pentatonic song material to support the curriculum in the United States. Much of it is from the American folk-song repertory, including many examples from the African-American song literature. Some is from Classical music litera-ture, and some from the folk repertories of other countries, including Hungary. Researchers and educators continually locate music that is indigenous to specific ethnic groups in the United States, and that is suit-able for the Kodály-inspired curriculum.

The most natural interval for children to sing, and one that they sing as part of play, is the descending minor third (sol-mi). Children usu-ally use this interval when they make up songs, taunt each other, and chant sing-song ditties. The next tone they learn is "la," which adds the major second and perfect fourth to the children's musical vocabulary. This, too, is part of the natural melodic language of young children. Probably every young child has chanted this sequence:

Soon children are musically and intellectually ready to expand their melodic vocabulary to include the other two notes of the pentatonic scale and the octave of the tonic.

When the pentatonic scale has been learned and execises mastered, children have acquired a vocabulary of intervals they can sing in tune, sight-read, and understand. When they have learned whole steps and perfect intervals, children are ready to conquer half steps. The fourth and seventh degrees are added, thus completing the major scale.

MINOR AND MODAL SCALES

Accidentals are introduced after students master the tones of the major scale and all of its intervals. This leads to minor and modal scales. As students progress, rhythmic and melodic experiences usually continue in a combined fashion. The value of movable *do* becomes more apparent as students progress farther from the basic keys. It allows them to feel at ease in any key. Children learn the difference between *do*- and *la*-ending melodies before accidentals are introduced.

HAND SIGNS

The Kodály concept fosters kinesthetic development. Both rhythm and melodic exercises utilize kinesthetic activity in the form of hand signs. Sarah Glover invented hand signs in nineteenth-century England, and John Curwen later improved them. Kodály adapted them for his own method on the conviction that learning to sight-read through a medium other than the voice greatly increases reading skills. The hand signs help children learn to read music by translating sound into body motion, and are used both rhythmically and melodically. Students use hand signs for musical dictation, for sight reading, and for performing duets and part songs.

Students can learn to play instruments if they wish, but only after developing sufficient vocal skill. They are ready for an instrument when their individual musical competency allows them to play with good tone and intonation, and in a musical manner. Children are usually encouraged to play the recorder, but they also play other wind and string instruments as well.

RESULTS OF THE KODÁLY CONCEPT

Students who complete several years of the Kodály-inspired curriculum are able to sight-read much of the folk and art music literature. They do this by means of melodic syllables, rhythmic syllables, and hand signs, and they can analyze form and harmony.

THE KODÁLY CONCEPT IN THE UNITED STATES

Several educators, including Tibor Bachmann, Lois Choksy, Mary Helen Richards, and Denise Bacon, have adapted Kodály's work for use in the United States.

Tibor Bachmann is a native of Hungary. He taught the Kodály method in a Hungarian state teachers college before emigrating to the United States in 1956. Bachmann's approach to the Kodály method is presented in a series entitled *Reading and Writing Music*.[29] His text contains few familiar songs because Bachmann believes that children can best learn to read music with unfamiliar musical material. The child is introduced to notation with a one-line staff, and additional lines are introduced as needed. Rhythm is stressed from the beginning. The book contains sections on rhythm designed to separate rhythmic from melodic development. It uses Kodály's rhythm syllables, the *sol–fa* syllables, and hand signs. Bachmann incorporates tone games to encourage individual response in matching tones to help children develop musical hearing, and dictation to develop tonal memory. Music writing is stressed because, according to Bachmann, students are able to handle music reading if they are familiar with music writing. They learn at an early stage that the music they write can be performed by themselves and others. Bachmann uses the movable *do* clef in order to spare children the necessity of learning key signatures before they are ready for them. Tone blending and intonation are developed in two-part singing exercises. After the G clef is introduced, key signatures are used to designate the location of *do*, and accidentals are introduced. Students analyze authentic Hungarian and American folk music to develop perception of the elements and structure of music.

Lois Choksy studied the Kodály method under Katinka Daniel, a student of Kodály. She traveled to Hungary in 1968 to attend the Danube Bend Summer University at Estergon, and returned to Hungary in 1970 to study music education at the Franz Liszt Academy. In her application of the Kodály method, children develop concepts of good intonation, and of feeling the beat and accent in duple meter during the first year of study. They learn to identify the rhythmic patterns of familiar songs and to step and clap the rhythm and beat. They also develop concepts of high and low, loud and soft, and fast and slow.

Choksy, like Kodály, prefers to avoid the intonation problems caused by half steps, but she permits them to be used occasionally. She utilizes Kodály's rhythmic syllables and hand signals. Choksy agrees with the current practice of the official Hungarian curriculum that restricts children in the second year of study to the keys of C, F, and G because they need to develop a strong feeling for key center, and familiarity with these keys helps them in future instrumental music study. Also, there are no accidentals in the C, F, and G pentatonic scales.

In a later stage of study, children undertake triple meter, the dotted half note, the anacrusis, syncopation, and sixteenth-note patterns, and learn the pentatonic scale. At that point childen learn *fa* and *ti*, and are introduced to the concept of major and minor keys and key signatures. They continue with dotted rhythms, learn triplets, other new meters, and modal melodies. Choksy identifies four sources of difficulty in adapting the Kodály method for American education: (1) the nature of American culture; (2) school organization and teaching practices; (3) teacher training; and (4) materials.[30]

Mary Helen Richards received her Bachelor of Music Education degree from the University of Nebraska. She studied choral repertoire at Stanford University and Smith College, and was later a student of Kodály in Hungary. The Richards curriculum progresses by units, from simple to complex. It begins with music reading in the first year and continues with increasingly advanced knowledge and skills to the sixth level. Her system is built on a sound rhythmic foundation that is taught with syllables and physical movement. Students use hand signs with a movable *do* for the pentatonic scale. The voice is the basic instrument, and students develop good intonation by means of two-voice singing parts. The pentatonic song literature includes African-American spirituals, American pioneer songs, mountaineer songs, and variety of other ethnic pieces. Singing begins with the natural chants of children, and the intervals of these chants are the basis of the approach to melody.

The Richards approach emphasizes music reading and intervallic recognition in conjunction with the recognition of rhythmic syllables. Key signatures, clefs, and accidentals are introduced only when they are needed to progress to the next step. Review continues throughout the entire process, and each element of music is coordinated with the other elements. Experience charts, used to present concepts to an entire class, help develop group musical response. The first-level charts take the class through four tones of the pentatonic scale. The fifth tone and the octave are introduced via the second-year charts. By the end of the third year, the complete diatonic scale and complex rhythm patterns have been learned. Richards continually emphasizes reading and singing because she considers them inseparable. Music writing is less important than in the Bachmann approach.[31]

Denise Bacon was director of the Dana School of Music in Wellesley, Massachusetts, when she traveled to Europe in 1967 to study the Orff and Kodály methods. She recognized the potential of the Kodály-inspired curriculum and returned to Hungary several times to become more thoroughly acquainted with it. In 1969 the Ford Foundation granted her $184,000 to plan and establish the Kodály Musical Training Institute (KMTI), originally located in Wellesley. Bacon was the first director of education at the Institute. When it later moved to the Hartt School of Music in Hartford, Connecticut, she founded the Kodály Center of America (KCA) in Wellesley. Bacon's major contributions are her early work in introducing American music educators to both the Kodály and Orff approaches, and her leadership in making Kodály training available to American music educators. She was one of the first to bring Hungarian music educators to the United States to teach American educators, and to arrange for Americans to study the Kodály method in Hungary.

KODÁLY TRAINING FOR TEACHERS

The Organization of American Kodály Educators endorses certificate programs that meet its standards. A Kodály certificate program must develop competency in musicianship, methodology, folk music, and conducting. Students are also expected to demonstrate voice and keyboard proficiency, and to have experience in choral ensembles. A number of institutions have approved Kodály teacher education programs. They include California State University at Los Angeles, Hartt School of Music, Holy Names College, Kodály Institute at Capital University, New York University, Sam Houston State University, Silver Lake College, the University of North Texas, the University of Oklahoma, and the University of St. Thomas. In addition, numerous other colleges, universities, and conservatories throughout the United States and Canada offer summer Kodály courses.

THE ORGANIZATION OF AMERICAN KODÁLY EDUCATORS

OAKE was founded in March 1974 to facilitate the growth and development of Kodály education in the United States. It sponsors an annual national conference, and its official journal is *The Kodály Envoy*. OAKE became an affiliated organization of MENC in 1984.

Orff and Kodály Combined

The names Orff and Kodály represented something new and exciting to American music educators in the 1960s. The two approaches were often confused with each other, however, because both arrived on the American music education scene at about the same time and Americans were often unaware of their differing philosophies and methodologies. To add to the confusion, the same people sometimes advocated both approaches simultaneously.

The two names were sometimes used interchangeably, or in conjunction with each other, as though Orff and Kodály were two aspects of one method. American music educators sometimes sought ways to combine the approaches, and this added to the confusion. "Combining" means the adaptation of appropriate parts of each to the general music program. These attempts were premature because rank-and-file music teachers did not know enough about either. Now each method has been clarified in publications, in the development of new teaching materials, and in teacher training programs. The separation between Orff and Kodály is distinct and clear, and each has its own legion of specialists and believers. Even so, the original tendency toward combining the two continues, but to a lesser extent than in the 1960s.

The creators of the two methods had defined their fundamental differences. Kodály conceived of his curriculum as a method to be developed in a systematic, predetermined manner. Orff did not consider his approach a method, nor did he intend it to be highly structured. He believed that it can be used successfully when modified and adapted for local conditions and musical traditions.

Denise Bacon discussed the two approaches when she returned from her 1967 European trip. She pointed out that although educators try to combine the approaches, that was not the intent of either Orff or Kodály, even though they held great professional and personal respect for each other. In fact, at that time the Orff Institute used elements of the Kodály method, and Hungarian teacher training institutes used Orff instruments. Bacon evaluated an early attempt to combine the two approaches:

> I still believe they should be used in the same curriculum, but whether fused as a teaching procedure I cannot say yet. . . . My class is now doing Kodály one day a week and Orff one day a week. Kodály can exist independently without the Orff, but I do not believe the Orff will accomplish the objectives as well without the Kodály. At this moment, I tend to think the two should be used in parallel fashion rather than fused, and that the Kodály should precede the Orff and the instruments should not be used as accompaniment to singing until children have acquired some musical skills.[32]

Arnold Walter, president of the Inter-American Music Council, opposed attempts to merge the two methods:

> The only question that concerns us here is whether it [Kodály] should be combined with basic Orff training. I am inclined to say that it should not. The Orff approach is the nearest thing to incidental learning a school can provide. It stresses impulse, fantasy,

improvisation—characteristics that have nothing to do with the deciphering of printed scores, however valuable that may be in itself. The Schulwerk does not attempt to teach all about music. On the contrary, it leaves a great deal out. It limits itself to laying a firm foundation for studies yet to come, be they vocal, instrumental theoretical, or historical. It is based on the premise that children can assimilate music in exactly the same way that they learn to speak. If that premise is false, the Schulwerk has obviously little value. If the premise is correct, we ought to be consistent, we ought to keep the pedagogical framework intact.[33]

Grace Nash perceived a need for both Orff and Kodály in combination with Laban's theory of motion in exploration of space, time, and weight, developed on the principles of Dalcroze. She discussed the dehumanizing environment of a mechanized society, in which there is an ever-increasing need to develop human sensitivity and awareness of the individual. As people become further removed from nature they have fewer opportunities for play and fantasy and less opportunity to develop those human attributes that can help them attain stability and satisfaction.[34] She wrote:

> . . . placed in the center of the curriculum, this [Orff-Kodály-Laban] program could help children express their verbal experiences in sound, movement, color (nonverbal media) and similarly nonverbal experiences can be translated into articulate and beautiful language. The five senses, movement, color, and feeling would be combined with language and sound. Every child would be shown how to sing and control pitch knowledgeably. Their songs, poetry, and dances would be self-accompanied on precision-tuned easy-to-play instruments (classroom instruments), an ensemble of beauty and excellence of aesthetic proportion—student inspired and achieved.[35]

The Orff and Kodály approaches, although philosophically different, have similarities that lend themselves to an eclectic method. Purists support one or the other, but most school music educators do not have the time, materials, equipment, or facilities to adopt either in its pure form. Conscientious and knowledgeable teachers have made effective use of certain elements of Orff and Kodály by combining them with traditional approaches, taking advantage of several similarities:

1. Bodily movement is an integral part of both methods, Orff for creating music, Kodály as an aid to learning music reading.
2. Both use melodies based on the same intervals, and begin with the pentatonic scale. Orff uses the pentatonic so children do not imitate familiar diatonic music, and Kodály because children have difficulty singing half steps in tune.

3. Both stress the development of a musical vocabulary: Kodály by assigning verbal and kinesthetic symbols to melody and rhythm, Orff through nonintellectual use of movement.

4. Both rely on rhythmic and melodic improvisation, Orff for the development of musical feeling and creativity, and Kodály for musical feeling and the development of music reading skills.

5. Both are group methods that build on children's interaction with each other.

6. Both begin with the child as the source of music, rather than with external music.

Suzuki Talent Education

Dr. Shinichi Suzuki developed his philosophy of education while searching for a way to help post–World War II Japanese children develop to their full potential in a nation devastated by the war. He wrote: "Talent Education has realized that all children in the world show their splendid capacities by speaking and understanding their mother language, thus displaying the original power of the human mind. Is it not probable that this mother language method holds the key to human development?" (Shinichi Suzuki, 1958).[36]

THE BACKGROUND OF TALENT EDUCATION

Suzuki was born in 1898 into a musical family. His father owned the first violin factory in Japan, and Suzuki played there as a child; he later worked there and learned about violin design and construction. His musical training began in Japan, but he later studied for eight years in Berlin with Karl Klinger. After World War II Suzuki adopted a young orphan in Matsumoto and gave him violin lessons. Violins were scarce in postwar Japan, and when Suzuki began to teach several other children, they had to share one instrument. Gradually, he procured more instruments and more students, and within a few years his method, "*Talent Education*," became the object of serious interest to parents and teachers.

THEORY OF TALENT EDUCATION

Talent Education is built on a philosophical foundation developed from Suzuki's theory of education. He called it the "mother-tongue method." It is based on what psychologists refer to as psycholinguistic development. Suzuki observed how easily and naturally children master their own mother tongue while adults learn a new language only with great difficulty. He recognized that this ability also permits young children to learn much more than is normally expected of them. His method helps children attain knowledge and skills through observation, imitation, repetition, and the gradual development of intellectual awareness.

FIGURE 5.1. Shinichi Suzuki performing with young artists

The Method

Suzuki Talent Education is predicated on the belief that people are products of their environment. The environmental conditions necessary to promote good learning by children are well defined and strictly adhered to by teachers of the method. These conditions are based on the informal process of learning the mother tongue. Each aspect of the method is related to one or more steps in the process of developing language communication skills. Talent education begins during infancy, when recorded music becomes part of the child's environment. Children begin playing the violin at age 3. By then, they have its sound in their minds and are physically capable of manipulating the instrument. They learn the violin by rote, as they do language. Imitation is an important part of the process, and so they listen frequently to the playing of their teacher and advanced students.

Technical mastery precedes music reading. Students first learn by rote, memorizing all of the music they learn. Actual note reading begins as an association process in which the students match what they are playing to the printed note. There is no emphasis on sight reading, and the development of reading skill is approached through the material that the student has already memorized. The musical materials are well defined; all talent education students progress through the same sequence of songs, exercises, and literature. New technical skills are introduced as they become necessary to perform the music being studied. Students master skills as they are needed for immediate application.

Talent education lessons are private and geared to individual needs. Their length is determined by each student's attention span. Parents are deeply involved in the process and learn along with the child. At least one of the parents attends lessons and helps with daily practice. Parental involvement is important for technical development, and it demonstrates to the child that the parents value violin study.

To help student relate as much as possible to the instrument, the physical environment is arranged so the students are not distracted or tempted to develop poor playing habits. Much of the paraphernalia that is part of traditional violin lessons is absent. Music stands, music, other unnecessary devices (cleaning cloths, tuning equiptment), and even chairs are out of sight during the lesson. Young violinists are more likely to develop good posture and position while standing. Standing also allows for more physical freedom, and the use of movement activities, such as walking or marching while playing.

Students learn by rote, which allows them to focus their attention solely on the instrument. Special recordings accompany the first several volumes of the literature, and standard commerican recordings provide examples for the most advanced music. The recordings serve as models in developing good tone and musicality. Rote teaching continues for at least two years, depending on the age of the students and their rate of progress. It continues even after students begin to read music to allow them to continue their technical development. Suzuki's concept of repetition is manifested throughout the entire period of study. Students continue to play music they learned earlier as they progress to more advanced music. The simpler music remains in the repertory, and is played even after students have mastered the most difficult repertoire. Ideally, lessons are private, but group instruction techniques are often used in the United States. It is easier for students to learn to read music in ensemble situations because printed music helps keep the group together.

Suzuki believes it to be of utmost importance for children to play with good tone and intonation from the very beginning. Young students only use the upper half of the bow to avoid the scratching and screeching sounds caused by playing with the lower half. Students whose hands are too small for the traditional bow grip use a simplified grip instead. Students constantly hear music performed in tune, and are kept aware of good intonation. Pieces of tape placed on the fingerboard to mark the exact location of finger placement help them with their own intonation.

The large Suzuki festivals held in Japan and in many parts of the United States represent the work of many teachers who collaborate to provide a musical outlet for their students. All Suzuki students play a common repertoire, which makes festivals easier to plan. Some include thousands of children, who represent every level of advancement. The festivals are arranged so that, as the number of performers increases, the level of the music's difficulty decreases. The most advanced students play first. After performing their repertoire, a less experienced group joins them and together they play the next lower level of music. This pattern continues until, when the youngest students join in, the entire assembly plays the beginners' literature, including the centerpiece of that level of Talent Education music, "Twinkle, Twinkle Little Star." Suzuki festivals are public showcases for students, for whose talents and skills they are especially created and designed, just as school band, orchestra, and chorus concerts are structured for the special skills of those performing groups. The festivals are excellent public relations devices, and they seldom fail to convince their audiences that Talent Education is a viable, successful method of bringing children to a much more advanced level than is normally expected of them in music, or any other endeavor.

TALENT EDUCATION IN THE UNITED STATES

Americans encountered Talent Education in 1958, when it was introduced at a meeting of the American String Teachers Association (ASTA) at Oberlin College. The teachers, viewing a film of 750 Japanese children playing the Bach Concerto for Two Violins, were awed by the technical and musical levels of the young musicians. ASTA decided to send a representative to Japan to observe the method in person. After Suzuki himself extended an invitation, John Kendall journeyed to Japan in 1959. He returned to Japan in 1962 to continue his study of the method. In 1964 Suzuki and a group of ten children, ranging in age from 5 to 14, gave several performances in the United States, including one for the MENC convention in Philadelphia. Again, both the outstanding performance and the demonstration of the method were a revelation to American teachers. An American string teacher noted that 4- and 5-year-old Japanese children were playing music of professional caliber, while American children usually did not begin to study the violin until age 9 or 10. Talent Education quickly began to develop in the United States. It was adjusted to suit American conditions, but its integrity was preserved. Several American string educators, including John Kendall, Paul Rolland, and Tibor Zelig, developed successful American Suzuki programs based on their own adaptations of the method. They published many articles and instructional materials to support American Talent Education.

One reason for the differences between the American and Japanese versions of the method was that, in the 1960s, most Americans did not recognize the feasibility of intense instruction for preschool children. This made it difficult for American teachers to find preschool students. Attitudes toward the education of young children have changed since then. Private Talent Education schools have been established, and public school systems also offer Suzuki instruction. In many cases, programs do not have much parental involvement because of work schedules. Japan, with its increase in two-income families, is beginning to experience the same problem. Undoubtedly, Japanese Talent Education teachers must make similar adjustments.

Suzuki Talent Education has proved beyond doubt that young children are capable of performing advanced string literature. It is controversial, though, because many Talent Education students do not join school orchestras. Talent Education advocates point out that training orchestra musicians is not their purpose. This controversy has prevented a greater proliferation of Talent Education programs in public schools. Despite criticisms, however, the Talent Education movement continues to grow and flourish.

After Talent Education became well established in the United States, it expanded to other instruments. It now includes violin, viola, cello, piano, flute, harp, guitar, and double bass instruction. These instruments are usually made in smaller sizes for children. In the case of the flute, a curved headjoint, similar to that of the bass flute, makes the instrument shorter and more easily manipulated, even by children with short arms and little fingers.

The Suzuki Association of the Americas sponsors biennial meetings, and publishes six issues of *The American Suzuki Journal* each year. SAA is located at P.O. Box 17310, Boulder, CO 80308.

Comprehensive Musicianship

The Manhattanville Music Curriculum Program

We must stop pretending that we have the sacrosanct perspective and the duty to inflict it, in our terms, on captive students. Real education is not a study about things; it is experience inside things. If music is an expressive medium, learning involves expressing. If it is a creative art, learning means creating. If music has meaning, personal judgments are fundamental to the learning process. If music is a communicative art, the educational process must involve students in communication. Facts may be taught, but meaning is discovered. There is nothing antecedent to discovering meaning.[37]

Ronald Thomas, Director
Manhattanville Music Curriculum Program

Thomas's statement is the basic premise of the Manhattanville Music Curriculum Program (MMCP). The MMCP, funded by a grant from the U. S. Office of Education, was named after Manhattanville College of the Sacred Heart in Purchase, New York, where it originated. Thomas's objective was to develop a sequential music learning program for the primary grades through high school. The project produced the *Synthesis* (a comprehensive curriculum for grades 3–12), *Interaction* (an early-childhood curriculum), and three feasibility studies: the Electronic Keyboard Laboratory; the Science-Music Program; and the Instrumental Program. On completion of these materials, there were twenty-three university-sponsored teacher reeducation workshops in various parts of the country.[38]

> In all phases of operation and in the curriculums which were produced, the project has presented alternatives to the status quo. . . . From the ground up, in rationales, objectives, musical perspectives, structure of concepts, learning processes, educational expectations, even in consideration of what a music class is, the MMCP curricula have been grounded in the logic of a viable art and contemporary educational ideas.[39]

EXPLORATORY STUDY

The MMCP began in 1965 with Thomas's exploratory study of ninety-two innovative and experimental music programs in thirty-six states. He discovered six common factors:

1. Each program had clearly defined objectives.
2. The students' frame of reference was a basic concern in planning instruction.
3. The relationship of skill and cognitive growth was a primary factor in program development.

4. Teachers assumed the role of resource persons and guided students rather than imposed knowledge on them.

5. Development of skills and cognitive learning depended on the individual student's ability to accept responsibility; students were given the opportunity to learn by trial and error and by hunch.

6. The teachers had active musical lives outside of their schools.[40]

THE PROJECT

During the first of the three phases of MMCP, Thomas reflected on the validity of traditional music education values and practices. He concluded that innovative procedures were needed because students do not learn as teachers expect them to. He found a contradiction between teachers' classroom style and students' learning styles. Thomas contemplated the unconventional classroom, stating: "A basic core of concepts and related factors of skill development, environment, process, and objectives were shaped from the observed logic and enthusiasm of students in the experimental classrooms."[41] The results of Phase One made it painfully clear that students neither heard music the way teachers thought they did, nor did they understand what teachers thought they should. They perceived music in a way that was valid for themselves, notwithstanding the teacher's values. Student perceptions were based on their own interests, observations, and ideas of form and structure.

In the second phase, Thomas approached the task of refining and synthesizing the Phase One data with the conviction that the curriculum had to consist of more than just information and concepts. It would have to be an integrated plan designed to meet the needs of the students, the subject matter, and the educational objectives. Before planning for this kind of curriculum, he had to define the fundamental characteristics of music that would serve as the basis of musical and educational decisions throughout the curriculum-writing process. The spiral curriculum took shape during Phase Two. "Spiral" means a sequence of concepts in the curriculum, each of which is presented several times at various stages of development. Every successive presentation of a concept is at a higher, more refined level. The results of Phase Two were tested in selected classrooms, which Thomas called experimental stations.

During Phase Three, Thomas found the spiral curriculum unsuitable for very young children, and he developed a precycle program for kindergarten through grade 2. Working with the Central Atlantic Regional Educational Laboratory (CAREL), he explored and tested the precycle program, just as he had done with the spiral curriculum during the previous two years.

The study of teacher in-service programs, which began during Phase Three, addressed four issues:

1. Teachers did not know enough about music to work with students creatively.

2. Teachers found it difficult to consider goals other than skill achievement and performance.

3. Many teachers were method oriented and found it difficult to work in a new framework.

4. Many teachers had not personally experienced creative accomplishment and were therefore not secure in an atmosphere of creativity.

THE PRODUCTS OF MMCP

In fulfillment of the original grant proposal for the MMCP, Thomas produced four items: (1) a curriculum guide and related material for a sequential music program; (2) a meaningful sequence of basic musical concepts in terms of the students' understanding; (3) a spiral curriculum that would unify the philosophies and directions of all levels of the music curriculum; and (4) a curriculum that would allow teachers to use MMCP effectively.

CURRICULUM GUIDES

The project's major curriculum was the MMCP *Synthesis*, which offers learning experiences that grow from the student perspective. The *Synthesis* is a flexible guide, rather than a tightly structured syllabus. The goal of *Interaction* is the musical experience in which children become involved as creative and active musicians. They make judgments and discover new ideas, sounds, and meanings. The inherent goals are sensitivity to the elements, materials, and expressive possibilities of music. Formal musical concepts are approached informally in five phases: free exploration; guided exploration; exploratory improvisation; planned improvisation; and reinforcement. Other Manhattanville curriculum guides include the *Electronic Keyboard Laboratory*, the *Science-Music Laboratory*, the *Instrumental Program*, the *Teacher Re-education Program*, and the *College Curriculum Study*.

THE APPLICATIONS OF MMCP

MMCP encourages children to listen to the sounds of their environment and to create their own sounds by clapping, stamping, tapping, snapping, scraping, whistling, moaning, and so on. Groups of children put together sounds to form compositions, which they analyze and discuss. As they develop concepts of form, balance, and contrast, their sound combinations become more refined and begin to reflect aesthetic sensitivity in their planning and execution. Children start using more musical sounds that involve melody and rhythm, and begin to develop their own notational systems. Eventually, this creative approach leads children through several stages of exploration and creativity until they develop the ability to perceive, perform, and create music that is satisfying to them.

Music, as defined by MMCP director Ronald Thomas, is a vehicle for communication. It also interprets one's environment, and is a means

FIGURE 5.2. MMCP Curriculum Concept Spiral

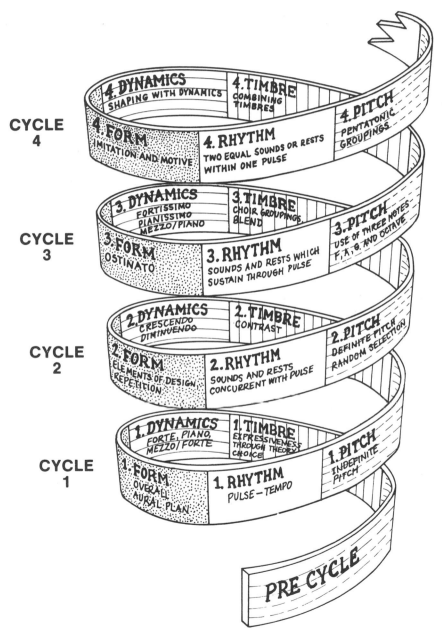

Note: Ronald B. Thomas, *MMCP Final Report*, Part 1 Abstract (United States Office of Education, ED 045 865, August 1970), pp. 39-49

of creative fulfillment. Children must develop certain skills to use music for these purposes. They must be able to hear music the way the composer does, to think in the medium of music, to conceptualize and recognize musical structure, and to comprehend the language of musical sounds.[42] Students need to study music in an unfragmented manner to experience all aspects of music. They compose, perform, conduct, listen, and evaluate. The purpose of this comprehensive approach is to stimulate the development of sensitivity to musical meaning so the student can get beyond the mechanics. Thomas writes, "He does not simply stand back and observe it with reverence—he uses it as a means of creating, exploring, and in his own way, achieving."[43]

CYCLE 1

TIMBRE. The quality or color of sound, the timbre, is a major factor in musical expressiveness. The timbre may be shrill, intense, dulcet, silvery, nasal, smooth, bright, or dull. The composer must select the most appropriate timbre for a particular piece.

DYNAMICS. The composer must also determine the dynamics of the sound. Volume affects the expressive result.

PITCH. The composer decides on the comparative highness or lowness of sounds. The choices deal with sounds of indefinite pitch like those produced by a triangle, a cymbal, or a drum. The highness or lowness of indefinite pitch are determined by the preceding or following sounds. A cymbal sounds low after a triangle, but high after a large drum.

FORM. The plan of a piece—its shape, or form—is another determination made by the composer. Plan refers to the aural design, the way the sounds are put together. The plan is based on the composer's intent.

RHYTHM. Tempo is the characteristic of music that makes it go fast or slow. The pulse is the underlying beat (sometimes not heard but only sensed) that may help to create a feeling of motion in music. These items must also be selected by the composer.

FIGURE 5.3. MMCP Spiral Level 1

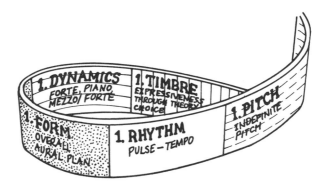

CYCLE 1 SKILLS

AURAL

Identify the general and comparative pitch characteristics of sounds of indefinite pitch (differences between drum sounds, cluster sounds made by objects, etc.).

Identify various timbres used in the classroom and the instruments used to produce them.

Identify volume differences in student compositions and in illustrative recordings.

Identify pulse and changes in tempo. Recognize simple sequences.

DEXTEROUS

In performing:

Produce sounds (vocal or instrumental) at the instant they are demanded and control the ending of the sound.

Produce the desired tone quality (vocal and instrumental).

Produce sounds of three volume levels (f, p, mf) when allowed by the nature of the instrument.

Maintain the tempo when necessary.

In conducting:

Indicate precisely when to begin and when to end.

Indicate pulse, where appropriate (not meter).

Indicate desired volume.

Indicate general character.

Translative

Devise graphic symbols, charts, or designs of musical ideas that allow for retention and reproduction.

Visual translations should represent the overall plan and include distinguishing signs for different instruments or timbres, and relative durational factors.

Volume should be indicated by the standard symbols: f, p, mf.

Words designating the character of the music, such as quietly, forcefully, smoothly, or happily, should also be used.

Vocabulary

Timbre	Form	Indefinite pitch	Volume
Dynamics	Tempo	Aural	Improvise
Forte	Pulse	Devised notation	Composer

Piano	Pitch	Cluster	Conductor
Mezzo	Forte		Performer

Cycle 1 Sample Strategy

The Quality or Color of Sound, the Timbre, Is a Major Factor in the Expressiveness of Music

- Each student selects an item or object in the room with which he can produce a sound. Preferably, the item or object will be something other than a musical instrument.

- After sufficient time has been allowed for students to experiment with sounds or selected objects, each student may perform his sound at the location of the item in the room.

- Focus on "listening" to the distinctive qualities of sounds performed. Encourage students to explore other sound possibilities with the item of their choice.

- Discuss any points of interest raised by the students. Extend the discussion by including the following questions:

  How many different kinds of sounds were discovered?

  Could the sounds be put into categories of description, i.e., shrill, dull, bright, intense, etc.?

  After categories of sound have been established, experiment with combinations of sounds.

- Is there any difference between sounds performed singly and sounds performed in combination?

- In listening to the recorded examples focus on the use of timbre.

- How many different kinds of sounds were used?

- Could we put any of the sounds in this composition into the categories we established earlier, i.e., bright, dull, shrill, etc."

- Were there any new categories of sounds? Could we duplicate these?

Assignment

Each student should bring one small object from home on which he can produce three distinctly different sounds. The object may be a brush, a bottle, a trinket or anything made of wood, metal, plastic, etc.

Suggested Listening Examples:

"Steel Drums," Wond Steel Band, Fold 8367

"Prelude and Fugue for Percussion," Charles Wuorinen, GC 4004

"Ballet Mechanique," George Antheil, Urania (5) 134

The Plan, the Shape, the Order of a Piece of Music Is Determined by the Composer

- Each student may perform his three sounds at his own desk. Focus on "listening" to distinctive qualities of sounds performed.

- Encourage students to focus attention on other exploratory possibilities by investigating the sound-producing materials with greater depth.

  Can you produce a sound on your object that is bright, dull, shrill, intense, etc.?

  How is this done?

- Discuss any points of interest relative to the activity.

- Extend the discussion by focusing on the following questions:

  Why is silence in the room necessary for performance to be effective?

  How did sounds vary or seem similar?

  Which objects produced the brightest, dullest, most shrill, most intense sounds?

  What makes a sound dull, bright, intense, etc.?

- Divide the class into groups of 5 or 6 students. A conductor-composer should be selected by each group. He will determine the order of sounds and the overall plan of the improvisation. Conducting signals should be devised and practiced in each group so that directions will be clear.

- Allow approximately 10 minutes for planning and rehearsal. At the end of the designated time each group will perform.

- Tape all improvisations for playback and evaluation. Discussion should focus around the following questions.

  Did the Improvisation have a good plan?

  Did the music hold together?

  What was the most satisfying factor in this piece?

  How would you change the improvisation?

  What are some of the conductor's concerns?

- In listening to the recorded examples, focus attention to the overall shape or plan of the music. In listening to a single example two or three times, students may map out a shape or a plan that represents the composition. These plans can be compared and used for repeated listenings.

  Suggested Listening Examples:

  "Construction in Metal," John Cage, KO8P-1498

  "Poéme Electronique," Edgar Varése, Col ML5478; MS6164

The Degree of Loudness or Softness, the Volume or the Dynamics of the Sound, Will Affect the Total Expressive Result

- Using the entire class as performers on object instruments, volunteer students will conduct an exploratory improvisation to investigate the effects of sounds used singly, sounds used in combination, and dynamics. It is suggested that before the improvisation the volunteer conductors choose 3 or 4 students who will play singly when directed. Conducting cues for entrances and exits should also be established.

- Tape the exploratory improvisations for immediate playback and evaluation. Discuss all perceptions verbalized by the students. Extend the discussion by including the following questions:

  How did volume or dynamics affect the total result?

  Can all the object instruments be heard at an equal level of volume when performed in a group?

- Groups consisting of 4 or 5 students will plan an improvisation. Focus attention to the quality of sounds used singly, the quality of sounds used in combination, and the expressive use of volume. Consideration for the overall shape of the piece should also be a concern.

- Following a short planning and practicing period (about 10 minutes), each group will perform the improvisation for the class.

- Tape the improvisations for immediate playback and evaluation. Discuss students' comments as they relate to the improvisations. Extend the discussion by focusing attention on the following questions.

  What degree of loudness or softness was used most frequently by the performing groups?

  Did the improvisations have an overall shape or design?

- Summarize the discussion by introducing forte (f), piano (p), and mezzo-forte (mf). In listening to the recorded examples, ask students to identify the dynamic level used most frequently by the composer.

- Did you get any musical ideas from this composition that you might be able to use?

  Suggested Listening Examples

  "Parade," Morton Gould, Columbia CL 1533

  "Te Deum, Judex Crederis," Hector Berlioz, Columbia ML 4897

  "Prélude á l'Aprés-midi d'un faune," Claude Debussy, London LS 503

- Allow 30 seconds for each class member to think of an unusual vocal sound. The sound can be made with the throat, voice, lips, breath or tongue.

- Each student may perform his\her sound for the class. Focus "listening" on the distinctive qualities of the vocal sounds performed.

- Discuss any points of interest raised by the students. Extend the discussion by including some of the following questions.

  Did anyone perform his\her sound long enough to communicate a feeling of motion?

  How would you describe the motion?

- Divide the class into groups consisting of 4 or 5 students. One person in each of the groups should be a conductor. Each group will concentrate on producing their individual sounds to the motion of an item of their choice or one that has been suggested to them, e.e., the steady motion of a carpenter hammering a nail, the steady motion of a worm crawling, the steady motion of a person jogging, the steady motion of a horse galloping, etc.

- Allow approximately 10 minutes for groups to plan and practice their improvisations. At the end of the designated time each group will perform.

- Tape each improvisation for immediate playback and analysis. Discuss any comments made by the students. Extend the discussion by including the following questions:

  How would you describe the motion, slow, medium, or fast? Did it have a steady beat or pulse?

- Summarize the discussion by introducing tempo as the characteristic that refers to the speed of music and pulse which is the underlying beat (sometimes not heard but only sensed).

- In listening to the recorded examples, focus attention on the use of tempo.

  How would you describe the tempo, slow, medium, or fast?

  Did the pulse or underlying beat change before the end of the composition?

  What was the effect?

  Suggested Listening Examples:

  "Flight of the Bumblebee," Nicolai Rimski-Korsakov, Epic LC 3759

  "String Quartet No. 79, Op. 76, No. 5, Joseph Haydn, Turnabout TV 34012S

The Contemporary Music Project

Comprehensive musicianship is the term used to describe the interdisciplinary study of music. Traditionally, music courses separate the various aspects of the subject. History and theory, for example, are taught as separate and unrelated courses, often by different instructors who make little attempt to relate the two subjects. This is even more true of applied music, in which students often do not learn the relationship between music literature, historical and stylistic periods, and the theoretical systems that underpin the literature. Their fragmented view of music prevents them from developing insights necessary for true musical understanding. The Contemporary Music Project, described in chapter 2, brought together a distinguished group of musicians and music educators to devise a systematic effort to solve the problem. Its recommendations served as the tenets of comprehensive musicianship:

1. The content and orientation of musicianship training should serve all music degree students regardless of their eventual specialization.

2. Comprehensive musicianship training incorporates conceptual knowledge with technical skills to develop the capacity to experience fully and the ability to communicate the content of a musical work.

3. The courses in musicianship training should be designed to synthesize knowledge acquired in all other musical studies.

4. All musicianship studies should relate contemporary thought and practices with those of former times.

5. Musicianship courses should be considered as evolving and open-ended disciplines. The student must be given the means to seek and deal with materials outside and beyond formal education in music.

6. The relevance of musicianship training to professional studies should be made clear to the student. The clarity of purpose may be achieved if musicianship training is based on the student's own musical development and expressive needs.

7. Courses constituting comprehensive musicianship training are directly related to each other. The study of any specific subject matter need not be confined to a given course but approached in several ways in other complementary disciplines.[44]

The Uses of Comprehensive Musicianship

Comprehensive musicianship practices were adopted gradually as the findings of the Contemporary Music Project were disseminated, but relatively few colleges instituted comprehensive musicianship programs. Those that did usually combined the study of performance, theory, and history. The concept had more impact in the elementary and secondary schools, especially in relation to performing ensembles. Directors of bands, orchestras, and choruses adopted comprehensive musicianship ideas and practices because traditional performance-oriented music programs, excellent though they were, often did little to enhance the musicality of individual students. Many music educators questioned the value of this kind of activity and concluded that individual growth and development are more important than collective results.

Traditionally, American school performance ensembles have had no formal curriculum. Instead, the music played by a group is the curriculum. If a high school band prepares twenty-five pieces during one school year, then the curriculum for one particular student might be the second clarinet parts of those twenty-five pieces. What the student learns about music history, style, theory, and analysis is usually serendipitous. R. Jack Mercer discussed the deficiency of this kind of curriculum:

> There are few band curricula that take the student through the basics of music theory and history. Instead, scores are selected to meet the requirements of the next performance, and the curriculum is the score. Consequently, the content of the course of study is fortuitous, depending almost entirely upon whether it is football season or concert season. . . . The goal of musical training is to present a polished musical performance.[45]

Often, the ensemble is a public relations unit of the educational system and provides an enjoyable recreational activity for its members. Charles Benner cautions, however, that this is not necessarily good music education: "It can be inferred that performing participation has little effect on musical behavior other than the acquisition of performance skills, unless there is a planned effort by the teacher to enrich the performing experience with additional kinds of musical understanding."[46]

The solution to the problem lies in the music performed; used properly, it can be the basis for learning about music. Joseph Labuta offers a definition of musicianship as it applies to student performers in a comprehensive sense: "The term 'musicianship' is often used when referring to comprehensive musical attributes and abilities of performers. It is theory applied to practice; it is knowledge and skill applied to practical music making."[47]

Authors have published many books and articles to help directors use music as the basis for broader musical learning. Instructional materials include analytical, theoretical, and historical information that is compatible with a comprehensive approach. In *Blueprint for Band*, Robert Garofalo describes the director's responsibilities in a comprehensive musicianship situation:

> To organize a viable program of studies that correlates instrumental music performance with the study of music structure and style, and encompasses a diversity of musical behaviors—performing, listening, analyzing, composing, conducting, arranging; and . . . to establish a stimulating musical environment in which students are continuously brought into contact with the "creative musical experience" either directly or indirectly.[48]

FIGURE 5.4. Blueprint of Objectives

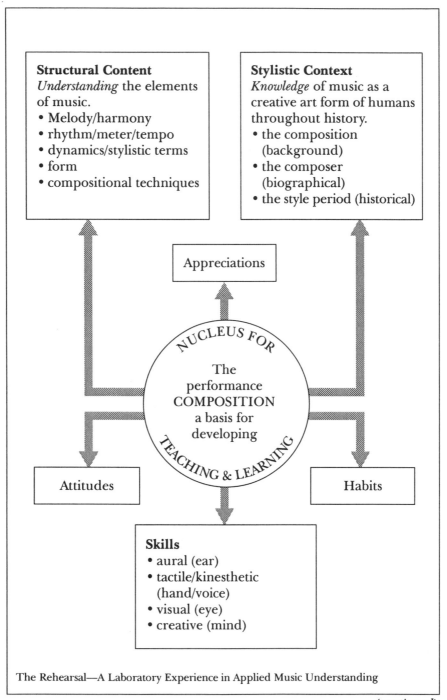

Structural Content
Understanding the elements of music.
• Melody/harmony
• rhythm/meter/tempo
• dynamics/stylistic terms
• form
• compositional techniques

Stylistic Context
Knowledge of music as a creative art form of humans throughout history.
• the composition (background)
• the composer (biographical)
• the style period (historical)

Appreciations

NUCLEUS FOR

The performance COMPOSITION a basis for developing

TEACHING & LEARNING

Attitudes

Habits

Skills
• aural (ear)
• tactile/kinesthetic (hand/voice)
• visual (eye)
• creative (mind)

The Rehearsal—A Laboratory Experience in Applied Music Understanding

(*continued*)

```
(Clarification of Skills)
Skills:
    Aural (ear)
        1. Identification of the elements of music(see under Content)
            a. melodies & harmonies (including intonation)
            b. rhythms, meters & tempos (including ensemble)
            c. timbres/textures (including tone quality and blend)
            d. intensities (including balance)
        2. extended listening skills (form and compositional techniques)
    Tactile/Kinesthetic (hand/voice)
        1. playing
        2. conducting
        3. singing
        4. music writing
    Visual (eye)
        1. music reading
            a. individual parts
            b. multiple parts
        2. sight reading
    Creative (mind)
        1. composing
        2. improvising
        3. arranging/transcribing
```

Used with permission, Meredith Music Publications, 170 N.E. 33rd Street, Fort Lauderdale, FL 33334

Garofalo takes understanding, knowledge, and skills into account. He suggests that rehearsals be planned to meet specific objectives that arise from each musical composition. The composition is both played and studied.[49] He provides an outline of the areas for which objectives might be developed. In his 1994 book, *Instructional Designs for Middle/Junior High School Band*,[50] Garofalo presents instructional units for teaching music through rehearsals of several standard band pieces.

This approach requires a different kind of preparation by the director, who must set long-term goals, and conduct each rehearsal as a combination of rehearsal, class, and laboratory. It necessitates outside work by individual students beyond regular daily practicing, as well as additional equipment and facilities. The performance ensemble can serve a valuable educational function for its individual members, but the addition of comprehensive music activities might prevent the ensemble from fulfilling all of its traditional functions, at least in terms of numbers of performances. The director risks not meeting community and school expectations. Garofalo argues, however, that performance standards should not be compromised:

It must be clearly understood that the proposed curriculum is not antiperformance. The band must continue to work toward achieving the highest level of performance it is capable of attaining. Performance standards must not be slighted in any way. Indeed, a high level of performance is a necessary condition for any comprehensive musicianship curriculum of this type. Furthermore, evidence has shown that when students are taught both concepts and skills through the performance repertoire, they perform as well or better because they understand the music they are playing.[51]

The Hawaii Music Curriculum Program

Comprehensive musicianship has also been explored in relation to general music, which provides broad musical knowledge for students, often to a greater degree than performance ensembles. Sometimes, however, children's experiences in general music classes are too narrow to permit them to develop musical concepts and knowledge of various styles of music. This can happen when children do not have in-depth performance experiences that validate the conceptual knowledge developed in class. Also, the curriculum is often based on discrete units that address nonmusical topics. This approach to the historical and sociological aspects of music does not explore the music itself in any depth. The practice is not, however, as widespread as it was before basal series began to incorporate sequential learning programs. A number of teacher education texts have also influenced teaching practices. One such text is *Comprehensive Musicianship through Classroom Music*, published in 1974.[52] It is the result of the Hawaii Music Curriculum Program, which began in 1968 at the Hawaii Curriculum Center in Honolulu. The Center was awarded the total ESEA Title III allotment for Hawaii, and designated some of that money for the statewide Fine Arts Exemplary Activities Program. The program's purpose was "to create a logical, continuous educational program ensuring the competent guidance of the music education of all children in the state's public schools and to test and assemble the materials needed by schools to realize this problem."[53] The initial plan for the project, described here, was carried out, although it evolved to something different from what was tested in schools.

According to the Hawaii Music Curriculum Program, the term "comprehensive" means that students will be involved with music in school in the same ways in which people are involved with music outside of the schools—as composers, performers, listeners, and scholars. The curriculum is based on seven concepts—tone, rhythm, melody, harmony, form, tonality, and texture—which are presented in the form of a spiral curriculum. A taxonomy of musical concepts that progressed from the general to the specific, and from the simple to the complex, was created. For example, the concept of rhythm forms early in a child's life.

FIGURE 5.5. The Hawaii Music Curriculum Project
Teaching Media Charted Relative to Instructional Zones

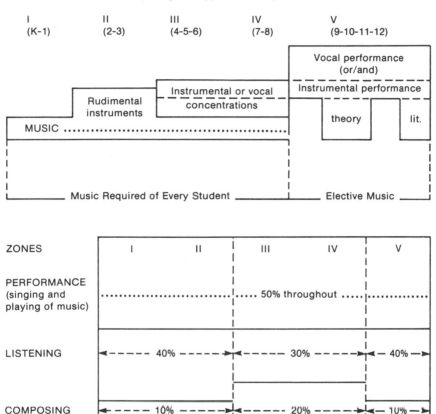

ZONES OF INSTRUCTION (with grade approximations)

Note: Reprinted by permission of Curriculum Research and Development Group, College of Education, University of Hawaii

The child deals with rhythm in an increasingly complex and sophisticated progression throughout the curriculum. The taxonomy of concepts was translated into a curriculum that covers the entire K–12 music experience. It is an ungraded curriculum that represents "levels of sophistication," rather than formal school grade levels. Students progress through the curriculm at their own rates. The curriculum has five divisions, or zones:

> *Zone I*: General music, consisting of singing; playing on rudimental instruments such as recorder, autoharp, bells, and the usual trappings of the traditional elementary music class; listening, composing, discussing, and a rudimentary kind of research; introduction to the graphic representation of musical sounds.
> *Zone II*: Essentially a continuation of Zone I, but with greater emphasis on performance with rudimentary instrument; introduction to reading and writing of standard musical notation.
> *Zone III*: Introduction to performance on various traditional instruments and singing as a technique; vocal, brass, woodwind, percussion, and string categories during the first third of the zone; selection of "major" instrument concentration (including vocal) during final two-thirds of zone; continuation of activities of previous two zones.
> *Zone IV*: Formation of ensemble groups that permit playing for special interest combinations; continuation of listening, composing, analyzing work along with ensemble performance.
> *Zone V*: Continuation of ensembles, addition (for those who so elect) of music theory, and/or music literature courses (grades 9–10); participation in a music ensemble as prerequisite for election of theory course; and/or advanced music literature course.[54]

Each area of instruction is divided into objectives, learning activities, and evaluative procedures. The objectives are stated in behavioral terms, and the learning activities involve students with music as composers, performers, listeners, and scholars. The evaluative procedures are of several kinds. Some require "high level cognitive behavior such as analysis, synthesis, and evaluation."[55]

Thomson states that, despite the traditional appearance of the curriculum, "the separate classes comprising the zones—including band, chorus, and orchestra—are to be regarded not as ends in themselves, but rather as contexts for learning musical concepts."[56]

Summary

Many ensemble directors have implemented comprehensive musicianship practices, and have been pleased to find that their students learn more about music and have more positive attitudes toward music. Those directors, however, have to be willing to accept a lower quality of performance from their ensembles. They have had to do more traditional teaching, which requires a different distribution of time, effort, and other resources. These problems are often difficult to overcome, as are the community expectations of normal performance and entertainment by school ensembles. Despite its promise of musicality in performance ensemble, comprehensive musicianship never took hold to the extent that it permanently influenced school performing groups. School districts that adopt the national arts education standards (see chapter 4), however, might find that the realization of comprehensive musicianship philosophy and practices will help them achieve their curricular goals.

Music Learning Theory

by Edwin E. Gordon[a]

I wanted to gather information on how we learn when we learn music, or, in current terminology, how audiation is developed and sustained. Unlike my colleagues, I had little interest in techniques, that is, in how to teach. I needed to know what should be learned, when it should be learned, and why it should be learned.

Edwin Gordon, 1991[57]

Music learning theory is primarily an explanation of how students of all ages learn music; it is not intended to explain how they should be taught music. Music learning theory offers a specific description of the ways in which the types and stages of audiation (hearing and comprehending music without the sound being physically present) ideally occur as students are exposed to and interact with tonal patterns and rhythm patterns in familiar and unfamiliar music.

The terms "music learning theory," "music learning sequences," and "learning sequence activities" will be used frequently. Learning sequences activities are used to put music learning theory into practice. The three music learning sequences are skill learning sequence; tonal content learning sequence, which includes tonal pattern learning sequence; and rhythm content learning sequence, which includes rhythm pattern learning sequence. All three are necessary because skill learning sequence can function only in conjunction with one of the other two learning sequences. When we first introduce, for example, skill learning sequence at the aural/oral level to students just beginning formal instruction in listening to and performing music through audiation, we must choose the music best suited to these students on the basis of either tonal content learning sequence or rhythm content learning

---

[a]This chapter is freely adapted from material found in two of my books: *Learning Sequences in Music: Skill, Content, and Patterns* (Chicago: GIA, 1993), and *A Music Learning Theory for Newborn and Young Children* (Chicago: GIA, 1990). For further information, particularly about audiation, music aptitudes, and rhythm, I recommend *Learning Sequences*, and particularly about preparatory audiation, *A Music Learning Theory*. Used with permission of GIA.

sequence. Skills are taught in conjunction with tonal content or rhythm content.

Discrimination and Inference

Discrimination learning is fundamental because it provides us with the necessary readiness for inference learning, which is the more conceptual of the two. Discrimination and inference learning occur together as one or the other receives the greater emphasis. Rote learning, in the form of imitation or memorization, is crucial to discrimination learning; it provides the basis for the later generalization and abstraction that occurs in inference learning. We make only simple inferences as we are engaging in discrimination learning, but we use much, if not all, of what we have discriminated as we engage in inference learning.

When students learn to sing a song by rote, or when they perform a piece of music after memorizing it from score, they have engaged in discrimination learning, having learned to discriminate among pitches and durations in a given piece. Inference learning occurs when students are unconscious of what they are learning or even that they are learning, because they are teaching themselves the unfamiliar by inferring from the familiar. The more facts and ideas students can discriminate among, the more inferences they will be able to make.

For the purpose of explaining music learning theory, I have outlined its levels and sublevels. After each level or sublevel of learning is achieved in skill learning sequence, it becomes incorporated into the next higher level or sublevel in the skill learning sequence. Just as inference learning incorporates and interacts with discrimination learning, so every level of learning incorporates and interacts with all the previous levels of learning. Only the first few minutes of a class period or rehearsal would ever be given over to learning sequence activities, and the remainder of the class time reserved for classroom or performance activities. Ideally, these activities are coordinated with learning sequence activities because all three enhance students' audiation skills by reinforcing one another.

Discrimination Learning

AURAL/ORAL

Achievement at the aural/oral level involves continuous back and forth interaction between the aural and the oral; when students hear tonal patterns or rhythm patterns and then sing or chant what they have heard, they learn to listen to those patterns with more precision, and can go on to perform them with yet more precision. Students develop audiation skill by means of this continuous learning loop.

Both listening and singing are necessary for the audiation potential to be realized. Learning to sing what one listens to enhances music

Figure 5.6. Levels and Sublevels of Skill Learning Sequence

I. Discrimination
    A. Aural/Oral
    B. Verbal Association
    C. Partial Synthesis
    D. Symbolic Association
         Reading-Writing
    E. Composite Synthesis
         Reading-Writing
II. Inference
    A. Generalization
      Aural/Oral
      Verbal
      Symbolic
    B. Creativity/Improvisation
      Aural/Oral
      Symbolic
    C. Theoretical Understanding
      Aural/Oral
      Verbal
      Symbolic

appreciation; when students sing without listening, they develop poor intonation and rhythm, and worse yet, they lack musical expression and style. Think of sports. Can you ever really appreciate what you see on the field if you have never, at some time, played the game yourself? Likewise, doesn't your own playing improve when you observe others playing with a higher degree of skill and sophistication? There might be so many sports fans because the "visual/kinesthetic" approach to learning in physical education is so common. It might be equally true that there are relatively few persons who appreciate music through understanding because the aural/oral level in music education is so rarely taught.

How well students learn to audiate depends not only on their music aptitude, but on the size of their vocabularies of aural and oral tonal patterns and rhythm patterns. Just as the word is the basic unit of meaning in language, so the pattern is the basic unit of meaning in music. It is words, not individual letters, that make possible our understanding of language, and so the more words students have in their listening and speaking vocabularies, the better they are able to think about what is said to them and the better able they are to draw conclusions of their own. Students with limited musical vocabularies are likely to imitate, rather than audiate. Thus, it is more important for students to audiate many patterns, even if they cannot read any of them, than to audiate a few patterns that they can read.

In accordance with music learning theory, students begin immediately at the aural/oral level to learn a variety of tonal patterns in various tonalities. The more tonal patterns they learn and the sooner they are able to identify them in Dorian, Mixolydian, major, and harmonic minor tonalities, the better. Students cannot learn too many tonal patterns and rhythm patterns at the aural/oral level of learning.

It is important when children are learning a language that stories be read aloud to them. A similar approach is recommended for students of all ages learning music. When students are at the aural/oral level in learning sequence activities, songs, chants, and larger forms of music should be performed for them in classroom activities.

VERBAL ASSOCIATION

In addition to carrying forth internal syntactic meaning, at the verbal association level we also give objective external nonsyntactic meaning to what we are audiating. External meaning may be, for example, the association of letter names, time value names, names of intervals, and tonal syllables and rhythm syllables with patterns.

Students learn to respond through audiation to a broader range of music as a result of developing their tonal pattern and rhythm pattern vocabularies. Without verbal association, however, students find it increasingly difficult to discriminate among the additional patterns they need to learn. When more and more patterns are learned with a neutral syllable, the patterns begin to sound alike to the students unless they can organize them by syllable names in audiation. Thus, verbal association makes possible students' retention and recall of patterns, tonalities, and meters for use in higher levels of discrimination learning and in all levels of inference learning. This is particularly true in creativity/improvisation, because without verbal association, even patterns that were once solid in audiation at the aural/oral level using a neutral syllable may be lost.

As we acquire language, the aural/oral and verbal association levels of learning naturally occur together because we develop our initial language skill to name the objects we see. A similar type of visual/verbal process is impossible in music development, however, because when we first hear tonal patterns and rhythm patterns performed, our immediate desire is simply to listen to, and discover, patterns (perhaps as a way to make what is unfamiliar appear familiar); we feel no internal need to apply names to what we are hearing. Thus in music, we need an additional level of learning to teach the verbal association of proper names and syllable names. If, for no other reason than that, general theories of learning cannot be applied to music learning theory.

To understand all that is involved in the verbal association level of learning, it is necessary to understand the distinction between signs and symbols as the terms are used in music learning theory. Consider that the signs are the sounds of the pitches and durations we hear, whereas symbols are the written notes we see as the representations of those sounds. In other words, signs present and symbols represent. When students learn to give names to the sounds they audiate at the verbal association level, the sounds (pitches and durations) and names (verbal associations) in a tonality or a meter seem inseparable, combining into one sign as a simple pitch or duration.

A comprehensive sign is any tonal pattern or rhythm pattern. Students learn how to audiate many comprehensive signs in different tonalities and meters at the verbal association level, once again using tonal syllables and rhythm syllables. Only when that is accomplished are students ready to move on to the symbolic association level, and to higher levels of audiation of the signs represented by the symbols. At these levels, written symbols are associated with audiated signs. Signs are audiated; they should never be read because they immediately lose their value as signs and are inadvertently transformed in the minds of students into symbols.

As students learn to audiate and to perform tonal patterns and rhythm patterns, they should also be learning about form, style, phrasing, dynamics, and tone quality, and to connect these musical ideas with their proper names. The performance of tonal patterns and rhythm patterns, being integral to musical performance, must be associated with one or more of those dimensions. Music learning theory, however, does not offer direction in sequencing those dimensions of music. This is because, whereas the tonal and rhythm dimensions constitute an observable and continuous sequence in music learning theory, the dimensions of form, style, phrasing, dynamics, and tone quality are relatively illusive. Each teacher must decide, depending on the interpretive demands of the music, how those dimensions may best be combined with the dimensions that lend themselves to music learning theory.

PARTIAL SYNTHESIS

In skill learning sequence, discrimination learning incorporates both the partial synthesis and composite synthesis levels of learning. The aural/oral and verbal association levels are synthesized into the partial synthesis level of learning, and the partial synthesis and symbolic association levels of learning are synthesized into the composite synthesis level of learning.

The partial synthesis level operates in two ways. First, as students synthesize the aural/oral and verbal association levels, they become aware of the internal logic of tonal syllables within and among tonal patterns, and of rhythm syllables within and among rhythm patterns. Thus, at the partial synthesis level of discrimination learning, inference learning begins to take place in the minds of students. At the partial synthesis level, students learn to synthesize individual patterns they are audiating into series of tonal patterns or rhythm patterns. When they hear a pattern as part of a series, students audiate and perform it differently, depending on the way the pattern interacts with the other patterns in the series. Thus, they learn to audiate pattern relationships as they are being established. To students' ears the whole becomes different from, but not necessarily greater than, the sum of its parts.

One of the purposes of the partial synthesis level is to teach students to recognize for themselves familiar tonalities and meters. Students are able to accomplish this because the tonal and rhythm patterns in each series interact with one another to establish a tonality or meter. In classroom activities and performance activities, however, tonality and meter must be established for students before they perform a piece of music in order to assist them in performing with better intonation and rhythm.

Although verb tense functions as an aspect of grammar in language, the sequential order of two or more consecutive adjectives is determined syntactically. One would say "the big red house," rather than "the red big house." Or "the big beautiful red house," rather than "the big red beautiful house." Tonal syntax, like grammar, involves orderly arrangements. Pitches are arranged within a tonal pattern, and tonal patterns within a series of tonal patterns. Rhythm syntax requires orderly arrangements of durations within a rhythm pattern, and rhythm patterns within a series of rhythm patterns. Intentionally or not, composers intend syntax in music, and conductors and performers ierpret syntax in music. Listeners must give syntax to music if they are to audiate it. Syntax cannot be taken from music; it must be given to music through audiation. However, a listener, conductor, or performer may not give the same syntax to a piece of music that a composer intended, which is why we generally speak about performance in terms of interpretation.

The importance of partial synthesis to all higher levels of learning in music learning sequence is obvious, but partial synthesis is difficult to teach. Thus, many teachers in both higher education and in the schools skip this level of discrimination learning entirely and go directly to the generalization-verbal level of inference learning. Before asking students to identify the functions of patterns, tonality, and meter in a familiar piece of music, teachers expect them to do so in an unfamiliar piece. As a result, students are never given the chance to develop skill at the partial synthesis level. They are not prepared to participate properly in higher levels of learning, including the reading of notation.

Partial synthesis skill enables students to listen to music in a musically intelligent manner. In addition to comprehending syntax in music, students become aware of humor in music. They become bored, if not annoyed, with simple-minded music that is repetitive and unnecessarily loud. They are not dependent on texts to give meaning to music, and antics and graphic displays are not interesting or useful to them as music teaching techniques.

SYMBOLIC ASSOCIATION

At the next level of discrimination learning, symbolic association, students are taught to read and write music by associating symbols with syllables, and sounds with the patterns they represent. They audiate the tonality and the meter, and perform the patterns they are reading or writing. This is called notational audiation. In the reading of notation in skill learning sequence activities (as opposed to the mere naming of notes), the sequential process moves from the symbolic association-reading level to the combined aural/oral and verbal association levels, and then to the partial synthesis level. At that point students are able to read the patterns they have learned through audiation. In writing notation, the sequential process is reversed; it moves from the combined aural/oral and verbal association levels to the partial synthesis level. Only then do students move to the symbolic association-writing level, where they write familiar patterns through audiation (as opposed to merely copying notation).

Children learn to read a language aloud before they begin to read silently. Similarly, they learn to read music notation by singing and chanting what they read before they begin to read silently. This is why it is imperative that the aural/oral and verbal association levels are taught first. It is even more important, however, that the partial synthesis level be taught as a readiness for symbolic association; otherwise, students will read and write notation without audiation, and thus without musical understanding.

Our verbal association of tonal patterns and rhythm patterns is determined by what we audiate. Therefore, our interpretation of the tonal and rhythm patterns that we perform is also determined by what we audiate, so that what we see in notation is, in a real sense, only incidental. We audiate music, and read and write music notation. Musicians should be expected to audiate everything they see in notation, but because of the imprecision of notation, they should not be expected to put into notation everything that they audiate. This means that unless we can audiate the music we read and write, we cannot expect notation to impart musical meaning. This limits us to faking when we read and write music notation. Many young pianists who cannot audiate, for example, use the piano keys like they do letter names and time-value names: as just another set of musically meaningless symbols that activate the decoding process.

Students learn to audiate tonal and rhythm syllables at the verbal association level of learning. At the symbolic association level, they learn to read and write by using the syllables that they have been taught to audiate. Let me stress again that students should be taught to read and write patterns, not individual notes. After all, reading means audiating, and then singing or chanting patterns that one sees in notation. Writing requires the same process, but in reverse.

COMPOSITE SYNTHESIS

Composite synthesis is the highest level of discrimination learning It synthesizes the partial and the symbolic association levels. At this level students learn to audiate the tonality or meter of one or more series of familiar tonal patterns or rhythm patterns in familiar or unfamiliar order as they are reading or writing the patterns. Specifically, they now audiate the tonality or meter at the same time that they are reading or writing a series of patterns. Musically intelligent reading, writing, and listening are taking place at this level.

Like the symbolic association level, the composite synthesis level has reading and writing sublevels. The same sequential process, moving from symbols to audiation when reading, and from audiation to symbols when writing, takes place at the symbolic association level and the composite synthesis level. At the symbolic association level students deal with individual patterns, whereas at the composite synthesis level they learn to deal with the simultaneous awareness of the tonality and the meter of those patterns.

At the symbolic association and composite synthesis levels of discrimination learning, students learn what music notation is, and how to read and write it. Only later, at the theoretical understanding level of inference learning, will students learn why music notation lacks consistency, and is often without internal and external logic. They learn that either a half step or a whole step, as it is audiated, may be notated on adjacent lines and spaces on the staff, and even though notes may go up on the staff, they go to the right on the piano keyboard, and down, or in another direction, on a string instrument finger board.

Inference Learning

In inference learning the instructor teaches students *how* to learn, and students teach themselves *what* to learn. Techniques using rote learning and imitation are inappropriate; instead, the teacher guides students in a process of discovery. When the teacher resorts to rote or imitation teaching, the intended inference level of learning automatically reverts back to a corresponding discrimination level of learning. In discrimination learning students recognize what is familiar, whereas in inference learning they are expected to identify what is unfamiliar on the basis of what they already know to be familiar. For example, students make inferences in audiation when they identify unfamiliar patterns by comparing their similarities and differences with patterns they already know and recognize. Students need to be taught, by rote or imitation, what and how to discriminate so they can then teach themselves through inference. The value of a good teacher to this process and the importance of the method, materials, techniques, and assessment procedures cannot be overestimated.

With continued use, skills, tonal patterns, and rhythm patterns that students teach themselves at inference levels of learning become familiar to them, and the number of patterns that they learn continually increases as long as the teacher exposes them to additional unfamiliar tonal patterns and rhythm patterns. Meanwhile, students continue to be engaged in inference learning, although they may become familiar with a particular pattern or skill; they are engaging in inference learning every time they teach themselves new and better ways to use them.

GENERALIZATION

At the generalization-aural/oral level the teacher first establishes the tonality, using a neutral syllable, and then performs two sets of familiar and unfamiliar tonal patterns. The students then indicate whether the sets sound the same or different. The same technique is used with rhythm patterns. Regardless of their musical aptitude, students find it easier to identify similar sets of patterns than different sets.

At the generalization-verbal level the teacher establishes tonality or meter using a neutral syllable, or the students repeat in solo the teacher's performance of one or more familiar and unfamiliar tonal or rhythm patterns. At this level, however, students use tonal syllables or rhythm syllables instead of the neutral syllable that the teacher used. As part of generalization-verbal learning, students are also expected to name the tonality and meter established by the teacher with patterns using a neutral syllable. If they are unable to do so satisfactorily, instruction is then be repeated at the partial synthesis level of discrimination learning, or at the generalization-aural/oral level of inference learning.

At the reading sublevel of generalization-symbolic learning, students are expected to read one or more of a mix of familiar and unfamiliar tonal and rhythm patterns, and identify the tonality and meter they are audiating as they read. This is done without the teacher's assistance.

When students are introduced to a new novel, teachers normally ask them to read it, not to sight read it. Because of the quality and quantity of guidance and instruction students receive in language-discrimination learning, they are expected to be familiar with most of the words, and they will easily make sense of most unfamiliar words in the context of the familiar ones. This is exactly what occurs in music when students are taught according to the principles of music learning theory. Because they constantly audiate what is familiar, building on what they already know, they can be expected to read a new piece of music as easily as they read a familiar piece. Thus, the term *sight reading* simply is not applicable in music any more than it is in language, at least not as it is used traditionally.

The role of music aptitude in inference learning is even more important than it is in discrimination learning. Those students with the highest tonal and rhythm development, and stabilized music aptitude, are the most successful in making generalizations. Because of the very nature of their generalizations, students automatically make similar generalizations in classroom activities and performance activities; when they perform a piece of music for the first time, for example, they might automatically associate syllables with the tonal patterns they discover, identify the tonality and meter, and engage in reading and writing activities connected with the needs of performance. When students develop skills in learning sequence activities, they soon find reason to use them in classroom activities and performance activities.

CREATIVITY/IMPROVISATION

All creativity is, to some extent, a form of improvisation, and all improvisation a form of creativity. Both embody an elaborate surface structure built on a deeper structure of essential pitches and durations. Thus, I combine creativity and improvisation into one level of learning. Nonetheless, differences exist between creativity and improvisation in terms of what is being emphasized. For example, a composer creates a composition with an internal logic of its own, whereas a jazz musician improvises a blues melody based on a standard chord progression.

Creativity and improvisation represent the unfolding of what students know, based on discriminations they have made in the past. Perhaps closer to the truth is what Bartók and Picasso have suggested: that the patterns we turn to in creativity and improvisation are likely those based on intuition and imagination developed during a child's artistic babble stages. The fact is that creativity and improvisation can be taught only indirectly. All that teachers can do is to assist students in acquiring the necessary skills and understanding that the first three levels of discrimination learning provide, allowing students to teach themselves the skills necessary for engaging in creativity and improvisation.

To create and improvise, one must have something to say. Unless students have acquired in discrimination learning the ability to audiate vocabularies of tonal patterns and rhythm patterns in various tonalities and meters, they will not possess the necessary foundation in audiation to enable them to know what they might want to say as they create and improvise. The larger the students' vocabularies, and the more varied the music they have heard in terms of style, expression, and harmonic progressions, the better able they will be to choose appropriate tonal patterns and rhythm patterns from their audiation dictionaries that contribute to the syntax and artistry of their music. Without the readiness that discrimination learning provides, students can engage only in aleatory exploration. Creativity and improvisation will become for them, as for many professional musicians, only what others can do.

Creativity/improvisation has two sublevels: aural/oral and symbolic. Further, creativity/improvisation-symbolic has two additional sublevels:

reading and writing. There is no verbal sublevel at the creativity/improvisation level, however, because after students complete the verbal association level in discrimination learning, the use of tonal and rhythm syllables to identify musical patterns, tonalities, and meters becomes simply another technique to aid in inference learning.

In creativity/improvisation-aural/oral without verbal association, the teacher establishes the tonality or meter using a neutral syllable. He or she then performs familiar and unfamiliar tonal patterns or rhythm patterns, also with a neutral syllable. The students respond by performing in solo, as if in conversation, new or different tonal patterns or rhythm patterns, also with a neutral syllable. Here, it is the aural/oral level of discrimination learning that provides the direct readiness for this activity.

At the reading sublevel of creativity/improvisation-symbolic learning, students learn to read chord symbols or figured bass. They then perform tonal patterns that correspond to the symbols, using either a neutral syllable or tonal syllables or rhythm syllables. Students learn to identify the tonality they are audiating as they read the symbols. At the writing sublevel of creativity/improvisation-symbolic learning, students write, rather than perform, in response to the patterns they are given.

THEORETICAL UNDERSTANDING

Music theory, as it is approached in learning sequence activities based on music learning theory, explains to students through intellectual understanding why we perceive, sensate, and audiate as we do in musical thought and performance. Many topics are relevant to why music is perceived, sensated, audiated, performed, read, written, created, and improvised as it is. Some examples are the structural basis and types of music syntax; the difference between intrinsic and extrinsic meaning in music and the relationship of each to the other; the identification of foreground, middle ground, and background in music and the relationships among them; and the nature of essential pitches and durations.

Having acquired skill at all levels of music learning sequence, except theoretical understanding, young musicians can nevertheless intelligently audiate, perform, read, write, create, improvise, and listen to music. The theoretical understanding level is approached only when students have achieved all previous levels of discrimination and inference learning, because every lower level of learning serves as a unique readiness for the theoretical understanding level.

Letter names, time-value names, interval names, key signature names, and measure-signature names serve as techniques at the theoretical understanding level of inference learning. Students use them to theorize about music after they are able to audiate. In theoretical understanding learning, only specific aspects of patterns and series of patterns are used.

The Importance of Audiation

Many music teachers, particularly those who specialize in music theory at the high school and college levels, direct their teaching to the symptoms that students manifest as a result of their deficiencies in audiation. Simply stated, to teach audiation is to teach through the ear. To teach intellectual understanding is to teach through the eye. If the eye is to take meaning from the printed page of music notation, the ear must be taught first.

NOTES

1 James L. Fisher, "Handbells in the Schools" (Sellinsville, PA: Schulmerich Carillons, 1971).

2 Ronald Lee, "Arts in Education: A Curricular Approach to Explore." Paper presented at National In-service Conference, Chicago, March 1984.

3 Ibid.

4 Charles E. Silberman, *The Opera Classroom Reader* (New York: Random House, 1973), 749.

5 Eunice Boardman Meske and Carroll Rinehart, comp. *Individualized Instruction in Music* (Reston, VA: Music Educators National Conference, 1963).

6 William C. Hartshorn, "The Study of Music: An Academic Discipline" (Washington DC: Music Educators National Conference, 1963), 23.

7 Karl D. Ernst and Charles L. Gary, eds., *Music in General Education* (Washington, DC: Music Educators National Conference, 1965).

8 M. E. Sadler, in Emile Jaques-Dalcroze, *The Eurhythmics* (Boston: Small Maynard, 1915), 32.

9 Ibid., 35.

10 Irwin Spector, *Rhythm and Life: The Work of Emile Jaques-Dalcroze* (Stuyvesant, NY: Pendragon, 1990), 334.

11 Ibid., 236.

12 Karl W. Gehrkens, "Rhythmic Training and Dalcroze Eurythmics," *Yearbook*, Music Supervisors National Conference (Chicago, 1932), 309f.

13 Charles R. Hoffer, *Introduction to Music Education* (Belmont, CA: Wadsworth, 1983), 123.

14 Spector, 70.

15 Emile Jaques-Dalcroze, "Teaching Music Through Feeling," *Etude* 39 (June 1921): 368.

16 Jo Pennington, *The Importance of Being Rhythmic: A Study of the Principles of Dalcroze Eurthymics Applied to General Education and the Arts of Music, Dancing, and Acting* (New York: Putnam's, 1925), 26–27. Used with permission.

17 Beth Landis and Polly Carder, *The Eclectic Curriculum in American Music Education: Contributions of Dalcroze, Kodály, and Orff* (Washington, DC: Music Educators National Conference, 1972), 23.

18 Ibid., 26–27.

19 Emile Jaques-Dalcroze, *Eurthymics, Art and Education*, trans. Frederick Rothwell, ed. Cynthia Cox (New York: Blom, 1972), 145–68.

20 Landis and Carter, *The Eclectic Curriculum*, 156.

21 Hermann Regner, Director, Orff-Schulwerk Zentrum, Salzburg, in Jane Frazee, *Discovering Orff: A Curriculum for Music Teachers* (Mainz: Schott, 1987), 5.

22 Brigitte Warner, *Orff-Schulwerk: Applications for the Classroom* (Englewood Cliffs, NJ: Prentice-Hall, 1991), 6.

23 Bjonar Bergethon and Eunice Boardman, *Musical Growth in Elementary School*, 4th ed. (New York: Holt, Rinehart, 1979), 231.

24 Arnold Walter, "Carl Orff's 'Music for Children,'" *The Instrumentalist* 13, no. 5 (January 1959): 39. Used by permission.

25 Arnold Walter, Introduction to *Music for Children* by Carl Orff and Gunild Keetman, trans. and adap. Arnold Walter and Doreen Hall, 5 vols. (Mainz: B. Scott's Sohne, 1955), vol. 1.

26 Carl Orff, "The Schulwerk and Music Therapy," *The Orff Echo* 26, no. 4 (Summer 1994): 10–13.

27 Loraine Edwards, "The Great Animating Stream of Music," *Music Educators Journal* 57, no. 6 (February 1971): 38–39. Reprinted by permission of Music Educators National Conference.

28 Zoltán Kodály, quoted in Lois Choksy, *The Kodály Method*, 2d ed. (Englewood Cliffs, NJ: Prentice-Hall, 1988), 3.

29 Tibor Bachmann, *Reading and Writing Music* (Elizabethtown, PA: Continental, 1968).

30 Lois Choksy, *The Kodály Method* (Englewood Cliffs, NJ: Prentice-Hall, 1974).

31 Mary Helen Richards, *Threshold to Music* (Belmont, CA: Fearon, 1964).

32 Denise Bacon, "Kodály and Orff: Report from Europe," *Music Educators Journal* 55, no. 88 (April 1969): 55–56. Reprinted by permission of the Music Educators National Conference.

33 Arnold Walter, "The Orff-Schulwerk in American Education" (Muncie, IN: American Orff-Schulwerk Association, 1969), copyright 1969. Used by permission.

34 Ibid., 173–74.

35 Grace E. Nash, "Media for Human Development," in *The Eclectic Curriculum in American Music Education* (Washington, DC: Music Educators National Conference, 1972), 173. Reprinted by permission of Music Educators National Conference.

36 John D. Kendall, *Talent Education and Suzuki*, quoting from a speech by Shinichi Suzuki, given at the National Festival, Tokyo, 1958 (Washington, DC: Music Educators National Conference, 1966), 9. Reprinted by permission of Music Educators National Conference.

37 Ronald B. Thomas, "Rethinking the Curriculum," *Music Educators Journal* 56, no. 6 (February 1970): 70.

38 Ronald B. Thomas, *MMCP Final Report*, part 1, Abstract (Washington, DC: U. S. Office of Education ED 045 865, August 1970), vii. Reprinted by permission.

39 Ibid., vii.

40 Ronald B. Thomas, "Learning Music Unconventionaly—Manhattanville Music Curriculum Program," *Music Educators Journal* 54, no. 9 (May 1968): 64. Reprinted by permission.

41 Thomas, *MMCP Final Report*, 2.

42 Ronald B. Thomas, *MMCP Synthesis* (Bardonia, NY: Media Materials, 1970), 4.

43 Ibid., 6.

44 *Comprehensive Musicianship: The Foundation for College Education in Music* (Washington, DC: Music Educators National Conference, 1965), 21. Reprinted by permission of Music Educators National Conference.

45 R. Jack Mercer, "Is the Curriculum the Score—or More?" *Music Educators Journal* 58, no. 6 (February 1972): 51–53. Reprinted by permission of Music Educators National Conference.

46 Charles H. Benner, *Teaching Performance Groups* (Washington, DC: Music Educators National Conference, 1972), 10.

47 Joseph A. Labuta, *Teaching Musicianship in the High School Band* (West Nyack, NY: Parker, 1972), 7.

48 Robert J. Garofalo, *Blueprint for Band* (Fort Lauderdale, FL: Meredith Music Publications, 1983), 98.

49 Ibid., 98.

50 Robert J. Garofalo, *Instructional Designs for Middle/Junior High School Band* (Fort Lauderdale, FL: Meredith Music Publications, 1994).

51 Ibid., 98.

52 William Thomson, *Comprehensive Musicianship through Classroom Music* (Belmont, CA: Addison-Wesley, 1974).

53 William Thomson, "Music Rides a Wave of Reform in Hawaii," *Music Educators Journal* 56, no. 9 (May 1970): 73.

54 William Thomson, *The Hawaii Music Curriculum Project: The Project Design* (Honolulu: Collge of Education, University of Hawaii), 14. Used by permission.

55 Allen W. Flock, "The Comprehensive Music Program," *PMEA News* (Pennsylvania Music Educators Association) 40, no. 4 (May 1976): 47.

56 Ibid., 47.

57 *The Quarterly Journal of Music Teaching and Learning*, 2, no. 1, 2. Quoted from cover.

6

Materials and Tools of Music Education

Popular Music

As music educators extended their boundaries to serve American society more comprehensively, they began to use musical materials that had previously not been acceptable to many music educators. The music is the heart of the curriculum, and despite the amount of attention given to how we teach, the character of the music is more foundational to school music programs than the method. In less than three decades, the music literature of school programs has radically and profoundly transformed American music education. Consider the diametrically opposed views of jazz and popular music throughout much of the twentieth century:

> *1926.* I share the view that jazz is the most distinctive contribution America has made to the world-literature of music. What we now need is proper guidance of the jazz germ. There are two kinds of germs in the physical world—those that kill and those that preserve human life. Jazz germs are of the same nature. It is for the open-minded American musicians and musical educators to discover, preserve, and develop the worthy elements of jazz. Jazz as an end in itself, except for dancing and the like, is to be deplored. Jazz as an idiom for something worthwhile, as a stepping-stone to something better than we now recognize, is, as Shakespeare put it, "a consummation devoutly to be wished."[1]
>
> Edwin Stringham, 1926

1967. Music of all periods, styles, forms, and cultures belongs in the curriculum. The musical repertory should be expanded to involve music of our time in its rich variety, including currently popular teenage music and avant-garde music, American folk music, and the music of other cultures.[2]

The Tanglewood Declaration, 1967

Popular music is sometimes referred to as "youth music" for the purpose of music education. MENC coined the phrase in the November 1969 issue of the *Music Educators Journal*, which was dedicated to the philosophical and practical aspects of popular music in American education.

Earlier, popular music had found little acceptance by the music education profession. For many years the dance orchestra had been on the periphery of the music curriculum. Later it was called the "jazz band," and then the "jazz lab band," but it still remained an extracurricular activity. In 1941 Peter Dykema and Karl Gehrkens, both of whom were authoritative voices of the profession, wrote pessimistically about jazz (or swing, or dance music) in *The Teaching and Administration of High School Music*. Having acknowledged that jazz had already gained a solid foothold in school music programs, and that it was already too late to eliminate it, they nevertheless warned of the dangers of using jazz in the school music program. They were especially concerned that playing in a dance orchestra was likely to cause poor playing habits and corrupt musical taste. They said:

> Swing music—which is merely a highly emotionalized style of playing jazz, and to which we are in no sense objecting to as a legitimate type of human experience—is primarily physical. It induces violent physical movement—note the jitterbug. It is "fleshly" in its entire conception. It does not lead toward the spiritual. It is "good fun" at the time, but it does not yield abiding satisfaction. To use such music in the school as a substitute for serious music is to cheat youth of a highly important experience which has the possibility of assisting in the development of spiritual resources.[3]

Throughout the 1940s and 1950s music education writers argued strongly in articles (especially in the *Music Educators Journal*) and books that jazz and popular music should not be part of school music programs. It was a moot argument, however, because as Dykema and Gherkens had noted earlier, jazz had been firmly entrenched for years. As late as 1963 the participants in the Yale Seminar recommended that schools have stage bands because they would draw students into music programs, where they might be attracted to ensembles that play more serious music. Some educators observed that the stage band had developed and grown in American education with little justification and planning, and that no substantial curricular need had been established for it.

They feared that by bowing to the pressure to include popular art forms in the curriculum, the schools would leave themselves open for well-deserved criticism. In 1966 William Sur and Charles Schuller stated: "The question of whether the dance band should be part of the school instrumental program is debatable. There seems to be general agreement that if it is offered it should be reserved for senior high school and should be considered a noncredit music activity."[4]

Conversely, many other music educators accepted popular music wholeheartedly as a legitimate subject of study and as a performance genre. They defended the stage band on grounds of student interest, the development of good technique and playing habits, and as a suitable aesthetic experience. Many, however, did not accept rock and roll. Thus, they continued the tradition of nonacceptance of current popular music in music education by identifying a kind of music that appeals strongly to youth, but which has no place in the schools.

The Youth Culture

The 1960s was a time of social movements. Many groups of Americans demanded something to which they were legally entitled but were denied because of societal mores or traditions. Despite constitutional guarantees of individual freedom, many Americans were openly discriminated against and little was done to help them, either by legislative mandate or court decree

The massive civil rights movement of the 1960s brought widespread recognition of the youth culture as a distinct element of American society. Adults were often shocked and dismayed by the bizarre youthful of sexual conduct, drug usage, and styles of dress and by various forms of illegal conduct. This behavior was so deviant from the accepted social norm that adults had little choice but to recognize youth as discrete culture. The youth culture was held together by its music, rock, and the 1969 Woodstock (New York) Music Festival was one of its strongest symbols. The pervasiveness of the youth culture awoke music educators to the fact that youth music had to be sanctioned in school music programs. This profound change constituted a music education revolution, which was blessed by the findings of the Tanglewood Symposium of 1967. MENC officially recognized the place of popular music in school programs when the Symposium agreed that all kinds of music were appropriate for school music programs: "The music repertory should be expanded to involve music of our time in its rich variety, including currently popular teenage music."

THE NATIONAL ASSOCIATION OF JAZZ EDUCATORS

When MENC bestowed its blessing on jazz and other popular musics in the curriculum, it opened the way for the full development of school stage bands. Music and education leaders—Stan Kenton, Louis Wersen,

John Roberts, Charles Gary, and others—founded the National Association of Jazz Educators (NAJE) in 1968, and MENC immediately granted it associated organization status, recognizing that it would lend legitimacy and credence to jazz education. Because the purpose of NAJE is "to further the understanding and appreciation of jazz and popular music, and to promote its artistic performance,"[5] the affiliation of MENC and NAJE at that particular time was all but inevitable. The specific objectives of NAJE, as stated by M. E. Hall, president of the organization, are:

1. To foster and promote the understanding and appreciation of jazz and popular music and its artistic performance.

2. To lend assistance and guidance in the organization and development of jazz and popular music curricula in schools and colleges to include stage bands and ensembles of all types.

3. To foster the application of jazz principles to music materials and methods at all levels.

4. To foster and encourage the development and adoption of curricula that will explore contemporary composition, arranging, and improvisation.

5. To disseminate educational and professional news of interest to music educators.

6. To assist in the organization of clinics, festivals, and symposia at local, state, regional, and national levels.

7. To cooperate with all organizations dedicated to the development of musical culture in America.[6]

NAJE, which has since become the International Association of Jazz Educators (IAJE), has promoted jazz-oriented curricula by encouraging students to perform, compose, arrange, and improvise jazz. The activities of the organization affect all levels of education, from elementary through graduate school. IAJE materials include lists of stage-band, choral, and string literature, listening materials, and materials for general music classes. Most state music eduactors associations have IAJE units, and many colleges and universities have student chapters. The official publication, *The IAJE Educator*, features philosophical and practical articles about all aspects of jazz education. Its plentiful advertisements for materials, supplies, and equipment indicate that the music industry supports jazz in schools wholeheartedly.

Many publications also support jazz and popular music. Elementary graded music series commonly contain popular music, and their accompanying recordings include representative jazz and rock music in addition to the traditional variety of folk and classical music, and children's songs. Many recently published elementary and secondary books and audiovisual materials teach music concepts and skills through popular music and introduce students to its historical and sociological implications.

Popular music has profoundly influenced school music performance practices. Its effect on marching bands is even greater than on other ensembles. Marching bands seldom play marches any more in halftime shows and parades. Their major literature now is jazz and popular music. Directors are able to select from a seemingly infinite variety of popular arrangements, some of which include complete halftime shows. Vocal jazz, complete with costumes and choreography, has blossomed into a large movement with its own literature, teacher training methods, competitions, musical, choreographic, and costuming traditions.

Colleges offer courses in jazz history and in other forms of popular music, and students often elect such courses in place of traditional music appreciation classes. Because music education majors must prepare themselves to work with popular music, music education curricula often include courses in jazz and rock history, improvisation, and in instruments particularly appropriate to popular music, especially the guitar.

The growth of stage bands reflects the impact of popular music in American education. Until the late 1950s commercial stock arrangements constituted the school dance band repertoire. By the early 1960s these groups were called jazz bands, jazz lab bands, or stage bands, and they were plentiful enough for publishers profitably to distribute arrangements and new music composed specifically for them. Most schools have jazz lab bands now, and many include smaller specialty units that play dixieland, blues, ragtime, or various kinds of rock. The quality and quantity of this music has increased to the point where it is used not only by student musicians, but by commercial bands as well.

The growth of the stage band at the college level has been a major factor in the development of the jazz major, which is offered by many institutions of higher education. College jazz lab bands often rival professional groups in quality, and some make commercial recordings. It is not unusual for some jazz major programs to attract more students than do other music major programs.

CONCLUSION

The rapid growth of popular music in American education has been phenomenal. The stage-band movement achieved maturity within the brief period of ten years, and popular music quickly became a part of almost every aspect of music education. David McAllister writes:

> We affirm that it is our duty to seek true musical communication with the great masses of our population. While we continue to develop and make available, to all who are interested, the great musics of the middle class and aristocracy, we must also learn the language of the great musical arts which we have labeled "base" because they are popular. . . . When we have learned that any musical expression is

music, we hope to be able to reduce the class barriers in our schools and our concert halls. The resulting enrichment of our music will, we hope, give it a new vitality at all levels, and provide a united voice that can speak, without sham, of our democratic ideals.[7]

Multicultural Music

The United States is probably the most multicultural nation on earth. Few, if any, other countries began with such a heterogeneous population, and continued to become more pluralistic as they grew and matured. Despite the actuality of multiculturalism, however, it has only been in recent years that Americans have begun to recognize the need to broaden their Eurocentric perception of the United States. Eurocentrism had been the traditional view since colonial times. It began to change when it was challenged by the many Americans whose roots are not European and who were denied many of the benefits of American citizenship because of their ethnic or cultural heritages. For much of the country's history, immigrants were welcomed by industry because they provided cheap labor, and, in fact, they were a major factor in the industrialization of the United States. The labor force consisted of Hungarians, Czechs, Italians, Slovaks, Poles, Serbs, Croats, Slovenes, Russians, Rumanians, Greeks, Chinese, and many others. As they continued to flood into the country, however, Americans began to fear that their culture would be diluted if their country continued to absorb so many newcomers. Congress restricted immigration sharply in 1921, and Emma Lazarus's poem "The New Colossus" ("Give me your tired, your poor, your huddled masses yearning to breathe free") became little more than a romantic fiction. Immigration was reopened again two decades later, this time with severe restrictions on who could enter. With the more recent waves of Asian and Hispanic immigration throughout the second half of the twentieth century, the United States continues to become increasingly multicultural. What was once called the "melting pot" is now referred to as a "salad bowl," in which the ingredients are mixed, but not blended.

The United States began to recognize officially the multicultural nature of its population shortly after World War II: "Beginning in the 1950s, American leaders, who before 1945 had tended to view the United States as an Anglo-Saxon or Euro-American society, redefined the United States as a 'nation of nations,' a federation of ethnic and racial groups united only by democratic idealism."[8]

Legislation Supporting Multiculturalism in Education

The passage of the Education Amendments Act of 1972 (P.L. 92-318) made multicultural education a legal requirement for educators. Multiculturalism was not new to educators at that time, but Title IX ("Ethnic Heritage Program") of P.L. 92-318 ("Educations Amendments

Act") clarified the official statutory intention of multicultural education, and helped set its focus and direction:

> In recognition of the heterogeneous composition of the Nation and of the fact that in a multiethnic society a greater understanding of the contributions of one's own heritage and those of one's fellow citizens can contribute to a more harmonious, patriotic, and committed populace, and in recognition of the principle that all persons in the educational institutions of the Nation should have an opportunity to learn about the differing and unique contributions to the national heritage made by each ethnic group, it is the purpose of this title to provide assistance designed to afford to students opportunities to learn about the nature of their own cultural heritage, and to study the contributions of the cultural heritages of the other ethnic groups of the Nation.

The bill declared that educational institutions should provide the opportunity for students to learn about their own cultural heritages and those of other ethnic groups. It also provided for the dissemination of curriculum materials, for training teachers, and for cooperations with people and organizations "with a special interest in the ethnic group or groups with which the program is concerned . . . ."

In addition to Title IX, P.L. 92-318 contained another section relevant to multicultural education. Title VII ("Emergency School Aid") was intended "to meet the special needs incident to the elimination of minority group segregation and discrimination among students and faculty in elementary and secondary schools." Title VII authorized grants to school systems in metropolitan areas to develop cooperative relationships between schools with significantly different ethnic and racial student bodies. Among other things the bill specified that funds could be used for remedial services, and for:

> The development and use of new curricula and instructional methods, practices, and techniques to support a program of instruction for children from all racial, ethnic, and economic backgrounds, including instruction in the language and cultural heritage of minority groups.

Following the enactment of this law, over half the states adopted formal policy statements on multicultural matters; several enacted laws relating to multiculturalism, including the legalization of bilingualism.

Another legislative act, Goals 2000, has given further support to multicultural education. Goal 3 identifies the core subject areas in which students are to develop competency. One of the objectives of Goal 3 is: "All students will be knowledgeable about the diverse cultural heritage of this Nation and about the world community." This objective relates funding of the national standards to multicultural education, and will be highly relevant for arts education.

Multicultural Music Education

Lois Weiner describes the beginnings of the current multicultural education efforts:

> Attempts by civil rights activists to remedy educational inequalities for black students sparked similar efforts by other ethnic groups . . . By 1970 writers had begun to describe American schools' "rich diversity" of students: Puerto Rican students in eastern cities; Chinese, Japanese, and Pacific Islands immigrants in the western states; Mexican Americans in the midwest and southwest; Cubans in Florida; and black and native Americans throughout the country.[9]

Multicultural music had been a peripheral part of American music education throughout much of the twentieth century. MENC, in fact, became involved in multicultural activities as early as 1929, when its new Committee on International Relations sponsored the first of several international meetings, this one held in Switzerland. Interest grew in the music of Latin America during the 1930s, and MENC undertook various cooperative activities with the Pan American Union in Washington, DC, and the U.S. Department of State. This interest expanded even more just before and during World War II, when the advantages of internationalism and mutual understanding became evident to the American people. The United Nations, founded in 1948, established the United Nations Educational, Scientific, and Cultural Organization (UNESCO), which in turn appointed an International Music Council (IMC). From IMC developed the International Society for Music Education (ISME) in 1953. Eventually, MENC became the official American representative to ISME, positioning the organization to be proactive in the promotion of multicultural musics. This did not necessarily translate into strong multicultural music programs in schools, however.

Despite the long-standing involvement of MENC, it was only in the 1960s that music educators began to recognize that the adoption of multicultural music was the right and necessary direction for them to take. It was not only desirable, but essential, to embrace multicultural music as an integral part of the music curriculum. The 1960s Civil Rights Movement, the Tanglewood Symposium, legislative acts, court decisions, and the general tenor of the times focused the attention on music educators their new responsibility.

The traditional emphasis on Western art music was too restrictive to meet the needs of a nation of immigrants. For too long, many American students did not recognize their own cultures in the traditional music curriculum. This was ironic because as citizens of the nation that has the greatest variety of ethnic backgrounds of any country, they were part of the most heterogeneous society in the world. Even so, few of their musics found a place in basal series or were sung by high school choruses. In a time of expanding cultural awareness, music educators found themselves in a key position. They had the tools and the moral imperative to help people understand each other through music. Bennett Reimer wrote, "Only the most provincial would assume that no one can or should share the musical benefits of a group other than the one to which he happens to belong."[10]

CULTURAL AUTHENTICITY

Effective teaching of multicultural music has proven to be an elusive pursuit for American music educators because school music had been focused primarily on Western music for so long. Teachers were not trained in musics other than their own, nor were they expected to acquire expertise in non-Western musics. When they became interested in other musics, they depended on publishers to prepare materials for them that could be presented without much actual knowledge of diverse cultures. Publishers had been doing this all along, to an extent. For a long time textbooks had introduced children to the cultures of other countries. These were brief, superficial glimpses of foreign lands and cultures, but they were considered exotic and many teachers incorporated them into their curricula. Basal music series, like other texts, also presented songs and colorful pictures of other cultures, and teachers would have their students sing and dance their music.[11]

Unfortunately, teachers usually presented multicultural musics in such a sterile manner that they were barren of the cultural traits that make music meaningful to a particular culture. Like Western music literature that had been transformed into "school music," ethnic musics were also reduced to shallow melodies in songbooks or superficial arrangements for instrumental and vocal ensembles. Lee Cloud wrote about the folk songs in *The World of Music*, published by Silver Burdett and Ginn in 1989. He described characteristically superficial editorial decisions that consisted of "alterations in the tune that change the melodic shape, structure, or rhythm, text alterations that either change or completely disguise the original meaning of the song, and recommended activities that are foreign to the folk song in particular or the folk culture in general."[12] Despite the inadequacy of cultural authenticity and meaning, however, at least the music of non-Western cultures was recognized in school programs. It remained for music educators to learn musics new to them in a meaningful way.

WORLD MUSICS OR MULTICULTURAL MUSICS?

For years, there was confusion about the definition of multicultural musics. The music education profession first approached the topic as "world musics," rather than as "multicultural musics." The difference is critical. The study of the music of other countries and cultures has often replaced entirely the study of the music of the many American cultures. These musics have evolved in the United States along with their contemporary ethnic cultures, and are different from what they had been for previous generations. Even the Tanglewood Declaration was vague about this issue in its statement, "Music of all periods, styles, forms, and cultures belong in the curriculum . . . including avant-garde music, American folk music, and the music of other cultures."[13] The last phrase of this germinal declaration seems to refer to the music of foreign, rather than American, cultures. In the early 1970s MENC began to publish articles about both American ethnic musics and foreign musics, having not yet officially distinguished between them. The November 1971 issue of *Music Educators Journal* emphasized African-American music. Conversely, the October 1972 issue carried the subtitle "Music in World Cultures" with the lead article by the distinguished anthropologist Margaret Mead. MENC conferences also featured sessions on world musics. Patricia Sheehan Campbell identifies the source of the dichotomy:

> A cultural exoticism often surfaced in these watershed years to color the manner in which musical diversity was defined by music teachers and by the Music Educators National Conference. The "world music" movement encouraged teachers to look beyond the U.S. for the musical content of their classes, with little attention paid to the music of minority American peoples whose musical heritages had yet to be explored.[14]

Campbell identified the events that signified the growing awareness of the need to focus on the musics of American minorities: the publication of *Source Book of African and Afro-American Materials for Music Educators* by Standifer and Reeder in 1972; the founding of the National Black Music Caucus; and the creation of the MENC Minority Concerns Commission in 1973. The name of the commission was later changed to the Minority Awareness Commission, and in 1979 to the Multi-Cultural Awareness Committee. By the 1980s multiculturalism, at least for music educators, had evolved from world musics to the musics of the American people. The May 1983 issue of *Music Educators Journal*, which featured articles on the music of American Hispanic and Asian peoples, symbolized the shift.

The world music movement has extended well beyond the United States. In 1994 the International Society for Music Education approved a new policy on world music education: "We believe that the musics of the world's cultures, seen individually and as a unit, should play a significant role in the field of music education, broadly defined."[15] The policy recommends that music education "Take as a point of departure the existence of a world of musics, all of which are worthy of understanding and study."[16]

Teaching Multicultural Music

The music education profession had been slow in evolving practical class-room approaches, but it finally began to address itself to that need. MENC continued releasing publications and other media, sponsoring conference sessions, appointing committees and commissions, and in general, implementing its official support for multicultural music education. It published an influential text, compiled by Anderson and Campbell, entitled *Multicultural Perspectives in Music Education*[17] in 1989. From 1986 through 1992 MENC released five audiocassette sets about multicultural teaching, accompanied by teaching materials. The tapes featured immigrant musicians discussing their own musics and cultures and how they had adapted to life in the United States. In 1990 MENC, with the Smithsonian Institution and the Society for Ethnomusicology, sponsored the Symposium on Multicultural Approaches to Music Education. It was scheduled immediately before the MENC biennial meeting to permit interested members to attend both. The symposium proceedings were published as *Teaching Music with a Multicultural Approach*.[18] The May 1992 issue of *Music Educators Journal* was dedicated to multicultural music education. In addition to MENC, the American Orff Schulwerk Association, the Organization of American Kodály Educators, and the American Choral Directors Association began to focus their attention on helping their members address multiculturalism.

C. Victor Fung describes three approaches to teaching multicultural musics, or world musics, at the college level. The first is organized geographically. In this approach, the class studies the music of a particular people for a certain length of time and then goes on to study another people's music. In the musical approach, focusing on such concepts as scales, meter, key signatures, and polyphony, the instructor draws illustrations from the musics of many world cultures. The third approach, and the most demanding on the instructor, is topical. The curriculum is organized around selected topics, which might include "healing, lullabies, entertainment, gender roles, and social hierarchies." The topics are socially significant, and by addressing the same topic as it applies to many musics, students are likely to make connections among the cultures.[19]

Preparing Music Educators for Multicultural Teaching

The professional music education organizations spent many years leading teachers toward effective multicultural education and helping them teach it effectively. Unless one grows up in a particular culture, however, he or she is unlikely truly to understand it. Teaching the music of a society other than one's own, on the basis of cognitive knowledge, does not elicit the affective response that is evoked in people who grew up in that culture. This is problematic for music educators, who spend years developing their musical proficiency only to find that those skills usually do not transfer to other musics. Whether they perform classical, jazz, or other mainstream musics, few Western musicians can authentically perform the music of other cultures. Violinists cannot realistically play Indian music, clarinetists cannot play Klezmer, and singers cannot sing Chinese opera. An important part of learning how to teach multicultural musics is recognizing that outsiders can learn about other cultures, but seldom to the degree needed to feel them deeply. Lois Weiner is not encouraging about the effectiveness multicultural education for future teachers. She describes a large-scale study of new teachers by the National Center for Research on Teacher Learning: "Despite coursework in multicultural education, teachers could not move beyond two contradictory moral imperatives: All children should be treated equally, and teachers should individualize to accommodate students' needs."[20]

A more realistic goal is to have students develop sensitivity and respect for cultures other than their own. Bennett Reimer warns against trying to superimpose one's own musical and cultural values on unfamiliar musics:

> There is no simple, singular, all-purpose solution to the reality confronting us—that foreign musics are, in essence, foreign . . . What we can do is honor and cherish the existence of the foreign. We can encourage diversity in music to exist as we encourage the diversity of species in the natural world to exist, by preserving and protecting each diverse manifestation of culture and of nature. We need not assume that we must personally benefit from the existence of foreign musics in the sense that we can own them or even borrow them for our personal aggrandizement. A world of diversity is simply a more interesting world. We can be satisfied to know our part of the world, to appreciate it for what it is, and also to understand what it is *not*— a standard applicable to other parts of the world.[21]

Knowing this, teachers must be especially sensitive to how they themselves communicate with people of other cultures, and how they convey knowledge of their musics. Teacher education programs do not usually cover this in depth, and music educators must learn them through experience. Fortunately, there is a wealth of publications, audio and visual recordings, summer workshops, and college and community-based courses available. Campbell refers to "cultural competence" as the goal that music educators continually strive for as they develop their skills and knowledge in multicultural music teaching. Carlesta Henderson expands on the issue:

> If music teachers expect to teach minorities effectively, they must go to the source of the various cultures and learn to understand how their music came to be. The societal forces that make up the culture interrelate to the culture's art, its religion, its family structures, it

sociopolitical ethos, its geography, and its history. When students learn the music of a culture from these multiple perspectives, authentic folk music takes on a new dynamic and meaning. College professors who teach music methods courses must return to school, but this "school" can often be far away. Reading about a culture is not as valid as an actual immersion into it.[22]

Music as a means of entry to other cultures raises another issue. Which is the primary subject—music or culture? A briefing paper issued by the arts education associations describes the emotional bond between works of art and the culture that produced them. It discusses implications for the content of instruction, especially as the emotional content of the music diminishes its intellectual substance.[23]

Obviously, the subject of multiculturalism still holds many unresolved issues for music educators. Unlike earlier educators in the days of the melting pot, they now try to preserve pluralism in the United States. The ways in which this is done are dictated by professional and personal philosophies of music education and by the ability of each music educator to deal sensitively with unfamiliar materials.

Technology and Music Education

The electronic revolution has had a dramatic impact on music and its related fields. Computer technology has been applied to music in every conceivable way in order to satisfy the needs of both the amateur and the professional musician.

The amateur musician has at his or her disposal a vast array of instruments that, with minimal human intervention, can practically play themselves. For example, some keyboard instruments use computer chips to provide harmonic and rhythmic accompaniments for any melody played on the keyboard. Instruments of this type seemingly make instant composers and performers of the novice. Nothing could be simpler.

On the other hand, the professional musician who enters the world of technology must be prepared for the demands and the rewards of that world. In addition to mastering his or her own instrument or area of specialization, a musician must gain a broader view of music. That view will include a thorough knowledge of the nature of sound and a familiarity with the articulations and idiosyncrasies of other instruments. In addition, he or she must know about sequencing techniques—how to record and how to edit. Finally, musicians must develop aesthetic judgment so that they can recognize when technology is used as an end in itself, or when it is used as a tool to enhance a truly musical performance.

The rewards of technology are many. First and foremost, a musician can be in total control starting with a musical concept and progressing through composition, notation, performance, and recording. Now, with a minimum amount of equipment, musicians can be desktop composers and desktop pub-lishers. Secondly, musicians now have the tools that can shape, color and articulate every sound. They have at their disposal a sonic palette that any of the great composers of the past would envy.

Technology has brought about many changes with more changes yet to come. In the final analysis, technology has the potential to make music better; the musicianship behind the technological application, however, will always make the difference in the music we hear.

Don Muro
statement to author, November 17, 1994

Technology has so permeated our society that it is now a common-place and unremarkable part of the everyday lives of most of the American population. It has revolutionized many aspects of modern life, including education. Music educators and students share in the technology revolution in many ways. Some find that learning has become highly individualized, making the instructional process more effective. Others have enriched their professional and personal lives by joining electronic communication systems that allow people, regardless of their location, to share information with each other.

Few music educators disagree that electronic technology can be of significant help to their profession, but many have not yet begun to take advantage of it. Some do not have the equipment and training. Others are intimidated by this relatively new field that seems never to stop developing and growing; its boundaries keep spreading, and no end is in sight. Regardless of how much one learns about technology and its uses in education, there will always be something new to learn. Some are discouraged by the fact that everything new becomes old very quickly, and teachers must continually develop their technological knowledge and skills to keep up with their students. Many, however, welcome technology with open arms. They are familiar with educational software, enter the "information superhighway" through the Internet or other communication services, and often develop new and innovative teaching practices. Some are so captivated by technology that it engages more of their attention than the subject matter itself. Eventually, however, this problem recedes as people become accustomed to technology and learn to regard it as the valuable tool that it is.

Technology is a new challenge for music educators. Its incredible potential can radically change music education practices, just as it has changed music, to the extent that performances recorded only forty years ago already strike us as archaic. As recently as the 1950s the electric (not electronic) guitar was highly advanced technology, and it was only in the 1960s that electronic synthesizers began to come to the attention of the public. Now we are completely accustomed to a seemingly infinite variety of electronically generated musical sounds. Music educators have found many applications for technology. They use it for:

Producing and manipulating music

Enhancing music learning

Accessing information

Communicating

Distance education

Producing and Manipulating Music

Electronic music consists of sounds that are generated, altered, and controlled by electronic means. It became viable in the 1950s with the establishment of the Columbia-Princeton Music Center in New York City. The composers Vladimir Ussachevsky, Otto Luening, and Milton Babbitt founded the center, which provided leadership in the development of electronic music. It was followed by the University of Illinois Electronic Music Center, and then by electronic music studios in many other colleges and universities. Because of the cost, imposing physical size, complexity of the equipment, and the strange sounds that it produced, electronic music was considered esoteric and not of great interest to most musicians or to the public. By the late 1960s conditions began to change. People were gradually becoming accustomed to electronic sounds in the public media and recordings. Television commercials, motion picture music, and many other venues helped accustom the public to new sounds.

Electronic music began to find its way into school music programs in the late 1960s. Opportunities for teacher preparation in electronic music were inadequate at that time because colleges were slow to adopt the new technology. Only a few offered appropriate courses, and they dealt mostly with composition, theory, and the techniques of musique concrète (electronic music composed with electronically processed natural sounds). Music education courses in electronic music were usually limited to a few summer workshops, and the cost of setting up an electronic music studio was prohibitive. Not having confidence in the future of the new phenomonem, many music educators adopted a cautious "wait and see" attitude.

At first music educators treated electronic music primarily as music literature, using the compositions of such composers as Babbitt, Leuning, and Ussachevsky as examples. Teachers considered the music to be a new musical form that was to be studied, but not necessarily produced, in the schools. A significant breakthrough came in 1967, when the Pilot Electronic Project (PEP) was established in eighteen schools in Connecticut by the State Department of Education. Title III of the

Elementary and Secondary Education Act provided funds that enabled PEP to offer a medium of creativity for students. Ussachevsky and Babbitt worked with educators to create curricula for electronic music composition. As students created music through the new medium they also developed original notational systems so their experiments (compositions) could be represented visually and modified. One of the first synthesizers suitable for school programs, the ElectroComp 200, was developed in response to the needs of Project PEP. By the end of the 1960s both the cost and size of synthesizers had dropped to the point where they became feasible for use in school programs. They became small, lightweight, and portable, and cost as little as $1,000. During the 1970s many schools throughout the country set up electronic music studios, some with minimal basic equipment and others with complex collections of sophisticated synthesizers, other sound-manipulation devices, and elaborate playback equipment.

Rapid technological advances have brought new types of equipment that are easy to use, versatile, and inexpensive. Nonprogrammable keyboards have become so commonplace that, like personal computers, they are now commodities sold in a variety of stores. More appropriate for the music classroom is the programmable keyboard, which is actually a synthesizer. These synthesizers use MIDI (Musical Instrument Digital Interface) technology, which is an international standard for communication between synthesizers.[a] MIDI permits a keyboard to be connected to any standard computer, regardless of its brand or operating system. With the proper software, it can then perform a number of technological functions like sequencing, voice editing, and even typesetting music played on a keyboard. The music can then be edited on screen and printed in score form or in individual parts. Sequencing is the programming of several sounds at once, each of which can have its own acoustical characteristics, such as frequency, intensity, timbre, resonance, and reverberation.[24] It has replaced tape splicing, the old technology that required the composer to record every individual sound on magnetic tape to be combined and manipulated as the composer wished. It was a tedious, arduous process that often took many months of cutting and splicing tape to create just one composition. Sequencing permits the composer or performer to experiment with sounds in real time and to combine sounds quickly and easily. The extreme versatility of this technology makes it a valuable tool for teaching almost any aspect of music, from listening skills to composition to instrumental and vocal performance.

---

[a]Before the invention of MIDI technology in 1983 software could be read only by the operating system for which it was programmed. Users were limited to the music software available only for their own particular system, whether DOS, Apple, Atari, Commodore, or another.

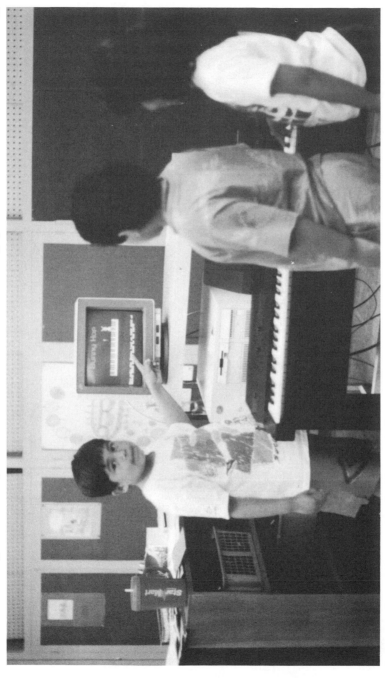

FIGURE 6.1. Ortega Elementary School, Austin, Texas. Students of Joyce Forrest use interactive technology.

Courtesy of Joyce Forrest. Used with permission

School synthesizers are often configured as workstations, and include a keyboard controller, a synthesizer for sound production and manipulation, and a sequencer. A student using an integral sequencer can record music generated by the synthesizer, edit the music, and play it back. Unfinished compositions can be stored, to be recalled and completed at a later time.[25]

The problems of electronic music in education are being solved as teachers and students become more knowledgeable about synthesizers and electronic music, and as new software proliferates. Synthesizers are used in an ever-increasing number of schools in performance to accompany soloists and ensembles, and even in synthesizer ensembles.[26]

Figure 6.2. Don Muro works with music educators at a technology workshop.

The Study of Music Through Technology

Computer Assisted Instruction (CAI) was made possible in the early 1970s, when Control Data Corporation, working with Indiana University, the University of Delaware, and the University of Illinois, inaugurated a new project called PLATO. PLATO provided linkages between universities using computers connected through telephone lines. Computers were still too large and too expensive to be feasible for use in most universities and schools. With the invention of the microcomputer in the latter part of the 1970s, however, the cost of the technology dropped, and the ensuing intense competition between manufacturers made it accessible to institutions and individuals. Numerous software companies were founded to make the new hardware even more useful. Music educators began to develop music instruction programs for the Apple II computer, which led the way for massive software development efforts in the near future. Now music instructional software is a normal part of music education, and teachers can select from a myriad of programs to serve their particular needs. CAI presents material to students in a manner that permits them to interact with the computer. Material is presented via computer, and the student selects the appropriate response to progress to new material or to review material not yet learned. Fred Hofstetter lists five capabilities of CAI for providing effective instruction: (1) it is a means of individualizing instruction because students progress through programs at their own rates; (2) it emphasizes "the intrinsic joy of learning and deemphasizes competition with peers as a motivating force"; (3) it encourages "students to tailor learning experiences to meet their own objectives"; (4) it gives immediate feedback, requiring each student to partake in a dialogue with the computer; and (5) it saves time because the level of instruction is adjusted for each student.[27]

The GUIDO (Graded Units for Interactive Dictation Operations) system is an example of CAI. It was developed at the University of Delaware and is now published and distributed commercially.[28] GUIDO helps students develop aural skills and is effective with groups that have wide learning differences. It is a series of programs to increase aural abilities in intervals, melodies, chord qualities, harmonies, and rhythms. Sitting at a computer, the student hears an interval played electronically while several intervals are displayed on the screen. He or she selects the correct one. The program tracks the correct and incorrect answers and keeps the student informed of how many more correct answers are necessary to complete the learning unit. GUIDO can be tailored to meet individual student needs, and incorporates a student record-keeping system. Intervals can be played melodically, harmonically, and melodically up or down. The top or bottom notes of the interval can be preset or selected randomly. The student can select simple or compound intervals, can repeat the interval, and can control the length of time it is heard.

Other CAI programs teach piano technique, give melodic dictation, offer tutoring in singing, reading, and writing music, and transform drills into games that make skill development an enjoyable activity for students. Innovative programs continually expand the limits of CAI. Blombach and Benward describe several new CAI ear-training capabilities as allowing a student to take dictation from an actual commercial recording and write or play back a part of the performance (whether a single voice or a piano score), develop aural perception skills while learning music analysis, explore musical forms by rearranging blocks of musical sound to compose, play "missing" parts of a composition, and improvise compositions within parameters indicated by the teacher.[29]

CAI is used with elementary and secondary students to develop aural skills and to study musical form, theory, and history. As early as 1983 the Verona Middle School Instrumental Music Department in Verona, Wisconsin, had a CAI Music Lab for developing music reading and composing skills, and for comprehensive musicianship. Its software—for drill and practice, tutorial, simulation, games, and computer-managed instruction—permitted a wide variety of musical activities.[30]

Music education technology continues to become more sophisticated. For example, the Yamaha program, "Music In Education," is an entire packaged keyboard curriculum that includes hardware (keyboards, mixer, remote control, compact disk player) and software that are coordinated with a complete curriculum. The technology permits the teacher to work with the entire class at one time, or with individual students. The program is based on six concepts:

1. Curriculum and instructional materials are central to the program, and provide a logical enhancement of teaching and learning into all areas of the curriculum.

2. Technology is an important component, and has been integrated so that it is an outgrowth of the *instructional* purposes of the program. The technology in the Music In Education program is a tool with which to teach, rather than a separate subject that has to be specifically taught.

3. The class group is the primary vehicle of instruction. Technology, the unique curricular design and cooperative learning experiences are directed toward reaching *groups* of learners, yet concurrently recognize the special learning and perceptual needs of the individual.

4. Instructional components include measures to assess student understanding, perception and achievement. The musical growth and understanding of the individual is essential to the success of the group.

5. Student musical experiences have an application beyond the music classroom experience, into other academic experiences,

personal use in the home, and in the development of lifetime participation with music.

6. Curriculum materials recognize and respect the traditions of classroom music and our rich cultural heritage and provide a bridge between those traditions and a contemporary setting for instructional materials.

The curriculum is divided into 145 nongraded modules; the teacher decides how much instructional content can be covered by a particular class. This program, like many others, uses sophisticated technology to support, rather than drive, music instruction.

The invention of the CD-ROM and its expansion to multimedia have made CAI even more powerful and versatile. The University of Delaware was a leader in developing this technology for music instruction. In 1982 the National Endowment for the Humanities awarded the University almost $350,000 to "demonstrate how the random access capabilities of educational videodiscs can enhance the teaching of stylistic and theoretical concepts in selected masterworks." The result, four years later, was an eight-sided, interactive Videodisc Music Series.[31]   There has been a remarkable amount of technological development throughout the 1980s, and compact discs have virtually replaced vinyl recordings. CDs, with their immense data storage capacity and magnificent sound reproduction ability, have increased the versatility of CAI. Interactive CD technology is beginning to find its way to the market, and as it becomes more readily available, educators will find more and more uses for it in classrooms. Koozin and Jacobson predict:

> Musical study tools will be able to incorporate interactive analytical insights, animated music graphics synchronized with a CD recording, historical pictures, video clips and information, real-time text translations, running commentary, and text-or audio-based quizzes. Advanced students will be able to examine various dimensions of a work in gradually superimposed layers of complexity, or see and hear long-range structural relationships that cannot be demonstrated through traditional methods.[32]

Steven Adams praises the use of CD-ROM for its ability to play standard audio compact disks:

> The advantage of a computer control is that any point on the audio CD can be accessed nearly instantly with precision to 1/75th of a second. This audio control can be combined with text and graphics on the computer screen providing students with carefully guided listening activities for training in any number of aural skills. Since the system uses CDs for the sound source, the audio output is of the highest quality.[33]

A great deal of CAI software is available, and teachers must remain informed of what is available and how well the various programs meet their needs. There are programs for listening skills, composing, ear training, music theory, instrumental methods, music appreciation, and music analysis. One problem is that software is developed for a large potential market and often does not closely match the needs of a particular teacher. Also, teachers must be aware that although much of the software is of high quality, some is not. Like textbooks and music, much software is irrelevant, trite, uninteresting, improperly sequenced, or inaccurate. Often, teachers with special needs learn programming so they can develop their own software.

Information Processing and Access

Information processing and access means collecting, storing, retrieving, and disseminating information. It can be as modest as using personal computers for word processing, spread sheets, and databases, or as far-reaching as using networks to access the vast amounts of information available to anybody with a computer equipped with a modem. Information retrieval services organize information data files that are located via search systems and retrieved by users. Lockheed and SDC are examples of companies that offer search systems to retrieve information from databases like the Educational Resources Information Center (ERIC).

ERIC (see chapter 4) is of special interest to music educators because it publishes *Current Index of Journals in Education (CIJE)*. *CIJE* contains the indices of *Music Educators Journal* and the *Journal of Research in Music Education*.[b] *Resources in Education (RIE)*, another subsection of ERIC, provides information on government grants for musicians and music educators. Users can access online catalogues for these databases. University Microfilms International, which publishes most American, and many foreign, doctoral dissertations, has three methods of accessing information about its publications in addition to the traditional library search. *Online Search* contains dissertation citations and is available in most libraries. *Disc Search* makes dissertation abstracts available on CD-ROM, and is also available in libraries. There is a fee for the third method, *Datrix Search*. Users can do their online keyword searches to scan the titles of over a million dissertations and master's theses written as early as the 1860s, and of dissertation abstracts since 1980. Datrix Search is an offline computer search service that is performed by University Microfilms International on request. University Microfilms has had a Dissertation Abstracts server on the Internet since 1994. Although the dissertations from only a few disciplines (not including

---

[b]*JRME* is also indexed in *Psychological Abstracts (PA)*.

music) are accessible through this server, it makes available the *University Microfilms International Copyright Handbook*, which contains valuable information about dissertations.

Electronic Communication

Communication via computer has become commonplace during the 1990s and millions of people all over the world take advantage of simple, inexpensive communication networks. Networks connect people so effortlessly that the technology replaces much of what would recently have been transmitted by telephone or mail at an earlier time. Harold Griswold foresees that, "by the turn of the century, 'network literacy' will be given as much emphasis in education as 'computer literacy' receives today."[34]

The major vehicle for electronic communication is the Internet. Ed Krol describes the Internet:

> Once you're connected to the Internet, you have instant access to an almost indescribable wealth of information. Through electronic mail and bulletin boards, you can use a different kind of resource: a worldwide supply of knowledgeable people, some of whom are certain to share your interest, no matter how obscure. It's easy to find a discussion group on almost any topic, or to find some people interested in forming a new discussion group.[35]

Among the various Internet services are mailing lists and news groups. Mailing lists are simply lists of people who share particular interests and correspond electronically with each other about that interest. Users join a news group by subscribing to it, after which any messages sent to the group are automatically forwarded to every other member. It has been estimated that more than 15,000,000 people use the Internet. This technology is making a reality of the "global village" cliché.

Music educators have many bulletin boards and discussion groups available to them. Electronic communication technology meets the needs of performers interested in stylistic interpretation, listeners who want to hear the latest rap recordings, researchers needing information on any subject, and even composers who want to share their music internationally. A few examples of the scores of discussion groups dedicated to specific musical interests are:

A Cappella

Beastie Boys

Blues

The Byrds

James Taylor

Karaoke

Led Zeppelin

MIDI

Moody Blues

Polkas

The Doors

Rock 'n' Roll Classic

Rock 'n' Roll Heavy Metal

Frank Sinatra

Marching Bands

Double Reed Instruments

Music Therapy

Some of the music education sources are *Research Studies in Music Education* (University of Southern Queensland, Australia), *Music and Brain Information Database* (University of California Irvine and National Association of Music Merchants), *Computer-Assisted Information Retrieval System* (University of Texas at San Antonio), *Music Research Information Services* (University of Utah), and *Music Education Resource Base* (University of Victoria, British Columbia). In 1994 the J.W. Pepper & Son Co. established the Pepper National Music Network (PNMN) for music educators as a source of information and communication. Music educators can both view and order music through PNMN, and as Pepper upgrades the system they will even be able to hear the music they are considering buying. PNMN also has bulletin boards to permit members to share ideas and ask questions of each other. The Music Educators National Conference established its own network area within PNMN, allowing MENC members access to news of the profession, contact with other music educators and with MENC leaders, and information about professional issues.

Many libraries are now online, making their resources available to Internet users. Users can access hundreds of public and university libraries as well as the Library of Congress. An especially useful feature of this service is interlibrary loan, through which users can order interlibrary loan materials from distant libraries and have them delivered either to themselves or to their own institutional libraries. The user requests interlibrary loans on-line, which makes the service accessible through a personal computer.

Even arts education advocacy efforts, such as those described in chapter 4, are enhanced by online communications. "Goal Line" is an education reform online network that provides a database for teachers, education activists, parents, social services, and civic and business groups to search for strategies and resources to achieve specific goals of the

Goals 2000 legislation. It is also an online conferencing system that permits people to have open discussions about education reform. The America 2000 Coalition, Inc. describes Goal Line as follows:

> Goal Line is an easy-to-use, interactive computer network for community activists involved in education reform. The network will offer a comprehensive database of the nation's most promising education programs, practices and resources and will be organized around the six National Education Goals. . . . The network is designed to increase the pace and scope of community efforts by connecting reformers around the nation, fueling their conversations and increasing the likelihood that they will learn from one another. It provides a meeting place where Coalition Members and Communities can become part of a productive, a national community striving for common goals.[36]

Distance Education

The U.S. Congress Office of Technology Assessment defines distance education as the "linking of a teacher and students in several geographic locations via technology that allows for interaction."[37] Joseph Maddy, the founder of the Interlochen Music Camp (now the Interlochen Arts Academy) was one of the first distance educators in music, when he taught instrumental music throughout Michigan via radio broadcasts. Distance education today is infinitely more sophisticated than in Maddy's time. In this interactive mode of instruction, students and teacher meet at the same time but not in the same place. They communicate electronically by means of two-way video. Instructor and students see and hear each other and have real-time discussions. The instructor can respond to a question signaled by the raised hand of a student who is hundreds, or thousands, of miles away. Interactive technology makes it possible for courses to be offered from a campus to distant sites where there is no qualified instructor available. This kind of instruction approximates normal classroom situations. The level of quality depends both on the electronic equipment available, and on the instructor's preparation for teaching via an electronic medium.

Another form of distance education uses the Internet for communication. Students and instructor communicate through electronic mail, bulletin boards, and electronic conferencing. Assignments are given, and student papers and other homework are returned via E-mail. This method of instruction allows all members of the class to communicate with each other and also permits private conferences with the instructor. This is a new mode of communication for a large proportion of adults, but many young people, having used it for years, are completely accustomed to it. Antonio Lasaga estimates that tens of thousands of elementary school students in many countries use the Internet, even to ask questions of the President of the United States. President Clinton has responded to students via the Internet. KIDLINK connects children from many countries, allowing them to have global dialogues. They have interactive discussions via KIDCAFE, and teachers discuss projects through KIDPROJ.[38]

The Gradual Adoption of Technology in Schools

Like every other aspect of education, the adoption of technology is uneven throughout the country. Its usage depends on the ability of school systems to obtain equipment and upon the preparation and propensity of individual teachers. Once teachers become comfortable with technology, however, they usually want to go on to explore new possibilities. New software programs are continually released for a multitude of uses in music education. Given its possibilities for improving education, technology will probably influence music instruction more and more, and teachers will consider it indispensable in the future. Although it is difficult for teachers to keep up with new technological developments in their field, there is help available to them. For example, the Institute for Music Research of the University of Texas at San Antonio periodically sponsors conferences on Technological Directions in Music Education. Its purpose is to "share information concerning current applications of technology in music education."

The Association for Technology in Music Education

ATMI offers another means of remaining current in technology as it affects music education. It was founded in 1973, (originally as the National Consortium for Computer-Based Music Instruction), as a forum for the exchange of ideas among developers and users of computer-based systems for music instruction. In 1987 its name was changed to ATMI to describe the organization more accurately. Until 1992 it was a special interest group of the Association for the Development of Computer-Based Instructional Materials, but in 1993, it adopted bylaws making it an international, independent not-for-profit organization. ATMI sponsors a listserver (ATMI-L), and is planning an archive site for software. It publishes a quarterly newsletter, *ATMI International Newsletter*, and the annual *ATMI Technology Directory*, a 450-page compendium of software and hardware for teaching music.[39]

NOTES

1 Edwin J. Stringham, "Jazz—An Educational Problem," *The Music Quarterly* 12, no. 2 (April 1926): 190–95.

2 The Tanglewood Declaration, article 2.

3 Peter W. Dykema and Karl W. Gehrkens, *The Teaching and Administration of High School Music* (Boston: Birchard, 1941), 455.

4 William R. Sur and Charles F. Schuller, *Music Education for Teen-Agers* (New York: Harper & Row, 1966), 147.

5 John T. Roberts, "MENC's Associated Organizations: NAJE," *Music Educators Journal* 55, no. 7 (March 1969): 44–46. Reprinted by permission of Music Educators National Conference.

6 M. E. Hall, "How We Hope to Foster Jazz," *Music Educators Journal* 55, no. 7 (March 1969): 44–46. Reprinted by permission of Music Educators National Conference.

7 David McAllister, "Curriculum Must Assume a Place at the Center of Music," in *Documentary Report of the Tanglewood Symposium*, 138.

8 John B. Judis and Michael Lind, "For a New Nationalism," *The New Republic* 4, no. 184 (March 27, 1995): 24.

9 Lois Weiner, *Preparing Teachers for Urban Schools: Lessons from Thirty Years of School Reform* (New York: Teachers College Press, 1993), 110.

10 Bennett Reimer, "General Music for the Black Ghetto Child," *Facing the Music in Urban Education* (Washington, DC: Music Educators National Conference, 1972), 89.

11 Patricia Shehan Campbell, "*Musica Exotica*, Multiculturalism, and School Music," *The Quarterly Journal of Music Teaching and Learning* 5, no. 2 (Summer 1994): 67.

12 Lee V. Cloud, "The Miseducation—and Missed Education—of Musicians about African-American Music and Musicians," *The Quarterly Journal of Music Teaching and Learning* 4, no. 2 (Summer 1993): 13.

13 Robert A. Choate, ed., *Documentary Report of the Tanglewood Symposium* (Washington, DC: Music Educators National Conference, 1968), 139.

14 Campbell, 68.

15 "ISME Writes World Music Policy," *Teaching Music* 2, no. 5 (April 1995): 12. See "Panel on Musics of the World's Cultures," *International Journal of Music Education* 23, 1994.

16 Ibid.

17 William M. Anderson and Patricia Sheehan Campbell, ed., *Multicultural Perspectives in Music Edication* (Reston, VA: Music Educators National Conference, 1989).

18 William M. Anderson, ed., *Teaching Music with a Multicultural Approach* (Reston, VA: Music Educators National Conference, 1991).

19 C. Victor Fung, "Approaches in World Music Curriculum," *Social Sciences SRIG Newsletter* (Westchester, PA) (Spring 1995): 3.

20 Lois Weiner, *Preparing Teachers for Urban Schools* (New York: Teachers College Press, 1993), 111.

21 Bennett Reimer, "Can We Understand the Musics of Foreign Cultures?" *Musical Connections: Traditions and Change* (Aukland, New Zealand: International Society for Music Education, 1994), 232.

22 Carlesta Henderson, "Preparing Future Music Teachers for Dealing with Minority Students: A Profession at Risk," *The Quarterly Journal of Music Teaching and Learning* 4, no. 2 (Summer 1993): 36.

23 *K–12 Arts Education in the United States: Present Context, Future Needs*, a briefing paper for the arts education community (Reston, VA: Music Educators

National Conference, National Art Educaton Association, National Dance Association, National Association of Schools of Music, National Association of Schools of Art and Design, National Association of Schools of Theatre, National Association of Schools of Dance, January 1986), 6.

24 Terry Griffey, "Review of CUBASE," *The Quarterly Journal of Music Teaching and Learning* 1, no. 1, 2 (Spring 1990).

25 Jackie Wiggins, *Synthesizers in the Elementary Music Classroom: An Integrated Approach* (Reston, VA: Music Educators National Conference, 1991), 7.

26 Don Muro, interview with author, 17 January 1984.

27 Fred T. Hofstetter, "Microelectronics and Music Education," *Music Educators Journal* 65, no. 8 (April 1979): 39–45.

28 *GUIDO*, published and distributed by Temporal Acuity Products, Inc., Bellevue, WA.

29 Ann Blombach and Bruce Benward, "The Unvarnished Truth about Commercial Ear-Training Software," *The College Music Society Newsletter* (September 1994): 6.

30 Brian Moore, "A CAI Music Lab in the Middle School," *Dialogue in Instrumental Music Education* 7, no. 1 (Spring 1983): 19–23.

31 Fred T. Hofstetter, *Computer Literacy for Musicians* (Englewood Cliffs, NJ: Prentice-Hall, 1988), 98.

32 Daniel Jacobson and Timothy Koozin, "The Challenges of Multimedia in the Music Curriculum," *The College Music Society Newsletter* (September 1994): 3.

33 Steven M. Adams, Interactive Audio as a Resource for Music Couseware Development," *The Quarterly Journal of Music Teaching and Learning*, 1, no. 1, 2 (Spring 1990): 116.

34 Harold E. Griswold, "Multiculturalism, Music and Information Highways," *Music Educators Journal* 81, no. 3 (November 1994): 41.

35 Ed Krol, *The Whole Internet: User's Guide and Catalog* (Sebastopol, CA: O'Reilly, 1992), xx.

36 GOAL LINE: The Education Reform Online Network Fact Sheet, "What Is Goal Line?" (Washington, DC: America 2000 Coalition, 1993).

37 United States Congress, Office of Technology Assessment, *Linking for Learning: A New Course for Education*, OTA–SET–430 (Washington, DC: U. S. Government Printing Office, 1989), 4.

38 Antonio Lasaga, "Collaboration and Technology," *On Common Ground: Strengthening Teaching through School-University Partnership* (New Haven, CT: Yale-New Haven Teachers Insistute, n. 2, Summer 1994), 16.

39 Barbara Murphy, ed., *Technology Directory: 1994–1995* (East Lansing, MI: Association for Technology in Music Instruction, 1994).

Part III

AREAS OF CONCERN FOR MUSIC EDUCATION

7

Music Education for Special Needs

Music in Special Education

Programs of teacher education must be expanded and improved to provide music teachers who are specially equipped .. to work with the very young, with adults, with the disadvantaged, and with the emotionally disturbed.[1]

The term "special education" refers to all or part of the process of educating exceptional children that is different from that of educating normal children. Exceptional children deviate sufficiently from normal children to require special or modified educational experiences. Many special institutions exist to help exceptional children overcome their problems and to educate them. The focus of this chapter, however, is on special education for exceptional children in the regular music classroom and by the regular music teacher. The new term for educating special students in regular classrooms is "inclusion." It is used interchangeably with the older term, "mainstreaming." Most students with special needs are already mainstreamed, and with the trend toward inclusion, the percentage increases steadily. According to the *Fifteenth Annual Report to Congress on the Implementation of the Individuals with Disabilities Act* (Department of Education, 1993), over 93 percent of approximately five million children with disabilities are educated in regular classrooms.

After many years of debate about whether exceptional children should be educated in regular classrooms or in special schools that are staffed and equipped to handle specific problems, the issue has been resolved in favor of the regular classroom. It is now a common practice.[a]

---

[a]Some exceptional children are uneducable, and cannot function in the regular classrooms. They are still provided special facilities.

Mixing exceptional and normal children not only accomplishes educational goals, but it is also mandated by law. Interaction with normal children helps them adjust to the conditions of the world outside of school. They are challenged by working with normal children and often achieve far beyond what they would have in a closed, protected environment. Not all of their time is spent in the normal situation because they often need additional help from specialists outside of the classroom. Special help might be in the form of remedial reading, speech therapy, counseling, and remedial or therapeutic assistance for physically handicapped children. Gifted children whose abilities allow them to achieve far more than normal children, and who do not find sufficient challenge in normal classroom activities, need special enrichment activities.

The foundation of a philosophy of special education was laid at about the same time that contemporary philosophical foundations were being developed in other subject areas. Dr. Leonard Mayo said in 1954:

> Above all, we believe in the exceptional child himself; in his capacity for development so frequently retarded by the limits of present knowledge; in his right to a full life too often denied him through lack of imagination and ingenuity on the part of his elders; in his passion for freedom and independence that can be his only when those who guide and teach him have learned the lessons of humility, and in whom there resides an effective confluence of the trained mind and the warm heart.[2]

Children classified as exceptional include the intellectually gifted, the mentally retarded, the emotionally disturbed, the physically handicapped, and individuals who for reasons unknown achieve less than might reasonably be expected of normal children.

Legal Bases for Special Education

Congress has enacted several bills to protect and enhance the rights of handicapped and disabled Americans. The *Education for All Handicapped Children Act* (P.L. 94-142) was passed in November 1975. The bill stated:

> It is the purpose of the Act to assure that all handicapped children have available to them, within the time periods specified in section 612 (2) (B), a free appropriate public education which emphasizes special education and related services designed to meet their unique needs, to assure that the rights of handicapped children and their parents or guardians are protected, to assist States and localities to provide for the education of all handicapped children, and to assess and assure the effectiveness of efforts to educate handicapped children.

Before P.L. 94-142 was enacted, millions of handicapped children had either limited access to educational opportunities or in some cases, none at all. Since 1975 such children have had a legal right to free public education with full educational opportunities. All of the states have complied with the law, although some to a greater extent than others. It has been difficult to find qualified personnel, provide suitable facilities, and fund an expansion of public education necessary to meet the requirements of the law. A great deal of progress has been made, however, and school systems continually work toward providing the best possible opportunities for handicapped children in public schools. There is still much to be done in music programs. Sona Nocera wrote in 1979:

> Of interest to music educators is the estimate that only about two million handicapped children (out of eight million) are currently receiving any kind of arts education. Certainly this situation will need to be rectified if schools are to comply with providing appropriate educational experiences and full educational opportunities for the handicapped as well as the nonhandicapped. Since music education programs are a part of the curriculum for nonhandicapped in virtually all parts of the United States, failure to provide a music education for handicapped children would clearly be discriminatory.[3]

Since enacting P.L. 94-142, Congress has also passed other legislation to further strengthen the rights of handicapped and disabled persons. The *Individuals With Disabilites Education Act* of 1975 (P.L. 94-119) ensures that students with disabilities have a free, appropriate education in the least restrictive environment possible. Many more students were mainstreamed after the passage of this act because it covered "disabled," as opposed to "handicapped," students. The words "disabilities" and "handicaps" have different legal meanings. In terms of legislation enacted in 1975 and later, "disabilities" identifies a broader population that is protected by law. For example, certain illnesses and substance abuse qualify as disabilities. The newer term was also introduced to reflect a movement away from what had become a somewhat derogatory term, handicapped, to disabled, which has a less negative implication. The law considers a person disabled if he or she "has a physical or mental impairment that substantially limits one or more major life activities, has a record of such impairment, or is regarded by others as having such an impairment."[4] This broadened the protection of the law to include students who had been physically unable to deal with public buildings. After the enactment of the 1975 legislation, school systems began to make their buildings more accessible to people unable to use normal facilities. For example, ramps were built and drinking fountains lowered for students in wheelchairs.

THE AMERICANS WITH DISABILITIES ACT OF 1990

P.L. 101-336 was signed into law by President Bush to extend federal civil rights protection to disabled people. P.L. 101-336 took the protection of disabled people in a different direction by relating their treatment to their civil rights. Built on the Rehabilitation Act of 1973 and the Civil Rights Act of 1964, it provides "a clear and comprehensive national mandate for the elimination of discrimination against individuals with disabilities."[5] Title III, "Public Accommodations Provisions," identifies a nursery, elementary, secondary, undergraduate or postgraduate private school, or other education sites as places where ADA applies.

Music educators need to be especially sensitive to the needs of disabled students, whether the disability is caused by a learning or physical impairment or is an addiction. Educators must make all reasonable efforts to accommodate disabled students in such a way that they enjoy the same experiences as other students. Supposedly all American educators receive information from their administrators about implementing ADA with students. Similarly, those who hire teachers and professors are required to do so in compliance with ADA. Persons with disabilities that would have prevented them from being hired in the past now obtain and hold positions, and probably have the same rate of success as their nondisabled colleagues.

Music and Special Education

Although P.L. 94-142 does not mandate mainstreaming, its language clearly implies that handicapped children must receive educational opportunities that are as nearly normal as possible. Therefore, the usual interpretation of the law usually results in mainstreaming. Nocera points out that mainstreaming can benefit normal children as well as those who are handicapped:

> It is important for us as educators to understand that P.L. 94-142 is a human rights issue and that we arrived at mainstreaming for social rather than educational reasons. Indeed, there is no research that proves mainstreaming to be a superior educational approach for children with learning difficulties. Mainstreaming came about on the heels of the civil rights legislation of the 1960s and the public demand for equal opportunities for all. No one can argue the potential social value to society as a whole when average children grow up working and playing with children who are different. Perhaps the greatest fruits of current mainstreaming efforts will be that the next generation of adults will not have the stereotyped ideas regarding handicapped individuals that are held by much of the adult population today.[6]

INDIVIDUALIZED INSTRUCTION FOR HANDICAPPED CHILDREN

P.L. 94-142 specifies that handicapped children must be provided individualized services, part of which is a written Individualized Education Program (IEP). The act states:

> A written statement for each handicapped child [shall be] developed in any meeting by a representative of the local educational agency or an intermediate educational unit who shall be qualified to provide, or supervise the provision of, specially designed instruction to meet the unique needs of handicapped children, the teacher, the parents or guardians of such child, and whenever appropriate, such child, which statement shall include (A) a statement of the present levels of educational performance of such child, (B) a statement of annual goals including short-term instructional objectives, (C) a statement of the specific educational services to be provided to such child, and the extent to which such child will be able to participate in regular educational programs, (D) the projected date for initiation and anticipated duration of such services and appropriate objective criteria and evaluation procedures and schedules for determining, on at least an annual basis, whether instructional objectives are being achieved.

Mainstreaming must be planned carefully and effectively by teachers who understand the needs of each handicapped child and who are familiar with the services the school is capable of providing. Beer and Graham suggest the use of the *Music Assessment Sheet* to establish the musical needs of handicapped children, and provide examples of IEPs for their musical education.

The Special Student

The various categories of special students who are often placed in the regular classroom for at least part of the school day are (1) the neurologically handicapped, the most likely of whom to be found in the classroom are the mentally retarded, the minimally dysfunctioning, the speech handicapped, the autistic, the psychologically disturbed, and the perceptually insufficient; (2) the physically handicapped; (3) the emotionally disturbed; and (4) the gifted.

NEUROLOGICALLY HANDICAPPED CHILDREN

Neurologically handicapped children behave in ways that exaggerate normal behaviors. It is the degree of exaggeration that makes their behavior other than normal. Such exaggerated behavior often prevents the child from responding to stimuli normally, and from learning in classroom situations as other children do. Neurologically handicapped children often exhibit behavioral signs that the teacher can use to devise effective teaching strategies. One such behavioral sign is rigidity, or lack of ability to accept change. The child desires order, and if objects are placed where they are not normally located, or if schedules deviate from the normal, such change represents disorder. The needs of this kind of child might include repetitious singing of the same music, performed in the same way each time. Another behavior is hyperirritable attention, which is manifested in what appears to be lack of attention. Some children may, for example, be unable to sort out and classify the sounds they hear, and may only hear certain sounds on a recording. Emotional lability, another behavioral sign, affects the child's emotional response to music and to other stimuli. This behavior may cause the child to react differently from other children to a particular stimulus, and the inappropriate response is difficult for others to understand. Initiatory delay causes the child to respond to stimuli after an abnormally long delay. Children who exhibit this behavior sometimes appear not to respond to music, but they do so after a few seconds, minutes, hours, or even days have elapsed. Children whose behavioral problem is caused by lack of ability to think abstractly are unable to perceive relationships and transfer knowledge to various situations. Speech, writing, and musical notation are often beyond the grasp of such children because of lack of understanding of symbols like a word, which represents a particular entity, or a printed musical note, which represents a sound.[7]

The music teacher is challenged not only to teach musical concepts, but also to discover how music can help children improve their behaviors. This is especially difficult because the degrees of behavioral deviance vary. Deviant behaviors may be quite intense at one time and seem to disappear a few minutes later. This behavior is similar to normal patterns, but highly exaggerated. Newell Kephart explains:

> To most teachers, as well as parents, the slow learner is a complete enigma. One day he learns the classroom material to perfection; the next he seems to have forgotten every bit of it. In one activity he excels over all the other children; in the next he performs like a two-year-old. His behavior is unpredictable and almost violent in its intensity. . . . Too often these aberrant performances are attributed to willful misbehavior, stupidity, or lack of interest. Actually, in many cases, the child's problems are not his fault. His central nervous system is treating these items in a different way. . . The teacher needs two basic competencies: a rationale which permits consistent interpretation of the child's learning behavior and a repertory of techniques by which information can be presented in myriad ways.[8]

Another complicating factor is that neurologically handicapped children may or may not have normal intelligence. They are of all intelligence levels and may have other physical handicaps, may be emotionally disturbed, and may also be gifted. The teacher is often faced with handicapped children of different learning abilities and must analyze the place of every child in the class and devise unique remedial and learning activities.

Like other children, the neurologically handicapped child usually moves naturally to music. Some can react only on this level, while others are capable of all the musical activities in which other children participate. Kinetic response strongly suggests a heavy reliance on rhythm for music activities. Rhythm seems to be perceivable by all children. It is a part of common body movements and functions (walking, running, dancing, speech), and it is used to diagnose and remedy problems. Children who do not move easily or gracefully can be helped with the use of rhythmic activities. Rhythmic speech helps some children memorize material. This activity can lead the student to poetry, which opens many new possibilities for mental and physical development, and which can be used effectively with music by most children. Many with learning problems are able to analyze rhythm and understand the relationship between beat, meter, and tempo after developing kinetic abilities in response to music. Melody, timbre, and dynamics are often most successfully presented in conjunction with, or in response to, rhythm. Carl Orff recognized this when he based his approach to music for children on rhythm.

MENTALLY RETARDED CHILDREN

There are many degrees of mental retardation. Three categories of retardation are recognized for educational and training purposes: educable, trainable, and dependent. It is unusual for trainable and dependent mentally retarded children to be placed in regular classrooms. Therefore, this section deals with educable mentally retarded children.

Two important goals for which teachers of the mentally retarded strive are social development and the ability to communicate, especially verbally. Mentally retarded children have the same social needs as normal children, but have difficulty relating to people. Musical activities allow them to be contributing members of a group that shares enjoyable experiences. Musical games and other activities are especially important because play is a major vehicle for learning. Rhythm and movement games that require children to follow instructions are more likely to be successful than drills and exercises, which are of little benefit to most retarded children.

Retarded children are usually not very imaginative and have difficulty dealing with the abstract. Both areas can be improved if the teacher is cognizant of individual needs and promotes activities to stimulate them. Games involving music and other arts, especially drama, are helpful. Rhythm and movement games help develop large muscles and the imagination. Melodic activities encourage socialization. Retarded children who join normal children in a music class often experience personal growth, which adds much pleasure to their lives and helps them function more effectively.

Music experiences that introduce concepts and vocabulary can help retarded children communicate more effectively and become more aware of their environment (see Fig. 7.1 for an example). Music and speech are closely related, and properly guided music activities help prepare children to deal with the abstract symbolism of language. In some cases it is even possible to place educable mentally retarded children in performance ensembles. Retarded children do not usually perform as well as normal children on musical instruments, but many develop enough skill to participate. Unfortunately, their participation sometimes lowers the performance standards of the ensemble, which presents a problem for ensembles that are intensely oriented toward performance. The teacher and students must evaluate the purpose of the group in making decisions about accepting special students who cannot meet the standards of the group. Decisions for and against membership of special students have been made in various schools. The choice between the highest possible musical standards, and personal growth and satisfaction for the special student, can be difficult to make.

FIGURE 7.1. Reinforcement of Selected Directionality Concepts

Frances A. Jones

Goal: Reinforcement of Selected Directionality Concepts Leading into Dancing Activities

Handicap: Trainable and Educable Mentally Retarded

Objective	*Learning Experience*	*Resource*
Student demonstrates understanding and identification of right and left.	Color code hand with color tape so that child will have a color to see and match. Sing songs with right and left hand directions.	Color tape. "Hokey Pokey" and "Looby Lou"
Student demonstrates the ability to understand the directions of stop and go.	Have children play games of stop and go. Children march, clap, play instruments. When music stops, children also stop. Integrate traditional colors of green and red in traffic directions. Without verbal cues, teacher holds green or red cards to give directions.	Chairs and piano or record player for playing musical chairs. Red and green construction paper.
Student demonstrates understanding of in and out.	Play circle games. To step out, go away from the circle. To step in, come back to the circle.	"Go in and out the Window" and "Bluebird Through My Window"

From Richard M. Graham, *Music for the Exceptional Child*, pp. 228, 229. ©
Copyright by Music Educators National Conference. Used with permission

EMOTIONALLY DISTURBED CHILDREN

Less is known about emotionally disturbed children than about other exceptional children. In fact, so little is understood about their problems that it is possible for a teacher to harm an emotionally disturbed child while trying to help. In some cases it is difficult to distinguish between the emotionally disturbed child and the mentally retarded child. Frequent and specialized testing is required to learn exactly what condition exists. Teachers who deal with emotionally disturbed children in the same manner as with retarded children might produce an adverse effect. Severely disturbed children are often physically aggressive, and so are

FIGURE 7.2. Improvement of Motor Coordination: A Therapeutic Exercise for Emotionally Disturbed Children

Harriet Heltman

Goal: To Improve Motor Coordination
Handicap: Emotionally Disturbed
Level: primary, intermediate

Objective	Learning Experience	Resource
To improve motor coordination skills.	As the children begin to know the words and tune of this song, set up a marching situation: follow the leader, with the children taking turns being the leader.	"Marching to Pretoria," *Making Music Your Own*, p. 116.
To improve motor coordination of the total body.	As the children learn the words of the song, have all do the actions the words indicate. Develop right and left concept.	"Busy," *Making Music Your Own* (Kindergarten), p. 129.
To develop keen awareness of all parts of the body.	For total body awareness: the children stand in a circle, a single line, or a double line facing each other. Sing words and do actions indicated to the tune of "Merrily We Roll Along": Touch your toes and then your knees, And let your hands go clap. Touch the floor and stand up tall, And let your feet go stamp. Lift your foot and kick the ball, And let your hands go clap. Hug yourself and turn around, And let your feet go stamp. Lift your knee up in the air, And let your hands go clap. Stand on tiptoe and turn around, And let your feet go stamp. Point your toe and take a bow, And let your hands go clap. Bend your body down and up, And let your feet go stamp. Rock your shoulders side to side, And let your hands go clap.	"Merrily We Roll Along" (traditional), *Teaching Music Creatively*, p. 168.

not usually placed in the regular classroom. Music experiences can be beneficial for them, but it is usually the music therapist, rather than the music teacher, who works with emotionally disturbed children (Fig. 7.2).

PHYSICALLY HANDICAPPED CHILDREN

Despite the severity of the handicaps of some physically disabled children, classroom and music teachers often find it easier to work with them than with disturbed or retarded children. Their problems are usually easy to identify and decisions concerning the best place for them to be educated have usually been made by experts before they enter regular classrooms. Many physically handicapped children also have emotional problems, and need more teacher and peer encouragement than other children normally require. Fortunately, the physically handicapped child is usually treated compassionately in the classroom, more so than other types of special students whose behavior problems may be disruptive.

Physically handicapped children include individuals who are completely or partially blind or deaf, who are mute, or who cannot function normally because of other physical impairments. They often enjoy music and the other arts, and gain much from participating in them. The arts offer handicapped children experiences that are not only educational, but often therapeutic, as well.

Schools such as the California School for the Deaf at Riverside, the Metropolitan School for the Deaf in Toronto, and the New York State School for the Blind at Batavia have developed music programs that prove the value of music education for blind and deaf children. That the blind enjoy and participate in music is well known. Indeed, the number of excellent blind professional musicians in our society is evidence that sight is not a prerequisite for musical participation on a high level. Deaf children lack the one sensory ability by which most people perceive music. Because of the nature of sound, however, people can also perceive vibrations through sense of touch. The sensation of rhythm is not affected by lack of hearing, and so it is possible for deaf children in a normal classroom to enjoy music without actually "hearing" it. Fahey and Birkenshaw describe how the deaf experience music:

> Those of us who work with the deaf have seen the face of a tiny child light up when he places his hands on a piano or organ and feels the vibrations of music or feels and hears amplified music on records. We have seen deaf children enjoying rhythm bands, and reciting words to music, deaf teenagers enjoying square dancing and social dancing, and deaf adults gathered around a piano singing songs.[9]

The deaf have difficulty in developing clear and accurate pronunciation because they do not hear themselves speak, and so an important goal of music education for deaf children is clear speech. Rhythm, movement, and vibratory perception activities all incorporate the use of speech. A. van Uden writes:

> Deaf children have a great and basic need for a total rhythmic edu-
> cation from childhood, the method of which must use sound per-
> ception to its full extent. . . . It may be clear, too, that music and
> dance continuously train the auditory-vibratory senso-motoric func-
> tions as such. They train the memory for such sequences and their
> "praxias" [the practice of an art, as opposed to theory] so indirectly
> the basic functions of speech and language [are developed]. . . . An
> intense training in rhythm of the whole body, of breathing and
> speech, integrated with sound perception auditory remnants and
> vibration/feeling, is a must in schools for the deaf.[10]

Blind students are capable of most activities in which sighted students participate. Many develop acute powers of perception and intensely focus their attention to compensate for lack of sight. This permits
many blind students to be successful in the study of voice or an instrument and to participate in bands, orchestras, and choruses.

Blind students who read braille can also learn to read braille music
because both use the same system of raised dots to form symbols.
Various agencies and publishers provide materials for the blind that can
be used by the music teacher. *The New Braille Musician, Young Keyboard
Junior, Overtones, Music Journal, The Musical Quarterly*, and *High Fidelity*,
for example, are available in braille or on magnetic tape. The American
Printing House for the Blind in Louisville, Kentucky, and the Division
for the Blind and Physically Handicapped of the Library of Congress
provide braille music and books. Mu Phi Epsilon sponsors a project in
which music is taped at slow speeds so blind people can learn the music
by ear. These tapes are distributed by the Library of Congress. The
Sigma Alpha Iota project for partially sighted musicians provides large
print music, and is also distributed by the Library of Congress.[11]

Children whose disabilities prevent them from normal usage of
their bodies are often able to participate in many normal music activities
that are physical in nature. Activities that require physical movement
(rhythm and movement games, for example) can often be modified to
permit handicapped children to participate from their chairs. The music
teacher must devise changes in activities, create special activities, and
alter materials that allow physically handicapped children to participate,
and to gain musical and therapeutic benefits from the music program.

A TRANSDISCIPLINARY APPROACH

Humpal and Dimmick recommend what they call a transdisciplinary
approach to mainstreaming special learners. They work with other specialists in special education, classroom teachers, and parents, as well as
occupational therapists, physical therapists, and speech/language pathol-

ogists to determine the best approach to teaching each individual child. This team approach engenders strategies for music teaching that involve creative uses of augmentative devices (symbol systems, electronic speech synthesizers), adaptive equipment for children with physical limitations, and conventional items to be used in unconventional ways.[12]

GIFTED CHILDREN

A category of exceptional children that in the past has received relatively little attention in public education is the gifted. Although more attention has been given to their problems in recent years, gifted children often do not receive the extra stimulation they need for motivation. This can be devastating for a child of superior intellect or talent. The gifted child who becomes bored with school work may do poorly, be criticized, and develop a negative attitude toward school and learning, resulting in a frustrated, unhappy individual and a waste of valuable human resources.

Giftedness in children does not necessarily imply a superior intelligence quotient (although children with an IQ above 115 are usually considered gifted). It can also mean superior talent in only one or two areas, such as music or mathematics. Some gifted children, however, have the ability to excel in almost everything they do. Strang describes giftedness:

> Giftedness is many-sided, many patterned. Among the intellectually gifted we find persons talented in many different fields. Different patterns of personality have been noted among children with different kinds of talent—scientific, artistic, musical, leadership ability. Giftedness may take many forms depending upon the particular circumstances. . . . Gifted children are far from being a homogeneous group; there are wide individual differences among children designated as gifted.[13]

Music can be especially stimulating for gifted children, regardless of the area of giftedness, because they sometimes respond more deeply to aesthetic stimuli than do other children. Many gifted children also have the ability to analyze, create, and perform music. Their study of music can be in greater depth than that of normal children. The music teacher must recognize the abilities and interests of gifted children, plan carefully for their musical experiences, and demand more of them. When gifted students are placed in a normal music class, the teacher needs to provide enrichment activities over and above those offered to normal students. Individualized instruction is especially valuable for this kind of situation. Some of the teacher's time should be reserved for guiding gifted children in individualized activities. The teacher must be aware of what resources are available—library facilities, electronic media, audiovisual hardware and software, community resources—and make the best possible use of them for gifted students. Students gifted in music

FIGURE 7.3. Lesson Plan: Special Education

Lesson Plan   **Date** _____

WHO   Class (describe: visually impaired, hearing impaired, moder-
       ately retarded, mainstreamed. This requires deline-
       ating individual disabilities within the group.)

       _____

       _____

WHY   Objectives:

       _____

       _____

       _____

WHAT   Activity:_____ Source:_____

       _____

       _____

       _____

HOW   Methodology: (Include materials needed, room preparation,
       as presentation format.) _____

       _____

       _____

       _____

OUTCOMES   Evaluation:_____

       _____

       _____

       _____

       INDIVIDUAL STRATEGIES OR ASSIGNMENTS

       Name   **Action**
Example: *Billy B.*   *Ignore covering face with hands;*

       _____   *praise him whenever he is sitting*

       _____   *with his face uncovered—"How*

       _____   *glad I am to see your face—*

       _____   *you're so handsome."*

       Sarah J.   *Be sure to keep promise of*

       _____   *beginning class with "Hey, Liley."*

       _____   _____

       _____   _____

From Kay W. Hardesty, *Music for Special Education* (Morristown, NJ: Silver
Burdett Company, 1979) © 1979 Silver Burdett Company. Reprinted by permission

present other kinds of problems and responsibilities for the music teacher because musicality takes many different forms. A musically gifted child might excel in several aspects of music, or perhaps be an excellent composer with little performance skill.

Many more opportunities are available for gifted children now than in the past. Boards of education have acknowledged their obligation to gifted children by creating magnet schools to afford a higher level of education and training. There are many high schools that specialize in the arts throughout the United States, and magnet elementary schools have been established as well. Some states also sponsor summer arts programs for gifted children (Fig. 7.3).

Music in Urban Education

The music education profession must contribute its skills, proficiencies, and insights toward assisting in the solution of urgent social problems as in the "inner city" or other areas with culturally deprived individuals.

The Tanglewood Declaration

In 1961 President John F. Kennedy established the White House Panel on Educational Research and Development to serve as an advisory board to the U.S. Office of Education and the National Science Foundation, and to his own science advisor. The panel's first goal was to examine the issue of urban education, which even then was generally conceded to be a failing enterprise. Since that time there has been little, if any, improvement. Federal, state, and local governments have initiated numerous projects to improve urban schools, teacher education programs have addressed themselves to preparing teachers for urban schools, and a great deal of attention has been given to helping individual students. The problems continue in the 1990s, but in many cases conditions are even worse than they were in 1961. Even so, music educators can make positive contributions to the education of urban students, many of whom are "at risk."

The Social Revolution and Education

The social revolution of the 1960s affected education profoundly. Until that time, schools operated as though the educational needs of middle-class white children in suburbs and small communities were the same as those of all other American children. Education had not yet completely shed the melting pot ideal of homogenizing American society, but the social revolution made it clear that the ideal was no longer feasible, or even desirable.

Minority populations lived in their own cultures in city ghettos, where they created their own social orders. Until the 1960s relatively few poor people living in inner-city areas had opportunities to rise above poverty to the middle class. Among other deprivations, their educational opportunities were often limited by inferior schools. The "separate but equal" system of school segregation that predominated in some parts of the country until 1954 was a legal, but thinly disguised, means of attempting to educate minority children to the social level of their parents. Having little political influence, minorities had to accept the educational system as it was. They had little control; education was governed by boards of education that perpetuated the middle-class philosophy of education on which school systems functioned. Frank Riessman wrote in *The Culturally Deprived Child* that the problem stemmed from the conflicting cultures of the school and of the family. He urged urban educators to work within the current urban culture. He also reminded educators that, despite the title of his book, deprived urban children were not culturally deprived. Rather, they lived within their own culture, which was different from that of middle-class America.[14] Paul Goodman was more forthright in his criticism of urban schools. He asserted that it was not middle-class values that the schools promoted, but petit bourgeois, meaning bureaucratic and timid. He accused the upper grades and university of exuding "a cynicism that belongs to rotten aristocrats." Goodman argued for learning that is "truly practical, to enlighten experience, give courage to initiate change, reform the state, deepen personal and social peace."[15]

Robert Havighurst defined three phases of education integration in his analysis of school desegregation.[16] The first, from 1954 to 1958, consisted of the response to the 1954 Supreme Court decision (Brown v. Board of Education of Topeka, Kansas) that established the illegality of school segregation. Many African Americans migrated from rural areas to large cities during this period to find employment, and the middle class flight to the suburbs began. The period from 1958 to 1963 was one of concern and controversy because school segregation actually increased, due to the 1958 economic depression. School segregation continued after that because of neighborhood residential patterns, and the poor economic conditions in ethnic communities. Court decisions upheld the legality of de facto segregation caused by residential patterns, but not by school attendance areas deliberately drawn to segregate schools. It was during this period that African Americans began to openly oppose the long-established patterns of segregation in American society. Martin Luther King, Jr. began to lead his nonviolent resistance movement against segregation practices at this time.

Havighurst classified the period from 1963 to 1966 as that of African American revolution. At that time school segregation and other racial problems erupted. The March on Washington, in August 1963, was a convincing protest against traditional racial policies and practices. King, with hundreds of thousands of African Americans, white leaders, and other citizens who believed in the Civil Rights Movement, made clear to the federal government and the American people that segregation and discrimination were no longer acceptable. The movement had help from Congress. The Civil Rights Act of 1964 prohibited many specific aspects of racial discrimination, and the Voting Rights Act of 1965 increased black political power, especially in the South. During this time boards of education began to take active measures against school segregation.

Martin Luther King, Jr. had been able to contain the African-American revolution and prevent it from becoming violent, but after his assassination in 1968 urban populations exploded in fury. The force of the violence made all Americans aware of the depth of frustration and resentment among many African Americans. Since then, the courts and school authorities have tried to hasten the implementation of school desegregation, and gains have been made toward racial equity in all areas of life, including employment and housing. Unfortunately, many federal policies designed to reduce or eliminate problems associated with poverty have actually created worse environments than had existed earlier. Policies created in the 1960s to alleviate the problems of substandard housing, juvenile crime, teenage pregnancy, illegal drugs, and other urban ills have often been corrupted, and have perpetuated the problems. The federal government has not, to date, found ways significantly to improve the lives of inner-city residents.

The violent phase of the social revolution was followed by a period of permissiveness in which students had greater freedom. Increased permissiveness made it virtually impossible to maintain discipline in schools, urban and suburban alike. Teachers and administrators were faced with a dilemma: enforcing strict discipline increased student dropout rates, but relaxing discipline caused achievement rates to decline. The introduction of student bills of rights throughout the country further reduced the ability to maintain discipline. It was not until the early 1980s that most superintendents began to give school principals solid support by insisting on strong disciplinary codes. Those principals then often brought about dramatic improvement in their schools. Success stories brought about by strong principals were about individual schools, however, and not urban school systems.

Shore identified three phases in the battle to restore quality to urban schools. In 1969 educators attempted to promote career education to relate schooling to the workplace. He called this movement "anti-liberal arts, anti-dissent, especially intellectual dissent, and . . . a movement which depressed rising expectations, particularly from minority group youngsters." The second phase, from 1975 to 1982, was known as the War on Illiteracy. This was the "back to basics" movement, in which educators, with the assistance of ESEA Title I programs, "did not so much argue for reduced expectations as attempt to implement them by eliminating elective programs in schools and concentrating on the 'three Rs.'" The third phase, which began in 1982 and continues to the present, is the War for Excellence against Mediocrity.[17] Unfortunately, except in individual, isolated cases, the quality of urban education has not responded to well-meaning reform efforts. Student achievement in reading, mathematics, and other skills continued to decline. School dropout and crime rates increased, and there was little, if any, improvement in student motivation. A variety of education experts, including researchers and experts in compensatory education, agreed at a 1992 U.S. Department of Education conference that federal programs had not helped, and that the research literature had little to contribute to the solution. Despite the infusion of huge amounts of money, time, and effort, the movement to reform urban education has not succeeded.

Students at Risk

A publication of the United States Department of Education succinctly addresses the problem of students at risk:

> One of the enduring rallying cries for school reform is the need to better serve students placed at risk of school failure. Parents, teachers, policymakers, and community leaders want to know which children are at risk, why they are at risk, and what can be done to improve these students' opportunities for success. While those questions seem straightforward, the answers often reflect the oversimplification and confusion surrounding complex educational and social issues.[18]

Students at risk are those who are unlikely to graduate from high school. The term also refers to students who might graduate from high school, but with inadequate educational skills.[19]

Franklyn G. Jenifer, president of Howard University, clarified the problem, referencing the then ten-year-old report *A Nation at Risk: The Imperative for Educational Reform* (see chapter 1). He expressed skepticism about its recommendations, saying, "The report's impact has been more rhetorical than real." He wrote:

> To advocate more homework . . . as the report does, makes academic sense, but what if Johnny and Susie don't have a home? Or, what if the home they do have is so impoverished or so chaotic that doing homework is impossible? Or, what if their interest in doing their homework is met with derision, or even ostracism, by their peers?[20]

There are students at risk in suburban, small town, and rural school systems, but the problem is endemic in urban schools. The federal government tried to deal with the problem through Chapter I of ESEA, but with little effect. Another approach to solving the problem was the

National Teacher Corps, which developed from the Project in Urban Teaching at Cardozo High School, in Washington, DC The Project in Urban Teaching focused on developing effective curricula for urban education, and on producing

> . . . teachers who can make the urban classroom a catalyst for those economic, social and intellectual changes which are needed if the public high school is to fulfill its role as a key long-range agent in combatting juvenile delinquency and encouraging youth opportunities.[21]

The Teacher Corps was established by Congress in 1965, and continued until 1975. Senator Gaylord Nelson introduced the legislation for the Teacher Corps with the expectation that it would provide quality education for urban youth. The Corps' goals were innovative because its graduates were expected, as individuals, to improve urban education one classroom at a time. Also, much of the college course work was situated in schools, rather than on campuses.

Beginning in the 1990s the Peace Corps, several urban school systems, and more than twenty universities began to cooperate by jointly establishing teacher education programs for returning Peace Corps volunteers. Many of the volunteers have had teaching experience in some of the world's poorest nations and are dedicated to working with deprived students. Most do not have undergraduate degrees in teacher education, and so they enroll in master's degree programs (usually the Master of Arts in Teaching) designed to earn teacher certification as well as a master's degree. The programs are experiential, and the students spend at least a year as interns in urban schools. These programs develop partnerships between universities and urban school systems and have the potential to lead to new, more pervasive collaborative efforts.

Trainers of Teachers Trainers (TTT) was another program designed to improve urban education. The Education Professions Development Act of 1967 (see chapter 4) funded it until it ended in 1973. Universities that received TTT grants had wide latitude in designing programs, and they developed many innovative models. Lois Weiner concludes that, although the Teacher Corps demonstrated that government involvement in urban education could be beneficial, there was little schoolwide or districtwide, impact because the focus was on individual teachers. Most evaluators, however, considered the TTT program successful in introducing change in urban schools, and some of the models have been continued and developed further in various universities.

Weiner, discussing both the returning Peace Corps Volunteers and TTT programs, points out:

> The political implications . . . of the culture of poverty encouraged researchers to examine the problem *either* as one of student defi-

ciency *or* as a limitation of teachers and schools, rather than analyzing the relationship between the components and locating them in a wider context. Because the explanations were presented as mutually exclusive, educators generally failed to recognize the difference among disadvantaged students.[22]

This prevented teachers from identifying many of the problems that needed to be addressed among various groups of urban students.

Slavin and colleagues identify three types of programs intended to help students at risk. The first, compensatory education, consists of government programs designed to help students complete their schooling. In 1987 almost 5,000,000 children received Chapter I services. These services focused primarily on improving reading and math skills. The second category was special education for students with disabilities. The third type was general education programs designed for students at risk.[23] The latter category is of greatest interest to music educators.

Music Education in Urban Schools

Urban school music programs were leaders in educational quality and innovative practices at one time. During the last several decades, however, many factors have come to bear on urban education, and the quality of both general education and music education has suffered. Although some individual urban music education programs function well and provide excellent music education for children, they do so mainly because of the superlative efforts of individual teachers and administrators. These educators find ways to minimize the negative effects of underfunded schools and a destructive social environment for students. Fortunately, there are many educators of this kind, but their impact is limited to localized situations.

Before the social revolution music instruction in urban schools had not been appreciably different from music in other kinds of school systems. It consisted of the same performing and general music experiences that constituted most music programs, and it utilized the same materials. Although this is still true of many urban music programs, beginning in the late 1960s more emphasis was placed on the music of minority cultures. In many cases music was actually taught to achieve a sociological goal: the awakening of self-awareness and development of self-pride through music. Now ethnic and popular musics form a major part of the music literature of urban school music programs, although many urban schools have excellent traditional performing ensembles. Teaching music, or any other subject, however, is difficult when the students come from deprived backgrounds. Echoing Franklyn Jenifer, Jerrold Ross, Director of the National Arts Education Research Center, describes the out-of-school lives of these children. He depicts many urban students as "ill-fed, ill-clothed and tired because they could not sleep the night before [and] cannot learn unless extraordinary attention is paid to their physical and emotional needs."[24]

Despite the overwhelming problems, there are bright spots in urban schools for music educators. In such difficult situations students need to feel that the body of knowledge that constitutes their education is relevant to them as individuals. The arts have always been relevant to young people, and perhaps even more important to deprived children. Music, as a reflection of the community musical life of minority groups, is sometimes a bright spot in urban education and holds promise not only for enriching the lives of at-risk students, but for helping to educate them as well. The Center for Music Research of Florida State University completed a project, "The Role of the Fine and Performing Arts in High School Dropout Prevention," in 1990.[25] The study found that participation in the arts is an opportunity for involvement that might not be available otherwise, and presents a challenge that many students accept enthusiastically. It gives them the opportunity to receive positive criticism and to respond to it by improving their performance. This motivates students and helps them develop confidence. The arts also engender social interactions approximating those of a family. The report states:

> Teachers and students are forced to deal with each other's short-comings and strengths in constructive ways, if the performance is to succeed. Positive outcomes of these experiences in team efforts are more than simply learning to accept different personalities and skills. They include the "family" concept—a close-knit team that is striving toward a mutual goal.[26]

Success in the arts requires discipline, and students are often willing to discipline themselves to focus on accomplishing an artistic task. This leads to pride in achievement and satisfaction with self. The project report continues:

> This project has provided some strong evidence that arts programs currently offered in Florida high schools provide a supportive, and in many instances, nourishing environment for students who border on dropping out of school. In many cases, at-risk in, and commitment to the band, chorus, orchestra, dance class, drama group, painting, sculpture, or other art project. Furthermore, some of these students remained in school, graduated, and successfully entered the business world—or received college scholarships.[27]

Other than this one project, there has been little research on the role of music, or of the arts in general, in serving at-risk students.

There are practical examples, however, of the success of the arts in supporting at-risk children. One is Ortega Elementary School, located in an area of Austin, Texas, that is overrun with drugs and gang activity; 90

percent of its students qualify for free or reduced-price lunches. Yet the school met a three-year academic goal in only two years: "All students will show a 15 percent gain over a three-year period of time" [on criterion-referenced tests of success in mathematics, reading, and writing, as well as higher-order thinking skills and problem-solving competence]. The school has received national recognition for its academic success, having been selected as one of America's best elementary schools by *Redbook*, and as a National Blue Ribbon School for Academic Excellence by the U.S. Department of Education.

Ortega's success began with a grant from the R.J.R. Nabisco Foundation, which designated it a Next-Century School. The purpose of the award was to restructure the school's programs for at-risk students. One of the components of Ortega's restructuring was "Labs to Enrich and Accelerate Learning," a group of technologically supported labs in science, math, computers, literature, music, art, and movement. In the music lab students are exposed to a wealth of listening, creating, and performing experiences. The arts-rich curriculum is credited with much of the school's success. Joyce Forest cites the College Board *Profile of SAT and Achievement Test Takers* (1990–1993) statement that test scores increase when the arts are integrated into the curriculum. "The district statistician reported that Ortega is 'off the charts' with scores that consistently exceed district predictions. . . . This remarkable increase is attributed to the interactive, accelerated, arts-rich curriculum that is being taught."[28]

Exemplary programs like Ortega's are examples of what can be done when a dedicated staff has sufficient resources. The school's success also demonstrates the effectiveness of partnerships between public schools and private foundations. This advantage, however, is not available to most schools. It can only be hoped that the 1990s educational reform movement will find ways to free enough resources to make such programs possible in all urban schools.

Preparing Music Educators for Urban Teaching

Only since the 1960s have teacher education institutions begun to address themselves to dealing specifically with urban, or inner city, teacher preparation. Urban students are often educationally disadvantaged and not motivated toward education. Unmotivated students must be treated differently from those who willingly pursue learning, and the inability to deal with passive students has resulted in many schools becoming more custodial than educational. Teacher preparation programs must include consideration of the most critical problems of urban children. Robert Strom wrote:

> Many opportunities for teaching and guidance are forfeited because [teachers] lack understanding regarding the customs, mores, and

values that govern behavior; the mechanism through which slum children can most be influenced; the structure and operation of powerful peer groups; [and] the indigenous system of incentives that affect motivation and discipline. . . . Although most prospective teachers need and desire training in these areas, seldom do college counseling, curriculum, and scheduling encourage it.[29]

Woock pointed out that with few exceptions, urban educators regarded urban students as "passive recipients of new programs and newly organized structures."[30] The problem still exists, but now it is addressed in teacher education programs. Agencies that accredit those programs[b] now require evidence of multicultural education in teacher preparation curricula.

The Tanglewood Symposium Committee on Critical Issues made recommendations to alleviate the lack of relevant preparation of music teachers in inner-city areas, recognizing that the arts can stimulate student motivation for learning. The January 1970 issue of *Music Educators Journal* was devoted to the topic of music in urban education. Inadequate teacher preparation was one of the major problems discussed in that issue:

> Many of the music teachers interviewed recalled the disillusionment they suffered during their first years of teaching when they found that what they were taught in college could not be used. They explained how they were forced to discard teaching techniques, concepts of curriculum and course content, educational philosophy, methods and materials that had been recommended to them as workable. Many felt that their college education was not only inadequate, but that it did them a disservice by actually leading them in the wrong direction.[31]

Lois Weiner points out that new urban teachers who are white or middle class "will confront such a cultural potpourri that no program of teacher education can prepare them with information about all the cultures they may see in the course of even a relatively brief career in an urban school."[32] Jerrold Ross asserts that teachers find it difficult to deliver music to all children because teacher education programs fail to provide sufficient cultural education. Most urban music teachers do not really understand why music is taught in schools; instead, they view music education as "some sort of performing experience that masquerades as education."[33]

---

[b]The predominant accrediting agencies for teacher education programs are the National Council for the Accreditation of Teacher Education (NCATE) and the National Association of State Directors of Teacher Education and Certification (NASDTEC).

The musical focus of many urban school music programs shifted in the late 1960s to ethnic, pop, and jazz. Teachers of ethnic, or any other kind of music, must be able to analyze, perform, and possibly create in the style of the music. Unfortunately, most teachers were not so expert. Students were often exposed to African music, for example, without the information and tools they needed to understand it. They could not comprehend it any more than they could Western art music that was presented without proper instruction. In these cases, the use of ethnic music was often self-defeating.

Colleges and universities began to institute black studies programs in the late 1960s. Despite their contribution to scholars by learning, however, they did not have much influence on music teacher education programs. The people who learned about black history and culture were not always the ones who would teach them to children. Music education methods courses incorporated African-American music only after college music departments began to offer courses in jazz, popular, and ethnic musics. Students preparing to teach music in urban schools began to have opportunities to learn the music and develop the skills that would be relevant to their particular teaching situations. Teacher preparation programs that included types of music new to school curricula had become commonplace by the early 1970s.

Music in Urban Schools: Conclusion

The problems of urban education are myriad, and conditions have improved little, if at all. The transfer of authority to more localized levels and the recognition of the need to develop curriculum according to local needs are hopeful signs, but as social problems increase, the schools must expect to deal with a wider range of problems, and usually with less money. The economic depression of the mid-1970s deprived music programs of teachers, facilities, equipment, and materials, and many urban school districts have never replaced them. As bleak as the picture is, however, music teachers are nonetheless meeting with success in many schools. At least part of their success is due to community support. As important as this support is for affluent schools, it is even more critical for urban schools that do not have sufficient material resources.

NOTES

1 The Tanglewood Declaration, article 8.1.

2 M. E. Frampton and Eleva D. Gall, *Special Education for the Exceptional Child* (Boston: Porter Sargent, 1955), xxvi.

3 Sona D. Nocera, *Reaching the Special Learner Through Music* (Morristown, NJ: Silver Burdett, 1979), 4.

4 *Basic 504 Compliance Guide* (Washington, DC: Thompson Publishing Group, 1992), tab 1000, 25.

5 Ibid.

6 Ibid.

7 Betty T. Welsbacher, "More than a Package of Bizarre Behaviors," in *Music in Special Education* (Washington, DC: Music Educators National Conference, 1972), 10–12.

8 Newell C. Kephart, *The Slow Learner in the Classroom* 2d ed. (Columbus, OH: Charles E. Merrill, 1971), v–vi.

9 Joan Dahms Fahey and Lois Birkenshaw, "Bypassing the Fear: The Perception of Music and Feeling and the Touch," in *Music in Special Education* (Washington, DC: Music Educators National Conference, 1972), 31.

10 A. van Uden, *A World of Language for Deaf Children* (Rotterdam: Rotterdam University Press, 1970), 179, quoted in John Grayson, "A Playground of Musical Sculpture," *Music Educators Journal* 58, no. 8 (April 1972): 51.

11 Muriel K. Mooney, "Blind Children Need Training, Not Sympathy," *Music Educators Journal* 58, no. 8 (April 1972): 59.

12 Marcia Earl Humpal and Jacquelyn A. Dimmick, "Special Learners in the Music Classroom," *Music Educators Journal* 81, no. 5 (March 1995): 21–23.

13 Ruth Strang, "The Nature of Giftedness," *Education of the Gifted*. Fifty-seventh yearbook of the National Society for the Study of Education, part 2 (Chicago: University of Chicago Press, 1958), 64.

14 Frank Riessman, *The Culturally Deprived Child* (New York: Harper & Row, 1976).

15 Paul Goodman, "The Universal Trap," in *The Urban School Crisis* (New York: League for Industrial Democracy and United Federation of Teachers, 1966), 67.

16 Robert J. Havighurst, *Education in Metropolitan Areas* (Boston: Allyn and Bacon, 1966), 169–76.

17 I. Shore, *Culture Wars: School and Society in the Conservative Restoration 1969–1984* (London: Routledge and Keegan Paul, 1986).

18 *Educational Reforms and Students at Risk: A Review of the Current State of the Art* (Pittsburgh: Superintendant of Documents, 1994), introduction.

19 Robert E. Slavin, Nancy L. Karweit, and Nancy A. Madden, *Effective Programs for Students at Risk* (Boston: Allyn and Bacon, 1989), 5.

20 Franklyn G. Jenifer, "Education in a Vacuum." *The Sun* (Baltimore), 3 May 1993, p. 3C.

21 Benetta Washington, "Cardoza Project in Urban Teaching: A Pilot Project in Curriculum Development Using Returned Peace Corps Volunteers in an Urban High School" (Washington, DC: ERIC Document Reproduction Service No. ED 001 653), introduction.

22 Lois Weiner, *Preparing Teachers for Urban Schools* (New York: Teachers College Press, 1993), 36–37.

23 Ibid., 6–17.

24 Jerrold Ross, "Research in Music Education: From a National Perspective," *Bulletin* of the Council for Research in Music Education, no. 123 (Winter 1994–1995): 126.

25 "The Role of the Fine and Performing Arts in High School Dropout Prevention," a curriculum development and renewal project developed by the Center for Music Research for the Florida Department of Education, Division of Public Schools, 1990.

26 Ibid., 12.

27 Ibid., 15.

28 Joyce Forest, "Music Technology Helps Students Succeed," *Music Educators Journal* 81, no. 5 (March 1995): 35–38, 48.

29 Robert D. Strom, *Teaching in the Slum School* (Columbus, OH: Charles E. Merrill, 1965), 33.

30 Roger R. Woock, "Urban Education in the United States of America," in Coulby, Jones, and Harris, eds., *World Yearbook of Education 1992: Urban Education* (London: Kogan Page Limited, 1992), 98.

31 "Overtones," *Music Educators Journal* 56, no. 5 (January 1970): 103–104. Reprinted by permission of Music Educators National Conference.

32 Lois Weiner, *Preparing Teachers for Urban Schools* (New York: Teachers College Press, 1993), 110.

33 Jerrold Ross, "Research in Music Education: From a National Perspective," *Bulletin*, Council for Research in Music Education, no. 123 (Winter 1994/1995): 129.

8

The Education of Music
Teachers

Competency-Based Teacher Education

Until the late 1960s music teacher education had changed very little
from what it had been decades earlier when it consisted of traditional
classroom courses in liberal arts, applied music, music theory, history,
and literature, music education method courses, and practice teaching.
In the 1960s, however, a new movement began as public interest awakened in educational accountability. When persistent school problems
made it clear that teacher education had to be overhauled, a new movement, "Performance-Based Teacher Education" (PBTE), came into
being. By 1970 PBTE was generally known as "Competency-Based
Teacher Education."[a]

The National Advisory Council on Education Professions
Development outlined the essential characteristics of CBTE in 1976:

> Students' progress depended on their ability to perform satisfacto-
> rily discrete teaching tasks or competencies. The competencies were
> to be based on actual teaching conditions, stated to teacher-candi-
> dates in advance so they would know what they were supposed to
> accomplish, and subjected to public scrutiny. The teacher prepara-
> tion program had to assist the student in acquiring these compe-

---

[a]The more recent terminology, "Outcomes-based Teacher Education," has been discontinued in many places because it has been equated with values, which many
regard as a code word for a particular religious or political agenda. The term has
become so controversial that both educators and community members purposely
avoid using it.

238

tencies, usually in an individualized format, known as an "instructional module."[1]

Competency-Based Teacher Education is a means by which the concept of accountability is extended from schoolteachers and administrators to the colleges and universities that educate teachers. CBTE is rooted in the social upheaval of the 1960s, which was also partially responsible for the movement toward educational accountability. The sit-ins, campus riots, and other manifestations of dissatisfaction with the inequities of American society in the 1960s were aimed not only at the government establishment but also at higher education. The insensitivity of colleges and universities to members of minority groups was bitterly protested on campuses across the country. Teacher education programs had given little recognition to the specific professional needs of those students who would become teachers of minority children. For the most part, programs were based on the needs of the American middle class, and their admission requirements often tended to exclude minority youth. The social, cultural, and educational requirements for entering students were sometimes unattainable by minority youth.

In the field of music, the problem was manifested by lack of technical development in performance, undeveloped music reading skills, inexperience with traditional Western art music, and lack of familiarity with the musics of other cultures, even those that are close neighbors in urban areas. Urban school systems had unique social and cultural needs, and their problems were perpetuated by teacher education institutions that did not prepare teachers adequately to meet those needs.

Traditionally, teachers themselves had had little part in the decision-making processes that affected education. When teacher associations and unions gained power during the 1960s teachers won a more equitable share in the governance of education. Recent developments in research and technology also encouraged the development of CBTE. The new technology of the sixties made innovative teaching techniques possible as it expanded the scope of learners. Television and other media offered an almost unlimited variety of vicarious experiences for children. Individualized instruction gave them the opportunity to assimilate knowledge in ways better suited to individuals than to groups.

As its component parts were minutely analyzed, the act of teaching itself became a subject of research. This helped establish a new science of teacher education. One of the major factors that brought about CBTE was the interest of the federal government in education. The government's financial support of educational research and curriculum development played a major part in bringing about a new mode of teacher education that has provided relevant education for preservice and in-service teachers. Also, it has made teacher education available to many students who could not otherwise afford it through its student aid programs.

Characteristics of Competency-Based Teacher Education

Students in outcomes-based programs must demonstrate teaching competencies as part of their program exit requirements. This replaces, in part, the traditional course examination concept. Competencies are stated in terms of behavioral objectives that make it possible to assess objectively the student's degree of success. The competencies determine assessment criteria, which set the level of mastery to be demonstrated and are disclosed to the student in advance. Assessment is based on student performance and takes into account the student's knowledge of the subject, ability to plan, analyze, interpret, and evaluate situations and behaviors.

Instruction is modularized, in keeping with the philosophy of individualization. Modules, rather than traditional courses, are the basic unit of progress of the teacher education program. A module consists of a set of learning activities, including objectives, prerequisites, preassessment, instructional activities, postassessment, and remediation. Modules allow for individualization in completion time, independent study, and alternative means of instruction. The learner is able to evaluate his or her effectiveness through continuous feedback from others. Learning activities are often assigned on an individual basis because there are constant indications of what modifications are required. The program is completed upon demonstration of the competencies that have been established as necessary for a particular teacher role or function. Exit requirements are emphasized and more importance is placed on the program requirements as the learner proceeds through it than on traditional matriculation requirements.

Competency-based teacher education is a field-centered approach that involves real students in authentic teaching-learning situations. Materials focus on concepts, skills, and knowledge that can best be gained in a specific instructional setting, usually an authentic classroom, but sometimes a simulation. Students and college faculty design the instructional system collaboratively. Because the student is preparing to become a teacher, part of the learning experiences includes making personal decisions about his or her own education. This leads the student to learn what is involved in educational decision making and helps ensure that programs are relevant to special skills and interests. As students develop understanding of the teaching process they proceed from mastery of specific techniques to combinations of techniques. This is called role integration and is usually not fully developed until the teacher is thoroughly experienced. For this reason, teacher education is considered by planners to be not only a preservice program, but a developmental process that extends throughout the teacher's entire career (Fig. 8.1).

FIGURE 8.1 Conceptual Model of Competency-Based Teacher Education

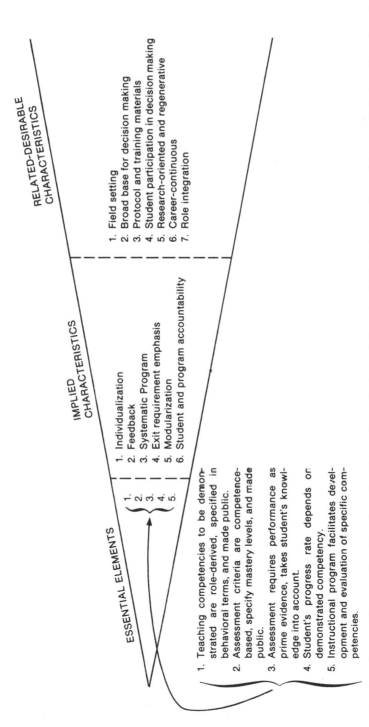

Stanley Elam, *Performance-based Teacher Education: What Is the State of the Art?*, PBTE Series no. 1 (Washington, DC: American Association of Colleges for Teacher Education, December 1971), p. 8. Reprinted with permission of the American Association of Colleges for Teacher Education

Competency-Based Certification of Teachers

Competency-based teacher education is intrinsically related to certification. In most states, the traditional certification procedures of evaluating courses and counting numbers of credit hours have been replaced by automatic certification of graduates of approved competency-based programs. Graduates of traditional programs are not certifiable in some states without having proved their competency through successful teaching experience elsewhere.

Competency-Based Music Education

In 1968 MENC President Wiley Housewright appointed a Commission on Teacher Education to make recommendations for the improvement of music teacher education. Commission Chair Dennis Holt wrote, "It was the judgment of the Music Educators National Conference that many teacher education programs had been overtaken by obsolescence. The Commission expressed concern for developing "mature teachers who could demonstrate identifiable competencies as musicians as well as educators"[2]:

> The development of music teacher competencies should result from the total program of the teacher training institution, The demonstration of competence, rather than the passing of a course, should be the deciding factor in certification. This means that proficiency tests, practical applications of historical, theoretical, and stylistic techniques, and advanced standing procedures should be enforced; and that an adequate means of final assessment should be developed and implemented.[3]

Music education majors in typical collegiate programs usually took courses for three years and spent much of the fourth year in their student teaching experience. In many cases the only other direct contact students had in school music programs occurred in their observation periods. New teachers had little practical experience in the classroom and were often unprepared for their responsibilities. Because of this, many new teachers found their first year in the profession extremely difficult. Another aspect of the same problem was that students did not have any teaching experience until the senior year, and could not know if they would like teaching until it was too late to change to a different major. Their college instructors had no opportunity to make judgments about their teaching effectiveness prior to student teaching, and could not give informed advice about becoming teachers. It is extremely difficult for college students to be faced with the necessity of finding a new major in the senior year, and of having to extend their collegiate careers to graduate. It is also a waste of university resources.

COMPETENCY-BASED TEACHER EDUCATION AND MUSIC EDUCATION

The accrediting agency for collegiate music and music education programs is the National Association of schools of Music (NASM). NASM recommendations are highly respected by member institutions and are usually implemented as thoroughly as possible. NASM recognized CBTE principles in its 1973 edition of *Proposed Revision of Standards for Baccalaureate Degrees and Recommendations for Graduate Study in Music,* which recommended the following:

1. The professional education component should be dealt with in a practical context, relating the learning of educational principles to the student's day-by-day musical experiences. Students should be provided opportunities for various types of teaching and observation experiences throughout the period of undergraduate study.

2. Laboratory experiences that give the conducting student opportunities to apply rehearsal techniques and procedures are essential.

3. Laboratory experience in teaching beginning instrumental students—individually, in small groups, and in large classes—is essential.

4. Institutions should encourage observation and teaching experiences prior to formal admission to the teacher education program; ideally, such opportunities should be provided in actual school situations. These activities, as well as continuing laboratory experiences, must be supervised by qualified music personnel from the institution and the cooperating schools.

Music Education Methods Courses

CBTE has become more flexible than the original Performance-Based Teacher Education model, and there is less reliance on exacting, discrete learning units. Nevertheless, learning is still arranged modularly, and students approach new material in an organized, linear fashion. Learning modules, based on predetermined competencies that successful teachers must achieve, often replace traditional courses in vocal, general, and instrumental methods. Each module specifies several activities, including research, observation, and practical application. Students often select different activities to achieve the same goal in deference to their own unique learning styles. As learning and skill development become more individualized, greater variation must be introduced into modules to develop skills, abilities, and interests. The activities require learners to spend extended periods in school music programs, where they observe, help teachers, and teach students prior to the actual student teaching experience. Simulated teaching situations like microteaching are also used. Students approach one task at a time by observing successful teachers, developing skills in a particular area through practice and study, learning new methods of teaching, and by actual practice teaching. A possible danger in this mode of education is that the student will achieve many teaching competencies without developing either a broad view of the teaching process or the ability to integrate the competencies into a comprehensive teacher role.

The most critical task of competency-based planners is identifying the competencies students are expected to achieve. The MENC Commission on Teacher Education published a list of competencies recommended as the basis for granting certification to music teachers:[4]

PERSONAL QUALITIES

Music educators must:

1. Inspire others
2. Continue to learn in their own and in other fields
3. Relate to individuals and society
4. Relate to other disciplines and arts
5. Identify and evaluate new ideas
6. Use their imaginations
7. Understand the role of a teacher

MUSICAL COMPETENCIES

All music educators must be able to:

1. Perform with musical understanding and technical proficiency
2. Play accompaniments
3. Sing
4. Conduct
5. Supervise and evaluate the performance of others
6. Organize sounds for personal expression
7. Demonstrate an understanding of the elements of music through original composition and improvisation in a variety of styles
8. Demonstrate the ability to identify and explain compositional choices of satisfactory and less satisfactory nature
9. Notate and arrange sounds for performance in school situations
10. Identify and explain compositional devices as they are employed in all musics
11. Discuss the affective results of compositional devices
12. Describe the means by which the sounds used in music are created

PROFESSIONAL QUALITIES

Music educators must be able to:

1. Express their philosophy of music and education

2. Demonstrate a familiarity with contemporary educational thought

3. Apply a broad knowledge of musical repertory to the learning problems of music students

4. Demonstrate, by example, the concept of a comprehensive musician dedicated to teaching

SPECIFIC APPLICATIONS OF COMPETENCY-BASED TEACHER EDUCATION

To demonstrate how a module is developed and used in music education, let us isolate one critical skill needed by junior high or middle-school choral directors. They must be able to listen to student singers and then analyze, evaluate, and place students in the proper section of the chorus. A teacher who is unable to do this successfully will have a poorly balanced chorus and the individual singers can develop vocal problems and poor attitudes toward singing. When the competencies for voice testing have been identified and agreed on by the class participants, various learning activities are decided on. Before the module is begun students are informed of the assessment criteria so they know in advance exactly what level of performance will be expected and under what conditions. The requirement might include listening to a certain number of children sing during a specified time span and making correct decisions about their placement in a chorus. Part of the assignment might include listening to individual singers and choruses for specific qualities that affect a teacher's ability to make predictions about singers; students will also be expected to read much of the literature available about the subject, explore sources of material for voice testing, view films and videotapes, and work with children in a school. When the various assignments have been completed, the students must demonstrate competence in the predetermined method. Students who do not develop the necessary competence receive advice and guidance to improve their performance before progressing to the next module. They review their own performance via videotape and are critiqued by the instructor, the classroom teachers, and fellow students. If the weakness is in the selection of material for voice testing, research may be required to find more suitable material. If the student has difficulty relating to children, more time might be needed in observing teachers and working with children. After remediation, the student is given another opportunity to demonstrate the particular required competency.

For anothers example let us segregate a competency required of instrumental music teachers: the ability to teach children to develop a suitable clarinet embouchure and produce an acceptable tone. To teach embouchure successfully one must know what constitutes a correct embouchure, be able to produce a good tone, impart the necessary information, guide skill development, and motivate children to learn. This module would probably be one of several in a unit on teaching the clarinet (or woodwind instruments). Prerequisite modules would have assured the student's competence in selecting reeds, assembling the instrument, and playing it at least at a minimum level of performance. Before students actually teach embouchure, they must read the appropriate literature, view films and videotapes, observe accomplished clarinetists to learn embouchure variations, and observe young clarinetists. Learners must also teach the skill in a simulated experience to college students. Finally, they work in a school, where they develop the confidence and ability to teach beginning clarinetists. The final task is to instruct a group of children of predetermined age or grade level in developing a good clarinet embouchure. The children's success in producing a satisfactory tone is the determining factor in evaluating the college student's competence.

The same pattern is followed for the various methods courses. Students learn to teach instruments, voice, musical knowledge, and concepts, and to direct ensembles by developing a sequence of competencies that eventually evolve into the ability to guide children in musical learnings and skills. Rather than being isolated from real-life experiences, students learn through participation in authentic activities. Competency development also provides realistic and meaningful evaluative criteria for the potential employer who evaluates applicants for teaching positions. If the teacher education program is accredited by its state department of education, its graduates are eligible automatically for teaching certificates.

ANOTHER VIEW OF COMPETENCY-BASED TEACHER EDUCATION

Many educators have expressed reservations about CBTE because some of its tenets and practices are based on assumption, opinion, and casual observation. Andrews identified four commonly held false assumptions:

1. A list exists which includes the basic competencies all teachers should possess and be able to demonstrate.
2. Techniques exist to evaluate objectively whether or not a candidate actually has these competencies.
3. Research has shown which teacher competencies are related to children's learning.
4. Developing a competency system of preparation and evaluation is a relatively simple task and not likely to be more expensive than present systems.[5]

Most states have, nevertheless, based their teacher certification requirements on competency-based teacher education.

Carroll Gonzo poses several questions to determine how to approach the subject: Who is competent to judge competence? What is competence? What is basic? Where are the philosophical roots to justify CBTE? In what learning theory is it nested? What teaching theory embraces it? He writes: "With the arrival of Competency Based Education, the pedagogical road to Eden has not unequivocally been found."[6] Probably the most frequently criticized aspect of this mode of teacher education is the fact that an aesthetically based subject does not lend itself readily to the requirements of behavioral objectives.

Abraham Schwadron commented:

> Aesthetic matters were neatly placed in "affective domains." Considering the highly subjective nature of the arts, the covertness of the aesthetic experience, and the longitudinal factors critical to any true attempts at evaluation, the entire design looms up as a convenient misconception, musically and aesthetically fallacious and insensitive. First, the nature of music. . . does not lend itself to the immediacy of quantitative measures. Hence it is disappointing to hear from music educators that since the aesthetic response cannot be overtly observed, or objectively measured, ergo it cannot significantly contend with the "pressing" need for accountability. Second, it has been stated . . . that aesthetic responses cannot be taught. May I suggest . . . that if something is learned, some mode of teaching is responsible.[7]

Despite its controversial nature and the difficulty of applying it to music education, performance-based teacher education has taken a firm hold in the education and certification of teachers. It is the norm and will probably continue to be the basis for teacher preparation in the future,

Examinations to Qualify for Teaching

The National Teacher Examination

As of 1992 forty states required applicants for certification to pass tests. Twenty-four of them required completion of at least one part of the National Teacher Examination (NTE) of the Educational Testing Service (ETS) of Princeton, New Jersey. The NTE consists of standardized examinations of academic achievement. There is a core battery of tests and seventy-eight specialty area tests. The three core battery tests cover general knowledge, communication skills, and professional knowledge. The music education examination tests for understanding of the basic content of undergraduate music courses. It covers basic musicianship (music history, theory, and performance skills), curriculum and instruction, and professional information.

Praxis

ETS developed The Praxis series in 1993. It is in three parts and includes "assessments for each stage of the beginning teacher's career, from entry into teacher education to actual classroom performance."[8] The Praxis series

> provides measures of academic achievements and proficiencies for students entering or completing college or provisional teacher preparation programs and for individuals in professional areas. Such testing may provide information helpful to policy makers in making licensing decisions, to educational institutions in evaluating programs, and to examinees in assessing their own qualifications regarding subject and/or pedagogical knowledge.[9]

Praxis I, *Academic skills Assessments*, measures competence in basic skills: reading, mathematics, writing. Praxis II, *Subjects Assessments*, measures knowledge of content area, which includes the major area. It includes the continuation of the NTE Programs Core Battery tests and tests for communication skills (listening, reading, writing), general knowledge (social studies, mathematics, literature and fine arts, science), and professional knowledge (planning instruction, implementing instruction, evaluating instruction, managing the instructional environment, professional foundations, professional functions).

Praxis III, *Classroom Performance Assessment*, was developed in response to increasing demands by state departments of education to measure performance in the classroom as a licensing criterion. It takes into account the complexity of the classroom milieu and divergent requirements for various subjects. It requires teachers to demonstrate the ability to make proper decisions, and to be guided by them. Praxis III employs trained observers, who use a common framework of criteria that reflects the licensure requirements of the various states.

Like the NTE, Praxis is not required in all states. In 1994 seventeen states required the music education test of Praxis II. Only one state required the music tests. The content of Praxis II is as follows:

MUSIC HISTORY AND LITERATURE

Music of all periods

Style periods (chronology)

Stylistic characteristics (melody, rhythm, harmony, texture, dynamics)

Composers

Genres

Music literature

Performance media (instruments, voice, and electronic media)

Music Theory

Compositional organization (pitch, rhythm, rhythm, texture, form, improvisation, expressive elements)

Acoustics

Performance skills

Conducting

Interpretation of style and symbols, including score reading

Improvisational techniques

Performance literature

Critical listening and performance error recognition

Acoustical considerations (rehearsal and performance areas)

Curriculum, Instruction, and Professional Concerns

Course offerings from K–12

Course content, including psychomotor, cognitive, and affective behaviors,conceptual elements of music, learning sequence, performance skills appropriate to grade level, interdisciplinary aspects, evaluation of students, pedagogical approaches, selection of appropriate vocal and instrumental materials, classroom management skills

Sociology, philosophy, psychology, and history of music education

Professional literature (journals, reference works, other source materials)

Professional practices and ethics

Professional organizations

Many questions are based on tape-recorded excerpts.[10]

MATCH

In 1994 Educational Testing service created a new computerized database called MATCH. lt is relational, and allows users to access both the content area requirements for teacher licensing and the math and science requirements for students in each state. Catherine Havrilesky writes, "Schools cannot achieve their educational goals if they hold their teachers and students to different academic standards."[11] MATCH makes it possible for future teachers and state certification officers to easily and quickly compare a college student's preparation in math and science with the public school curriculum to determine whether there is a match. It is possible that ETS will expand MATCH in the future to include all of the subjects for which national standards have been developed.

Professional Certification

Professional certification is a new vehicle for certifying deserving teachers as outstanding. It is an entirely different process from that of certification by state departments of education. The National Board for Professional Teaching Standards was instituted in 1987 "to establish high and rigorous standards for what teachers should know and be able to do and to certify teachers who meet those standards." The first certifications were granted in 1993. Professional certification is not mandatory, but it is desirable to those whose performance warrants recognition by a national certifying body. Assessment of teaching effectiveness is done with objective measures, essays, interviews, simulated performances, documentation, and observation by trained examiners. When enough teachers have achieved national certification, that recognition is expected to carry some weight in hiring preferences, salary adjustments, and promotions. Earlier, MENC had instituted its own Professional Certification Program as a vehicle to recognize excellence in music teaching, but in 1994 its National Executive board voted to discontinue it because it duplicated the work of the National Board for Professional Teaching Standards.

Partnerships in the Education of Music Teachers

With the development of competency-based teacher education and assessment requirements, it has been necessary for the process of teacher education to expand beyond universities to involve educators in schools. One developing trend is the transformation of the student teaching experience from the status of classroom visitor to an intensive internship in a professional development center staffed by expert teachers and university personnel. Professional development centers are similar in concept to university laboratory schools, which have come to be regarded by some as elitist. Laboratory schools were usually of the highest quality, but being laboratories, most of their students were the children of the faculty of the institution to which the schools belonged. Being so selective, many laboratory schools did not reflect a realistic view of the schools in which education majors would eventually teach. Professional development centers, on the other hand, are schools that already exist in a public school system, and are operated in cooperation with one or more universities. As an entity of the school system they are able to identify and meet the teacher training needs of the schools.

The MENC Task Force on Music Teacher Education for the Nineties

In 1984 MENC appointed the Task Force on Music Teacher Education for the Nineties to gather and synthesize information from music educators and other interested individuals throughout the country, and to make recommendations for change. Gerald B. Olson, chair of the task force, wrote:

> The time to implement positive changes for teacher education is now. Specifically, we must implement in such a way that needed change can evolve through procedures and structures put in place for the future. To that end, the task force is calling for a focus on partnership and process in music teacher education—a partnership of all parties that have an expressed interest in the preparation of school music educators, and a process for preparing teachers that addresses and accommodates inevitable change, personal differences, and personal growth.[12]

The task force considered research-based education improvement, alternative schools, magnet schools, voucher plans, and the increasing school population before suggesting a view of the future and proposing fundamental changes in music teacher education. It described possible changes in the recruitment, selection, and retention of music educators, teacher certification, professional development programs, and the proposed partnership for music teacher education involving cooperating school music educators, music education professors, and music professors. Many of the recommendations of the task force have been implemented in teacher preparation programs.

Music Education Research

Research, or systematic inquiry, is the major interest of many music educators. They seek solutions to practical problems in music education, to satisfy personal curiosity about problems that can be solved only by the application of research techniques, and to contribute to a body of knowledge that is of interest to other researchers, practitioners, and curriculum developers. Music education research has been conducted throughout most of the twentieth century, but it became a serious aspect of the profession only when the *Journal of Research in Music Education* (JRME) began publication in 1953 under the auspices of MENC. Since that time, MENC has been the principal supporter of research activities in the United states outside of colleges and universities. Although most music education research is undertaken by higher education faculty and graduate students, it is MENC that has sponsored publications and various research events that are beyond the means of colleges and universities. Virtually all graduate music education students take at least one research course designed to introduce them to systematic inquiry, including the rationale, techniques, and tools of research. These courses prepare students to become researchers, or at least give them enough expertise to be able to read research reports and articles knowledgeably and critically.

The Music Education Research Council

The impetus for MENC involvement in the sponsorship of research was the Educational Council. Established in 1918, the Council was the forerunner of the Music Education Research Council (MERC), the body that now governs MENC research activities. Educational Council publications consisted of reports, curriculum guides, information on the training of music supervisors, and a variety of topics concerning music education. Most of the reports were based on survey data, from which the Council drew its recommendations. One of the most significant reports was *The Present Status of Music Instruction in Colleges and High schools, 1919–1920*, which was published as Bulletin Number 9 by the U.S. Bureau of Education.

The name of the Council was changed in 1923 to the National Research Council of Music Education. The National Research Council continued to publish bulletins reporting on survey studies of various aspects of music education. In 1932 its name was changed again, this time to the Music Education Research Council (MERC), which has remained the research branch of MENC to the present day. MERC continued the research bulletin series, covering such topics as rural schools, music supervision, standard courses of study in music, basic programs of study, and music in the senior high school, among others. Nineteen bulletins had been published by the time the series ended in 1940. The most influential of the bulletins was the seventeenth, *Music Rooms, Buildings and Equipment,* which was published in 1934, and published in new editions in 1949, 1955, and 1966.

The responsibilities of MERC are:[13]

1. To serve as the governing body of the SRME [Society for Research in Music Education] and implement the objectives of the society.

2. To organize and administer a suitable variety of research sessions at the national conventions of the MENC.

3. To coordinate and guide the work of the divisional and state research chairmen.

4. To cooperate, individually or collectively, with any agency or organization in any project likely to enhance the status of research in music education improve the quality or increase the quantity of such research, or facilitate the application of the results of such research; and to support, encourage, and promote all types of

research in music education and fields related to music education.

5. To advise and cooperate with the Curator of the MENC historical Center and the University of Maryland in developing and administering the Center.

6. To function as a source of information, coordination, and communication in all matters affecting research in music education nationally and internationally.

7. To recommend for publication, position papers relating to research problems (evaluation, design, measurement, value of inferential statistics, bibliography, curriculum, etc,) with a view to establishing guidelines in research practices in music education.

8. To sponsor institutes and publish proceedings for the purpose of critically examining current research findings in specific subject areas with a view toward their application and implementation in educational practice.

9. To cooperate with the President, National Executive Board, publication committee, or any other MENC committee or unit in matters relating to research in music education.

MERC was relatively inactive from 1940 until 1960, when it began a collaborative relationship with the *Journal of Research in Music Education. JRME* and MERC cosponsored the *Bibliography of Research Studies in Music Education, 1949–1957,* the *American Index to the Musical Quarterly, 1915–1957, Music Education Materials—A Selected Bibliography,* and *Basic Concepts in Music Education* (1958). These publications and other projects helped revitalize MERC, which has provided important service to the profession since then.

The Society for Research in Music Education

The Society for Research in Music Education (SRME) was established in 1960 under the governance of MERC. The objective of SRME is "the encouragement and advancement of research in those areas pertinent to music education." Its aims are:[14]

1. Sponsor meaningful sessions at MENC national conventions devoted to reports of research studies and relevant topics.

2. Through its divisional and state units, sponsor similar sessions at the divisional and state levels.

3. Provide an effective framework for the exchange of information among persons engaged in or interested in research in music education.

4. Encourage all research in music education and in fields related to music education.

In 1963 the *Journal of Research in Music Education* became the official publication of SRME. MENC members who subscribe to JRME are automatically members of SRME. SRME also oversees the publication of *Update: The Applications of Research in Music Education.*

SPECIAL RESEARCH INTEREST GROUPS

In 1978 several Special Research Interest Groups (SRIG) were formed at the MENC national convention. The SRlGs, which operate under the governance of MERC, serve music educators who share similar research interests. Each SRIG publishes a newsletter and meets at MENC national conventions. The apportionment of the eleven SRIGs' 1994 membership[15] suggest the distribution of research interests in the music education profession:

Affective	180
Creativity	72
Early Childhood	180
General Research	200
History	436
Instructional Strategies	200
Learning and Development	200
Measurement and Evaluation	700
Perception	100
Philosophy	300
Social Sciences	242

THE MENC HISTORICAL CENTER

The MENC Historical Center was established at the University of Maryland, College Park, in 1965 as the official MENC archive. MENC and the University of Maryland share governance. Its purpose is "to preserve the documents and materials that have reflected and influenced the history of musical instruction in the United States."[16] An outstanding archival collection of MENC materials and other important documents and artifacts, the Center is part of a group of collections called Special Collections in Music.[b]

---

[b]Special Collections in Music embraces the archival collections of the American Bandmasters Association, American String Teachers Association, Association for Recorded Sound Collections, College Band Directors National Association, International Association of Music Libraries (U. S. Branch), International Clarinet Association, International Society for Music Education, Maryland Music Educators Association, Music Educators National Conference, Music Library Association, Music OCLC Users Group. Mid-West International Band and Orchestra Clinic, National Association of College Wind and Percussion Instructors, National School Orchestra Association, Organization of American Kodály Educators, and Society for Ethnomusicology.

The Journal of Research in Music Education

The *Journal of Research in Music Education* began publication in 1953 under its founding editor, Allen P. Britton, whose title was Chairman of the Editorial Committee, and whose first editorial working space was his dining room table. The original purpose of JRME was to publish "articles which report the results of research in any phase of music education." Initially, many of the articles were based on historical and descriptive research. In the early 1960s music educators, like those in other educational disciplines, started to value experimental methods, and articles based on that kind of research began to appear in *JRME*. By the time Robert G. Petzold became editor in 1972 the majority of articles were based on experimental and descriptive research techniques. James C. Carlsen became editor in 1978, George L. Duerksen (acting editor) in 1981, Jack A. Taylor in 1982, Rudolph Radocy in 1986, and Harry Price in 1994. *JRME* now publishes "reports of research that clearly make a contribution to theories of music education."

The Council for Research in Music Education

The Council for Research in Music Education (CRME) was established in 1963 by Richard Colwell and sponsored by the University of Illinois and the Illinois Office of the Superintendent of Public Instruction. The *Bulletin of the Council for Research in Music Education* is published by the University of Illinois. Each issue contains a few research-based articles and several reviews by CRME members of doctoral dissertations. CRME also publishes indices of recently completed music education doctoral dissertations available for review in the *Bulletin*.

Other Research Journals

Although the *Journal of Research in Music Education* has been the major outlet for music education research since 1963, several others have been established to satisfy the needs of specialized research interests, or to provide more opportunity for persons in particular states to publish the results of their research.

The *Missouri Journal of Research in Music Education*, established in 1962, is a publication of the Missouri State Department of Education. The journal publishes "contributions of a philosophical, historical or scientific nature which reports the results of research pertinent in any way to instruction in music in the educational institutions of Missouri."

The *Bulletin of Research*, sponsored by the Pennsylvania Music Educators Association, was founded in 1963. Its editorial policy is as follows:

> The Editorial Board encourages and solicits written reports of innovative teaching efforts which show positive results in actual practice.

Although some researchers feel that informality results in question-able validity and reliability, the Editorial Board of the Bulletin feels that many valuable projects go unrecognized. In our opinion, certain of these efforts are true research and deserve to be reported. The more formal and characteristic research reports are nonetheless important, and the Editorial Board feels a continued need to report them as well as applied research that may not conform to tradition-al research patterns. Articles which synthesize research studies from a variety of sources also are solicited.

Contributions to Music Education, founded in 1972, is the research Journal of the Ohio Music Educators Association. Its purpose is

to support scholarly work in Music Education conducted in Ohio primarily and in the field of Music Education as a whole secondari-ly. The intent of the Journal is to provide a needed addition to the existing journals of research in Music Education in the United states. . . . Contributions contains research reports, speculations about research, book reviews, and discussions about knowledge in music education and research methodology. All forms of inquiry are to be included—descriptive, experimental, historical, and philosophical as well as unusual speculative articles.

The Bulletin of Historical Research in Music Education was founded by George Heller in 1980 as an outgrowth of the newly established history special Research Interest Group of MENC. Published by the University of Kansas, it is a forum for music education historians, an outlet for the publication of research findings in the history of music education, and a source of information pertinent to research in the history of the profession. It publishes "research of a philosophical and historical nature per-tinent in any way to music education."

The *Southeastern Journal of Music Education*, established in 1989, is published by the University of Georgia. It "is offered as a service to the profession, providing for the distribution of a broad spectrum of research across all levels and areas of education within music."

Update: The Applications of Research in Music Education, established in 1982 by Charles Elliott, was originally published by the Department of Music of the University of South Carolina and is now a publication of the Music Educators National Conference. lt contains research-based articles reported in nontechnical language and articles about research. The arti-cles may take the form of a "review of the literature or may report the findings of a single research study if that study is of sufficient scope." Emphasis is on interpretation and application in the classroom rather than research procedures and statistics.

The Quarterly Journal of Music Teaching and Learning was established by Richard Colwell in 1989 at the University of Northern Colorado to present scholarly essays and a forum for music education scholars. It covers a broad range of topics related to music education, with occasional special interest issues.

Philosophy of Music Education Review was founded in 1993 by Estelle Jorgensen and is published by the School of Music of Indiana University. Its purpose is "to disseminate philosophical research in music education to an international community of scholars, artists, and teachers."

In addition to the above, several foreign journals publish research articles pertinent to music education, the International Society for Music Education (ISME) sponsors a variety of special interest organizations, one of which is its Research Commission. The Commission meets before each biennial ISME meeting to share research findings of international interest.

Handbook of Research on Music Teaching and Learning

The publication of the *Handbook of Research on Music Teaching and Learning* in 1992 was one of the most significant events in the recent history of music education research because "It is the definitive guide to the sources, methodologies, issues, and controversies surrounding international music education."[17] The *Handbook*, edited by Richard Colwell, was sponsored by MENC and published by Schirmer Books. It contains original essays by fifty-five scholars from the United states, the United Kingdom, Canada, and Australia.

Research Symposia and Conferences

THE ANN ARBOR SYMPOSIUM

MENC, the University of Michigan, and the Theodore Presser Foundation cosponsored the three segments of the Ann Arbor symposium "The Applications of Psychology to the Teaching and Learning of Music" at the University of Michigan in 1978, 1979, and 1981. The purpose of the symposium was to explore the relationship between research in certain areas of behavioral psychology and music education. The event provided a forum for researchers in the psychology of music education and those in the psychology of learning to discuss the results of their research and to discourse on the relationships of their work. The subject was of particular interest to the music education profession because of the growing interest on the part of music educators in cognitive psychology.

In session I (1978) papers were presented by leading music education researchers to acquaint the participating psychologists with music education practices, and to present issues to which research psychologists might contribute their knowledge and expertise. Session II (1979) consisted of presentations of papers by psychologists on the topics discussed by the music educators the year before. The 1981 session allowed further structured contacts between music education researchers and psychologists.

THE WESLEYAN SYMPOSIUM ON THE APPLICATION OF SOCIAL ANTHROPOLOGY TO THE TEACHING AND LEARNING OF MUSIC

The Wesleyan Symposium was held in August 1984 under the sponsorship of Wesleyan University, MENC, and the Theodore Presser Foundation at Wesleyan University in Middletown, Connecticut. Like the Ann Arbor Symposium, this event reflected current interest by music educators in world musics and pedagogical practices in teaching them.

OTHER SYMPOSIA AND CONFERENCES

The two symposia describe above were the first major events of this type since the Tanglewood Symposium of 1967. Having proved the value of this kind of scholarly meeting to the profession, many other symposia and conferences have taken place since, most of them dedicated to specialized professional interests. Their topics have been philosophy of music education, general research, general music, early childhood education, conducting, history, and social psychology. Occasional symposia have also been held to honor such events as college centennials and outstanding individuals such as Charles Leonhard of the University of Illinois. Each symposium has resulted in a notable publication. One event, the Research Conference on Qualitative Methodologies in Music Education I, was of special interest to all music education researchers because its topic embraces virtually every research specialty. The conference took place in May 1994 under the sponsorship of the School of Music of the University of Illinois. A second qualitative methodologies conference took place in 1996, also at the University of Illinois. It is possible that increased interest in qualitative methods will be reflected in research journals in the future. Jerrold Ross was outspoken about the need for qualitative research as a means of helping to solve some of the problems of music education:

> [There is a] need for a war on research as it is now conducted at the university level akin to the war on poverty once declared by Lyndon Johnson. For it is poverty of education, poverty of cultural knowledge, and poverty of spirit that now confronts our field. We need qualitative research, frequently and appropriately supported by quantitative data, to move music education into the forefront of educational thought in this country.[18]

Ross urges doctoral students to focus their research on such relevant topics as how children learn music and benefit from it; music teacher preparation; the results of collaboration among classroom teachers, music teachers, and arts-in-residence; the lifelong effects of music education;

what it is that general educators, administrators, and general policy makers expect as the outcomes of music education; and links between music and cognition.[19]

Conclusion

There has never been a strong relationship between music education research and practice, and the research community remains somewhat isolated from that of practitioners. Except for occasional exceptions, such as the work of Edwin Gordon, researchers have often taken the position that as the body of research literature increases practitioners will find ways to use it. In an unpublished speech before the MENC research community in 1986, Robert Petzold said:

> Education and music education have not yet satisfactorily solved the perennial problem of how to narrow that gap between what research has learned about ways to improve practice and what the practitioner is doing. Educational practice, based largely on tradition, common sense, experience, and common consensus is unlikely to change as a consequence of isolated studies which are seen to have little relationship to the music teaching-learning process.[20]

It is possible that the movement toward assessment in education will bring researchers and practitioners closer together as they cooperate in meeting the demands of educational accountability. The research community has enough members with the skill and experience to support the profession's need for research-based practices.

NOTES

1 National Advisory Council on Education Professions Development, *Competency Based Teacher Education: Toward a Consensus* (Washington, DC: National Advisory Council on Education Professions Development, 1976), 6, 7.

2 Dennis M. Holt, "Competency Based Music Teacher Education: Is Systematic Accountability Worth the Effort?" *Bulletin* of the Council for Reserach in Music Education, no. 40 (Winter 1974): 1.

3 Robert Klotman, ed., *Teacher Education in Music: Final Report* (Washington, DC: Music Educators National Conference, 1972).

4 Ibid., 4–7.

5 T. E. Andrews, "What We Know and What We Don't Know," in Houston, ed., *Exploring Based Education* (Berkeley, CA: McCutchan, 1979).

6 Carroll Gonzo, "A Critical Look at Competency Based Education," *Contributions to Music Education* (1981/1982): 181.

7 Abraham A. Schwadron, "Music Education and Teacher Preparation: Perspectives from the Aesthetics of Music," *Journal of Musicological Reasearch* (1982): 181.

8 The Praxis Series, *Arts* (Princeton, NJ: Educational Testing Service, 1994), 3.

9 The Praxis Series, *Core Battery Tests and Multiple Subjects Assessment for Teachers* (Princeton, NJ: Educational Testing Service), 4.

10 Ibid., 23.

11 Catherine Havrilesky, "New Database 'MATCH'es Teacher Requirements and Curriculum Standards," *ETS Developments* 40, no. 1 (Fall 1994): 2.

12 Gerald B. Olson, "Preface," *Music Teacher Education: Partnership and Process* (Reston, VA: Music Educators National Conference, 1984), 11.

13 "Handbook of the Society for Research in Music Education," *Journal of Research in Music Education*, 9, no. 2 (Summer 1971): 243.

14 Ibid., 239.

15 Charles A. Elliot, ed., "Comments from the Editor." *Update: Applications of Research in Music Education* 13, no. 1 (Fall–Winter 1994): inside front cover.

16 Ibid., 249.

17 Richard Colwell, ed., *Handbook of Research on Music Teaching and Learning* (New York: Schirmer Books, 1992), front flap.

18 Jerrold Ross, "Research in Music Education: From a National Perspective." *Bulletin*, Council for Research in Music Education, no. 123 (Winter 1994/1995): 131.

19 Ibid., 130–31.

20 Reported in Michael Mark, "A History of Music Education Research," *Handbook of Research on Music Teaching and Learning* (New York: Schirmer Books, 1992), 57.

Part IV

FINALE

9

The Assessment of Music Education

Assessment and Educational Reform

Assessment is a key word in every educational reform movement. Common sense dictates that teachers must know what their students learn and how effective their own methods are. Policymakers rely heavily on assessment before making critical decisions, whether about education or national security. Without assessment, there can be no realistic planning for change and improvement. Yet, for over 150 years accurate, reliable assessment has eluded music educators, as it has the education profession as a whole. A profession cannot grope in the dark in the vague hope of finding the right path, however, and so assessment, accurate or not, takes place regularly at the individual, classroom, local, state, and national levels.

The first attempt at state-wide assessment of music education practices occurred in 1837. Henry Barnard, the Connecticut state superintendent of schools, persuaded the legislature to sponsor a survey of teachers. The survey included eight questions on music. The eight questions reveal the undeveloped state of survey research at that time, but they could have elicited rudimentary data that might have had some use in planning:

Can you sing by note?

Can you play any instrument?

Do you teach or cause singing in school, either by rote or by note?

Do you use singing as a relieving exercise for ill humor or weariness in schools?

Do you use any instrument, or have any used, as an accompaniment to singing?

263

Do you teach your pupils to use the proper musical voice in singing?

Do you do so from ear, or from knowledge of the physiology of the vocal organs?

How many of your pupils prove on trial unable to understand

music, or acquire even a moderate degree of proficiency in the practice?[1]

Unfortunately, Mr. Barnard's position was eliminated soon after the survey, and the first attempt at statewide music education research proved to be the last for a long time. There is no evidence that the survey results had any affect on practices in schools.[2] The most recent Connecticut survey of arts education is described later in this chapter.

The educational reform movements of the contemporary era of music education have fostered interest in national assessments of several subject areas, including music. The broadest in scope, and possibly the most controversial, is the National Assessment of Educational Progress.

The National Assessment of Educational Progress

Until the 1970s there had been no evaluation of the results of music education on a national scale. American education methods, standards, and goals are extremely diversified, and a nationwide evaluation would be complex and expensive. The need for a national assessment of education became apparent in the early 1960s, when the education reform movement was well under way. The tremendous increase in education expenditures in the late 1950s and early 1960s was for education input (personnel, teacher retraining, curriculum development, equipment, and facilities). During this time of government generosity for educational research and development grants, however, many people suspected that increased input did not necessarily improve the output. There was no accurate way to correlate the enormous resources being invested in education with the results of the investment. Standardized achievement tests had been in use for decades, but they indicate comparative levels of achievement rather than what students have actually learned. Thus, standardized tests were unsuitable for a national assessment of education.

In 1963 Dr. Francis Keppel, U.S. Commissioner of Education, initiated several conferences to explore ways of obtaining the needed information. The result was the formation of a committee called the Exploratory Committee on Assessing the Progress of Education (ECAPE) in 1964. ECAPE was "to examine the possibility of conducting an assessment of educational attainment on a national basis."[3] Having determined that such an assessment was feasible, ECAPE selected ten disciplines for the initial assessment: art; career and occupational development; citizenship; literature; mathematics; music; reading; science; social studies; and writing. The committee in charge of the project was called the Committee on Assessing the Progress of Education (CAPE). CAPE began its work in 1969 under the auspices of the Carnegie Corporation, but later in the same year control was shifted to the Education Commission of the States, which still operates it. The U.S. Office of Education (USOE), now the U.S. Department of Education, provides funds and monitors the National Assessment of Educational Progress (NAEP).

The first assessment could only establish baseline data by which future ratings were to be measured. Keppel was warned by educators of the inherent danger of misinterpreting data from the first assessment and was urged to take care in reporting its results to the public. Unfortunately, the press repeatedly neglected to report that the data from the first assessment would have meaning only in relation to future assessments. Negative headlines usually highlighted newspaper reports of the raw data. This shook the confidence of the public and dealt a blow to education. The second music assessment was done in 1978 and 1979. It provided the comparison with the first assessment that was so badly needed.

The Goals of NAEP

NAEP provides information to educational decision makers and teachers that can be used to establish educational priorities and determine national progress in education. Its goals are (1) to measure changes in the educational attainments of young Americans; (2) to make available on a continuing basis comprehensive data on the educational attainments of young Americans; (3) to utilize the capabilities of NAEP to conduct special interest "probes" into selected areas of educational attainment; (4) to provide data, analyses, and reports in a form that could be understood by a variety of audiences; (5) to encourage and facilitate interpretive studies of NAEP data, thereby generating implications useful to educational practitioners and decision makers; (6) to facilitate the use of NAEP technology at state and local levels when appropriate; (7) to continue to develop, test, and refine the technologies necessary for gathering and analyzing NAEP achievement data; (8) to conduct an ongoing program of research and operational studies necessary for the resolution of problems and refinement of the NAEP model.[4]

Methodology of NAEP

The first NAEP asked questions of respondents at four age levels; the second queried respondents at three age levels. Each question, or task (exercise), reflects a previously defined educational goal or objective. The exercises are administered to scientifically selected samples that take into account demographic factors—community size and socioeconomic status of the respondents—as well as ethnic categories (only for the second assessment). Respondents were selected from all parts of the country. Students were sampled at three age levels that represent educational milestones: age 9, when most are near the completion of their primary education; age 13, when most have completed their elementary school education; and age 17, when most are still in school and completing their secondary education. The first assessment also sampled 17-year-olds who were not in school in order to gain a more accurate picture of their skills, knowledge, and attitudes; this group was not sampled in the second assessment. Another group, young adults (ages 26 to 35), was included only in the first assessment to determine the educational results for people who had completed their formal education and had been away from school for years.

NAEP does not score or rank individual respondents. It determines how groups at the four age levels perform on specific exercises and, within each age level, how groups of individuals perform, taking into consideration demographic and sociological variables. It is unnecessary for each respondent to take every exercise. The exercises are divided into booklets, and each respondent takes only one. The samples for each booklet are statistically equivalent, which allows comparisons to be made across them. This allows NAEP to assess performance on more exercises than is possible in the usual testing situation.

Most exercises are multiple-choice questions, but there are also open ended exercises that require responses varying in length from a few words to a long essay. Some employ pictures, tapes, films, or practical everyday items as stimuli. Individual interviews, the manipulation of appropriate apparatus to solve a problem, and observations of the respondents' problem-solving techniques supplement the paper-and-pencil tasks. For example, in music, respondents were asked to sing a song or perform on an instrument; in science, to conduct a small experiment; in math, to make change from a change drawer; in social studies, to interpret an election ballot. Affective exercises and attitude questions are also included because positive attitudes and opinions about the various learning areas are considered important educational attainments.

NAEP exercises are administered either to individuals or to small groups (not larger than twelve) by specially trained personnel, but individuals are not ranked according to their performance. Because the aim of NAEP is to describe attainment, it does not emphasize exercises that require high discrimination ability. The exercises cover the entire spectrum of difficulty, from very easy tasks to the most difficult.

NAEP differs from standardized achievement tests in several ways.[5]

Standardized Tests	**NAEP**
Norm-referenced.	Content or objective-referenced.
All respondents take every exercise, are scored for their performance, and are ranked with respect to a reference group.	No individual respondent takes all of the exercises, receives a score, or is ranked.
Mass administered.	Administered to individuals or small groups.
Multiple-choice format.	Variety of exercise formats.
Focus on the cognitive domain.	Exercises relate to cognitive and affective domains.
Respondents read the items for themselves.	Exercises are read to respondents by a paced tape recording or by the exercise administrator in an interview situation.
Test items are not made public.	Half of the exercises are released so the public can understand NAEP methods.

NAEP in Music

Before constructing assessment instruments for each subject area, NAEP set basic guidelines for the development of objectives. Its objectives had to be acceptable to scholars, educators, and thoughtful lay citizens, and stated in behavioral terms. NAEP brought together scholars, teachers, and curriculum specialists to develop objectives and prototype exercises. The Educational Testing Service (ETS) of Princeton, New Jersey, won the contract to develop music objectives in 1965. It appointed a committee of experts to assist in its work, and disseminated the results of that group's deliberations to research organizations and various individuals for further recommendations. The committee developed broad categories of objectives:

I. Perform a piece of music

A. Sing (technical proficiency not required)

B. Play or sing (technical proficiency required)

C. Invent and improvise (technical proficiency required)

II. Read standard musical notation

A. Identify the elements of notation, such as clefs, letter names of notes, duration symbols, key signatures, and dynamic markings

B. Identify the correct notation for familiar pieces

C. Follow notation while listening to music

D. Sight-sing

III. Listen to music with understanding

A. Perceive the various elements of music, such as timbre, rhythm, melody and harmony, and texture

B. Perceive structure in music

C. Distinguish some differing types and functions of music

D. Be aware of (and recognize) some features of historical styles in music

IV. BE KNOWLEDGEABLE ABOUT SOME MUSICAL INSTRUMENTS, SOME OF THE TERMINOLOGY OF MUSIC, METHODS OF PERFORMANCE, SOME OF THE STANDARD LITERATURE OF MUSIC, AND SOME ASPECTS OF THE HISTORY OF MUSIC

A. Know the meanings of common musical terms to be used in connection with the performance of music, and identify musical instruments and performing ensembles in illustrations

B. Know standard pieces of music by title, or composer, or brief descriptions of the music, or of literary-pictorial materials associated with the music from its inception

C. Know something of the history of music

V. KNOW ABOUT THE MUSICAL RESOURCES OF THE COMMUNITY AND SEEK MUSICAL EXPERIENCES BY PERFORMING MUSIC

A. Know whether or not there are music libraries and stores in the community, and know where concerts are given

B. Seek to perform music by playing, singing, taking lessons, joining performing groups, etc.

VI. MAKE JUDGMENTS ABOUT MUSIC, AND VALUE THE PERSONAL WORTH OF MUSIC

A. Distinguish parodies from their models

B. Be able to describe an important personal "musical" experience.[6]

The 1978–79 assessment provided a measure of change in performance since the 1971–72 assessment. About half of the exercises in the first assessment were repeated in the second under roughly identical administrative conditions. It revised the objectives of the first assessment, and created additional exercises for the new objectives. The second assessment involved approximately 20,000 9-year-olds, 25,000 13-year-olds, and 22,000 17-year-olds.[7] The objectives of the 1978–79 assessment were as follows:

I. VALUE MUSIC AS AN IMPORTANT REALM OF HUMAN EXPERIENCE

A. Be affectively responsive to music

B. Be acquainted with music from different nations, cultures, periods, genres, and ethnic groups

C. Value music in the life of the individual, family, and community
Make and support aesthetic judgments about music

II. PERFORM MUSIC

A. Sing (without score)

B. Play (without score)

C. Sing or play from a written score

D. Play or sing a previously prepared piece

III. CREATE MUSIC

A. Improvise

B. Represent music symbolically

IV. IDENTIFY THE ELEMENTS AND EXPRESSIVE CONTROLS OF MUSIC

A. Identify the elements of music

B. Identify the relationships among elements in a given composition Demonstrate an understanding of a variety of musical terms, expression markings, and conducting gestures m a musical context

V. IDENTIFY AND CLASSIFY MUSIC HISTORICALLY AND CULTURALLY

A. Identify and describe the features that characterize a variety of folk, ethnic, popular, and art music

B. Identify and describe the music and musical style of the various stylistic periods in Western civilization (e.g., Medieval, Renaissance, Baroque, Classical, Romantic).

C. Identify representative composers of each period. Cite examples of ways in which people utilize music in their social and cultural life.[8]

Musical Achievement: The First Assessment

The 1971 music assessment contained fifteen performance exercises, some of which included several parts. The exercises were divided into five groups—singing familiar songs, repeating unfamiliar musical material, improvising, performing from notation, and performing a prepared piece. An administrator read the instructions to each individual, played the stimulus on a tape recorder, and recorded the response on a second one. Individuals were encouraged to record their voices before the administration began to minimize anxiety caused by singing into a microphone. A group of music professionals listened to samples of the responses and constructed scoring guidelines that were sufficiently comprehensive to encompass the wide range of quality in performances, and objective enough to ensure that any given performance would receive the same score from any scorer.

Performance

SINGING FAMILIAR SONGS
About 20 percent of the 9-year-olds, 30 percent of the 13-year-olds, and 40 percent of the 17-year-olds and adults gave performances rated "good" in the unaccompanied singing of "America." Singing with accompaniment, approximately 93 percent of all four age levels were able to keep an acceptable rhythm. Acceptable pitch ranged from 70 percent for adults to 50 percent for 9-year-olds. Success levels were relatively similar for singing a familiar round, but were considerably lower. Forty-five percent of the adults were able to perform a familiar round acceptably.

REPEATING UNFAMILIAR MUSICAL MATERIAL
About half of the older groups and 30 percent of the 9-year-olds were able to repeat a rhythm pattern successfully. Success in repeating a four-measure melodic pattern ranged from 2 percent for 9-year-olds to 9 percent for adults. Acceptable repetition of a harmonic pattern was performed by 8 percent of the 13-year-olds and by 15 percent of adults. This section was not administered to 9-year-olds.

IMPROVISING
From 70 to 90 percent of the various age groups of respondents were successful in improvising a rhythmic accompaniment to a short jazz selection of moderate tempo, but less than 20 percent in any age group added embellishments. Success in improvising a complementary melody to a given one ranged from less than 50 percent to about 60 percent. Those judged "good" ranged from about 20 to 40 percent. Only about 10 percent of the 13-year-olds and adults were able to improvise a harmonic accompaniment acceptably, and many individuals did not attempt to respond to this exercise.

PERFORMING FROM NOTATION
There were four sight-reading exercises. In the simplest, not more than 12 percent of any age group was successful in overall quality, although success rates were higher for the separate aspects of rhythm and pitch.

PERFORMING A PREPARED PIECE
Twenty-five percent of the 9-year-olds, 35 percent of the 13-year-olds, 25 percent of the 17-year-olds, and 15 percent of the adults claimed to play a musical instrument. Approximately half played a prepared piece for the assessment, and about half of those performed a simple piece acceptably. About 60 percent of the respondents were successful in singing a selection of each individual's choice. Females did slightly better than males in all age groups. There was little racial difference in overall performance, although variations occurred in many exercises. In rhythm exercises, for example, 9-, 13-, and 17-year-old blacks attained percent-

ages of 7 or 8 points higher than whites of the same ages. Black adults were at or above the national average in the familiar song, rhythm, melody, and harmony exercises. Children of parents with some post–high school education attained percentages from 5 to 20 points higher than respondents whose parents had no high school education. Respondents from the central United States did slightly better than those from other regions. Respondents from rural communities scored lower in improvising and instrumental performance, especially at the adult level. The younger groups in inner city areas scored considerably lower than the national average, although 9-year-olds in this group attained percentages 7 or 8 points higher than the rest of the nation in tapping a rhythm. The suburban group performed consistently well on practically all of the exercises at every age level.

The NAEP report stated:

> If there is a pattern emerging from all this, it is that people can enjoy and perform music in a rudimentary way but that they are not famil iar with the more technical aspects of music. They can sing, and they like to sing; they hear enough music to recognize the instruments, and they like to listen to music. Only the technical skills and the spe cialized vocabularies that have been constructed to describe music are lacking from the musical background of most individuals. The majority of Americans do enjoy listening to music and can perform music in a rudimentary way.[9]

Knowledge of Musical Notation and Terminology

VOCABULARY

Between 90 and 95 percent of each age group were able to identify which musical element changed in a certain place in a recorded piece of music. Given a choice of "louder," "softer," "slower," or "exactly the same," most respondents correctly identified "louder." This was the only vocabulary exercise in which a majority chose the correct response. Approximately 60 percent of the 17-year-olds, 50 percent of the 13-year-olds, and 25 percent of the 9-year-olds correctly identified a four-phrase structure. But when asked to identify changes in rhythm, melody, and harmony in a heard piece, less than 60 percent identified rhythm, and less than 50 percent identified melody and harmony.

BASIC NOTATION

About 60 percent of the 13-year-olds and 40 percent of the adults were able to identify the note D from a printed list of five choices. Less than 30 percent of any group knew that two eighth notes are equal to a quarter note in duration. In score reading, when asked to mark in the score the place where the recorded music stopped, less than 20 percent of the 9-year-olds were successful, but about 50 percent of the 13-year olds, 70 percent of the 17-year-olds, and 55 percent of the adults succeeded. Not more than 30 percent of any group could identify a discrepancy between a heard melody and a printed score.

Listening to Music with Understanding

AURAL RECOGNITION
All groups did well in identifying the timbres of various instruments, and all groups scored about 90 percent in identifying a piano's timbre. Success rates were also high in identifying a trumpet and a piccolo. Respondents had more difficulty identifying instrumental timbres in a jazz idiom. About 60 percent of the upper age groups were able to identify the tone of a violin and 'cello. In visual recognition tests approximately 80 percent of the upper three age levels could identify a picture of a trumpet among other instruments. The success rate was about 40 percent in visual identification of 'cellos and bassoons.

Music History and Literature

The music history and literature section tested knowledge about music history, genres, styles, and literature. Traditional Western art music, popular, folk, electronic music, and music of earlier periods were included.

PERIODS IN MUSIC HISTORY
Approximately 60 percent of the respondents identified the correct chronological order of five historical periods. When asked to identify the periods of a variety of musical selections, success varied among 17-year-olds from 60 percent (Tchaikovsky) to less than 10 percent (Schoenberg). For adults, the range was from approximately 54 percent to 10 percent. Fewer adults recognized Vivaldi than Schoenberg.

MUSIC GENRES AND STYLES
When asked to recognize style similarities, about 60 percent of the three upper age groups succeeded. Approximately the same percentage was correctly classified jazz pieces as ragtime, boogie-woogie, Chicago school, or modern when they heard boogie-woogie and Dave Brubeck. Between 30 percent and 40 percent identified the styles of Cannonball Adderly, Earl Hines, and Scott Joplin.

MUSIC LITERATURE
Approximately 40 percent to 50 percent of the respondents of the three upper age groups recognized "America the Beautiful." Success in recognizing "This Land Is Your Land" and "When the Saints Go Marching

FIGURE 9.1. Sample NAEP Exercises: Improvising Melody

In Exercise 1H, individuals were asked to listen to the following phrase and then improvise a concluding phrase (m.m. 152):

An acceptable phrase was one which complemented the first phrase and ended with a cadence. About half of the individuals from all four age groups attained acceptable scores. Percentages of good responses were lower, ranging from about 20% for 9-year-olds to about 40% for adults, but criteria for good responses were far more stringent.

SCORING CRITERIA FOR EXERCISE 1H, IMPROVISING MELODY

Good
Acceptable
Poor

Three basic criteria separated the acceptable responses from the poor responses. To be considered acceptable, a response must have begun within two measures of the end of the stimulus, must not have deviated in tempo by more than 10% and must not have contained more than two unidentifiable pitches (pitches a little sharp or flat were acceptable).

Three other criteria separate good responses from other acceptable responses:

A good response must have lasted at least two measures, while other acceptable responses could have been as short as one measure.

Good responses maintained the key, while other acceptable responses could establish and retain a new tonal center in a closely related key (dominant, subdominant, relative minor or parallel minor). Temporary dominant modulation with return to the tonic was not considered to be a change of key.

A good response must have ended on the first, third or fifth degree of the tonic chord with a definite feeling of finish, while other acceptable responses could end on any note in the same key in a clear cadence or half-cadence.

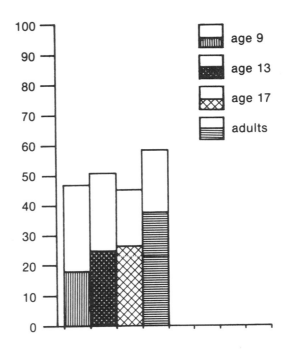

EXHIBIT 8
Percentages of Success for Exercise 1H, Improvising Melody

Note: Example provided by National Assessment of Educational Progress, 860 Lincoln Street, Denver, CO

FIGURE 9.2. Sample NAEP Exercises: Musical Genres

Exercise 5E was administered individually to 9-year-olds, 13-year-olds, 17-year-olds and adults. Administrators read from and recorded responses on pages like the following.

A. Are there any kinds of music that you like to listen to?

		Age Level		
	9	13	17	Adult
Yes (Go to B)	83%	96%	99%	99%
No (Go to D)	16	4	1	1
No response (After 10 seconds, go to D)	1	0	0	0

B.*What one kind of music do you MOST like to listen to?

If no response is given in 10 seconds, go to D.

If respondent names more than one kind of music or says "ALL kinds" ask, *Which kind do you MOST like to listen to?* If respondent gives a general response such as "Popular" or "Classical," ask, *What TYPE of (popular, classical, etc.) music?* Probe to find out the specific kind of music such as rock, blues, opera, symphonic, etc. If respondent names a performer or composer, ask, *What kind of music do you MOST like by that person?*

Go to C.

	Age Level			
	9	13	17	Adult
Instrumental art (e.g., classical, symphonic)	3%	4%	5%	12%
Vocal art (e.g., opera)	1	0	0	1
Jazz	4	5	4	6
Folk	4	2	4	5
Rock	32	57	62	14
Country-western	8	7	5	29
Soul	1	3	5	0
Popular ballads (e.g., barbershop, male vocalists, romantic)	2	2	2	8
Blues	1	1	2	2
Background music	0	0	0	3
Other popular	3	5	4	8
Other types (e.g., unclassifiable responses)	17	7	6	11

C. What other kinds of music do you like to listen to?

(1) _____   (6) _____
(2) _____   (7) _____
(3) _____   (8) _____
(4) _____   (9) _____
(5) _____   (10) _____

Note: Example provided by National Assessment of Educational Progress, 860 Lincoln Street, Denver, CO

If respondent answers "None" OR no response is given in 10 seconds, go to D.

If respondent pauses after first response ask, *What other kinds do you like to listen to?* Probe to find out the specific kinds of music, as in B.

Stop after 10 responses OR when respondent answers "None" OR no response is given in 10 seconds.

	Age Level			
	9	**13**	**17**	**Adult**
At least one additional type named	40%	73%	85%	92%
At least two additional types named	11	38	51	66
At least three additional types named	3	14	26	37

D. Are there any kinds of music that you do NOT like to listen to?

⬭ Yes (Go to E)	62	73	78	82
⬭ No (End the exercise)	36	26	22	18
⬭ No response (After 10 seconds, end the exercise)	2	1	0	0

E. * What one kind of music do you LEAST like to listen to?

If no response is given in 10 seconds, end the exercise.

If respondent names more than one kind of music or says "ALL kinds," ask, *Which kind do you LEAST like to listen to?* If respondent gives a general response such as "Popular" or "Classical," ask, *What TYPE of (popular, classical, etc.) music?* Probe to find out the specific kind of music such as rock, blues, opera, symphonic, etc. If respondent names a performer or composer, ask, *What kind of music do you LEAST like by that person?*

Go to F.

	Age Level			
	9	**13**	**17**	**Adult**
Instrumental art (e.g., classical, symphonic)	4%	9%	14%	9%
Vocal art (e.g., opera)	5	16	15	24
Jazz	2	4	4	7
Folk	2	3	2	1
Rock	8	7	11	25
Country-western	6	12	18	10
Soul	1	1	2	1
Popular ballads (e.g., barbershop, male vocalists, romantic)	4	3	1	0
Blues	1	1	2	1
Other popular	3	5	2	3
Other types (e.g., unclassifiable responses)	18	7	4	1

In" was considerably higher. The three upper levels were less successful in recognizing several" familiar" classical selections (from 3.1 percent to 38.6 percent). Success in matching composers and compositions ranged from 3.6 percent for 13-year-olds hearing Prokofiev's *Peter and the Wolf*) to 52.5 percent for adults hearing Sousa's "Stars and Stripes Forever" (Figs. 9.1, 9.2).

Attitudes Toward Music

The national assessment included exercises designed to elicit information about attitudes toward music. NAEP's survey conditions do not permit the measurement of musical sensitivity. Instead, the exercises measure "approach tendencies," which are assumed to correlate to aesthetic sensitivity. It was found that a majority of people in all four age groups seek out and listen to music at least once a week on television, radio, or recordings. Most people attend live musical programs outside of school, although not frequently. Rock is the kind of music to which 9-, 13-, and 17-year-olds prefer to listen. The greatest percentage of adults (29%) prefer country and western music. Fourteen percent of the adults prefer rock and 12 percent instrumental art music. Lower percentages expressed preferences for vocal art music, folk, soul, popular ballads, blues, background music (3% of adults and no others), other popular musics, and other unclassifiable types. A large majority of respondents at all age levels said that they like to sing "very much" or "somewhat." Twenty percent of the 9-year-olds, 40 percent of the 13-year-olds, and 30 percent of the 17-year-olds most enjoy singing rock, and adults folk (10%), country and western (13%), and popular ballads (12%).

The data indicate that fewer people in each successively higher age group play instruments and that there is a decrease in the amount of time spent playing in each successive group. This is true of all instruments except keyboard and strings, which remain fairly stable through the adult group. A sometimes large majority of each age level indicated that they "strongly agree" or "somewhat agree" that singing or playing an instrument with a large or small group is enjoyable. This exercise indicated a growing interest in small-group participation, which may have implications for music education programs. In response to the exercises concerning membership in musical groups, 22 percent of the 9-year-olds, 27 percent of the 13-year-olds, 20 percent of the 17-year-olds, and 5 percent of the adults indicated that they belonged to a school or community vocal group. Membership in school and community instrumental groups included 8, 17, 10, and 1 percent of the age groups, respectively.

Generally, females of all ages expressed more positive attitudes toward music than did males. Blacks listen more often and enjoy musical participation more than whites and expressed more positive attitudes toward music. Children of parents with some post–high school education enjoy singing and playing more, and were more willing to participate in musical groups than were children of parents with no high school education. There is a slight difference in attitudes between various types of communities, but the greatest differences were in the suburban areas, where there is more playing of instruments, and in the rural areas, where there is more participation in musical groups.

Response to the First NAEP

After the results of the first music assessment were tabulated, the MENC executive board appointed a six-member panel to meet with the National Assessment staff to study the implication of the survey. The panel members, Paul Lehman, Jo Ann Baird, William English, Richard Graham, Charles Hoffer, and Sally Monsour, discussed each group of exercises and identified implications that were "to be interpreted not as statements of fact, but as hypotheses which need further testing." Three statements were offered as a guide to interpretation of the results:

1. The assessment results are based on a random sample of the entire population regardless of musical background or preparation. The data provide valuable insights into the musical competence of the "average" citizen; a study of persons with some degree of training or interest in music would presumably produce quite different findings.

2. Not all of the musical knowledge and skills assessed are directly attributable to formal instruction in schools. Television, radio, and social environments play major roles in developing musical knowledge as well as in influencing musical tastes and attitudes. Thus, the ability of the music teacher to influence the results is limited.

3. Each exercise represents a single, specific skill from a broad array of related skills. It is tempting but hazardous to generalize from one or two discrete bits of information to a more sweeping conclusion. Although certain patterns of results may appear to emerge, the validity of any generalization must be considered in light of a number of related skills and the extent to which they are representative of the generalized array of skills. The variety of skills included in the assessment is so great that the number of exercises devoted to each skill must be very small. As a result, attempts to generalize should be undertaken with the greatest caution.[10]

The Second Music Assessment

Achievement Results for the 1978–1979 Assessment

About three-fourths of the students at each age appear to have positive feelings about music and are able to make simple judgments about it. Many students have some knowledge of musical elements and expressive devices of music. On forty-five questions about elements and devices, the average success rate for 9-year-olds was 52 percent; on 50 questions, the average for 13-year-olds was 61 percent; and on 49 questions, the average for 17-year-olds was 57 percent. Students appear strongest at identifying the elements and devices and weakest at identifying the relationships among them in a given composition. Knowledge about music history and style is less widespread: on 18 exercises assessing these areas, the average success rate for 9-year-olds was 58 percent; on 55 items, the average success rate for 13-year-olds was 36 percent; and on 61 such exercises for 17-year-olds, the average success rate was 39 percent.

Changes in Achievement

Fewer 9- and 17-year-olds were successful in answering their respective exercises in the 1978–79 assessment than in the 1971–72 assessment. The decline between assessments for 9-year-olds was 3.3 percent; for 17-year-olds, it was 2.5 percent. About 41 percent of 13-year olds responded correctly to the music exercise in both assessments. Fewer 9- and 17-year-olds in the second assessment were successful on exercises that required knowledge of the elements and expressive devices of music than in the first assessment. The decline between assessments was 3.4 percent for 9-year-olds and 4.9 percent for 17-year-olds. Knowledge about music history and style did not decline between assessments among 9-, 13-, or 17-year-olds.

Exposure to Music

Nine-year-olds who indicated that they had had music instruction in school during the two year period of 1977 to 1979 performed about 4 percentage points higher on all music exercises than those who had music in school for only one year, and 6 percentage points higher than those who had not had music instruction in school in either year. Seventy-four percent of the 9-year-olds indicated that they "listen to music," 45 percent indicated that they "sing just for fun," and nearly 30 percent that they "play a musical instrument just for fun" in the school music class. More 13- and 17-year-olds participated in general music classes than in choir, band, or orchestra. However, approximately 28 percent of the 13-year-olds and 18 percent of the 17-year-olds had never taken a general music class or music appreciation. Forty-eight percent of the 13-year-olds and 46 percent of the 17-year-olds had never enrolled in choir, chorus, or glee club; 50 percent of the 13-year-olds and nearly 52 percent of the 17-year-olds had never taken band or instrumental music; and slightly more than 90 percent of the 13- and 17-year-olds had never taken orchestra. Those 13- and 17-year-olds who had taken part in school musical activities and classes performed better on the achievement exercises than those students who had not. Achievement results were 12 to 13 percentage points different between students who had no band or orchestra experience and those who had at least three years of participation in this activity. There is also a difference of 6 to 9 percentage points between students who had not participated in choir or glee club and those who had participated for at least three years.[11]

NAEP also gathered data on the musical training background of students. All students participating in the 1978–79 music assessment were asked the same questions about their exposure to musical activities outside of school. More 13- and 17-year-olds than 9-year-olds listen to music, sing alone for fun, and sing with friends for fun. However, percentages for 9- and 13-year-olds are more similar to each other than the percentages of 17 year-olds who sing with friends for fun. Conversely, more 9-year-olds than 13- or 1 7-year-olds indicated that they sing in a church or community music group. Percentages of 9-, 13-, or 17-year-olds who do at least one of the singing activities are very similar. More 13- and 17-year-olds than 9-year-olds play a musical instrument alone for fun, while more 9-year-olds than 13- or 17-year-olds indicated that they play a musical instrument with friends for fun and play a musical instrument in a community group. In addition, more 9-year-olds than 13- or 17-year-olds indicated at least one activity involving playing an instrument. More 9-year-olds than 13- or 17-year-olds take music lessons and make up their own music.[12]

Comparative Results of the Two Assessments

The exercises common to both assessments provided a basis for comparison over a period of several years, but funding limitations prevented the collection of data on students' abilities to perform and to create music during the second assessment. The comparative results indicate that fewer 9- and 17-year-olds were successful in answering their respective exercises in the 1978–79 assessment than in the 1971–72 assessment. The decline between assessments for 9-year-olds able to respond correctly to the music exercises was about 41 percent in both assessments. Achievement results on the objectives indicate fewer 9- and 17-year-olds in the second assessment were successful on exercises that required knowledge of the elements and expressive devices of music than in the first assessment. The decline between assessments was 3.4 percent for 9-year-olds and 4.9 percent for 17-year-olds, but knowledge about music history and style did not decline between assessments among 9-, 13-, or 17-year-olds (Figs. 9.3, 9.4, 9.5).

The results of the second assessment were lower than those of the first in almost every category. Music enrollments had declined by the time of the second assessment, and it tested many more students who had not participated in school music programs. Many of the societal factors discussed in chapters 1 and 2 also influenced the second assessment. School

FIGURE 9.3. National Mean Percentages and Changes on Correct Responses for 9-, 13-, and 17-Year-Olds in Two Music Assessments

	Mean % Correct 1971–72	Mean % Correct 1978–79	Change in Mean % Correct 1971–72, 1978–79
Age 9 Total exercises—25	53.6	50.3	−3.3*
Age 13 Total exercises—69	41.8	41.3	−0.5
Age 17 Total exercises—80	45.7	43.2	−2.5*

*Asterisk indicates percentages statistically significant at the 0.5 level

Music 1971-79. Results from the Second National Music Assessment, no. 10-MU-35, National Institute of Education (pamphlet)

conditions had worsened in the period between the two assessments, and there were fewer music teachers. The increased emphasis on verbal and qualitative learning skills probably contributed to the decline in performance on the second assessment as well. The profession was reflected positively, however, in the increased scores of students who had had music instruction in schools. That finding was significant because it is a positive indication that musical knowledge and skills increase with instruction.

The information in the National Assessment reports was of great potential value to the music education profession, but actually had little influence on practices. Other subjects indicated results similar to those of the music assessment. Reading and writing, for example, both showed declines on the 1992 assessment, although math and science achievement improved slightly. There was less publicity about the second assessment and relatively little public feedback. This might have been because the media had given so much attention to education that the public was overloaded with information, and perhaps even jaded.

The 1997 Assessment of Educational Progress

Two of the major components of the national standards for arts education were an assessment framework, and specifications for a national assessment of knowledge and ability in grades 4, 8, and 12. In 1991, the National Assessment Governing Board, which oversees NAEP, voted to

FIGURE 9.4. National Assessment of Educational Progress in Music: 1971–1972 and 1978–1979

Mean Selected characteristics of participants	Age 9			Age 13			Age 17[a]		
	Mean Percentage correct		Mean change	Mean Percentage correct		Mean change	Mean Percentage correct		Mean change
	1971–1972	1978–1979		1971–1972	1978–1979		1971–1972	1978–1979	
All participants	53.6	50.3	-3.3	41.8	41.3	-0.5	45.7	43.2	-2.5
Region									
Northeast	56.5	51.7	-4.8	42.1	41.8	-0.4	46.6	43.3	-3.3
Southeast	51.0	47.2	-3.9	40.0	39.4	-0.7	43.8	41.3	-2.6
Central	55.0	52.0	-3.1	43.3	42.4	-0.9	47.3	44.1	-3.2
West	51.3	50.4	-1.0	41.3	41.6	+0.3	44.4	43.9	-0.5
Sex									
Male	52.8	49.9	-3.0	40.4	40.2	-0.2	44.4	41.6	-2.8
Female	54.3	50.8	-3.5	43.2	42.4	-0.8	46.9	44.6	-2.2
Race									
Black	43.3	41.0	-2.3	36.1	35.6	-0.4	38.1	36.5	-1.5
White	56.0	52.3	-3.6	42.9	42.4	-0.5	47.0	44.4	-2.6
Hispanic	45.1	42.8	-2.3	36.6	35.1	-1.5	36.4	36.4	0.0
Parental Education									
Not High School Graduate	48.1	44.2	-3.9	38.5	36.8	-1.7	40.2	37.3	-2.9
Graduated High School	53.5	50.5	-3.0	41.8	40.9	-0.9	45.0	41.1	-4.0
Post High School	58.4	54.6	-3.8	45.2	44.2	-1.0	49.2	46.5	-2.7
Size and Type of Community									
Extreme Rural	51.7	45.8	-5.9	40.9	39.3	-1.6	43.4	40.4	-3.0
Low Metropolitan	43.4	42.0	-1.4	36.5	35.1	-1.4	40.7	37.9	-2.8
High Metropolitan	59.8	56.0	-3.8	45.2	45.5	+0.3	49.5	46.5	-3.0
Main Big City	48.9	49.1	+0.2	40.8	40.3	-0.4	44.5	42.7	-1.8
Urban Fringe	56.4	52.9	-3.6	42.4	43.2	+0.8	47.0	43.2	-3.8
Medium City	55.9	49.2	-6.8	41.7	40.0	-1.6	47.2	43.5	-3.6
Small Place	53.2	50.2	-2.9	41.8	41.1	-0.7	44.8	43.3	-1.6

[a]All participants of this age were in school.

Note: The mean change is equal to the difference in the mean correct of each year but may differ in this table because of rounding.

Source: National Assessment of Educational Progress, *Music 1971-79: Results from the Second National Music Assessment,* 1981. Reprinted from Grant, Vance W., and Elden, Leo J., *Digest of Education Statistics,* 1982 (Washington, DC: National Center for Education Statistics), p. 30

FIGURE 9.5. National Assessment of Educational Progress in Music 1971–1972 and 1978–1979

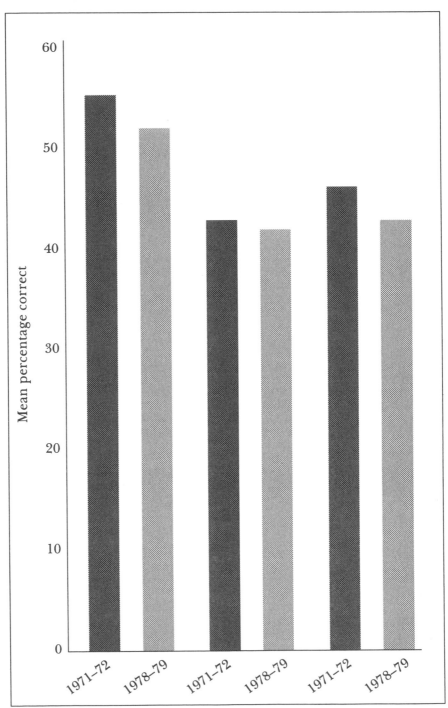

assess arts education in 1996, but in 1994 the Board decided to postpone it until 1997. The arts are the first curricular discipline to be submitted to national assessment on the basis of the national standards, possibly because the National Endowment for the Arts and the Getty Center for Education in the Arts of the J. Paul Getty Trust agreed to fund the assessment.

Ramsay Selden of the Council of Chief State School Officers (CCSSO) and A. Graham Down of the Council for Basic Education co-chaired the Steering Committee for the development of the 1997 assessment. The twenty-eight-member committee includes representatives from professional education organizations, artist organizations, parent organizations, representatives of business and industry, policymakers, and the general public. The function of the Steering Committee is to develop policies and procedures, and a second committee, the thirty-two-member Planning Committee, is responsible for the content and the assessment framework. Its members are K–12 and higher education arts specialists, artists, and assessment specialists. Frank Philip of CCSSO is the chair. The assessment and national standards projects were developed in parallel so they could be coordinated.[13] The fact that A. Graham Down served both as co-chair of the Steering Committee and chair of the Consortium of National Arts Education Associations, which oversaw the development of national arts education standards, assures close coordination of the two processes. Two subcontractors were employed for the project: the College Board wrote the specifications document, and the Council for Basic Education assisted in the consensus process.[14]

Philip explains that achievement in arts education needs to be measured because teachers and students have to be informed about the outcomes of school experiences. Also, arts education, like general education, exists in a world in which priorities are ordered partly on issues other than education. To satisfy political and other community interests, arts education has to prove that its content is substantive, and that student experiences and achievement are similar to those of other subjects. He writes:

> In an age of accountability driven by fewer and fewer resources for education, arts education must join the competition and demonstrate effective learning in an area of the curriculum that provides unique knowledge, skills, and experience not found anywhere else. And while the assessment of arts education cannot accomplish this task alone, it is clearly one key prerequisite to achieving parity in the curriculum.[15]

Despite the high level of visibility of arts education in the new reform movement, Richard Colwell expresses concern about submitting the standards to the NAEP process:

If the standards are voluntary, it follows that the assessment should be. Meaningful assessment in core subjects can never be voluntary. They can be random or stratified but a voluntary assessment can provide data only at the local level. Local evaluations are context specific and based on local objectives and expectations. . . . The best match between a voluntary national assessment would be a voluntary national curriculum and perhaps that is the intent of these individuals working on the national standards project.[16]

He also mentions that the results of the first two assessments were so negative that "curriculum writers elected to ignore the results rather than wrestling with the meaning of the puzzling data." Colwell expressed further concern because the music education profession has little history of systematic evaluation of student achievement, except for performance. Edwin Gordon's work is the lone exception, but because his research and that of his students do not match the national standards, it is not applicable to the national assessment.[17]

It remains to be seen whether the results of the 1997 assessment will affect practice so it can serve as a baseline for future assessments. The first two assessments were intended to be used in this way, but

FIGURE 9.6. Standards & NAEP Arts Assessment

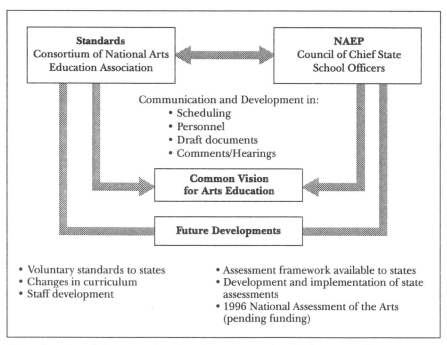

Note: Reprinted from *Arts in Education: From National Policy to Local Community Action*, a publication of the National Assembly of Local Arts Agencies, produced in cooperation with the National Endowment for the Arts

were not. Perhaps the involvement of the arts education community in all phases of the 1997 assessment will assure that the results are used constructively to strengthen and improve arts education in the future.

State Assessments

Because the national standards are voluntary, there is no uniformity in state assessments, and in fact, most states have not assessed arts instruction. There is some pressure, however, from the United States Department of Education for statewide assessments based on the NAEP model. It is possible that new legislation will withhold monies from Chapter 1 (of the Elementary and Secondary Education Act) to states that do not develop acceptable assessment programs. This would be too expensive for any state to bear because Chapter 1 provides numerous support services for underprivileged children, and states could not take on that expense with their own funds.

In 1994 the Council of Chief State School Officers established a program, the State Collaborative on Assessment and Student Standards (SCASS), to assist the states in developing standards and assessment tools:

> SCASS projects are designed to meet a state's assessment development needs, now and under the opportunities offered by Goals 2000. They will develop and provide assessments that can elevate the level of teaching and learning. The projects are an important way of realizing the objectives of the Goals 2000 legislation for improved student assessment programs.[18]

The NAEP/State Collaborative Assessment of Student Standards (a NAEP/SCASS Arts Project) is a sixteen-state consortium to develop state assessment programs based on NAEP, although only a few member states have begun to plan their assessments. Phase 1 of SCASS included the development of prototype exercises appropriate for an NAEP assessment of both large-scale and classroom groups for music, the visual arts, dance, and theater. In Phase 2 the focus shifted from NAEP assessment to prototypes of classroom assessment exercises.

The Illinois assessment was based on multiple choice questions, California developed a performance-based assessment, and Connecticut adopted the NAEP standards for assessment purposes. Activities in other states do not necessarily include arts assessments yet, but are worthy of note because they might eventually embrace arts education.

NEW YORK
New York State is a member of the SCASS Arts Project. In 1994 the New York State Board of Regents, the governing body for education,

adopted a₁ framework for the arts in which state arts standards are related to the national goals. The framework contains four broad standards:

Creating, performing, and participating in the arts
Students will actively engage in the processes that constitute creation and performance in the arts (dance, music, theatre, and visual arts) and participate in various roles in the arts.
Knowing and using arts materials and resources
Students will be knowledgeable about and make use of the materials and resources available for participation in the arts in various roles.
Responding to and analyzing works of art
Students will respond critically to a variety of works in the arts, connecting the individual work to other works and to other aspects of human endeavor and thought.
Understanding the cultural dimensions and contributions of the arts
Students will develop an understanding of the personal and cultural forces that shape artistic communication and how the arts in turn shape the diverse cultures of past and present society.[19]

The New York State Education Department (SED) cooperated with the New York State School Music Association (NYSSMA) to facilitate the adoption of the standards in each community. NYSSMA established Operation Music: New York State (OMNYS) "to lead the State to a uniformly higher level of musical achievement, with the new SED Assessment Frameworks and MENC National Goals as the levels to attain." OMNYS is a two-part curriculum assessment process. Phase I consists of an inventory to be used by individual teachers, or by groups of teachers, to list curriculum content and compare them with the state framework. NYSSMA has regional councils in all parts of the state, and in Phase II, the councils assist teachers in developing local assessment strategies.

MARYLAND

Maryland is also a member of NAEP/SCASS Arts Project, but, as in New York State, no arts assessment has been planned. In 1990 the state adopted a unique assessment program, called the Maryland State Performance Assessment Program (MSPAP). Authentic testing, which has students write, solve practical problems, locate and cite evidence, speak, and listen, is the basis for MSPAP. MSPAP replaces standardized tests, which have had the effect of classifying students for placement in tracks according to achievement and ability. Higher-level skills like problem solving and critical and creative thinking are usually integral to the higher tracks, but not to the lower ones. Thus tracking has a serious negative influence on lower-track students for the rest of their lives, and is discriminatory. The National Association for the Advancement of Colored People Legal Defense Fund, the American Civil Liberties Union, and the Children's Defense Fund have all identified tracking as a major cause of what is called "second-generation" segregation.[20]

The most unusual aspect of MSPAP is that individual student scores are not reported. Instead, schools are rated and held accountable. Rating is based on individual achievement in certain subjects as well as other factors such as average attendance, promotion rate, and dropout rate. MSPAP provides comparative data for the State Department of Education, local boards of education, and communities. In rare cases, schools have scored so low that the State Department of Education has raised the issue of placing them under state control until their scores improve. The relevance of this innovative system to arts educators is that, although it initially disregarded achievement in the arts, in 1994 the Maryland State Board of Education formally adopted arts goals with this resolution:

> By the year 2000, 100 percent of Maryland's students will participate in fine arts (arts education) programs that enable them to meet the content and achievement standards established by State standards for the arts.

FLORIDA

Also in 1994, the Cabinet of the State of Florida endorsed the national standards. Shortly after, the Florida Department of Education began incorporating the arts standards into the state educational reform plan, and they will be assessed with other subject areas. Mary Palmer commented: "In Florida, the arts are a multibillion dollar industry. Three of ten jobs in Florida are arts related. The arts provide connections and understandings among our culturally diverse populations. The arts help keep kids in school and make Florida a better place to live."[21]

These are positive developments for Florida arts educators, but their effects can only be seen when local school system funding issues are resolved. The issues include numbers of teaching positions needed, school time dedicated to arts instruction, state certification standards, and ability to provide suitable facilities and equipment.

MINNESOTA

Minnesota is not a member of NAEP/SCASS Arts Project, but it has developed an assessment plan modeled after NAEP. The state had voluntary assessments in the 1970s, and in 1989 its legislature mandated that school districts use the NAEP in certain subjects. This was the result of increasing public demand for accountability "at the district, building, and learner levels." By law each school district is required to have a curriculum review and improvement cycle for all subjects, and each subject has to be assessed on a cycle of not more than six years.

The Minnesota Department of Education wanted to ensure a "systematic, continuous, census-like survey of knowledge, skills, understanding, and attitudes of students across three age/grade levels and across each subject area."[22] Each subject has a group of "essentials" that specify "what students know, do, create, or value at the time of graduation from high school." The Minnesota Frameworks in Arts Curriculum Strategies Project (FACS) was created to meet the legislative mandate. It is based on the national standards in music, theater, dance, and visual art. FACS then developed the Frameworks of Performance Standards in the Arts. The frameworks are guides for instruction, and are expected to lead to satisfactory assessments. The purpose of the Minnesota Assessment Program is to evaluate program effectiveness and provide a basis for strengthening the curriculum. Susan Vaughan writes:

> The MDE assessment was created to minimize costs of developing and scoring assessment exercises while maximizing the quality of the product over time. The Minnesota model also provided a means for making comparisons of results within the state and to national and central states' students.[23]

In 1980 and 1984, Minnesota replicated the NAEP for music. The findings were as follows:

1. Students in three large cities performed lower than students in the rest of the state in all standards, and at all three grade levels (grades 4, 8, 11).
2. Girls consistently performed higher than boys, and the difference increased at all grades on the 1984 assessment.
3. In 1984, Minnesota students scored higher than students at all grade levels in the central United States and throughout the country.
4. On the items that were tested during both years, fourth graders improved, eighth graders declined slightly, and eleventh graders performed at about the same level.[24]

The 1993 assessment measured knowledge and values in music history and theory, listening, reading and writing, cultural analysis, and the making of musical judgments, as well as attitudes and opinions. Being based on standards that did not exist at the time of the earlier assessments, the 1993 assessment results were not compared with those of the previous assessments.

Data Collection: Another Kind of Assessment

During a time of declining economic support for arts education, it is especially important for the profession to have a variety of data on arts offerings in schools. Such data are necessary to support advocacy efforts and should be of interest to professional associations and individual teachers who need to be knowledgeable about the health of their profession. The information usually describes quantity, rather than quality, and is nonjudgmental. It provides overall pictures of arts offerings nationally and at state and local levels; it is limited, however, because it does not indicate trends, having been collected over a relatively short period of time. Also, the data do not report specific local conditions and circumstances that affect arts education at the grass roots level.

Data Collection by the National Arts Education Research Center

The Status of Arts Education in American Public Schools[25] is the report of a survey by the National Arts Education Research Center at the University of Illinois. Charles Leonhard was the research director. The survey collected and interpreted quantitative baseline data on the status of music, visual art, dance, and drama/theater education in American public schools. The questionnaire gathered demographic and curricular data and information about adequacy of instructional materials and financial and parental support for arts education.[26] The sample consisted of 1,326 schools out of a possible 80,000 schools throughout the country in the 1986–1987 school year.

The closing statement summarizes the findings of the survey:

> Since no set of validated criteria for the evaluation of arts programs exists, the emphasis in this report has been on reporting and interpreting data, not on assessment. The data do, however, provide a basis for a few general conclusions:
>
> 1. Arts specialists are essential to viable arts programs. Music and visual art programs have benefited greatly from the presence of specialists at every level of the public school. Drama/theatre and dance education have urgent need of a larger presence of specialist teachers.
>
> 2. Music educators need to give serious consideration to broadening the music program beyond performance to include greater emphasis on music history, criticism and aesthetics. Significant reduction in student enrollment in performance groups in large secondary schools may be a harbinger of the future.

3. The concept of Discipline Based Art Education has influenced art education to broaden the thrust of art programs beyond production.

4. There is evidence of substantial progress in the development of viable drama/theatre and dance programs, especially in large secondary schools where larger numbers of specialist teachers are present.

5. The small amount of time allotted to the arts in elementary schools represents nothing more than lip service to their value. A substantial increase in time allotment is essential.

6. There exists an urgent need for increased funding for all programs of arts education. Large percentages of schools reported than many essential items of instructional materials and equipment were either inadequate or absent in music programs, art programs and drama/theatre programs. Furthermore, large percentages of music educators and drama/theatre educators are burdened with the task of fund raising which inevitably forces them t spend an inordinate amount of time and energy at the expense of their achievement as educators.

7. Arts educators have good reason to be proud of their programs which, on the whole, have met the societal and educational needs of the past in excellent fashion. They must, however, come to terms with two significant developments that will inevitably affect arts education in the future: the educational reform movement and the rapidly changing ethnic composition of the student population.[27]

Data Collected by the Music Educators National Conference

The Music Educators National Conference Executive Board created the MENC Information Service to "identify information needs, gather existing information, collect new data, identify trends, and disseminate information about music, music education, and the arts."[28] MENC will continue collecting information for future comparisons against its baseline data. This will allow the organization to help "develop a national consensus and plan of action" for the music education profession. The data also have significance for music educators who wish to compare their conditions with those of other states, or nationwide, and they provide information for arts education advocates who need data to support their efforts.

MENC released the results of three major surveys of the status of music and arts education in schools. It published *Music and Music Education: Data and Information*[29] in 1984. The survey covers the following topics:

Occupational conditions: salaries, certification, and job availability

Degrees awarded by level in various fields

Achievement test results (NAEP, *Scholastic Aptitude Test*)

Participation in the arts

Attitudes and opinions toward education and music

In 1985 MENC published *Arts in Schools: State by State.*[30] This is especially valuable for state music education organizations that need information on the status of their discipline as compared with other states.

Data on Music Education,[31] published in 1990, provides statistics on the following:

Employment rates for teachers in public and private schools

Employment opportunities in various fields, including music

Degrees awarded in education and the arts

Examination results (NAEP, *Scholastic Aptitude Test, Graduate Record Examination*)

Secondary school offerings in selected subjects and enrollments

School district policies and practices concerning arts education

SAT Scores: Comparative Success of Arts Students

Arts education is also assessed by drawing inferences from Scholastic Achievement Test scores of students who have had arts education and those who have not. According to the College Board *Profile of SAT and Achievement Test Takers* for 1990 through 1993 students who had taken some arts courses (music, theater, art, dance, photography) had higher mean scores (21–23 points higher) on the verbal section than those with no arts courses. Math mean scores were from 11 to 14 points higher for arts students. In all four years, from 1990 to 1993, students who had taken music appreciation or had performance experience scored considerably higher than the average on both sections. The data also indicated that scores increased even more with the length of arts education. These data do not prove a causal relationship between arts education and success on the SAT, but because they indicate a positive relationship, they are used by educators who are called upon to discuss the benefits of arts education. The data should be of interest to researchers who wish to examine the possibility of a cause-and-effect relationship.

Teaching to Prepare for the National Assessment

In October 1994 MENC announced a new series of publications to assist music educators in their efforts to implement the national standards. The series includes separate volumes for band, orchestra and strings, chorus, general music, keyboard, guitar, and special ensembles, each divided by the levels used in the standards (pre–K, K–4, 5–8, 9–12). The publications include both teaching strategies and achievement standards. MENC requested that music educators participate in the development of the series by contributing their own ideas on sample forms published in *Teaching Music* (Figs. 9.6, 9.7).

Ensuing editions of the journal contained suggestions from music educators on how they conduct the activities related to specific standards, with one standard covered in each issue. In this way, the series helps prepare the profession for the 1997 NAEP, which will evaluate the learning outcomes of the standards.

FIGURE 9.7. Teaching Strategy Submission Form

Please consider sharing your successful teaching ideas with your colleagues by filling out the Teaching Strategy Submission Form on page 295.

Guidelines for Completing Teaching Strategy Submission Form
1. Identify the precise content standard and the achievement standard to which your strategy will apply. Remember that the content and achievement standards for PreK and for grades K–4, 5–8, and 9–12 are exit-level standards specifying what every student should know and be able to do at age 4 and upon exiting grades 4, 8, and 12. PreK strategies written for children younger than grade 4, and 5–8 or 9–12 strategies for students in grades earlier than grade 4 or grade 8, should lead toward attainment of the particular exit-level standard that is listed. *Note:* The complete K–12 music standards are listed in both the *National Standards for Arts Education* and *The School Music Program: A New Vision.* The Prekindergarten Standards appear only in the latter.

2. Keep in mind that each strategy should be no longer than a typical class session or portion of a class session. (PreK strategies may include information about how musical activities will be integrated into the children's daily experiences.) If you need more space for a strategy, please attach an additional page.

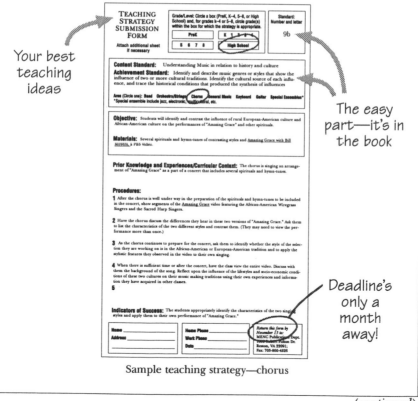

Your best teaching ideas

The easy part—it's in the book

Deadline's only a month away!

Sample teaching strategy—chorus

(continued)

Fig. 9.7. (*continued*)

3. At the K–4 and 5–8 levels, strategies are especially needed for grade 4 and for grade 8. Of course, strategies for other grades within those levels are also welcome.

4. Each strategy should include: an *objective* (a clear statement of what the student will be able to do), a list of necessary *materials,* information on what *prior knowledge and experiences* are necessary as well as how this strategy fits into the course curriculum, a set of *procedures* to develop the strategy, and what will be the *indicators* that students have been successful in meeting the standard.

5. You may duplicate this form and submit as many teaching strategies as you wish. (This form is also available through America Online. Please direct your message to PSenko and request that a copy be sent to your e-mail address.)

6. Please return completed forms to the MENC Publications Department *no later than November 15, 1994,* by mail, by fax (703-860-4826), or via America Online (PSenko).

Teaching strategies selected may be subject to revision. Contributors of strategies used in the series will be acknowledged in a listing in the publication for which the their strategies are selected. Your help in this very important project is greatly appreciated.

—*Carolynn A. Lindeman, Series Editor*

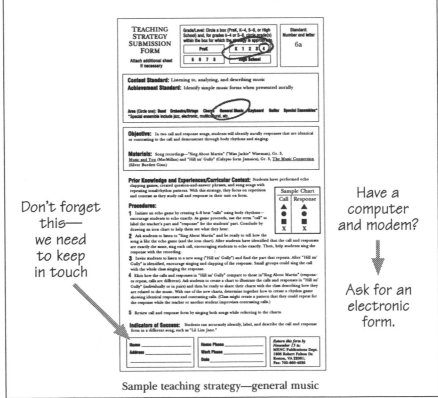

Don't forget this— we need to keep in touch

Have a computer and modem?

Ask for an electronic form.

Sample teaching strategy—general music

(continued)

TEACHING STRATEGY SUBMISSION FORM Attach additional sheet if necessary	Grade/Level: Circle a box (PreK, K–4, 5–8, or High School) and, for grades k–4 or 5–8, circle grade(s) within the box for which the strategy is appropriate.	Standard: Number and letter

PreK	K 1 2 3 4
5 6 7 8	High School

Content Standard:

Achievement Standard:

Area (Circle one): **Band   Orchestra/Strings   Chorus   General Music   Keyboard   Guitar   Special Ensembles***
*Special ensemble include jazz, electronic, multicultural, etc.

Objective:

Materials:

Prior Knowledge and Experiences/Curricular Context:

Procedures:

1

2

3

4

5

Indicators of Success:

Name _____

Address _____

_____

Home Phone _____

Work Phone _____

Date_____

Return this form by November 15 to: MENC Publications Dept. 1806 Robert Fulton Dr. Reston, VA 22091; Fax: 703-860-4826

From *Teaching Music*, October 1994. © Copyright 1994 by Music Educators National Conference. Used with permission

NOTES

1 "Mr. Barnard's Labors in Connecticut from 1838 to 1842," *Barnard's American Journal of Education* (1956), 695.

2 Michael L. Mark, "A History of Music Education Research," *Handbook of Research on Music Teaching and Learning* (New York: Schirmer Books, 1992), 49.

3 National Assessment of Educational Progress, *National Assessment of Educational Progress: General Information Yearbook*, report no. 0304 SGY (Washington, DC: U. S. Office of Education, 1974), 1.

4 NAEP, *General Information Yearbook*, 2.

5 Ibid.

6 Ibid.

7 NAEP, Education Commission of the States, *Procedural Handbook 1978–79 Music Assessment*, December 1981, report no. 10-Mu-40, xi.

8 Ibid., 2, 3.

9 National Assessment of Educational Progress, *The First National Assessment of Musical Performance*, report no. 02-MU-01 (Washington, DC: U.S. Government Printing Office, 1974), 29.

10 National Assessment of Educational Progress, *A Perspective on the First Music Assessment* (Washington, DC: U. S. Government Printing Office, 1974), 2.

11 NAEP, Education Commission of the States, *Music 1971–79; Results from the Second National Assessment*, November 1981, report no. 10-MU-01, xiii.

12 NAEP, Education Commission of the States, "Music 1971–79: Results from the Second National Music Assessment" (brochure), no. 10-MU-35.

13 Frank Philip, "Council of Chief State School Officers Begins National Assessment of Educational Progress Project on Arts Education Assessment," *Special Research Interest Group in Measurement and Evaluation*, no. 14 (Winter 1993): 1, 2.

14 Ibid., 3.

15 Ibid., 2, 3.

16 Richard Colwell, "Editor's Desk," *Special Research Interest Group in Measurement and Evaluation*, no. 14 (Winter 1993): 16.

17 Ibid.

18 "Current Information about the Arts SCASS Project" (Washington, DC: Council of Chief State School Officers, 1994).

19 New York State Education Department, "Preliminary Draft Framework Sampler," November, 1994.

20 Anne Werps, "A New Way of Measuring," *Baltimore Sun*, 13 May 1994, p. 27A.

21 "Florida Cabinet Accepts Standards," *Teaching Music* 2, no. 5 (April 1995): 22.

22 Susan Vaughan, "Evaluation of Arts Education in Minnesota: A Description of Minnesota's Arts Assessment Programs," *Special Interest Research Group in Measurement and Evaluation*, no. 14 (Winter 1993): 6.

23 Ibid.

24 Ibid., 10.

25 Charles Leonhard, *The Status of Arts Education in American Public Schools* (Urbana-Champaign, IL: Council for Research in Music Education, 1991).

26 Ibid., v.

27 Ibid., 210.

28 Daniel V. Steinel, comp., *Music and Music Education: Data and Information. National Data Review* (Reston, VA: Music Educators National Conference, 1984), 2.

29 Daniel V. Steinel, comp., *Music and Music Education: Data and Information* (Reston, VA: Music Educators National Conference, 1984).

30 Daniel V. Steinel, comp., *Arts in Schools: State by State* (Reston, VA: Music Educators National Conference, 1985).

31. Daniel V. Steinel, comp. *Data on Music Education: A National Review of Statistics Describing Education in Music and the Other Arts* (Reston, VA: Music Educators National Conference, 1990).

10

Contemporary Music Education: Conclusion

Music Education: A Collaborative Venture

The scope of topics in this book illuminates the remarkable breadth of activities and interests that constitute the world of music education. Music educators range from classroom music teachers to performing musicians, arts administrators, association executives and officers, technology experts, and corporate staffs that produce and merchandise a wealth of publications and paraphernalia. All of the parts are interdependent. While they do not fit together as neatly as a jigsaw puzzle, neither do any of them operate without some influence from the others, and without affecting the others. The collaboration of interests and specialties has produced impressive results. In fact, most of the profession's accomplishments result from collaborations or partnerships. The inclusion of arts education in the Goals 2000 legislation illustrates a healthy form of professional cooperation and collaboration. Music educators worked closely with other arts educators, community members, policymakers, and many others, without whom the arts would not have been included in the Goals 2000 legislation.

Another kind of cooperation exists with inventors, engineers, developers, manufacturers, and marketers. Here, music education is not normally the leading partner. Technology is usually ahead, and for years has led music education in new directions. From the beginning of the technological age music educators have used new tools to expand the limits of teaching and performance. They need more advanced equipment as they continue to refine their technological expertise, and the music industry has continually satisfied their requirements. Advanced technology has made other kinds of inroads as well. For example, music educators have welcomed the introduction of modern plastics into school music programs for innovations like inexpensive, lightweight, often brilliantly colored musical instruments, and uniforms and robes made of synthetic materials.

The business and industry sector of the greater society can also influence music education in other unexpected ways. For example, a seemingly trivial aspect of American life demonstrates how the profession is influenced by marketing practices that affect musical taste. When radio became available to the general public in the 1920s, the advertising industry recognized the capability of the new medium to capture the public's attention. The short advertising jingle—simple, clever, informative, and persuasive—was born. Advertising music is even more effective on television, where it is combined with magnificent visuals. The general public is probably more familiar with this kind of music than any other. As music educators labor to educate children about the breadth and depth of all kinds of music, their students' musical tastes have already been formed, to some extent, by advertising music. This music pervades the national subconscious and conveys the impression to many people that a clever, catchy melody is all that is needed to make a good piece of music.

A Unified Profession

The breadth of interests within music education is undeniably a positive aspect of the profession, but the continual expansion of interest areas has also brought problems. There are so many narrowly specialized interests now that few music educators take a professionwide view of their field. Even the Music Educators National Conference, as the umbrella association for all music educators, has had to find ways to manage interests so parochial that they sometimes exclude other areas of music education. Since the 1960s MENC has had Associated Organization and Affiliated Organization status for these special interest groups. They include organizations that represent Kodály educators, choral directors, string teachers, jazz educators, and many others. There are numerous other organizations of music educators as well that do not have formal affiliations with MENC. Good teachers need to invest themselves as completely as possible in their particular areas of interest, but their professional associations should continually cooperate as closely as possible with other interest groups to present a unified structure to policy makers and the public. The profession is best served by a membership with a broad view and empathetic attitude.

Belief in the Value of Music Education

Despite the inclusion of the arts in the Goals 2000 legislation, many music educators have difficulty justifying their discipline as a basic subject. The legislation affords the legitimacy that the profession has sought for so long, but that achievement was really a political act that transpired because of the political know-how of professional arts education organizations. Now that their profession has been recognized as a core subject, music educators must still arrive at a common belief that will allow them to truly integrate their subject into the curriculum.

The profession's interests are pluralistic, but there is a basic commonality that permeates every aspect of it: music education exists to serve society, and every component of it must contribute in some way to the betterment of the social order that sponsors it. To do this, music educators need a fundamental belief in the purpose of their profession and in its value to society. If every member of the music education profession believes that what he or she does improves the neighborhood, community, town, city, or nation, then it is possible for them to make people outside the profession aware of the value of musically educated populace.

There remains among music educators, however, a fundamental unease about the purpose and value of music education. Bennett Reimer's quotation about lack of professional "inner peace" in chapter 3 eloquently portrays the problem, and other writers have made reference to the same problem that has haunted the profession for over a century. There is still little agreement on the appropriate balance between school music as an educational discipline and as entertainment. Indeed, the line between the two is often hazy, and many music educators have to balance their activities to meet both educational goals and community expectations. There is another fundamental disparity about whether music should be used as a tool to teach other subjects or whether it should be treated as a discrete discipline. These are not issues that can be decided only by music educators. Communities and boards of education also participate in setting such fundamental agendas. Music educators should have a professional opinion on these matters, however, and be persuasive in expressing them to the people responsible for making policy decisions.

Music educators should have no doubt that society needs their services. A review of the many laws passed by the Congress of the United States that involve music, or arts, education, illuminates the fact that music education has responded to a number of national needs throughout the long period of educational reform. Music education has shared a place with the other education disciplines in implementing civil rights legislation, creating a multicultural view of the nation, and improving the quality of the nation's work force. As discussed in chapter 4, most of the critical developments in the profession during the last several decades have occurred in response to the needs of the greater society. Federal, state, and local policymakers recognize the value of music education, and the profession stretches itself to meet the mandates of public policy. These challenging requirements that have originated outside the profession have been beneficial to music education. It has had to seek new ways to operate and to serve. In doing this, it has modernized and improved its practices and has remained vital and current.

Music Education and the Local Community

Music education is a integral part of many local communities because it reflects community values, beliefs, and hopes. School music teachers who are sensitive to their community's needs are usually well appreciated and their programs valued. It would be ideal, however, if more music educators would create an active role for themselves in the out-of-school musical lives of their communities. There is a vigorous musical life beyond the schools throughout the country, and people have countless opportunities to study music and to perform in community activities. Unfortunately, one of the historic realities of American music education is that except in isolated cases it has had little association with community music activities. If school music educators could find more ways to build bridges to community musical organizations and institutions, both school and community would benefit. A close relationship would offer opportunities for school music teachers to become leaders in community cultural life. Multicultural music activities that are directly relevant to specific communities could be an integral part of school music programs. The school program could gain a significant number of community advocates, and teachers might find new musical opportunities for their students outside of school.

Another consequential benefit of relating school and community music is the opportunity to extend music education to adults of all ages. Lifelong music education has been discussed and recommended for decades by music educators but little has been done to set the process in motion. It is even possible that after they establish a close relationship between school and community, teachers could prepare their students for the musical life of their own specific communities. If this were done, school music programs would be their own best advocates, and communities could not help but appreciate the need for music in schools. This, of course, is asking much of music educators, who are very busy people. Building bridges to the community could easily add too heavy a burden, but the rewards are so promising that it is a worthwhile future goal for the music education profession.

Research to Serve Practical Needs

Another area to which the profession needs to address itself is its research community. Research is vital and healthy, as evidenced by the many new journals of the past two decades that have opened fresh outlets for research reports. Music education research is uncoordinated, however, and except in some extraordinary cases, is not directed toward the solution of practical problems. Music education had been a successful enterprise long before music education research was a serious endeavor. Practitioners do not usually feel a need for the services of researchers, and practice and research have never been completely at ease with each other. Nor do researchers necessarily believe themselves to be obliged to extend their activities beyond pure research that might or might not eventually find applications in practical situations. Not all research has to be of a practical nature, but so many studies are published now that one might hope to find a more direct relationship between research and practice.

Unfortunately, large-scale practical, or applied, research is usually expensive. Its attractiveness to the profession is obvious from the many research projects of the 1960s and early 1970s that were funded by the federal government. When that funding was no longer available, large-scale applied research projects had to be discontinued. Although this kind of project is beyond the reach of most music education researchers, the recent trend toward qualitative research might encourage many new studies that focus on classroom practices.

Researchers who are interested in undertaking practical projects might examine the extensive literature about current educational trends that often pose important research questions and suggestions. *Arts Education Research Agenda for the Future*, for example, published in 1994 by the National Endowment for the Arts and the U. S. Department of Education, offers suggestions for needed research. As the profession continues to grow and expand, new research opportunities are continually revealed. In addition to the traditional kinds of reports found in research journals, new studies are needed in the area of technology and its applications to music education, arts education policy studies, the uses of multicultural musics, music for children at risk, lifelong music education, and many other subjects.

An Active, Vital Profession

The number of new activities in which the profession has been involved in the second half of the twentieth century is remarkable. It has adopted new curricula and found ways to refine and improve their delivery; involved itself in the long-term effort to improve teacher education; sought means to improve urban education; established an internationally recognized and respected research community; sought to embrace and serve all of the peoples of a pluralistic society; continued to improve its performance component to the point where many student ensembles perform at an extraordinarily high level; and added a welcome, contemporary dimension to music learning and teaching by incorporating technology.

Despite its excellent record, music education, like many other professions in times of economic hardship, remains troubled. Clearly, financial support is the most critical issue for American music education.

Education policymakers, as well as the general public, must keep hearing the message that music instruction is well worth its cost. This is why advocacy has played such an important role for well over two decades.

Conditions never remain static, and the music education profession must always be in a position to make the right choices for the future. Allen Britton discusses one of the hazards inherent in preparing for the future and cautions the profession to proceed prudently and in an informed manner:

> Many American music educators have demonstrated what may be considered an easy readiness to climb aboard any intellectual bandwagon which happened to be near by, and to trust it to arrive at destinations appropriate for music educators, or worse, to adopt its destinations as their own without careful enough scrutiny of the intellectual properties involved.[1]

Given the changing nature of contemporary society, music education will undoubtedly continue to undergo both evolutionary change and radical transformation in the future, just as it always has. As time goes on there will be more and more choices to make and more groups of constituents to satisfy. Music educators must remain aware of philosophies, methods, techniques, materials, and the changing needs of society to be sure that their choices are judicious and appropriate. This will allow them to provide the highest quality of service, which in turn will keep the profession viable, sensitive to the needs of society, and dynamic. Even though economic problems continually threaten the profession, history tells us that the American people want their children to be educated musically. Music education will be valued as long as its practitioners continue to play a central role in creating a musically literate and informed American public.

NOTE

1 Allen P. Britton, "Music in Early American Public Education: A Historical critique," National Society for the Study of Education, *Basic Concepts in Music Education*, ed. Nelson B. Henry (Chicago: University of Chicago Press, 1958), 107.

Bibliography

CHAPTER 1: HISTORICAL FOUNDATIONS OF MUSIC EDUCATION

Allen, Dwight W. *Schools for a New Century*. New York: Praeger.

Barrett, Peter A. *Doubts & Certainties: Working Together to Restructure Schools*. Washington, DC: National Education Association, 1991.

Birge, William Bailey. *History of Public School Music in the United States*. Washington, DC: Music Educators National Conference, 1966.

Broudy, Harry S. "How Basic Is Aesthetic Education? or Is'RT the Fourth R?" *Bulletin*, Council for Research in Music Education, no. 57 (Winter 1978): 1–10.

Bruner, James S., ed. *Learning About Learning: A Conference Report*. Washington, DC: U.S. Department of Health, Education, and Welfare, 1966

Bulletin, Council for Research in Musical Education, Special Issue: Accountability, no. 36 (Spring 1974).

Cohen, Sol, ed. *Education in the United States: A Documentary History*. Vol. 1. New York: Random House, 1974.

Fiske, Edward B., Sally Reed, and R. Craig Sautter. *Smart Schools, Smart Kids*. New York: Simon & Schuster, 1991.

Friedman, Milton. "Busting the State Monopoly." *Newsweek* (5 December 1983): 96.

Gardner, Gordon, Leonard Grindstaff, and Evelyn Wenzel. "Balance the Selection of Content." *Balance in the Curriculum*. Washington, DC: Association for Supervision and Curriculum Department, 1961.

Goodlad, John I. *The Changing School Curriculum*. New York: Fund for the Advancement of Education, 1966.

Hechinger, Fred M. "Caution: Avoid Confusion on School Reforms." *Bulletin*, American Association for Higher Education, 36, no. 1 (September 1983): 2–4.

Henry, Nelson B., ed. *Basic Concepts in Music Education*, Fifty-seventh Yearbook of the National Society for the Study of Education, part 1. Chicago: Universty of Chicago Press, 1958.

Lee, Gordon C. "The Changing Role of the Teacher." In *The Changing American School*, Sixty-fifth Yearbook of the National Society for the Study of Education, part 2. Ed. John I. Goodlad. Chicago: University of Chicago Press, 1966, 9–31.

Leonhard, Charles. "Toward a Contemporary Program of Music Education." *Bulletin*, Council for Research in Music Education, no. 63 (Summer 1980): 11–19.

Mahlmann, John J. "Don't Let the Education Critics Drown Out Music." *School Board News* (21 September 1983): 2.

Miles, Matthew B. "Education Innovation: The Nature of the Problem." *Innovation in Education*. New York: Bureau of Publications, Columbia University Teachers College, 1974.

Murphy, Joseph. *Restructuring Schools: Capturing and Assessing the Phenomena*. New York: Teachers College Press, 1991.

Ravitch, Diane. *The Troubled Crusade: American Education, 1945–1980*. New York: Basic Books, 1983.

Rickover, Hyman. "We Have Lost That Realistic Sense of Purpose." *Washington Post*, 19 June 1983, B8.

Ross, Jerrold. "Research in Music Education: From a National Perspective." *Bulletin*, Council for Research in Music Education, no. 123 (Winter 1994/1995): 123–35.

Sand, Ole, and Richard Miller. *Schools for the Sixties*. New York: McGraw-Hill, 1963.

Silberman, Charles E. *Crisis in the Classroom*. New York: Random House, 1970.

Tellstrom, A. Theodore. *Music in American Education: Past and Present*. New York: Holt, Rinehart, 1971.

1980s National Reports on Higher Education

Adler, Mortimer Jerome. *The Paideia Proposal*. New York: Macmillan, 1982.

Boyer, Ernest L. *High School: A Report on Secondary Education in America*. New York: Harper & Row, 1983.

Business Higher Education Forum. *America's Competitive Challenge: The Need for a National Response*. Washington, DC, 1983.

College Entrance Examination Board. *Academic Preparation for College: What Students Need to Know and Be Able to Do*. New York: The College Board, 1983.

Goodlad, John I. *A Place Called School: Prospects for the Future*. St. Louis: McGraw-Hill, 1983.

K–12 Arts Education in the United States: Present Context, Future Needs, a briefing paper for the arts education community. Reston, VA: Music Educators National Conference, National Art Education Association, National Dance Association, National Association of Schools of Music, National Association of Schools of Art and Design, National Association of Schools of Theater, National Association of Schools of Dance, 1966.

Lake, Sara. *The Educator's Digest of Reform: A Comparison of 16 Recent Proposals for Improving America's Schools*. Redwood City, CA: San Mateo County Office of Education, 1984.

National Commission on Excellence in Education. *A Nation at Risk: The Imperative for Educational Reform*. Washinngton, DC: U.S. Government Printing Office, 1983. Stock L965-000-00177-2.

National Science Board Commission on Precollege Education in Mathematics, Science and Technology. *Educating Americans for the 21st Century*. Washington, DC: National Science Foundation, 1983.

Sizer, Theodore A. *Horace's Compromise: The Dilemma of the American High School*. New York: Houghton Mifflin, 1984.

Smith, Carleton Sprague. *The Study of Music: An Academic Discipline*. Washington, DC: Music Educators National Conference, 1963.

Southern Regional Education Board. *Meeting the Need for Quality: Action in the South*. Atlanta: Southern Region Education Board, 1983.

Task Force on Education for Economic Growth. *Action for Excellence: A Comprehensive Plan to Improve Our Nation's Schools*. Denver: Education Commission of the States, 1983.

CHAPTER 2: PIVOTAL EVENTS OF THE CONTEMPORARY ERA

The Contemporary Music Project

Bess, Michael. "Comprehensive Musicianship in the Contemporary Music Project's Southern Region Institutes for Music in Contemporary Education." *Journal of Research in Music Education* 39, no. 2 (Summer 1991): 101–13.

Britton, Allen. "MENC: Remembrances and Perspectives." *The Quarterly Journal of Music Teaching and Learning* 5, no. 2 (Summer 1994): 6–15.

———. "The Tanglewood Symposium," in "Music: A New Start." In *Britannica Review of American Education*. Vol. 1. Chicago: Encyclopedia Britannica, 1969.

Lowry, W. McNeil, ed. *The Arts and Public Policy in the United States*. Englewood Cliffs, NJ: Prentice-Hall, 1984.

Music Educators Journal 54, no. 7 (March 1968). A section entitled "Contemporary Music Project: Comprehensive Music Education" includes articles and reports about several aspects of the CMP.

Music Educators Journal 59, no. 9 (May 1973). A section entitled "Contemporary Music Project: Comprehensive Musicianship" describes the philosophy, history, and uses of comprehensive musicianship.

The Quarterly 1, no. 3 (Autumn 1990). This is a focus issue subtitled "The Contemporary Music Project."

Publications of the Contemporary Music Project (CMP)

CMP 1. *Contemporary Music for Schools* (1966). A catalog of works written by composers participating in the Young Composers Project, 1959–64.

CMP 2. *Comprehensive Musicianship* (1965). A report of the seminar sponsored by the Contemporary Music Project at Northwestern University, April 1965.

CMP 3. *Experiments in Musical Creativity* (1966). A report of pilot projects sponsored by the Contemporary Music Project in Baltimore, San Diego, and Farmingdale, New York.

CMP 4. *Creative Projects in Musicianship* (1967). A report by Warren Benson of pilot projects sponsored by the Contemporary Music Project at Ithaca College and the Interlochen Arts Academy.

CMP 5. *Comprehensive Musicianship: An Anthology of Evolving Thought* (1971). A discussion of the first ten years of the Contemporary Music Project, particularly as they relate to the development of comprehensive musicianship.

CMP 6. *Comprehensive Musicianship and Undergraduate Music Curricula* (1971). A discussion by David Willoughby of curricular implications of comprehensve musicianship as derived from 32 experimental college programs.

CMP 7. *Source Book of African and Afro-American Materials for Music Education* (1972). James A. Standifer and Barbara Reeder provide lists of books, articles, recordings, and other materials dealing with African and African-American music traditions.

CMP Library Catalogs

Volume I. *Works for Band*
Volume II. *Works for Orchestra*
Volume III. *Works for Chorus*

The Yale Seminar

Arberg, Harold, and Claude V. Palisca. "Implications of the Government Sponsored Yale Seminar in Music Education." *College Music Symposium* 4 (1964).
Beglarian, Grant. Review of *Music in Our Schools* by Claude V. Palisca. *Journal of Music Theory* 1 (1965): 187–89.
Bulletin, Council for Research in Music Education, no. 60 (Fall 1979). Entire issue consists of articles on the Yale Seminar.
Lehman, Paul. Review of *Music in Our Schools: A Search for Improvement. Notes* 22 (1965): 728–30.
Palisca, Claude V. *Music in Our Schools: A Search for Improvement.* Report of the Yale Seminar on Music Education. Washington, DC: U.S. Department of Health, Education and Welfare, Office of Education, OE-33033, Bulletin 1964, No. 28.
"Seminar on Music Education: Musicians Meet at Yale University." *Music Educators Journal* 50, no. 1 (1963): 86–87.

The Tanglewood Symposium

Choate, Robert A. "Music in American Society." *Music Educators Journal* 53 (1967).
————, ed. *Documentary Report of the Tanglewood Symposium.* Washington, DC: Music Educators National Conference, 1968.
Jones, William M. "Functions of Music in Music Education Since Tanglewood." *Bulletin*, Council for Research in Music Education, no. 63 (Summer 1980): 11–90.
Murphy, Judith, and George Sullivan. *Music in American Society.* Washington, DC: Music Educators National Conference, 1968.
Music Educators Journal 55, no. 1 (1968). Includes several articles on the Tanglewood Symposium.
Schwadron, Abraham. "The Tanglewood Symposium Summons." *Music Educators Journal* 26 (1968): 40–42.

The GO Project

"Goals and Objectives for Music Education." *Music Educators Journal* 57, no. 4 (December 1970): 24–25.

"The 'GO' Project: Where Is It Heading?" *Music Educators Journal* 50, no. 6 (February 1970): 24–25. Reprinted by permission of Music Educators National Conference.

Hoffman, Mary E. "Goals and Objectives for the Eighties." *Music Educators Journal* 67, no. 4 (December 1980): 48–49, 60.

Mark, Michael L. "The GO Project: Retrospective of a Decade." *Music Educators Journal* 67, no.4 (December 1980): 42–47.

The School Music Program: Description and Standards. Reston, VA: Music Educators National Conference, 1974; 2d ed., 1986.

National Standards for Arts Education

Goals 2000 legislation (Public Law 103-227). Can be obtained from either House Document Room, Room B-18, Ford House Office Building, Washington, DC 20515, or Senate Document Room, Room SH-4, Hart Senate Office Building, Washington, DC 20510.

Goals 2000 Fact Sheets. Can be obtained at no cost from Department of Education, Office of Public Affairs, 400 Maryland Avenue, SW, Washington, DC 20202.

Langan, Nancy. "Arts in Education: From National Policy to Local Community Action." National Assembly of Local Arts Agencies *Monographs* 3, no. 3 (April 1984). National Assembly of Local Arts Agencies, 927 15th Street, NW, 12th Floor, Washington, DC.

Lehman, Paul R. "Focus: The MENC Goals for 1990." *Music Educators Journal* 73, no. 8 (April 1987). Special insert.

———. "The National Standards: From Vision to Reality." *Music Educators Journal* 81, no. 2 (September 1994). Special insert.

National Education Goals Panel Community Tool Kit. Can be obtained from National Goals Panel, 1850 M Street, NW, Suite 270, Washington, DC 20036.

National Standards for Arts Education: What Every Young American Should Know and Be Able to Do in the Arts. Reston, VA: Music Educators National Conference, 1994.

Opportunity-to-Learn for Music Instruction: Grades PreK–12. Reston, VA: Music Educators National Conference, 1994.

Perspectives on Implementation: Arts Education for America's Students. Reston, VA: Music Educators National Conference, 1994.

The School Music Program: A New Vision. Reston, VA: Music Educators National Conference, 1994.

Steinel, Daniel V., comp. and ed. *Arts in Schools: State by State.* Reston, VA: Music Educators National Conference, 1988.

Summary Statement: Education Reform and the Arts. Reston, VA: Music Educators National Conference, 1994.

The Vision for Arts Education in the 21st Century. Reston, VA: Music Educators National Conference, 1994.

Young Audiences NEWS. New York: Young Audiences, Inc., 115 East 92nd Steet, New York, NY 10128. Spring–Summer 1993; Spring–Summer 1994.

Zinar, Ruth. "Music and Progressive Education." *Music Educators Journal* 70, no. 5 (January 1984): 33, 34.

The Music Educators National Conference publishes *Music for a Sound Education:
A Tool Kit for Implementing the World Class Standards* (1994).
   White Papers
      Fighting the Good Fight
      Q & A
      *Setting the Record Straight—Give and Take on the National Standards
         for Arts Education*
      The National: Moving from Vision to Reality
   Implementing the Arts Education (brochure series)
      What School Boards Can Do
      What School Administrators Can Do
      What State Agencies Can Do
      What Parents Can Do
      What the Arts Community Can Do
   Summary Statement: Education Reform and the Arts
   "Oh Say, can you sing . . .?"

CHAPTER 3: INTELLECTUAL CURRENTS IN THE CONTEMPORARY ERA

Philosophy of Music Education

Birge, William Bailey. *History of Public School Music in the United States.*
   Washington, DC: Music Educatiors National Conference, 1966.
Coates, Patricia. "Alternatives to the Aesthetic Rationale for Music Education."
   Music Educators Journal 69, no. 7 (March 1983): 31, 32.
Colwell, Richard J. *An Approach to Aesthetic Education.* Urbana: University of
   Illinois, ERIC Document Reproduction Service, 1970.
———, ed. *Basic Concepts in Music Education, II.* Niwot: University Press of
   Colorado, 1991.
Elliott, Charles A. "Behind the Budget Crisis, A Crisis of Philosophy." *Music
   Educators Journal* 70, no. 2 (October 1983): 36, 37.
Fowler, Charles, and David J. Elliott. *Winds of Change.* Ed. Marie McCarthy.
   Proceedings of a colloquium in music education at the University of
   Maryland at College Park, April 3, 1993. New York: American Council for
   the Arts in cooperation with the University of Maryland at College Park,
   1994.
Goodlad, John I. *The Changing School Curriculum.* New York: Fund for the
   Advancement of Education, 1966.
Harvey, Arthur W. "James L. Mursell: A Developmental Philosophy of Music
   Education." *Bulletin*, Council for Research in Music Education, no. 37
   (Spring 1947): 1–21.
Henry, Nelson B., ed. *Basic Concepts in Music Education*, Fifty-seventh Yearbook of
   the National Society for the Study of Education, part 1. Chicago:
   University of Chicago Press, 1958.
Jorgensen, Estelle R., ed. *Philosophy of Music Education Review.* Bloomington:
   Indiana University, published semiannually.
Knieter, Gerard L. "Aesthetics for Art's Sake." *Music Educators Journal* 69, no. 7
   (March 1983): 661–64.
Lee, Gordon C. "The Changing Role of the Teacher." In *The Changing American
   School*, Sixty-fifth Yearbook of the National Society for the Study of

Education, part 2. Ed. John I. Goodlad. Chicago: University of Chicago Press, 1966.

Mark, Michael L. "The Evolution of Music Education Philosophy from Utilitarian to Aesthetic." *Journal of Research in Music Education* 30, no. 1 (Spring 1982): 16–21.

————. "The Need for a Utilitarian Philosophy of Music Education." In *International Music Education: Tradition and Change in Music and Music Education*. Ed. Jack Dobbs. Papers of the 15th International Conference of the International Society for Music Education, Bristol, England, 1982.

Phillips, Kenneth H. "Utilitarian vs. Aesthetic." *Music Educators Journal* 69, no. 7 (1983):

Reese, Sam. "Teaching Aesthetic Listening." *Music Educators Journal* 69, no. 7 (1983): 36–38.

Reimer, Bennett. "Music Education as Aesthetic Education: Past and Present." *Music Educators Journal* 75, no. 6 (February 1989): 22–28.

————. "Music Education as Aesthetic Education: Toward the Future." *Music Educators Journal* 76, no. 7 (March 1989): 26–52.

————. *A Philosophy of Music Education.* 2d ed. Englewood Cliffs, NJ: Prentice-Hall, 1989.

————, and Ralph A. Smith, eds. *The Arts, Education, and Aesthetic Knowing.* Chicago: National Society for the Study of Education, 1992.

————, and Jeffrey E. Wright, eds. *On the Nature of Musical Experience.* Niwot: University Press of Colorado, 1992.

Schwadron, Abraham A. *Aesthetics: Dimensions for Music Education.* Washington, DC: Music Educators National Conference, 1967.

————. "Philosophy and Aesthetics in Music Education: A Critique of the Research." *Bulletin*, Council for Research in Music Education, no. 79 (Summer 1984): 11–32.

————. "Philosophy in Music Education: Pure or Applied Research?" *Bulletin*, Council for Research in Music Education, no. 19 (Winter 1970): 22–29.

Silberman, Charles E. *Crisis in the Classroom.* New York: Random House, 1970.

Tellstrom, A. Theodore. *Music in American Education: Past and Present.* New York: Holt, Rinehart, 1971.

Toward an Aesthetic Education. Washington, DC: Music Educators National Conference, 1971. Report of an institute sponsored by CEMREL, Inc.

Cognitive Psychology

Beyond Creating: The Place for Art in the American Schools. Los Angeles: Getty Center for Education in the Arts, 1985.

Broudy, Harry S. "A Common Curriculum in Aesthetics and Fine Arts." In *Inidivdual Differences and the Common Curriculum*, Gary D. Fenstermacher and John I. Goodlad, eds. Eighty-second Yearbook of the National Society for the Study of Education, part 1. Chicago: National Society for the Study of Education, 1983.

Bruner, Jerome, S. *The Process of Education.* Cambridge, MA: Harvard University Press, 1960.

————, Rose R. Oliver, and Patricia Greenfield, eds. *Studies in Cognitive Growth: A Collaboration at the Center for Cognitive Studies.* New York: Wiley, 1966.

Colwell, Richard J., ed. *Basic Concepts in Music Education, II*. Niwot: University Press of Colorado, 1991.

Deutsch, Diana, ed. *The Psychology of Music*. New York: Academic Press, 1982.

Documentary Report of the Ann Arbor Symposium: Applications of Psychology to the Teaching and learning of Music. Reston, VA: Music Educators National Conference, 1981.

Dowling, W. Jay, and D. L. Harwood. *Music Cognition*. New York: Academic Press, 1987.

Eisner, Elliott, ed. *Learning and Teaching*. Chicago: National Society for the Study of Education, 1965.

Elliott, David J. "Music, Education, and Musical Values." In *Musical Connections: Tradition and Change*. Ed. Heath Lees. Aukland, New Zealand: International Society for Music Education, 1994.

————. "Music, Education, and Schooling." In *Winds of Change: A Colloquium in Music Education*. New York: American Council for the Arts, 1993.

Fowler, Charles. "Redefining the Mission of Music Education: Teaching the Value of Music." In *Winds of Change: A Colloquium in Music Education*. New York: American Council for the Arts, 1993.

Gardner, Howard. "The ARTS PROPEL Approach to Education in the Arts." *Kodály Envoy* 20, no. 2 (Winter 1994): 4–11.

————. *Frames of Mind: The Theory of Multiple Intelligences*. New York: Basic Books, 1983.

————. *The Mind's New Science: A History of Cognitive Revolution*. New York: Basic Books, 1985.

Gary, Charles L., ed. *The Study of Music in the Elementary School—A Conceptual Approach*. Washington, DC: Music Educators National Conference, 1967.

Herrnstein, Richard J., and Charles Murray. *The Bell Curve: Intelligence and Class Structure in American Life*. New York: Free Press, 1994.

Hirst, P. H. *Knowledge and the Curriculum*. Boston: Routledge and Kegan Paul, 1974.

Jorgensen, Estelle R. "Towards an Enhanced Community of Scholars in Music Education." *The Quarterly Journal of Music Teaching and Learning* 1, no. 1, 2 (Spring 1990): 36–42.

Mittler, Gene A., and John A. Stinespring. "Intellect, Emotion, and Art Education Advocacy." *Design for Arts in Education* 92, no. 6 (July/August 1991): 13–19.

Phenix, Phillip. *Realms of Meaning*. New York: McGraw-Hill, 1964.

The Quarterly Journal of Music Teaching and Learning 2, no. 3 (Fall 1991). This focus issue is subtitled "Philosophy in Music Education" Debating the Issues."

Radocy, Rudolf E., and J. David Boyle. *Psychological Foundations of Musical Behavior*. Springfield, IL: Charles C. Thomas, 1979.

Reid, L. A. *Ways of Understanding and Education*. London: Heinemann, 1986.

Reimer, Bennett, and Ralph A. Smith, eds. *The Arts, Education, and Aesthetic Knowing*. Chicago: National Society for the Study of Education, 1992.

————, and Jeffrey E. Wright, eds. *On the Nature of Musical Experience*. Niwot: University Press of Colorado, 1992.

The Reimer/Gordon Debate on Music Learning: Complimentary or Contradictory Views? Reston, VA: Music Educators National Conference, 1994.

Report of the Commission on the Humanities. New York: American Council of Learned Societies, 1964.

Roehmann, Franz L. "On Philosophies of Music Education: Selected Issues Revisited." *The Quarterly Journal of Music Teaching and Learning* 2, no. 3 (Fall 1991): 40–46.

Serafine, Mary Louise. *Music as Cognition: The Development of Thought in Sound.* New York: Columbia University Press, 1988.

Bloboda, John A. *The Musical Mind: The Cognitive Philosophy of Music.* Oxford: Clarendon, 1985.

——, ed. *Generative Processes in Music: The Psychology of Performance, Improvisation, and Composition.* Oxford: Clarendon, 1988.

Stokes, Ann. "Thinking and Feeling in Music." *The Quarterly Journal of Music Teaching and Learning* 5, no. 3 (Fall 1994): 37–48.

Discipline-Based Arts Education

DBAE and Cultural Diversity. Proceedings of the seminar Discipline-based Art Education and Cultural Diversity, August 6–9, 1992, Austin, TX. Santa Monica, CA: Getty Center for Education in the Arts, 1993.

Dobbs, Stephen M. *The DBAE Handbook: An Overview of Discipline-Based Art Education.* Santa Monica, CA: Getty Center for Education in the Arts, 1992.

CHAPTER 4: ADVOCACY: CONNECTING PUBLIC POLICY AND ARTS EDUCATION

Alliance for Arts Education. *Interchange.* Washington, DC: John F. Kennedy Center for the Performing Arts. Official newspaper of the Alliance for Arts Education. Published bimonthly.

American Association of Colleges for Teacher Education. *Teacher Education Policy in the States: A 50-State Survey of Legislative & Administrative Actions.* Washington, DC: American Association of Colleges for Teacher Education.

"Amount of Money Allotted to Each Discipline by State." *Bulletin,* Council for Research in Music Education, no. 58 (Spring 1979): 18–52.

Arts Education Research Agenda for the Future. Washington, DC: National Endowment for the Arts and the United States Department of Education, 1994.

The Arts and Education: Partners in Achieving Our National Educational Goals. Washignton, DC: National Endowment for the Arts and the United States Department of Education, 1995.

Arts, Humanities, and Museum Services Act of 1979: Hearings before the Subcommittee on Education, Arts, and Humanities of the Committee on Labor and Human Resources, United States Senate, Ninety-sixth Congress, First Session on S. 1386 to Amend and Extend the National Foundation on the Arts and Humanities Act of 1965, And for Other Purposes. Washington, DC: United States Government Printing Office, 1979.

Backas, James. "The Environment for Policy Development in Arts Education." *Proceedings of the 56th Annual Meeting.* Reston, VA: National Association of Schools of Music, 1981.

Barresi, Anthony L., and Gerald Olson. "The Nature of Policy and Music Education." *Handbook of Research on Music Teaching and Learning.* New York: Schirmer Books, 1992.

Boyle, David, ed. *Arts IMPACT: Curriculum for Change.* University Park, PA: Pennsylvania State University Press, 1973.

Bulletin, Council for Research in Music Education, no 43 (Summer 1975). Special Issue: CEMREL Aesthetic Education Program.

Coming to Our Senses: The Significance of the Arts for American Education. Panel report, David Rockefeller, Jr., Chairman. The Arts, Education and Americans Panel. New York: McGraw-Hill, 1977.

Department of Education, Fund for Innovation in Education: Innovation in Education Program—State Content Standards for English, History, Geography, Civics, Foreign Languages, and the Arts. *Federal Register* 59, no. 69 (April 11, 1994).

Diez, Mary E., P. David Pearson, and Virginia Richardson. *Setting Standards and Educating Teachers: A National Conversation.* Washington, DC: American Association of Colleges for Teacher Education, 1994.

Fowler, Charles. *Can We Rescue the Arts for America's Children?* New York: ACA Books, 1988.

Gibbs, Nancy. "Home Sweet School." *Time* 144, no. 18 (October 31, 1994): 62–63.

———. "Schools for Profit." *Time* 144, no. 16 (October 17, 1994): 48–49.

Glazer Judith S. "The New Politics of Education: School Districts for Sale." *Education Week* 14, no. 10 (November 9, 1994): 36, 44.

Glidden, Robert. "The Implementation of National Standards in the Arts for American K–12 Education." *The College Music Society Newsletter.* The College Music Society, 202 West Spruce Street, Missoula, MT 59802. 1993.

Goals 2000 Legislation (Public Law 103-227). See above.

Goals 2000 Fact Sheets. See above.

Goekjian, Annie. "State Arts Agencies: An Overview." *Bulletin*, Council for Research in Music Education, no. 58 (Spring 1979): 1–8.

Goodlad, John I., Renata von Stoephasium, and M. Francis Klein. *The Changing School Curriculum.* New York: Fund for the Advancement of Education, 1966.

Hope, Samuel. *Policy Questions in Music Education: Opportunity, Content, Partnership, Funding, and Politics.* Reston, VA: Music Educators National Conference, 1985.

———. "The Standards Challenge." *The College Music Society Newsletter.* The College Music Society (see above). May 1994.

K–12 Arts Education in the United States: Present Context, Future Needs: A Briefing Paper for the Arts Education Community. Reston, VA: Music Educators National Conference, 1986.

Langan, Nancy. "Arts Education: From National Poilcy to Local Community Action." National Assembly of Local Arts Agencies *Monographs* 3, no. 3 (April 1984). National Assembly of Local Arts Agencies, 927 15th Street, NW, 12th Floor, Washington, DC 20036.

Lehman, Paul. "The National Standards: From Vision to Reality." *Music Educators Journal* 81, no. 2 (September 1994). Special insert.

Lineberry, William P., ed. *Status of Arts Education.* Urbana, IL: Council for Research in Music Education, 1991.

Lowry, W. McNeil, ed. *New Trends in Schools.* New York: Wilson, 1967.

McLaughlin, John T., ed. *Toward a New Era in Arts Education.* New York: American Council for the Arts, 1988.

Mahlmann, John J. "Maximizing the Power of Coalitions." *Association Management* 47, no. 9 (September 1995): 32–39.

Miller, Samuel D. "Music Education, Recent History, and Ideas." *Bulletin*, Council for Research in Music Education, no. 77 (Winter 1984): 1–19.

Murphy, Joseph. *Restructuring Schools: Capturing and Assessing the Phenomena*. New York: Teachers Press, 1991.

Murray, Kate Ruchford. "A Description of Various Projects of the State Arts Councils." *Bulletin*, Council for Research in Music Education, no. 58 (Spring 1979): 9–17.

National Coalition for Music Education. *Building Support for School Music: A Practical Guide*. Reston, VA: Music Educators National Conference, 1991.

National Commission on Music Education. *Growing Up Complete: The Imperative for Music Education*. Reston, VA: Music Educators National Conference, 1991.

National Education Goals Panel Community Tools Kit. See above.

National Education Commission on Time and Learning. *Prisoners of Time*. Washington, DC: U.S. Government Printing Office, 1994.

National Endowment for the Arts. *Guide to Programs*. Washington, DC: National Endowment for the arts annual. Available from the Superintendent of Documents, U.S. Government Printing Office, Washington, DC 20402.

National Endowment for the Humanities. *Program Announcement*. National Endowment for the Humanities annual. Available from the Superintendent of Documents (see above).

National Standards for Arts Education. Reston, VA: Music Educators National Conference, 1994.

"The New National Endowment for the Arts-in-Education Program: A Briefing Paper for the Arts Education Community." Reston, VA: Music Educators National Conference, National Art Education Association, National Dance Association, National Association of Schools of Music, National Association of Schools of Art and Design, National Association of Schools of Theatre, National Association of Schools of Dance, November 1986.

Olson, Gerald, Anthony Barresi, and David Nelson, eds. *Policy Issues in Music Education*. Report on the proceedings of the Robert Petzold Symposium, CIC Conference, October 1990. Madison: University of Wisconsin School of Music, 1990.

Pankratz, David B., and Kevin V. Mulcahy, eds. *The Challenge of Reform Arts Education: What Role Can Research Play?* New York: American Council for the Arts, 1989.

Patchen, Jennrey H. "Where Do We Go from Here?" *Music Educators Journal* 78, no. 1 (September 1991): 21–24.

Smith, Ralph. "Trends and Issues in Policy-Making for Arts Education." In *Handbook of Research on Music Teaching and Learning*. Ed. Richard Colwell. New York: Schirmer Books, 1992, 749–59.

Soundpost. Reston, VA: Music Educators National Conference, September 1992, November 1992, May 1993.

Straub, Dorothy. "Reflections on a MENC Presidency." *The Quarterly Journal of Music Teaching and Learning* 5, no. 2 (Summer 1994): 28–33.

Suber, Charles, and Betty J. Stearns. "Music Alert: The Chicago Story" (pamphlet). Washington, DC: Music Educators National Conference, 1972.

Sykes, Gary, and Peter Plastrik. *Stand Setting as Educational Reform*. Washington,

DC: American Association of Colleges for Teacher Education, 1993. Published jointly with the ERIC Clearinghouse on Teaching and Teacher Education.

"Time and Learning Study Supports Music Education." *Teaching Music* 2, no. 1 (August 1994): 9–11.

Toward Civilization: A Report on Arts Education. Washington, DC: National Endowment for the Arts, 1988.

Try a New Face! A Report on HEW-Supported Arts Projects in American Schools. Washington, DC: U.S. Department of Health, Education, and Welfare, 1979. U.S. Government Printing Office, Stock No. 017-080-01799-7.

The Vision for Arts Education in the 21st Century. Reston, VA: Music Educators National Conference, 1994.

Wallis, Claudia. "A Class of Their Own." *Time* 144, no. 18 (October 31, 1994): 52–57.

Warrener, John J. "The Effects of Proposition 2-1/2 on Music Education in Massachusetts." *Massachusetts Music Educator* 31, no. 3 (Spring 1983): 7–8.

———. "The Effects of Proposition 2-1/2 on the Position of Supervisor in Massachusetts." *Massachusetts Music Educator* 31, no. 4 (Summer 1983): 28–29.

Williams, Harold M. "Public Policy and Arts Education." Los Angeles: The J. Paul Getty Trust, 1993. Remarks presented at the Symposium on Public Policy and the Arts, Ohio State university.

Young Audiences NEWS. New York: Young Audiences, Inc. Spring–Summer 1993; Spring–Summer 1994.

The Music Educators National Conference offers an *Action Kit for Music Education* that includes the following:

Music Makes the Difference (brochure)

Music Education and Your Child (brochure)

America's Culture Begins with Education

Growing Up Complete: The Imperative for Music Education

Growing Up Complete: The Imperative for Music Education—An Executive Summary (brochure)

Building Support for School Music: A Practical Guide

Let's Make Music/A Way of Learning (video featuring Henry Mancini and Tim Lautzenheiser)

School Music and "Reverse Economics" (video featuring John Benham)

Teachers' Guide for Advocacy

Numerous documents of the United States Department of Education are available on the Internet. The address is gopher.ed.gov.

CHAPTER 5: MUSIC EDUCATION METHODS

Conceptual Learning

Bruner, Jerome S. *The Process of Education.* Cambridge, MA: Harvard University Press, 1960.

Gary, Charles, L., ed. *The Study of Music in the Elementary School—A Conceptual Approach.* Washington, DC: Music Educators National Conference, 1967.

Ernst, Karl D., and Charles L. Gary. *Music in General Education.* Washington, DC: Music Educators National Conference, 1965.

Smith, Carleton Sprague, and William C. Hartshorn. *The Study of Music as an Academic Subject*. Washington, DC: Music Educators National Conference, 1963. Speeches presented to the 1962 biennial meeting.

The Dalcroze Method

Books

Abramson, Robert, Lois Choksy, Avon Gillespie, and David Woods. *Teaching Music in the Twentieth Century*. Englewood Cliffs, NJ: Prentice-Hall, 1985.

Brown, Margaret, and Betty K. Sommer. *Movement Education: Its Evolution and a Modern Approach*. Reading, MA: Addison-Wesley, 1969.

Carder, Polly. *The Eclectic Curriculum in American Music Education*. Reston, VA: Music Educators National Conference, 1990.

Driver, Ann. *Music and Movement*. London: Oxford University Press, 1936.

———. *A Pathway to Dalcroze Eurhythmics*. London: Thomas Nelson, 1963.

Findlay, Elsa. *Rhythm and Movement: Application of Dalcroze Eurhythmics*. Evanston, IL: Summy-Birchard, 1971.

Gehrkens, Karl W. "Rhythmic Training and Dalcroze Eurythmics." *Yearbook*. Chicago: Music Supervisors National Conference, 1932.

Jaques-Dalcroze, Emile. *The Eurhythmics*. Boston: Small Maynard, 1915.

———. *Rhythmic Movement*. 2 vols. London: Novello, 1920–21.

———. *Rhythm, Music and Education*. Trans. Harold F. Rubenstein. Abridged reprint edition. London: Riverside, 1967.

Landis, Beth, and Polly Carder. *The Eclectic Curriculum in American Music Education: Contributions of Dalcroze, Kodály, and Orff*. Washington, DC: Music Educators National Conference.

Mead, Virginia Hoge. *Dalcroze Eurhythmics in Today's Music Classroom*. New York: Schott Music, 1994.

Spector, Irwin. *Rhythm and Life: The Work of Emile Jaques-Dalcroze*. Stuyvesant, NY: Pendragon, 1990.

Steinitz, Tony. *Teaching Music in Rhythmic Lessons: Theory and Practice of the Dalcroze Method*. Tel Aviv: OR-TAV, 1988.

Weikart, Phyllis. *Teaching Movement and Dance*. Ypsilanti, MI: High-Scope, 1982.

Yelin, Joy. *Movement That Fits*. Evanston, IL: Summy-Birchard, 1990.

Periodicals

Aranoff, Frances W. "Games Teachers Play: Dalcroze Eurythmics." *Music Educators Journal* 57 (February 1971).

Bennett, Peggy. "When 'Method' Becomes Authority." *Music Educators Journal* 72, no. 9 (May 1986): 38–40.

Brody, Viola A. "The Role of Body-Awareness in the Emergence of Musical Ability." *Journal of Research in Music Education* 1 (Spring 1953): 21–29.

Farber, Anne, and Lisa Parker. "Discovering Music through Dalcroze Eurhythmics." *Music Educators Journal* 74 (November 1987): 43–45.

Gehrkens, Karl W. "A Page or Two of Opinions." *Educational Music Magazine* 29 (September–October 1949): 11–13.

———. "Trends in Music Education." *Yearbook of the Music Supervisors National Conference* (1932).

Grentzer, Rose Marie. "Eurhythmics in the Elementary School Program." *Etude* 62 (January 1944): 22.

Hall, Lucy Duncan. "The Value of Eurhythmics in Education." *Yearbook of the Music Educators National Conference* (1936): 150–53.

Music Educators Journal 72, no. 6 (February 1986). This is a focus issue on foreign methodologies.

Naumberg, M. "The Dalcroze Idea: What Eurhythmics Is and What It Means." *Outlook* 106 (January 17, 1914): 127–31.

Scholl, Sharon. "Music for Dancers." *Music Educators Journal* 52 (February–March 1966): 99–102.

The Orff Approach

Carder, Polly. *The Eclectic Curriculum in American Music Education.* Reston, VA: Music Educators National Conference, 1990.

Carley, Isabel McNeill, ed. *Orff Re-Echoes* (selections from *The Orff Echo*, 1969–1975). Cleveland, OH: American Orff-Schulwerk Association, 1977.

Ebinger, V., and B. Stewart. *Index to the Orff Echo, Vols. 1–23.* Cleveland, OH: American Orff-Schulwerk Association, 1991.

Frazee, Jane. *Discovering Orff: A Curriculum for Music Teachers.* New York: Schott Music, 1987.

Glasgow, Robert B., and Dale Hamreus. "Study to Determine the Feasibility of Adapting the Carl Orff Approach to Elementary Schools in America." Monmouth: Oregon School of Education. ERIC document no. ED 010 804.

Guidelines for Orff-Schulwerk Training Courses Levels I, II, III. Cleveland, OH: American Orff-Schulwerk Association, 1980.

Guidelines for Orff Teachers. Level I Course Outline. Cleveland, OH: American Orff-Schulwerk Association. 1976.

Landis, Beth, and Polly Carder. *The Eclectic Curriculum in American Education.* Washington, DC: Music Educators National Conference, 1972.

Olson, Rees Garn. "A Comparison of Two Pedagogical Approaches Adapted to the Acquisition of Meloduc Sensitivity in Sixth Grade Children: The Orff Method and the Traditional Method." PhD dissertation, Indiana University, 1967.

———, ed. *Orff Re-Echoes II* (selections from *The Orff Echo*, 1975–1983). Cleveland, OH: American Orff-Schulwerk Association, 1985.

Steen, Arvida. *Exploring Orff.* Valley Forge, PA: Schott Music, 1992.

Thomas, Werner. *Carl Orff: A Report in Words and Pictures.* Mainz: B. Schott's Sohne, 1955.

Warner, Brigitte. *Orff-Schulwerk: Applications for the Classroom.* Englewood Cliffs, NJ: Prentice-Hall, 1991.

Periodicals

Breuer, Robert. "The Magic World of Carl Orff." *Music Journal* (March 1967): 56.

Flagg, Marion. "The Orff System in Today's World." *Music Educators Journal* 53 (December 1966).

Hamm, Ruth Pollock. "The Challenge of the Orff Approach for Elementary Music Education." *Musart* 22 (April–May): 16–17, 44.

————. "Orff Defended." *Music Educators Journal* 50 (April –May): 90–92.

Keller, Wilhelm. "What Is the Orff-Schulwerk—and What It Is Not." *Musart* (April–May): 16–18.

Klie, Ursula. "Principles of Movement in the Orff-Schulwerk." *Musart* (April–May 1970):

Nash, Grace C. "Orff." *The Instrumentalist* 20, no. 3 (October 1965): 47–51.

————. "The Orff-Schulwerk in the Classroom." *Music Educators Journal* 50 (April–May 1964): 92.

Nichols, Elizabeth. "Adapting Orff to the Music Series." *The Orff Echo* (February 1970): 2.

Olson, Rees Garn. "Orff-Schulwerk . . . Innovation at Bellflower." *The Instructor* (May 1967):

Ponath, Louise, and Carol Bitcon. "A Behavioral Analysis of Orff-Schulwerk." *Journal of Music Therapy* 9, no. 2 (Summer 1972): 56–63.

Siemens, Margaret. "A Comparison of Orff and Traditional Methods in Music." *Journal of Research in Music Education* 17 (Fall 1969): 292.

Methods

Birkenshaw, Lois. *Music for Fun, Music for Learning*. Toronto: Holt Rinehart, 1977.

Bitcom, Carol. *Alike and Different*. Santa, Ana, CA: Rosha, n.d.

Keetman, Gunhild. *Elementaria*. St. Louis: Magnamusic-Baton, 1974.

Nash, Grace, Geraldine W. Jones, Barbara A. Potter, and Patsy S. Smith. *Do It My Way: The Child's Way of Learning*. Sherman Oaks, CA: Alfred, 1977.

Orff, Carl, and Gunild Keetman. *Orff-Schulwerk*. 5 vols. Mainz: B. Schott's Sohne, 1955.

Wampler, Martha, ed. *Design for Creativity*. ESEA Title III Project. Bellflower, CA: Bellflower Unified School District, 1968.

Warner, Brigitte. *Orff-Schulwerk: Applications for the Classroom*. Englewood Cliffs, NJ: Prentice-Hall, 1991.

The Kodály Method

Bachmann, Tibor. *Reading and Writing Music*. Elizabethtown, PA: Continental, 1968.

————. *Growing with Music*. Elizabethtown, PA: Continental, 1968.

————. *Songs to Read*. Elizabethtown, PA: Continental, 1970.

Bennett, Peggy. "From Hungary to America: The Evolution of Education through Music." *Music Educators Journal* 74, no. 1 (September 1987): 36–45.

Carder, Polly. *The Eclectic Curriculum in American Music Education*. Reston, VA: Music Educators National Conference, 1990.

Chosky, Lois. "Kodály in and out of Context." *Music Educators Journal* 55 (April 1969):

————. *The Kodály Context*. Englewood Cliffs, NJ: Prentice-Hall, 1981.

————. *The Kodály Method*. 2d ed. Englewood Cliffs, NJ: Prentice-Hall, 1988.

Daniel, Katinka. "The Kodály Method." *Clavier* 7 (September 1968):

Darazs, Arpad, and Stephen Jay. *Sight and Sound*. New York: Boosey and Hawkes, 1965.

Edwards, Lorraine. "Hungary's Musical Powerline to the Young—the Great Animating Stream of Music." *Music Educators Journal* 57 (February 1971): 38–40.

Eosze, L. *Zoltán Kodály: His Life and Work.* Trans. Istvan Farkas and Gyula Gulyas. Boston: Crescendo, 1962.

Erdei, Peter and Katalin Komlos, eds. *150 American Folk Songs to Sing, Read, and Play.* New York: Boosey and Hawkes, 1974.

KCA News. Published periodically by the Kodály Center of America, 14 Denton Road, Wellesley, MA 02181.

Kodály Curriculum Guide for Silver Burdett Music. Morristown, NJ: Silver Burdett, 1983. Grades 1–3, Harold L. Caldwell; Grades 3–5, Peter R. Allen; Grade 6, Lorna Zemke.

Kodály, Zoltán. "Folk Song in Pedagogy." *Music Educators Journal* 53 (March 1962): 59.

———. *The Kodály Method Applied to the Teaching of Instruments.* Wellesley, MA: Kodály Musical Training Institute, 1974.

Teaching Music at Beginning Levels Through the Kodály Concept. 3 vols. Wellesley, MA: Kodály Musical Training Institute, 1973.

Kraus, Egon. "Zoltán Kodály's Legacy to Music Education." *International Music Educator* 16 (September 1967): 513–32.

Landis, Beth, and Polly Carder. *The Eclectic Curriculum in American Music Education.* Washington, DC: Music Educators National Conference, 1972.

Lewis, Aden. *Listen, Look and Sing.* Morristown, NJ: General Learning Corporation, 1971.

McLaughlin, Elizabeth. "The Significance of the Kodály Conception in America." *Musart* (January 1971).

Richards, Mary Helen. "The Kodály System in the Elementary Schools." *Bulletin,* Council for Research in Music Education, no. 8 (Fall 1966).

———. *Threshold to Music.* Belmont, CA: Fearon, 1964.

Strong, Alan D. *Who Was Kodály?* Organization of American Kodály Educators, 1992.

Szonyi, Erzebet. *Kodály's Principles in Practice.* New York: Boosey and Hawkes, 1973.

———. *Musical Reading and Writing. Teacher's Manual.* 2 vols. London: Boosey and Hawkes, 1974.

———. *The Child in Depth.* Portola Valley, CA: Mary Helen Richards, 1966.

———. *Teaching Music Through Songs.* Palo Alto, CA: Fearon, 1966.

Orff and Kodály

Abramson, Robert, Lois Choksy, Avon Gillespie, and David Woods. *Teaching Music in the Twentieth Century.* Englewood Cliffs, NJ: Prentice-Hall, 1985.

Bacon, Denise. "On Using Orff with Kodály." *Musart* 21, no. 4 (April –May 1969): 53.

Bergethon, Bjonar, and Eunice Boardman. "Ancillary Procedures for Teaching Music." in *Musical Growth in the Elementary School.* 4th ed. New York: Holt, Rinehart, 1979.

Carder, Polly. *The Eclectic Curriculum in American Music Education.* Reston, VA: Music Educators National Conference, 1990.

Landis, Beth, and Polly Carder. *The Eclectic Curriculum in American Music Education*. Washington, DC: Music Educators National Conference, 1974.

Nash, Grace C. "Kodály and Orff." *Clavier* 7 (September 1968): 23–25.

Stone, Margaret, L. "Kodály and Orff Music Teaching Techniques: History and Present Practice." Ph.D. dissertation, Kent State University. Ann Arbor, MI: University Microfilms, 1971.

Wheeler, Lawrence, and Lois Raeback. *New Approaches to Music in the Elementary School*. Dubuque, IA: William C. Brown, 1974.

———. *Orff and Kodály Adapted for the Elementary School*. Dubuque, IA: William C. Brown, 1985.

The Manhattanville Music Curriculum Program

Fisher, Renee. "Learning Music Unconventionally—Manhattanville Music Curriculum Program." *Music Educators Journal* 54 (May 1968): 61–64.

Gibbs, Robert. "Effects of the Manhattanville Music Curriculum Program in the Musical Achievement and Attitude of Jefferson County, Colorado, Public School Students." Ph.D. dissertation, University of Colorado, 1972.

Thomas, Ronald B. "Rethinking the Curriculum." *Music Educators Journal* 56, no. 6 (February 1970): 68–70.

———. "Objectives of the MMCO Curriculum." In *Instructional Objectives in Music: Resources for Planning Instruction and Evaluating Achievement*. Ed. David Boyle. Vienna, VA: Music Educators National Conference, 1974.

———. *Manhattanville Music Curriculum Program: Final Report*. Washington, DC: U.S. Office of Education, Bureau of Research, August 1970. ERIC document ED 045 865.

———. "Sound of a Revolution." *Catholic School Journal* (April 1970): 14–18.

———. *A Study of New Concepts, Procedures, and Achievement in Music Learning as Developed in Selected Music Programs*. Washington, DC: U.S. Office of Education, Bureau of Research (Project no. V-oo8), 1966.

Suzuki Talent Education

Berardocoo, Diana B. "A Study of the Philosophy and Method of Shinichi Suzuki." Master's thesis, The Catholic University of America, 1974.

Books

Cook, Clifford A. *Suzuki Education in Action*. New York: Exposition Press, 1970.

Kendall, John D. *Talent Education and Suzuki: What the American Music Educators Should Know About Shinichi Suzuki*. Washington, DC: Music Educators National Conference, 1966.

———. *Suzuki Violin Method in American Education*. Washington, DC: Music Educators National Conference, 1973.

Mills, Elizabeth, and Therese Cecile Murphy, eds. *The Suzuki Concept*. Berkeley, CA: Diablo, 1973.

Suzuki, Shinichi. *Nurtured by Love*. Trans. Waltroud Suzuki. Athens, OH: Senzay, 1989.

Wickes, Linda. *The Genius of Simplicity*. Princeton, NJ: Summy-Birchard, 1982.

Periodicals

Brunson, Theodore. "A Visit with Doctor Suzuki." *Music Educators Journal* 55 (May 1969): 54–56.
"Fiddling Legions." *Newsweek* (23 March 1964), 73.
Garofalo, Robert. "The Suzuki Method at the Campus School." *Musart* 23, no. 4 (February–March 1971): 13.
Garson, Alfred. "Learning with Suzuki: Seven Questions Answered." *Music Educators Journal* 56 (February 1970): 64.
Gerard, Sister Jane Elizabeth, CSJ. "Some Thoughts on Suzuki." *American String Teacher* 16, no. 3 (Summer 1966): 3.
Kendall, John. "A Report on Japan's Phenomenal Violinists." *Violins and Violinists* (November–December 1959): 241–44.
———. "The Resurgent String Program in America." *Music Educators Journal* 50 (September–October 1963): 45–48, 51. Also published in *Perspectives in Music Education: Source Book III*. Washington, DC: Music Educators National Conference, 1966.
Publisher's Newsletter. Princeton, NJ: Summy-Birchard. Published periodically.
Shultz, Carl. "Shinichi Suzuki: The Genius of His Teaching." *American String Teacher* 19 (Summer 1964): 40–41.
The Suzuki Journal. Athens, OH: Suzuki Association of the Americas. Published bimonthly.
Wassell, Albert. "Suzuki Answers Questions." *The Instrumentalist* 18 (March 1964).
———. "Visit with Shinichi Suzuki in Japan." *American String Teacher* (Summer 1964): 9.
Zelig, Tibor. "A Direct Approach to Preschool Violin Teaching in California." *The Strad* (January 1966): 310.

Methods

An Introduction to the Suzuki Method. Princeton, NJ: Suzuki Method International, 1984.
Kendall, John D. *Listen and Play*. 3 vols. Evanston, IL: Summy-Birchard, 1965.
Sato Cello School. *The Suzuki Method*. Evanston, IL: Summy-Birchard, 1971.
Suzuki, Shinichi. *Suzuki Violin School: Suzuki Method*. 10 vols. Tokyo: Zen-on-Music, 1955.
Zahtilla, Paul. *Suzuki in the String Class*. Evanston, IL: Summy-Birchard, 1971.

Comprehensive Musicianship

Benner, Charles H. *Teaching Performing Groups*. Washington, DC: Music Educators National Conference, 1972.
Bess, David Michael. "Comprehensive Musicianship in the Contemporary Music Project's Southern Regions Institutes for Music in Contemporary Music Education." *Journal of Research in Music Education* 38, no. 2 (Summer 1991): 111–12.
Boyle, David J. *Instructional Objectives in Music*. Vienna, VA: Music Educators National Conference, 1974.
Burton, Leon. "Comprehensive Musicianship—The Hawaii Music Curriculum Project." *The Quarterly* 1, no. 3 (Autumn 1990): 67–76.

Comprehensive Musicianship: The Foundation for College Education in Music. Washington, DC: Music Educators National Conference, 1965.

Garofalo, Robert J. *Blueprint for Band.* Fort Lauderdale, FL: Meredith Music, 1983.

———. *Rehearsal Handbook for Band and Orchestra Students.* Fort Lauderdale, FL: Meredith Music, 1983.

———. *Instructional Designs for Middle/Junior High School Band.* Fort Lauderdale, FL: Meredith Music, 1984.

Labuta, Joseph A. *Teaching Musicianship in the High School Band.* West Nyack, NY: Parker, 1972.

The Quarterly 1, no. 3 (Autumn 1990). This is a focus issue subtitled "The Contemporary Music Project."

Texter, Merry. *Musicianship in the Beginning Instrumental Class.* Washington, DC: Music Educators National Conference, 1973.

Thomson, William. *Comprehensive Musicianship through Classroom Music.* Belmont, CA: Addison-Wesley, 1974.

———. *The Hawaii Music Curriculum Project: The Project Design.* Honolulu: College of Education, University of Hawaii.

Music Learning Theory

Brink, Emily. "A Look at E. Gordon's Theories." *Bulletin,* Council for Research in Music Education, no. 75 (Summer 1983): 2–13.

Gordon, Edwin. "A Factor Analysis of the Musical Aptitude Profile, the Primary Measures of Music Audiation, and the Intermediate Measures of Music Audiation." *Bulletin,* Council for Research in Music Education, no. 87 (Spring 1986): 17–25.

———. "A Longitudinal, Predictive Validity Study of the Intermediate Measures of Music Education." *Bulletin,* Council for Research in Music Education, no. 78 (Spring 1984): 1–23.

———. "Research Studies in Audiation: I." *Bulletin,* Council for Research in Music Education, no. 84 (Fall 1985):

———. "A Response to Volume II, Numbers 1 & 2 of *The Quarterly.*" *Quarterly Journal of Music Teaching and Learning* 2, no. 4 (Winter 1991): 62–72.

———. *Learning Sequences in Music: Skill, Content, and Patterns.* Chicago: GIA, 1993.

———. *A Music Learning Theory for Newborn and Young Children.* Chicago, GIA, 1990.

Grunow, Richard F. "The Evolution of Rhythm Syllables in Gordon's Music Learning Theory." *Quarterly Journal of Music Teaching Learning* 3, no. 4 (Winter 1992): 56–66.

The Quarterly Journal of Music Teaching and Learning 2, no. 1, 2 (Spring/Summer 1991). This is a focus issue subtitled "The Work of Edwin Gordon."

CHAPTER 6: MATERIALS AND TOOLS OF MUSIC EDUCATION

Popular Music

Anderson, William. "A Reprise for Jazz." *Stereo Review* 33 (July 1974): 6.

Anslinger, Walter. "The Stage Band: A Defense and an Answer." In *Perspectives in Music Education.* Washington, DC: Music Educators National Conference, 1966, 533–35.

Bulletin, Council for Research in Music Education, no. 95 (Winter 1987). This is a focus issue subtitled "Research in Jazz Education."

Choate, Robert A., ed. *Documentary Report of the Tanglewood Symposium*. Washington, DC: Music Educators National Conference, 1968.

Dykema, Peter, and Karl W. Gehrkens. *The Teaching and Administration of High School Music*. Boston: Birchard, 1941.

Hall, M. E. "How We Hope to Foster Jazz." *Music Educators Journal* 55, no. 7 (March 1969): 44–46.

Mark, Michael L. "The Acceptance of Jazz in the Music Education Curriculum: A Model for Interpreting a Historical Process." *Bulletin*, Council for Research in Music Education, no. 92 (Summer 1987): 15–21.

———. "Youth Music: Is It Right for the Schools? *Quarterly Journal of Music Teaching and Learning* 5, no. 2 (Summer 1994): 76–82.

McAllister, David. "Curriculum Must Assume a Place at the Center of Music." In *Documentary Report of the Tanglewood Symposium*. Ed. Robert Choate. Washington, DC: Music Educators National Conference, 1968.

Roberts, John T. "MENC's Associated Organizations: NAJE." *Music Educators Journal* 55, no. 7 (March 1969): 44–46.

Scott, Allen. "NAJE Convention: Casualty Rates." *Radio Free Jazz*, no. 3 (March 1976): 9.

Stringham, Edwin J. "Jazz—An Educational Problem." *Musical Quarterly* 12, no. 2 (April 1976):

Sur, William R., and Charles F. Schuller. *Music Education for Teenagers*. New York: Harper & Row, 1966.

Multicultural Music Education

Anderson, William M., comp. *Teaching Music with a Multicultural Approach*. Reston, VA: Music Educators National Conference, 1991.

———, and Patricia Sheehan Campbell. *Multicultural Perspectives in Music Education*. Reston, VA: Music Educators National Conference, 1989.

Bringing Multicultural Music to Children (video). Reston, VA: Music Educators National Conference, 1992.

Campbell, Patricia Sheehan. "*Musica Exotica*, Multiculturalism, and School Music." *Quarterly Journal of Music Teaching and Learning* 5, no. 2 (Summer 1994): 65–75.

Fung, C. Victor. "Approaches in World Music Curriculum." *Social Sciences SRIG Newsletter*. West Chester, PA: West Chester University, 1995, 2, 3.

Han, Kuo-Huang, and Patricia Sheehan Campbell. *Teaching the Music of Asian Americans* (video). Reston, VA: Music Educators National Conference, 1991.

Judis, John B., and Michael Lind. "For a New Nationalism." *The New Republic* 4, no. 184 (March 27, 1995): 19–21, 24–27.

Keller, Marcello Sorce. "Multiculturalism: Can We Really Face a Different Music?" *Quarterly Journal of Music Teaching and Learning* 3, no. 4 (Winter 1992):

K–12 Arts Education in the United States: Present Context, Future Needs. A briefing paper for the arts education community. Reston, VA: Music Educators National Conference, National Art Education Association, National Dance Association, National Association of Schools of Music, National Association of Schools of Theatre, National Association of Schools of Dance, January 1986.

McAllester, David P., and Edwin Schupman. *Teaching the Music of the American Indian* (video). Reston, VA: Music Educators National Conference, 1991.

Multicultural Arts Education: Guidelines, Instructional Units and Resources for Art, Dance, Music and Theater, Grades K–12. Orlando: University of Florida, 1993.

Music Educators Journal 78, no. 9 (May 1992). This is a focus issue subtitled "Multicultural Music Education."

O'Brien-Rothe, Linda. *Teaching the Music of Hispanic Americans* (video). Reston, VA: Music Educators National Conference, 1991.

Olsen, Dale A., and Daniel E. Sheehy. *Teaching the Music of Hispanic Americans.* Reston, VA: Music Educators National Conference, 1991.

The Quarterly 1, no. 4 (Winter 1990). This is a focus issue subtitled "The International Issue."

The Quarterly Journal of Music Teaching and Learning 4, no 2 (Summer 1993). This is a focus issue subtitled "Has Music Education Turned Its Back on Minorities?"

Reagon, Bernice Johnson, and Luvenia A. George. *Teaching the Music of African Americans* (video). Reston, VA: Music Educators National Conference, 1991.

Reimer, Bennett. "Can We Understand the Music of Foreign Cultures?" In *Musical Connections.* Aukland, New Zealand: International Society for Music Education, 1994.

———. "General Music for the Black Ghetto Child." In *Facing the Music in Urban Education.* Washington, DC: Music Educators National Conference, 1972, 89.

———. "Selfness and Otherness in Experiencing Music of Foreign Cultures." *Quarterly Journal of Music Teaching and Learning* 2, no. 3 (Fall 1991): 4–13.

Teaching Tolerance. 400 Washington Avenue, Montgomery, AL 36104. Published semiannually.

Volk, Terese M. "The History and Development of Multicultural Music Education as Evidenced in the *Music Educators Journal,* 1967–1992." *Journal of Research in Music Education* 41, no. 2 (Summer 1993): 137–55.

———. "Folk Musics and Increasing Diversity in American Music Education: 1900–1916." *Journal of Research in Music Education* 42, no. 4 (Winter 1994): 285–305.

Weiner, Lois. *Preparing Teachers for Urban Schools: Lessons from Thirty Years of School Reform.* New York: Teachers College Press, 1993.

Technology in Music Education

Adams, Steven M. "Interactive Audio as a Resource for Music Courseware Development." *Quarterly Journal of Music Teaching and Learning* 1, no. 1, 2 (Spring 1990): 112–15.

Arenson, Michael, ed. *Courseware Directory.* National Consortium for Computer-Based Music Instruction. Published annually.

Berz, William L., and Judith Bowman. *Applications of Research in Music Technology.* Reston, VA: Music Educators National Conference, 1994.

Blombach, Ann, and Bruce Benward. "The Unvarnished Truth about

Commercial Ear-Training Software." *The College Music Society Newsletter* (September 1994): 2, 3.

Bonner, Paul. "The Sound of Software." *Personal Computing* 8, no. 6 (June 1984): 94–102.

Boody, Charles G., comp. *TIPS: Technology for Music Educators*. Reston, VA: Music Educators National Conference, 1990.

Cartwright, G. Phillip. "Distance Learning." *Change* (July/August 1994).

Dialogue in Instrumental Music Education 7, no 1 (Spring 1983). Entire issue.

Eddins, John M., ed. *Journal of Computer-Based Instruction* 7, no. 3 (February 1981).

Feldstein, Sandy. "Technology for Teaching." *Music Educators Journal* 74, no. 7 (March 1988):

Griffey, Terry. "Review of CUBASE." *Quarterly Journal of Music Teaching and Learning* 1, no. 1, 2 (Spring 1990): 116–19.

Griswold, Harold E. "Multiculturalism, Music, and Information Highways." *Music Educators Journal* 81, no. 3 (November 1994): 41–46.

Forest, Joyce. "Music Technology Helps Students Succeed." *Music Educators Journal* 81, no. 5 (March 1995): 35–38, 48.

Hahn, Harley, and Rich Stout. *The Internet Complete Reference*. New York: McGraw-Hill, 1994.

Hofstetter, Fred T. *Computer Literacy for Musicians*. Englewood Cliffs, NJ: Prentice-Hall, 1988.

———. "Evaluation of a Competency-Based Approach to Teaching Aural Interval Identification." *Journal of Research in Music Education* 27, no. 4 (Winter 1979): 201–13.

———. "Microelectronics and Music Education." *Music Educators Journal* 65, no. 8 (April 1979): 39–45.

Keyboard. Articles on technology in music and reviews of new equipment and software. Published monthly.

Krol, Ed. *The Whole Internet: User's Guide & Catalog*. Sebastopol, CA: O'Reilly, 1992.

Lasaga, Antonio. "Collaboration and Technology." *On Common Ground: Strengthening Teaching through School-University Partnership*. No. 2 (Summer 1994): 3, 4. New Haven: Yale-New Haven Teachers Institute.

Margolis, Jerome N. " A School Synthesizer Program Comes of Age." *Music Educators Journal* 73, no. 4 (December 1987): 32–36.

McGee, Deron. "Artificially-Intelligent Tutoring: An Assessment for the Future." *The College Music Society Newsletter* (September 1994): 2–4.

Muro, Don. *The Art of Sequencing*. Merrick, NY: Electronic Music Products & Services, 1995.

Murphy, Barbara, ed. *Technology Directory: 1994–1995*. East Lansing, MI: Association for Technology Instruction, 1994.

Music and Computer Educator Magazine. Hicksville, New York.

Online Answers. Ann Arbor, MI: University Microfilms International, 1993.

PNMN (Pepper National Music Network). J. P. Pepper & Son, Inc., P.O. Box 850, Valley Forge, PA 19482. Published periodically.

Powell, Steven. "The ABCs of Synthesizers." *Music Educators Journal* 73, no. 4 (December 1987): 27–31.

Sound Tree (Music Technology Services for Education), a division of Korg USA, 89 Frost Street, Westbury, NY 11590. Published periodically.

Swanzy, David, and William English, eds. *The Collection, Organization, and Dissemination of Information on Music*. Report fof the Third Annual Loyola Symposium. New Orleans: School of Music, Loyola University, 1960.

The Technology Directory. Annual software directory published by the Association for Technology in Music Instruction.

Wiggins, Jackie. *Synthesizers in the Elementary Music Classroom: An Integrated Approach*. Reston, VA: Music Educators National Conference, 1991.

Williams, David Brian, and I. Sue Beasley. "Computer Information Search and Retrieval: A Guide for the Music Educator." *Bulletin*, Council for Research in Music Education, no. 51 (Summer 1977): 23–40.

CHAPTER 7: AREAS OF CONCERN FOR MUSIC EDUCATION

Music in Special Education

Atterbury, Betty W. "The Perplexing Issues of Mainstreaming." *Bulletin*, Council for Research in Music Education, no. 94 (Fall 1987): 17–27.

———. "Preparing Teachers for Mainstreaming." *Quarterly Journal of Music Teaching and Learning* 4, no. 1 (Spring 1993): 20–26.

Bradley, R. C. *The Education of Exceptional Children*. Wolfe City, TX: University Press, 1970.

Cruickshank, William M. *Misfits in Public Schools*. Syracuse, NY: Syracuse University Press, 1969.

Darrow, Alice Ann. "Beyond Mainstreaming: Dealing with Diversity." *Music Educators Journal* 76, no. 8 (April 1990): 36–39.

Dunn, Lloyd, ed. *Exceptional Children in the Schools*. 2d ed. New York: Holt, Rinehart, 1973.

Erikson, Marion J. *The Mentally Retarded Child in the Classroom*. New York: Macmillan, 1965.

Gaston, E. Thayer. *Music in Therapy*. New York: Macmillan, 1968.

Gfeller, Kate, and Alice-Ann Darrow. "Ten Years of Mainstreaming: Where Are We Now?" *Music Educators Journal* 74, no. 2 (October 1987): 27–30.

Giangreco, C. Joseph, and R. Marianna. *Education of the Hearing Impaired.* Springfield, IL: Thomas, 1970.

Graham, Richard M. "Barrier-Free Music Education: Methods to Make Mainstreaming Work." *Music Educators Journal* 73, no. 5 (November 1988):

———. *Music for the Exceptional Child*. Reston, VA: Music Educators National Conference, 1975.

———, and Alice S. Beer. *Teaching Music to the Exceptional Child*. Englewood Cliffs, NJ: Prentice-Hall, 1980.

Hardesty, Kay W. *Music for Special Education*. Morristown, NJ: Silver Burdett, 1979.

Havighurst, Robert J., ed. *Education of the Gifted*. National Society for the Study of Education, Fifty-seventh Yearbook, part 2. Chicago: University of Chicago Press, 1958.

Hewett, Frank M. *The Emotionally Disturbed Child in the Classroom*. Boston: Allyn and Bacon, 1968.

Howell, Carol. "A Survey of General Music Education for Children with Special Needs in Maryland." *Maryland Music Educators* 41, no. 2 (November–December 1994): 28–33.

Humpal, Marcia Earl, and Jacquelyn A. Dimmick. "Special Learners in the Music Classroom." *Music Educators Journal* 81, no. 5 (March 1995): 21–23.

Kephard, Newell. *The Slow Learner in the Classroom.* 2d ed. Columbus, OH: Merrill, 1971.

Levinson, Sandra, and Kenneth Bruscia. "Putting Blind Students in Touch with Music." *Music Educators Journal* 72, no. 2 (October 1985).

Kirk, Samuel A. *Educating Exceptional Children.* 2d ed. Boston: Houghton Mifflin, 1972.

McCaslin, Nellie. *Creative Dramatics in the Classroom.* 2d ed. New York: David McKay, 1974.

McReynolds, James C. "Helping Visually Impaired Students Succeed in Band." *Music Educators Journal* 75, no. 1 (September 1988): 36–38.

Music Educators Journal 76, no. 7 (March 1990). This is a focus issue subtitled "The Gifted and Talented."

Music Educators National Conference. *Music in Special Education.* Music Educators National Conference, 1972. Washington, DC. Published originally in *Music Educators Journal* 58, no. 8 (April 1972).

The National Committee, Arts for the Handicapped. *Federal Legislation, The Arts and Handicapped People: Questions and Answers Concerning P.L. 94-142 "The Education for All Handicapped Children" Act and Section 504 of P.L. 93-112 "The Vocational Rehabilitation Acts Amendments of 1973."* Washington, DC: The National Committee, Arts for the Handicapped, 1978.

Nocera, Sona D. *Reaching the Special Learner Through Music.* Morristown, NJ: Silver Burdett, 1979.

The Role of Music in the Special Education of Handicapped Children. Conference Proceedings. Albany, NY: University of the State of New York/The State Education Department Division for Handicapped Children and the Division of the Humanities and the Arts, 1971.

Siegel, Ernest. *Special Education in the Regular Classroom.* New York: John Day, 1969.

Music in Urban Education

Bell, David. "A Positive Approach to Inner-City Teaching." *Music Educators Journal* 72, no. 1 (December 1985):

Choate, Robert A., ed. *Documentary Report of the Tanglewood Symposium* Washington, DC: Music Educators National Conference, 1970.

———. *Facing the Music in Urban Education.* Washington, DC: Music Educators National Conference, 1970.

Coulby, David, Crispin Jones, and Duncan Harris, eds. *World Yearbook of Education 1992: Urban Education.* London: Kogan Page, 1992.

Forest, Joyce. "Music Technology Helps Students Succeed." *Music Educators Journal* 81, no. 5 (March 1995): 35–38, 48.

Johnson, J. L. "A Use of Music to Reduce Discipline Problems in an Inner-city Junior High School." Ph.D. dissertation, United States International University, 1984. *Dissertation Abstracts International* 26, 1861A.

Geore, Luvenia A. *Teaching the Music of Six Different Cultures in the Modern Secondary School.* West Nyack, NY: Parker, 1976.

Goodman, Paul. "The Universal Trap." *The Urban School Crisis.* New York: League for Industrial Democracy and the United Federation of Teachers, 1966.

Hanshumaker, James. "Forging Instrumental Programs for an Instrumental Society." *Music Educators Journal* 76, no. 3 (November 1989): 33–37.

Haskins, Jim, ed. *Black Manifesto for Education*. New York: Morrow, 1973.

Havighurst, Robert J. *Education in the Metropolitan Areas*. Boston: Allyn and Bacon, 1966.

Jones, Leroi. *Blues People: Negro Music in White America*. New York: Morrow, 1963.

Kozol, Jonathan. *Savage Inequalities: Children in America's Schools*. New York: Crown, 1991.

Lee, Ronald Thomas. "A Study of Teacher Training Experiences for Prospective Inner-City Instrumental Music Teachers." Ph.D. dissertation, University of Southern California, 1983. *Dissertation Abstracts International* 44, 1270A.

Marshall, A. T. H. "An Analysis of Music Curricula and Its Relationship to the Self-Image of Urban Black Middle-School-Age Children." Ph.D. dissertation, The State University of New Jersey. *Dissertation Abstracts International* 38, 6594A.

Murphy, Judith, and Ronald Gross. *The Arts and the Poor*. Washington, DC: United States Government Printing Office, 1968.

Music Educators Journal 73, no. 6 (February 1987). This is a focus issue subtitled "The Present and Future of Music Teacher Education."

Music Educators National Conference. *Facing the Music in Urban Education*. Washington, DC: Music Educators National Conference, 1970. Originally published in the *Music Educators Journal* 56, no 5 (January 1970).

Riessman, Frank. *The Culturally Deprived Child*. New York: Harper & Row, 1962.

———. *The Inner City Child*. New York: Harper & Row, 1976.

Roberts, Joan I., ed. *School Children in Urban Slums*. New York: Free Press, 1967.

Ross, Jerrold. "Research in Music Education: From a National Perspective." *Bulletin*, Council for Research in Music Education, no. 123 (Winter 1994/1995): 123–35.

The Role of the Fine and Performing Arts in High School Dropout Prevention. Tallahassee: Florida Department of Education, Division of Public School, 1990. Available from the Center for Music Research, Florida State University, Tallahassee, FL 32306-2098.

Shore, I. *Culture Wars: School and Society in the Conservative Restoration 1969–1984*. London: Routledge & Kegan Paul, 1989.

Silberman, Charles E. *Crisis in Black and White*. New York: Vintage, 1964.

Slavin, Robert E., Nancy L. Karweit, and Nancy A. Madden. *Effective Programs for Students at Risk*. Boston: Allyn and Bacon, 1989.

Stronge, James H., ed. *Educating Homeless Children and Adolescents*. Newbury Park, CA: Sage, 1992.

Strother, Deborah Burnett, ed. *Learning to Fail: Case Studies of Students at Risk*. Bloomington, IN: Phi Delta Kappa, Maynard R. Bemis Center for Evaluation, Development, and Research.

U.S. Department of Education Office of Educational Research and Improvement. *Educational Reforms and Students at Risk: A Review of the Current State of the Art*. Pittsburgh: Superintendent of Documents, 1994.

Washington, Benetta. "Cardozo Project in Urban Teaching: A Pilot Project in Curriculum Development Utilizing Returned Peace Corps Volunteers in an Urban High School." Washington, DC: ERIC Document Reproduction Service No. ED 001 653, January 1964.

Washington, DC, Public Schools. "The Urban Teacher Corps 1963–1968:

Description and Philosophy." ERIC Reproduction Service No. ED 038 350, 1968.

Weiner, Lois. *Preparing Teachers for Urban Schools*, New York: Teachers College Press, 1993.

CHAPTER 8: THE EDUCATION OF MUSIC TEACHERS

American Association of Colleges for Teacher Education. *Academic Achievement of White, Black, and Hispanic Students in Teacher Education Programs*. Washington, DC: American Association of Colleges for Teacher Education, 1993.
————. *Performance-Based Teacher Education: An Annotated Bibliography*. Washington, DC: American Association of Colleges for Teacher Education, 1972.

Brand, Manny. "Toward a Better Understanding of Undergraduate Music Education Majors: Perry's Perspective." *Bulletin*, Council for Research in Music Education, no. 98 (Fall 1988): 22–31.

Brookheart, C. Edward, ed. *Graduate Music Teacher Education Report*. Reston, VA: Music Educators National Conference, 1982.

Bulletin, Council for Research in Music Education, no. 117 (Summer 1993). This is a focus issue subtitled "The Future of Arts Education: Arts Teacher Education—Do We Need a New Breed of Arts Educator?"

Burke, Caseel. *The Individualized Competency-Based System of Teacher Education at Weber State College*. Washington, DC: American Association of Colleges for Teacher Education, 1972.

Burnsed, Vernon, and Gretchen Jensen. "Teacher Education in Music: The Development of Leaders." *Quarterly Journal of Music Teaching and Learning* 5, no 3 (Fall 1994): 5–10.

Colwell, Richard J. "Program Evaluation in Music Teacher Education." *Bulletin*, Council for Research in Music Education, no. 81 (Winter 1985):

Dilworth, Mary, ed. *Diversity in Teacher Education: New Expectations*. Washington, DC: American Association of Colleges for Teacher Education, 1992.
————. *Reading Between the Lines: Teachers and Their Racial/Ethnic Cultures*. Washington, DC: American Association of Colleges for Teacher Education, 1992.

Duerksen, George. "Music Teacher Education Reform: An Example." *Quarterly Journal of Music Teaching and Learning* 2, no. 4 (Winter 1991): 50–61.

Elam, Stanley. *Performance-Based Teacher Education: What Is the State of the Art?* Washington, DC: American Association of Colleges for Teacher Education, 1971.

Elfenbein, Iris M. *Performance-Based Teacher Education Programs: A Comparative Description*. Washignton, DC: American Association of Colleges for Teacher Education, 1972.

Erbes, Robert. *Certification Practices and Trends in Music Teacher Education*. 4th ed. Reston, VA: Music Educators National Conference, 1992.

"New Database 'MATCh'es' Teacher Requirements and Curriculum Standards." *ETS Developments* 40, no. 1 (Fall 1994): 2.

Gonzo, Carroll. "A Critical Look at Competency-Based Education." *Contributions to Music Education*, no. 5 (1981/82): 181.

Holmes Group. *Tomorrow's Teachers: A Report of the Holmes Group*. East Lansing, MI: Holmes Group, 1986.

Leonhard, Charles. "Toward Reform in Music Teacher Education." *Bulletin,* Council for Research in Music Education, no. 81 (Winter 1985): 65–73.

Madsen, Clifford K., and Cornelia Yarbrough. *Competency-Based Music Education.* Englewood Cliffs, NJ: Prentice-Hall, 1980.

Meske, Eunice Boardman. "Teacher Education, A Wedding of Theory and Practice." *Bulletin,* Council for Research in Music Education, no. 81 (Winter 1985): 65–73.

Mountford, Richard D. "Competency-Based Teacher Education: The Controversy and a Synthesis of Related Research in Music from 1964 to 1974." *Bulletin,* Council for Research in Music Education, no 46 (Spring 1976): 1–12.

National Advisory Council on Education Professions Development. *Competency Based Teacher Education: Toward a Consensus.* Washington, DC: National Advisory Council on Education Professions Development, 1976.

National Association of Schools of Music. *Handbook.* Reston, VA: National Association of Schools of Music, 1974.

National Commission on Accrediting. *Accreditation in Music.* Reston, VA: National Commission on Accrediting, 1969.

The Praxis Series: 1994–1995 Registration Bulletin. Princeton, NJ: Educational Testing Service, 1994.

The Praxis Series: Core Battery Tests and Multiple Subjects Assessment for Teachers. Princeton, NJ: Educational Testing Service, 1994.

The Praxis Series: ARTS. Princeton, NJ: Educational Testing Service, 1994.

The Quarterly Journal of Music Teaching and Learning 4, no. 1 (Spring 1993). Focus issue subtitled "Music Teacher Education."

Schwadron, Abraham A. "Music Education and Teacher Preparation: Perspectives from the Aesthetics of Music." *Journal of Musicological Research* (1982): 176–92.

Task Force on Music Teacher Education for the Nineties. *Music Teacher Education: Partnership and Process.* Reston, VA: Music Educators National Conference, 1987.

Task Force on Shortage/Surplus/Quality Issues. *The Impact of Teacher Shortage and Surplus on Quality Issues in Teacher Education.* Washington, DC: American Association of Colleges for Teacher Education, 1983.

Teacher Education Commission. *Teacher Education in Music: Final Report.* Washington, DC: Music Educators National Conference, 1972.

Wolfe, Irving. *State Certification of Music Teachers.* Washington, DC: Music Educators National Conference, 1972.

Research in Music Education

Arts Education Research Agenda for the Future. Washington, DC: National Endowment for the Arts, United States Department of Education, 1994. May be purchased from United States Government Printing Office, Superintendent of Documents, Mail Stop: SSOP, Washington, DC 20401-9328.

Barnes, Stephen H. *A Cross-Section of Research in Music Education.* Washington, DC: University Press of America, 1982.

Bash, Lee, and John Kuzmich. "Survey of Jazz Education Research: Recommendations for Future Researchers." *Bulletin,* Council for Research in Music Education, no. 82 (Spring 1985): 14–28.

Boisen, Robert. "Selected Recent Art Research: Its Implications for Research in Music Education." *Bulletin*. Council for Research in Music Education, no. 64 (Fall 1980): 1–11.

The Bowling Green State University Symposuum on Music Teaching & Research. Bowling Green, OH: Bowling Green State University, 1980.

Bresler, Liora. "Teacher Knowledge in Music Education Research." *Bulletin*, Council for Research in Music Education, no. 118 (Fall): 1993.

Bulletin, Council for Research in Music Education, no. 85 (Fall 1985). This is a focus issue that presents the papers of the Tenth International Seminar on Research in Music Education, University of Victoria, British Columbia, 1984.

Bulletin, Council for Research in Music Education, no. 91 (Spring 1987). This is a focus issue that presents the papers of the Eleventh International Seminar on Research in Music Education, Frankfurt am Main, Federal Republic of Germany, 1986.

Bulletin, Council for Research in Music Education, no. 119 (Winter 1993/1994). This is a focus issue subtitled "The 14th ISME International Research Seminar."

Bulletin, Council for Research in Music Education, no. 122 (Fall, 1994; Winter 1994). These are special issues subtitled "Qualitative Methodologies," and include the papers presented at the University of Illinois conference of the same name from May 1994.

Colwell, Richard, ed. *Handbook of Research on Music Teaching and Learning*. New York: Schirmer Books, 1992.

Deihl, Ned C., and Kenneth C. Partchey. "Status of Research: Educational Technology in Music Education." *Bulletin*, Council for Research in Music Education, no. 35 (Winter 1973): 18–19.

Documentary Report of the Ann Arbor Symposium: Applications of Psychology to the Teaching and Learning of Music. Reston, VA: Music Educators National Conference, 1981.

Documentary Report of the Ann Arbor Symposium III: Applications of Psychology to the Teaching and Leaning of Music. Reston, VA: Music Educators National Conference, 1983.

Documentary Report of the Wesleyan Symposium of the Application of Social Anthropology to the Teaching and Learning of Music. Reston, VA: Music Educators National Conference, 1985.

Gonzo, Carroll. "Research in Choral Music: A Perspective." *Bulletin*, Council for Research in Music Education, no. 33 (Summer 1973): 21–33.

Grashel, John W. "Doctoral Research in Music Student Teaching: 1962–1971." *Bulletin*, Council for Research in Music Education, no. 78 (Spring 1984): 24–32.

———. "Research in Music Teacher Education." *Music Educators Journal* (July 1993):

Greenberg, Marvin. "Research in Music in Early Childhood Education: A Survey with Recommendations." *Bulletin*, Council for Research in Music Education, no. 45 (Winter 1976): 1–20.

"Handbook of the Society for Research in Music Education." *Journal of Research in Music Education* 19, no. 2 (Summer 1971): 238–52.

Heller, George, and Bruce Wilson. "Historical Research in Music Education: A Prolegomenon." *Bulletin*, Council for Research in Music Education, no. 69 (Winter 1982): 1–20.

Hylton, John. "A Survey of Choral Education Research: 1971–1981." *Bulletin*, Council for Research in Music Education, no. 76 (Fall 1983): 1–29.

International Society for Music Education. Papers of the Second International Seminar on Research in Music Education. *Bulletin*, Council for Research in Music Education, no. 22 (Fall 1970).

———. Papers of the Sixth International Seminar on Research in Music Education. *Bulletin*, Council for Research in Music Education, no. 59 (Summer 1979).

———. Papers of the Eighth International Seminar on Research in Musical Education. *Bulletin*, Council for Research in Music Education, no. 66–67 (Spring–Summer 1981).

Jellison, Judith A. "The Frequency and General Mode of Inquiry of Research in Music Therapy, 1951–1972." *Bulletin*, Council for Research in Music Education, no. 35 (Winter 1973): 1–18.

Klemish, Janice. "A Review of Recent Research in Elementary Music Education." *Bulletin*, Council for Research in Music Education, no. 34 (Fall 1973): 23–40.

Kratus, John. "Eminence in Music Education Research as Measured in the Handbook of Research on Music Teaching and Learning." *Bulletin*, Council for Research in Music Education, no. 118 (Fall 1993): 21–32.

———. "Subjects in Music Education Research, 1961–1990." *Quarterly Journal of Music Teaching and Learning* 3, no. 4 (Winter 1992): 50–54.

Leglar, Mary. "A Profile of Research in Music Teacher Education." *Quarterly Journal of Music Teaching and Learning* 4, no. 1 (Spring 1993): 59–67.

Lehman, Paul R. *Tests and Measurements in Music*. Englewood Cliffs, NJ: Prentice-Hall, 1968.

Leonhard, Charles, and Richard J. Colwell. "Research in Music Education." *Bulletin*, Council for Research in Music Education, no. 49 (Winter 1976): 1–30.

Madsen, Clifford K. and Charles H. Madsen. *Experimental Research in Music Education*. Raleigh, NC: Contemporary Publishing, 1978.

———, and Randall S. Moore. *Experimental Research in Music Education* (workbook). Raleigh, NC: Contemporary Publishing, 1978.

Mark, Michael L. "A History of Music Education Research." In *Handbook of Research on Music Teaching and Learning*. Ed. Richard Colwell. New York: Schirmer Books, 1992.

Moog, Helmut. "Psychological Research in Music as the Basis of Music Education, Especially the Education of the Handicapped." *Bulletin*, Council for Research in Music Education, no. 62 (Spring 1980): 22–30.

Nelson, David, J. "String Teaching and Performance: A Review of Research Findings." *Bulletin*, Council for Research in Music Education, no. 74 (Spring 1982): 39–48.

Phelps, Roger P. *A Guide to Research in Music Education*. 2d ed. Metuchen, NJ: Scarecrow, 1980.

Porter, Lewis. "Guidelines for Jazz Research." *Bulletin*, Council for Research in Music Education, no. 95 (Winter 1987):

Price, Harry E. "Applications of Research to Music Teacher Education." *Quarterly Journal of Music Teaching and Learning* 4, no. 1 (Spring 1993): 36–44.

Rainbow, Edward. "Instrumental Music: Recent Research and Considerations for Future Investigations." *Bulletin*, Council for Research in Music Education, no. 33 (Summer 1973): 8–20.

————, and Hildegard C. Froehlich. *Research in Music Education: An Introduction to Systematic Inquiry.* New York: Schirmer Books, 1987.

Richardson, Carol Peterson. "Creativity Research in Music Education: A Review." *Bulletin*, Council for Research in Music Education, no. 74 (Spring 1983): 1–21.

Ross, Jerrold. "Research in Music Education: From a National Perspective." *Bulletin*, Council for Research in Music Education, no. 123 (Winter 1994/1995): 123–35.

Saffle, Michael. "Aesthetic Education in Theory and Practice: A Preview of Recent Research." *Bulletin*, Council for Research in Music Education, no. 74 (Spring 1983): 22–38.

Schwadron, Abraham A. "Philosophy in Music Education: State of the Research." *Bulletin*, Council for Research in Music Education, no. 34 (Fall 1973): 41–53.

Serafine, Mary L. "Piagetian Research in Music." *Bulletin*, Council for Research in Music Education, no. 62 (Spring 1980): 1–21.

Simons, Gene. "Early Childhood Musical Development: A Survey of Selected Research." *Bulletin*, Council for Research in Music Education, no. 86 (Winter 1986): 36–52.

Smith, Ralph A., and Christiana M. Smith. "Research in the Arts and Aesthetic Education" *A Directory of Investigators and Their Fields of Inquiry.* St. Louis, CEMREL, 1978.

Turrentine, Edgar. "Historical Research in Music Education." Bulletin, Council for Research in Music Education, no. 33 (Summer 1973): 1–7.

Wapnick, Joel. "A Review of Research on Attitude and Preference." Bulletin, Council for Research in Music Education, no. 48 (Fall 1976): 1–20.

Warren, Fred. "A History of the Music Education Research Council and *The Journal of Research in Music Education of the Music Educators National Conference*." Ph.D. dissertation, University of Michigan, 1966. University Microfilms no. LC-66-14612.

Whybrew, William E. "Research in Evaluation in Music Education." *Bulletin*, Council for Research in Music Education, no. 35 (Winter 1973): 9–17.

Zimmerman, Marilyn Pflederer. "Music Development in Middle Childhood: A Summary of Selected Research Studies." *Bulletin*, Council for Research in Music Education, no. 86 (Winter 1986): 18–35.

Music Education Research Journals

British Journal of Music Education. York: Cambridge University Press, Department of Music, University of York.

Bulletin, Council of Research in Music Education. Champaign-Urbana: School of Music, the University of Illinois.

Bulletin of Historical Research in Music Education. Lawrence: Department of Music Education and Music Therapy, the University of Kansas.

Bulletin of Research. University Park: Pennsylvania Music Educators Association.

Contributions to Music Education. Kent: Ohio Music Educators and Kent State University.

International Journal of Music Education. Reading, UK: International Society for Music Education.

Journal of Music Teacher Education. Reston, VA: Music Educators National Conference.

Journal of Research in Music Education. Reston, VA: Music Educators National Conference.

Missouri Journal of Research in Music Education. Jefferson City: Missouri State Department of Education.

Philosophy of Music Education Review. Bloomington: School of Music, Indiana University.

Psychomusicology: A Journal of Research in Music Cognition. Normal: College of Fine Arts, Illinois State University.

The Quarterly Journal of Music Teaching and Learning. Greeley: School of Music, University of Northern Colorado.

Research Perspectives in Music Education. Tampa: School of Music, University of South Florida.

Southeastern Journal of Music Education. Athens: School of Music and Center for Continuing Education, University of Georgia.

Update: Applications of Research in Music Education. Reston, VA: Music Educators National Conference.

CHAPTER 9: THE ASSESSMENT OF MUSIC EDUCATION

Arts Education Research Agenda for the Future. National Endowment for the Arts and United States Department of Education. Washington, DC: U.S. Government Printing Office, 1994.

Colwell, Richard. "Authentic Assessment and Portfolios: What Do They Measure?" *Special Research Interest Group in Measurement and Evaluation,* no. 16 (Spring 1994).

Diez, Mary, et al. *Essays on Emerging Assessment Issues.* Washington, DC: American Association of Colleges for Teacher Education, 1993.

Gates, J. Terry. "The Politics of Portfolio Assessment." *Special Research Interest Group in Measurement and Evaluation,* no. 16 (Spring 1994).

Mark, Michael L. "A History of Music Education Research." In *Handbook of Research on Music Teaching and Learning.* Ed. Richard Colwell. New York: Schirmer Books, 1992, 48–59.

Miller, Ross. "In New York State: Assessment and 'A New Compact for Learning.'" *Special Research Interest Group in Measurement and Evaluation,* no. 15 (Spring 1992).

National Education Goals Panel. *Measuring Progress Toward the National Education Goals: Potential Indicators and Measurement Strategies* (compendium of interim resource group reports). Washington, DC: National Education Goals Panel, March 25, 1991.

———. *Measuring Progress Toward the National Education Goals: Potential Indicators and Measurement Strategies* (discussion document). Washington, DC: National Education Goals Panel, March 25, 1991.

Ross, Jerrold. "The National Arts Educatiuon Research Center at New York University: Challenging Tradition." *Quarterly Journal of Music Teaching and Learning* 1, no. 1, 2 (Spring 1990): 17–21.

Philip, Frank. "Council of Chief State School Officers Begins National Assessment of Educational Progress Project on Arts Education Assessment." *Special Research Interest Group in Measurement and Evaluation,* no. 14 (Winter 1993).

Steinel, Daniel V., comp. and ed. *Arts in Schools: State by State*. 2d ed. Reston, VA: Music Educators National Conference, 1988.

——, comp. *Data on Music Education: A National Review of Statistics Describing Education in Music and Other Arts*. Washington, DC: Music Educators National Conference, 1990.

——, comp. *Music and Music Education: Data and Information*. Reston, VA: Music Educators National Conference, 1984.

Vaughan, Susan. "Evaluation of Arts Education in Minnesota: A Description of Minnesota's Arts Assessment Programs." *Special Research Interest Group in Measurement and Evaluation*. no. 14 (Winter 1993).

The National Assessment of Educational Progress

An Assessment of Attitudes Toward Music. Report no. 03-MU-03, 1971–72 Assessment. Denver: National Assessment of Educational Progress, Education Commission of the States, 1974. ERIC no. ED 099 270.

The First Assessment: An Overview. Report no. 03-MU-00, 1971–72 Assessment. Denver: National Assessment of Educational Progress, Education Commission of the States, 1974. ERIC no. ED 155 126.

The First National Assessment of Musical Performance. Report no. 03-MU-01, 1971–72 Assessment. Denver: National Assessment of Educational Progress, Education Commission of the States, 1974. ERIC no. ED 155 126.

Music Objectives. Report no. 03-MU-10, 1971–72 Assessment. Denver: National Assessment of Educational Progress, Education Commsssion of the States, 1970. ERIC no. ED 063 197.

Music Objectives, Second Assessment. Report no. 10-MU-10, 1978–79 Assessment. Denver: National Assessment of Educational Progress, Education Commsssion of the States, 1980. ERIC no. ED 183 434.

Music Technical Report: Exercise Volume. Report no. 03-MU-20, 1971–72 Assessment. Denver: National Assessment of Educational Progress, Education Commission of the States. ERIC no. ED 120 086.

Musical Technical Report: Summary Volume. Report no. 03-MU-21, 1971–72 Assessment. Denver: National Assessment of Educational Progress, Education Commission of the States, 1975. ERIC no. ED 114, 348.

A Perspective on the First Music Assessment. Report no. 03-MU-02, 1971–72 Assessment. Denver: National Assessment for Educational Progress, Education Commission of the States, 1974. ERIC no. ED 097 276.

Procedural Handbook: 1978–79 Summary Assessment. Report no. 10-MU-40. Denver: National Assesment of Educational Progress, Education Commission of the States, 1981.

The Second Assessment of Music, 1978–79: Released Exercise Set. Report no. 10-MU-25. Denver: National Assessment of Educational Progress, Education Commission of the States, 1980.

For a list of articles, reprints, and miscellaneous documents about the first two national assessments of music or NAEP in general, see "NAEP Publications List," which can be ordered from:

National Assessment of Educational Progress
1860 Lincoln, Suite 700
Denver, CO 80203

Index